Trade Liberalization and APEC

Trade and investment liberalization under Asia-Pacific Economic Cooperation (APEC) looked to be going well in the mid-1990s. However, the subsequent Early Voluntary Sectoral Liberalization (EVSL) initiative, which was an ambitious attempt to stimulate comprehensive regional liberalization by accelerating tariff reduction in selected sectors, turned out to be a failure.

This book analyses the attempted trade liberalizations under the APEC framework by conducting case studies on policy processes of six members. Using the 'two-level game' model as an analytical framework, the volume is an incredibly useful tool for understanding trade liberalization and its implementation.

An impressive cohort of contributors come together in this wonderful collection to provide a book that will be of great use to students and academics involved with international trade and economic integration as well as being a useful reference tool for policy-makers across the world.

Jiro Okamoto is a researcher at the Institute of Developing Economies, Chiba, Japan.

Routledge Studies in the Modern World Economy

Trade Liberalization and APEC

Edited by Jiro Okamoto

Routledge
Taylor & Francis Group

LONDON AND NEW YORK

First published 2004
by Routledge
2 Park Square, Milton Park, Abingdon, Oxfordshire OX14 4RN

Simultaneously published in the USA and Canada
by Routledge
711 Third Avenue, New York, NY 10017

Routledge is an imprint of the Taylor & Francis Group

First issued in paperback 2012

© 2004 Selection and editorial matter, Jiro Okamoto;
individual chapters, the contributors

Typeset in Garamond by Taylor & Francis Books Ltd

British Library Cataloguing in Publication Data
A catalogue record for this book is available from the British Library

Library of Congress Cataloging in Publication Data

A catalog record of this book has been requested

ISBN 978-0-415-31806-8 (hbk)
ISBN 978-0-415-65288-9 (pbk)

Contents

Illustrations

Tables

Figures

Contributors

Fumio Nagai
Associate Professor, Graduate School of Law, Osaka City University

Tatsushi Ogita
Research Associate, Economics and Social Security, Fuji Research Institute Corporation

Jiro Okamoto
Senior Research Fellow in Canberra, Institute of Developing Economies and Visiting Fellow, Australia-Japan Research Centre, Australian National University

Yutaka Onishi
Associate Professor, Graduate School of Law, Osaka City University

Satoshi Oyane
Professor, Faculty of Law, Doshisha University

Hanafi Sofyan
Research Director, Institute for International Finance and Commodities

Michael Wesley
Senior Lecturer, School of Politics and International Relations, University of New South Wales

Akiko Yanai
Researcher, Regional Integration Studies Group, Inter-disciplinary Studies Center, Institute of Developing Economies

Preface and acknowledgements

It is already fourteen years since the establishment of the Asia-Pacific Economic Cooperation (APEC) forum in 1989. Over this period, APEC has been expanding its areas of activity based on three pillars: trade and investment liberalization, trade and investment facilitation, and economic and technical cooperation. This book focuses on trade liberalization under the APEC framework, especially the Early Voluntary Sectoral Liberalization (EVSL) consultations that became one of the main APEC agenda items between 1997 and 1999.

Trade liberalization in the region has been one of the main objectives of APEC since its establishment. In the early stages, nevertheless, it did not have any concrete measures or goals. Rather, APEC members' 'will' for regional trade liberalization was used as a lever to encourage the promotion of the Uruguay Round. It was around the same period as the conclusion of the Uruguay Round (December 1993) that APEC turned more substantively to regional trade liberalization. After the inaugural Leaders Meeting in November 1993, trade liberalization under APEC looked to be going well for several years. In 1994, the Bogor Declaration set a target of realizing 'free and open trade and investment' in the region by 2010 for developed members and 2020 for developing ones. In 1995, the modality for APEC liberalization was set in the Osaka Action Agenda and, in 1996, the first Individual and Collective Action Plans were compiled as the Manila Action Plan for APEC. However, the subsequent EVSL consultations ended in failure.

Why did the 'APEC way,' which emphasized a cooperative approach that avoided crucial conflicts among members, not function during the EVSL consultations? What were the causes that led EVSL to failure? These questions form the basis of this book. As will be clarified in this book, EVSL consultations brought the vagueness and contradictions that accompanied the APEC liberalization process to the surface. In other words, the APEC 'consensus' on regional trade liberalization has never been shared by its members. In general terms, it is unthinkable that the consensus was not shared. However, in APEC it was possible and, as a matter of fact, necessary for the smooth operation of the forum. Yet, the absence of a 'shared' consensus on regional liberalization became a serious obstacle when concretely advancing early liberalization.

To examine why EVSL failed, a two-year research project was organized in 1999 at the APEC Study Center in the Institute of Developing Economies (IDE). The result of the project was published in Japanese by the IDE at the end of 2001. When working for the publication of the book in Japanese, my wish to publish an English version grew because, to my knowledge, there were no books or articles in any language that conducted detailed analysis on the EVSL consultations from the perspective of the policy process. I wished to have feedback from a wider audience. Routledge kindly provided this valuable opportunity and I would like to express my sincere appreciation for that.

This means that publication of this book was not planned when the research project was started. I admit that I placed considerable additional burdens on the author of each chapter. I am grateful that they were all supportive and contributed to making discussion at meetings very lively and important. Their intellectual guidance was critical. I also thank all those involved in the editorial process, and those to whom I have had to delegate some of this work.

As readers will see when going through the book, descriptions in this book depend heavily on declarations, statements and summaries of related meetings, media reports, and interviews with government officials and private business organizations, because of the contemporary nature of the research topic. We should be thanking all interviewees by naming each of them for their cooperation and invaluable inputs. In most cases, however, we did not because many of them still work for the same organization and prefer to remain anonymous. Here, as an editor, I would like to express our deep appreciation.

After the failure of EVSL consultations, APEC liberalization seems to have lost its momentum. However, development in the international and regional economic environments never stops. On the one hand, the new WTO round (the Doha Development Agenda) has been launched and is to be concluded by the end of 2004, but the negotiations have encountered difficulties almost from the beginning. On the other, new types of free trade agreements have been proliferating very rapidly in the region. In these circumstances and after the EVSL experience, what roles can APEC play in trade liberalization and facilitation and economic cooperation aspects? To consider these important questions, it is necessary to understand the APEC forum as it is, not overestimating or becoming too pessimistic about its strengths and weaknesses. I do hope this book will help in this respect.

Jiro Okamoto
Canberra
November 2003

Abbreviations

ABAC	APEC Business Advisory Council
AEA	American Electronics Association
AF&PA	American Forest and Paper Association
AFTA	ASEAN Free Trade Area (Agreement)
ALP	Australian Labor Party
APEC	Asia Pacific Economic Cooperation
APKINDO	Asosiasi Panel Kayu Indonesia (Indonesian Wood Panel Association)
ASEAN	Association of Southeast Asian Nations
ATL	Accelerated Tariff Liberalization (WTO)
CAP	Collective Action Plan (APEC)
CIEP	Committee for International Economic Policy (Thailand)
CTI	Committee on Trade and Investment (APEC)
CUA	Concerted Unilateral Approach (Actions), (APEC)
DBE	Department of Business Economics (Ministry of Commerce, Thailand)
DFAT	Department of Foreign Affairs and Trade (Australia)
DISR	Department of Industry, Science and Resources (Australia)
DIT	Department of Industry and Trade (Indonesia)
EAEC	East Asian Economic Caucus
EC	Economic Committee (APEC)
EU	European Union
EVSL	Early Voluntary Sectoral Liberalization (APEC)
FPO	Fiscal Policy Office (Ministry of Finance, Thailand)
FTI	Federation of Thai Industries
GAPKINDO	Gabungan Pengusah Karet Indonesia (Indonesian Rubber Entrepreneurs Association)
GAPPINDO	Gabungan Perusahaan Perikanan Indonesia (Indonesian Fishery Entrepreneurs Association)
GATT	General Agreement on Tariffs and Trade
HS	Harmonized Commodity Description and Coding System
IAP	Individual Action Plan (APEC)
IMF	International Monetary Fund
ISO	International Organization for Standardization
ITA	Information Technology Agreement (WTO)
ITO	International Trade Organization
JA Zenchu	Central Union of Agricultural Co-operatives of Japan

JPMA	Japan Plywood Manufactures' Association
KADIN	Kamar Dagang dan Industri Indonesia (Indonesian Chamber of Commerce and Industry)
KIEP	Korean Institute for International Economic Policy
KMI	Korean Maritime Institute
LDP	Liberal Democratic Party (Japan)
MAFF	Ministry of Agriculture, Forestry and Fisheries (Japan)
MAPA	Manila Action Plan for APEC
MFA	Ministry of Foreign Affairs (Thailand)
MFN	most-favored nation (status/treatment)
MITI	Ministry of International Trade and Industry (Japan, Korea)
MOAF	Ministry of Agriculture and Forestry (Korea)
MOC	Ministry of Commerce (Thailand)
MOF	Ministry of Finance (Japan, Thailand)
MOFA	Ministry of Foreign Affairs (Japan, Korea)
MOFAT	Ministry of Foreign Affairs and Trade (Korea)
MOFE	Ministry of Finance and Economy (Korea)
MOMAF	Ministry of Maritime Affairs and Fisheries (Korea)
MRA	Mutual Recognition Agreement
NAFTA	North American Free Trade Agreement
NEC	National Economic Council (the United States)
NESDB	National Economic and Social Development Board (Thailand)
NGO	non-governmental organization
NPO	non-profit organization
NTB	non-tariff barrier
NTM	non-tariff measure
OAA	Osaka Action Agenda (APEC)
OECD	Organization for Economic Cooperation and Development
OMT	Office of the Minister for Trade (Ministry of Foreign Affairs and Trade, Korea)
PMV	passenger motor vehicles and parts (products/industries)
RTL	Informal Group on Regional Trade Liberalization (APEC)
SOM	Senior Officials Meeting (APEC)
TCF	textile, clothing and footwear (products/industries)
TBA	Thai Bankers Association
TCC	Thai Chamber of Commerce
TIA	Telecommunications Industry Association (the United States)
TPCC	Trade Promotion Coordination Committee (the United States)
TPSC	Trade Policy Staff Committee (the United States)
USTR	United States Trade Representative
WTO	World Trade Organization
Zengyoren	National Federation of Fisheries Co-operative Associations (Japan)

Introduction

Jiro Okamoto

One of the important objectives of the Asia-Pacific Economic Cooperation (APEC) forum is to realize 'free and open trade and investment' in the region by 2010 for developed members and by 2020 for developing members (APEC Leaders Meeting 1994). In 1996, the first action plans for regional liberalization by all members were presented and endorsed as the *Manila Action Plan for APEC*.

In reality, however, the APEC members offered not much more in these action plans than they had already committed to in the Uruguay Round. In other words, as the APEC members were internationally 'obliged' to undertake such policy changes under the Uruguay Round negotiations, their 'APEC promises' were merely repackaged 'Uruguay obligations.' The inability of APEC to deliver more liberalization caused deep frustration amongst the governments and private sectors of pro-liberalization members, such as the United States, Australia, New Zealand and Singapore, and it was during this time of deep frustration that the EVSL initiative, with the strong support of the pro-liberalization members, rose to the surface of APEC debate.

The Early Voluntary Sectoral Liberalization (EVSL) initiative was an ambitious attempt to accelerate regional trade liberalization by opening up selected sectors earlier than others. Good results for the EVSL were expected to give momentum to APEC liberalization as a whole and secure the achievement of the 2010/2020 goal set in Bogor in 1994. The actual results of the EVSL, however, were much fewer than expected. Participants in the EVSL consultations could not agree on tariff reductions and gave up on early liberalization under the APEC framework. Some measures for the implementation of other elements of the EVSL – non-tariff measures (NTMs), trade facilitation and Ecotech – were agreed upon, but those measures announced by ministers did not cover all the EVSL sectors. Considering these results, the EVSL cannot avoid being labeled as a 'failure.' Although APEC had focused on maintaining cooperative attitudes amongst its members as it pushed for trade liberalization, this case was the first time since its inception in 1989 that divisions between members had so clearly surfaced and consultations had so clearly failed.

The failure of EVSL 'to deliver' caused lingering suspicions to re-emerge, particularly with regard to APEC's ability to implement regional liberalization successfully. Fred Bergsten, who was a US representative and the chair of the APEC Eminent Persons Group (1993–5), stated that APEC was at that point 'dead in the water' (Bergsten 1999). Aggarwal and Morrison (1999: 2) also pointed out that, because APEC was an under-developed and weak institution, its vision of free and open trade and investment by 2010/2020 could not be realized.

The EVSL 'failure' raises some important questions about free trade and the role of APEC in the region. First, has the EVSL failure effectively closed the door on achieving the Bogor goals? And second, what implications does the failure have for APEC as an institution and for APEC's activities as a whole? To analyze these important questions, it is necessary first to understand why the EVSL episode ended as it did. This is the main question that this volume tries to answer. By conducting case studies on several of the participants in the EVSL process, the various contributors to this volume will analyze why the EVSL consultations failed.

The two years of EVSL consultations (1998–9), especially the first year that determined the fate of the EVSL, involved intense debates over the APEC principles of 'voluntarism,' 'flexibility' and 'comprehensiveness,' which were supposedly characteristics of the APEC liberalization process. It seemed that APEC members did not share common perceptions on any of these principles, though they were said to be the 'consensus.' Although the problems and limitations of APEC liberalization were especially concentrated in the EVSL process, no extensive study on the EVSL has so far been conducted. This book will attempt to fill this gap the literature. By doing so, it also attempts to contribute to the understanding of APEC as a framework for trade liberalization, in a manner which is neither excessively idealistic nor unnecessarily pessimistic, but, rather, which appreciates and accounts for the realities of the Asia-Pacific political economy.

This book is divided into three parts. Part I has four main aims: first, to introduce the characteristics of the liberalization that has taken place under the APEC framework; second, to explain the development of the EVSL consultations at the international level; third, to transpose the more abstract aspects of research on APEC and trade liberalization into more concrete research questions relating to the development of the EVSL; and, finally, to introduce an analytical framework for the case studies and conclusion. In Chapter 1, Akiko Yanai elaborates on the historical and institutional aspects of APEC and its liberalization process as they compare with the GATT/WTO. In Chapter 2, Jiro Okamoto outlines the development of the EVSL consultations. The picture of EVSL development begins with the origin of the EVSL at the Leaders Meeting in 1995 and concludes with the Ministerial Meeting in 1999. Then, the chapter subdivides our abstract research interests into more manageable research questions for Part II. Chapter 3 sets up an analytical framework for the book. Okamoto and

Michael Wesley begin by reviewing the existing literature on foreign policy making, before setting out the argument that the 'two-level game' model of Robert Putnam (1988) is the most suitable tool to analyze the EVSL. Okamoto and Wesley also argue, however, that several phenomena in the EVSL process cannot be readily explained by the original two-level game model, and thus, in order to analyze these extra phenomena, the original model needs to be extended with some additional concepts.

Part II is the case study section. With the broad outline of the EVSL development as well as the book's analytical framework having been covered in Part I, the authors of the case studies will focus on the accounts of the individual participants in the EVSL consultations. Six members have been chosen for discussion: Japan, the United States, Australia, Korea, Thailand and Indonesia. The cases include members who strongly pushed the EVSL, others who opposed the 'packaging' (see Chapter 2) of EVSL, and others again who were ambivalent as to whether they would promote or oppose the EVSL initiative. The range of economic development between members has also been taken into account in order that the studies reflect the diversity that exists amongst the APEC membership.

Tatsushi Ogita analyzes Japan's EVSL policy in Chapter 4. In terms of Japan's domestic EVSL policy making process, because the Ministry of Agriculture, Forestry and Fisheries was able to veto liberalization in sectors under its jurisdiction, the width of an acceptable agreement (called a 'win-set' in the 'two-level game' model) was significantly restricted. Moreover, as Ogita demonstrates, Japan's 'win-set' was reduced to zero when the EVSL-promoting members, such as the United States, demanded that the EVSL be implemented as a package.

In Chapter 5, Satoshi Oyane examines the United States. Oyane explains that under the Clinton government the APEC (EVSL) policy of the United States differed (in terms of the way in which it was formulated) from its traditional policy making process. The government actively involved itself in manipulating domestic preferences for the EVSL and created 'excessive' domestic expectations. The US government – backed by these domestic expectations, which were, in a sense, of its own making – strongly pushed the packaging of the EVSL initiative. Oyane argues that the US government did not realize that Asian members saw the packaging as a departure from APEC's principles, at least in the early stage of the EVSL consultations, and that, even if the government had realized its misunderstandings at a later stage, the task of changing policy had become almost impossible.

Written by Michael Wesley, Chapter 6 looks at Australia. For Australia, APEC has not only been a place to promote and realize the economic benefits from freer trade, but has also been an important institution in terms of achieving political and diplomatic goals. During the EVSL process, however, the Australian government also manipulated domestic preferences towards the EVSL. With an approach similar to that of the United States, the Australian government created domestic expectations and persisted with packaging the initiative. This tendency in Australia's EVSL policy, Wesley argues, reveals a loss of balance between the country's various policy objectives for APEC.

Yutaka Onishi analyzes the Korean case in Chapter 7. Onishi argues that the Korean government had little interests in the potential economic effects of EVSL on its domestic economy. Instead, the government, which was reeling from the currency and economic crisis at the time, decided to employ an EVSL policy that would gain the maximum domestic political support. In other words, Korea developed its EVSL policy after weighing up the benefits of regaining international economic credibility by actively participating in the EVSL against the loss of support that such participation would bring from some domestic industries because of liberalization.

In Chapter 8, Fumio Nagai deals with the Thai case. Nagai explains that the Thai government basically supported the EVSL initiative, but remained cautious during the consultation process. Thailand was a strong advocate of AFTA (ASEAN Free Trade Area) in the early 1990s and, since then, it has taken the initiative in promoting a deeper and wider AFTA scheme. Nagai argues that AFTA was the most important regional liberalization framework for Thailand, and its commitments to the EVSL were within, not beyond, the scope of AFTA.

Hanafi Sofyan analyzes Indonesia's policy in Chapter 9. The Indonesian government announced that its basic support for APEC liberalization was unchanged for the EVSL, and reiterated this support even as the country faced the economic and political crisis of the late 1990s. Sofyan argues that the Indonesian government felt a moral responsibility to support APEC liberalization in general, because of the central role played by then President Soeharto when the APEC leaders set the Bogor target in 1994. At the same time, the government urgently needed to restore international credibility to its economy. Thus, to show an active stance towards the EVSL, and for liberalization in general, supporting the EVSL was seen as a necessary policy for Indonesia. In reality, however, Indonesia's interests in the EVSL were focused only on the fishery and forestry sectors and it remained rather reluctant to liberalize the other thirteen EVSL sectors. The two sectors of most interest to Indonesia, however, were identical to those rejected by Japan, and when it became clear that these sectors would not be liberalized, the Indonesian government quickly lost interest in the EVSL.

Part III concludes the volume. In this section, Okamoto compares the different case studies in an attempt to answer the research questions of Chapter 2 by utilizing the analytical framework of Chapter 3. In answering these questions, attention will be paid to the following issues: each member's EVSL policy making process and win-set structure; the characteristics of domestic policy preferences for the EVSL; the EVSL sector selection process and the extent of each member's expectations concerning the EVSL; the nature of the choice that the members faced at the international and domestic consultation table; the influence of the economic crisis that occurred in July 1997; and each member's liberalization strategy and perception of cost of non-agreement. By using this multi-dimensional analysis, it is possible to understand the ultimate question of 'why the EVSL failed.' Lastly, this section will briefly consider how the failure of the EVSL consultations is likely to affect APEC and its activities.

Part I
Setting the research agenda

1 Characteristics of APEC trade liberalization

A comparative analysis with the WTO

Akiko Yanai

Introduction

In Kuala Lumpur in November 1998, the Ministerial Meeting of the Asia-Pacific Economic Cooperation (APEC) failed to reach a conclusion on the Early Voluntary Sectoral Liberalization (EVSL) consultations after heated and prolonged argument. As a consequence, APEC Ministers decided to call on the World Trade Organization (WTO) to take charge of the consultation process in order to maintain momentum in the liberalization negotiations. This decision had significant implications for the APEC process. As mentioned in the Introduction, the main objective of this book is to consider why the EVSL episode ended as it did. To address this issue, this chapter will focus on the statement that 'APEC is not a negotiative but a consultative body. If there is a need for negotiation, it should be done at the table of the WTO.' The statement was the explanation offered by Ministers when the EVSL consultations were passed to the WTO.

Both APEC and the WTO have played leading roles with regard to trade liberalization. The WTO is the only organization to promote trade liberalization on the multilateral level. APEC, on the other hand, as a result of its membership size and economic significance, has come to be regarded as an important regional trade arrangement. Most of the world's major states, with the exception of the European Union (EU), are APEC members. This gives APEC a total trade equivalent to half of the entire globe.

The two institutions share the common objective of trade liberalization. Accordingly, although this is not immediately obvious, they actively collaborate to achieve their goals. However, their approaches to trade liberalization are totally different, resulting in the general recognition of the WTO as a locus of negotiations and rulemaking and of APEC as a consultative body. In the EVSL consultations, one of the focuses of the arguments was the characteristics of the APEC trade liberalization and the role of APEC under the WTO system, which has been kept ambiguous. In order to analyze why EVSL consultations failed, it is necessary first to distinguish APEC from the WTO. In the section below, substantial differences between APEC and the WTO are clarified in the context of historical development, institutional principles and objectives. Operational differences in relation to the binding force of agreements, decision making processes and measures for liberalization are examined in the section which follows. In the fourth section, the modes of cooperation between APEC and the WTO will be discussed. After examining the consistency of APEC with the GATT/WTO, the case of the GATT Uruguay Round (1986–94) is highlighted in order to illustrate the relationships between the two bodies.

Substantial differences

Formation

Formation of the GATT

Recognition of the importance of creating an international trade and tariff institution has its origins in the bitter experience of the period running up to World War II. During this period, major countries such as the United Kingdom and France built economic blocs within their autonomous territories and colonies to protect their own industries, using the imposition of high tariffs and other trade barriers. These countries established preferential treatment systems so as to discriminate against non-allied states. This economic bloc trading system and the associated currency devaluation began a chain of events that resulted in a substantial reduction in world trade, contributing to the Great Depression of the 1930s worsening in terms of length and severity. Moreover, economic nationalism led to a phase of expansionism in order to enclose export markets, which eventually caused World War II.

Shortly after the commencement of hostilities, the United States and its allies began making their plans for the postwar economic order and the establishment of institutions to promote liberalization of world trade. These ideas were first incorporated into the Atlantic Charter of July 1941, which advocated a free and open market economy (Reisman 1996: 82–3). These notions developed slowly during the war, reaching fruition in the Bretton Woods Conference of July 1944. The focus of this conference was how best to create an international institutional framework in the monetary and banking sector. No specific discussion was held concerning the establishment of institutions to promote trade liberalization. Instead, the trade-related debates centered on how to obtain immediate benefits through reductions in tariffs and other trade barriers.[1] Therefore, only the International Monetary Fund (IMF) and the International Bank for Reconstruction and Development (the World Bank) were established at the conference.

In December 1945, the United States proposed to form the International Trade Organization (ITO) as the third pillar of the postwar international economic order, which was an unresolved agenda of the Bretton Woods

Conference. The proposal called for the preparatory conferences for creating the ITO,[2] and finally resulted in adoption of the ITO Charter in March 1948 in Havana; thus, it is known as the Havana Charter. Though the United States had taken the initiative in adopting the ITO Charter, the US government faced rejection of the ratification of the Charter by Congress, which was concerned with the impact of free trade on its domestic industries. Finally, in 1950, the government stopped trying to persuade Congress to ratify the Charter. As most other states thought that the ITO could not function efficiently without the United States, only two nations ratified the Charter.[3] Consequently, the plan for establishing the ITO lost momentum.

Alongside the ITO Preparatory Committee, the first multilateral negotiation for tariff reduction was held in Geneva.[4] Both the United States and the United Kingdom were in a hurry to begin tariff reduction, due to fear that the liberalization process might be significantly delayed when the rest of Europe and the developing countries joined the negotiating table (Diebold 1996: 157).[5] In order to assure and enforce the results of the trade round, part of the provisions of the draft ITO Charter were selected to form the core of the General Agreement of Tariffs and Trade (GATT) in 1947. In its early stages the GATT was regarded as a provisional agreement pending the formal establishment of the ITO. The 'ITO Charter' was originally expected to frame international trade rules, and it was the 'ITO' created by the ITO Charter that assumed the role of the implementing body. As the Charter was not able to come into effect, the GATT was forced to fulfill two simultaneous roles: as 'a permanent agreement' ruling the world trading system and 'a core institution' for promoting trade liberalization through multilateral negotiations. Though the GATT was not an institution established by a treaty-based instrument like the United Nations but merely a general agreement, it has had an actual secretariat and has functioned as a de facto international institution. In this chapter, therefore, the term 'the GATT' will denote the institution and the term 'the GATT agreement' the international agreement.

The lack of an institutional legal basis has hindered its ability to function as an efficient implementing body. This became more problematic 'as the GATT grew in scope and detail to cope with a fascinating set of concrete problems of international economic relations' (Jackson 1998: 13). At the Uruguay Round, many substantive trade rules were agreed. Some contracting parties called attention to the idea that the GATT should grow stronger organizationally in order to assure the implementation of agreements in the Uruguay Round and promote liberalization more effectively. Consequently, the GATT was reformed into a new institution, the WTO, in 1995.

Formation of APEC

On 31 January 1989 at a luncheon hosted by the Korean Business Association in Seoul, Robert Hawke (the then Prime Minister of Australia) presented a proposal for regional economic intergovernmental cooperation in the Asia-Pacific region, which led to the idea known as APEC.[6] He stated:

> I believe the time has come for us substantially to increase our efforts towards building regional cooperation and seriously to investigate what areas it might focus on and what forms it might take. ...
>
> We want to assess what the region's attitudes are towards *the possibility of creating a more formal intergovernmental vehicle of regional cooperation. A meeting of ministers from throughout the region would be a useful forum to investigate the question.*
>
> (Hawke, in Snape *et al.* 1998: 535. Italics added)

Australia decided to take the initiative in promoting APEC mainly because it strongly feared being excluded from new economic blocs that were in the process of developing. The European Community was pursuing the establishment of monetary union and the United States was in the process of concluding the North American Free Trade Agreement (NAFTA). In Australia there was a strong feeling of isolation from the global economy at this time. Hence, Australia advocated APEC as a regional group to which it could belong. At the same time, however, it made efforts to apply the brakes on expansion of regionalism with the slogan that 'APEC was outward-looking and did not aim to form a trading bloc' (APEC Ministerial Meeting 1990: paragraph 6). This was because Australia itself took a position against bloc economy, and, in addition, because it had to conciliate ASEAN countries that had a skeptical attitude towards forming a group.

At the beginning, most ASEAN countries hesitated over the Australian proposal. They were concerned that the creation of a regional arrangement would increase opportunities for the large players in the Asia-Pacific, such as Japan, China and the United States, to intervene in their affairs. Conversely, they also feared that failure to join such an arrangement would leave them isolated and vulnerable. ASEAN countries, which by undertaking to establish a 'world production base' had put themselves on the path to rapid economic expansion, were beginning to be incorporated into global market economy. They thought that APEC would be useful in terms of expanding export markets and promoting foreign direct investments.

After careful consideration of the pros and cons, the ASEAN countries decided to participate in APEC about six months after the original concept had been proposed. One of the most important influences on this decision was the position adopted by Australia and Japan, the two main initiators of APEC, which guaranteed that the ASEAN countries would be core to the institution and that APEC would maintain the non-binding nature of any principles agreed.[7] These promises to ASEAN significantly shaped the evolution of APEC. As a result, APEC was launched as a consultative forum to discuss the region's economic development with no organizational framework.

In the five years since it was established, however, APEC had made steady progress in the scope and prominence of its expanding activities (Davidson 1997: 124–31). In order to coordinate APEC activities and facilitate communication among its members, a permanent secretariat was established in Singapore in January 1993. At the same time, the Committee on Trade and Investment (CTI) was promoted from an informal group to the first standing committee. Further progress was made in November 1993, when the first Leaders Meeting was held at Blake Island and the agreement to regularize it was reached. This significant event dramatically changed the characteristics of APEC. Western members such as the United States, Canada and Australia have an interest in promoting the institutionalization of APEC. They consider APEC not only as a forum to discuss economic policies among its members, but also as an organization with specific goals of trade and investment liberalization in the Asia-Pacific region. They believe that the evolution of APEC's institutional structures and procedures will strengthen its effectiveness for reaching consensus and the implementation of meaningful work programs. As such, reinforcement of institutional structure and binding agreements are regarded as indispensable means of enforcing member economies to commit themselves on liberalization of trade and investment.[8] By contrast, ASEAN and several Asian governments have been reluctant to institutionalize APEC in a formal and legal fashion.[9] They were concerned about rapid institutionalization, which would make APEC an inflexible organization, and about accelerating excessive liberalization of trade and investment, which might be imposed on them without due consideration of their special circumstances. For this reason, the ASEAN countries insisted on informal arrangements rather than rigid institutionalization of APEC. Regarding institutionalization, APEC Ministers reconfirmed at the Osaka Meeting in 1995 that APEC should be a consultative body whose primary role is to discuss promotion of economic cooperation in the Asia-Pacific region. Furthermore, it was agreed by consensus that APEC should have no legally binding power at all.[10]

Although both APEC and the GATT similarly lack an institutional treaty clause, APEC should be distinguished from the GATT that has been institutionalized into the WTO, which itself has an establishment treaty. Furthermore, even though both APEC and the GATT/WTO included developing countries in their membership from the very beginning, APEC differs from the GATT/WTO in that ASEAN countries played a significant role in establishing the institution's principles. The views of developing economies have strongly influenced the institutional development process of APEC.

Principles

Principles of the GATT/WTO

The GATT system was established in order to proscribe the discriminatory trade treatment that had caused international trade to develop into economic blocs. The GATT, therefore, emphasized the principle of non-discrimination in trade. This principle was further divided into two parts: external non-discrimination prescribed in Article I and internal non-discrimination prescribed in Article III. The former is the so-called most-favored-nation (MFN) clause, which proscribes bilateral or regional tariff preferences. Article III deals with the regulation of foreign products and indicates that, once they are imported and tariffs are paid, they should be treated on equal terms with domestic products in respect of taxes and other requirements. In other words, Article III enforces the National Treatment rule.

Reciprocity is the second principle of the GATT. Essentially, reciprocity can be defined as the fundamental rule through which plural parties maintain a balance of treatment by granting the same or equivalent rights and benefits, or by fulfilling obligations to each other (Yamamoto 1988: 245). A reciprocal relationship can be explained as a balanced condition in which one side gives the other certain treatment while the other returns equivalent treatment (Kuwahara 1975: 417).[11] After the mid-eighteenth century, reciprocity was incorporated into a series of bilateral trade agreements, which had comprised a fairly elaborate network until the late 1930s (Finger 1991: 126–7). The ITO Charter aimed to encompass most of these bilateral treaties. Hence, as successor to the ITO Charter, the GATT was inevitably based on the principle of reciprocity.

In the early history of the GATT, reciprocity could be described as a guiding beacon for states to begin the process of dismantling trade protectionism (Winham 1992: 49). The principle of reciprocity, however, faced serious challenges as the GATT process developed. First, there was a problem of free riding. In the GATT agreements, the unconditional MFN clause prescribes that any bilateral agreement should be applied to other members. This implies that states signing the GATT agreement could take advantage of benefits without any binding agreement with others.[12] Early GATT tariff negotiations were multilateral only in name. In reality, they were conducted bilaterally between the principal supplier states and principal consumer states based on reciprocity. Such a condition made free riding more problematic. Complaints about free riding were raised by some states that were required to reduce tariffs as a result of trade negotiations. To solve this problem, the GATT not only obliged all member countries to participate in consensus building, but also decided to deal with the whole problem as an integrated package. Thus, following the Kennedy Round (1964–7), GATT negotiations became based on 'diffuse reciprocity' that is suitable for multilateral relationships.[13]

The second problem concerning reciprocity came to the surface when developing countries acceded to the GATT (Winham 1992: 50). In applying the reciprocity principle, it is extremely difficult to require the same level of concessions between states at different levels of economic development. Hence, it is questionable whether equal treatment of unequal partners in trade negotiations could be considered reciprocal. Developing countries demanded advantageous treatment for themselves and emphasized the new concept 'relative reciprocity,' which considers divergence in measuring equivalence of benefits. Following protracted negotiations, numerous exceptions to reciprocity were granted by industrialized GATT signatories in favor of developing countries at the Kennedy and subsequent Tokyo Rounds (1973–9). These exceptions are referred to as 'special and differential' treatments. According to Article XXXVI-8, which sets the exceptions to reciprocity, '[t]he developed contracting parties do not expect reciprocity for commitments made by them in trade negotiations to reduce or remove tariffs and other barriers to the trade of less-developed contracting parties.'[14] In this way, the principle of reciprocity in practice has been gradually altered to a new set of relationships based on 'diffuse reciprocity' and 'relative reciprocity.'

Principles of the APEC process

The Asia-Pacific region has its own distinctive features. These are: sociopolitical diversity; differing levels of economic development among member states; and a market-driven economic integration process. As such, it has been difficult for APEC to adopt the Western-style approach based on legislative and institutional integration found in the EU and NAFTA. Instead 'open regionalism'[15] and 'voluntarism' have been emphasized from the start as key principles of the APEC process.

Within APEC, 'open regionalism' is taken to mean regional economic integration without discrimination against outsiders. This involves the gradual elimination of internal barriers and the lowering of barriers against non-members. This concept manifested itself as one of the general principles of APEC liberalization and the facilitation process in the Osaka Action Agenda (OAA) that was endorsed by the Leaders Meeting in 1995.

<NON-DISCRIMINATION>

APEC economies will apply or endeavor to apply the principle of non-discrimination between and among them in the process of liberalization and facilitation of trade and investment.

The outcome of trade and investment liberalization in the Asia-Pacific region will be the actual reduction of barriers *not only among APEC economies but also between APEC economies and non-APEC economies.*

(APEC Leaders Meeting 1995b: Part One, Section A, 4. Italics added)

In arguing that APEC is different from NAFTA and other regional trade arrangements, Drysdale characterizes this concept of 'open regionalism' as follows:

> This new form of regionalism is *open* in a number of ways. It is open in that it is non-discriminatory; all liberalisation is to be on an MFN basis. It does not involve the negotiation of legally binding treaties. It is premised on strong support for the WTO. It is open in that the process is market-driven rather than institutional-driven. And it is open in that other non-players, on the periphery of the region and elsewhere in the world economy, are free to join in the process by liberalising in the same way.
>
> (Drysdale 1997: 6. Italics by Drysdale)

If liberalization within APEC is carried out strictly on the basis of open regionalism, preferential treatment that one member gives the other member economies will apply equally to outsiders as well. There can therefore be no logical objection to the claim that open regionalism is consistent with the non-discriminatory principle of the GATT/WTO embodied in the MFN clause. That is beside the point, since what is being discussed is the free riding problem. The main criticisms of open regionalism relate to the issue of free riding. For example:

> [M]ost proponents of regional economic programs for Asian economies generally advocate some form of 'open' regionalism. One approach would be for APEC nations to negotiate tariff reductions that would then be extended on a most favored nation basis to all trading partners. APEC's trading partners would undoubtedly welcome such an initiative, but some APEC nations themselves might find it hard to justify extending 'free-rider' benefits to nations from outside the region.
>
> (Lawrence 1996: 93)

Lopez and Matutes assert that trade liberalization in APEC is facing a stalemate situation because it is based on open regionalism; they examine the feasibility of open regionalism as follows:

> • Feasible in large integrated regions, but likely to converge to either multilateral negotiations or restricted trade agreements under Article XXIV, as the weight of free riders increases.
> • Unfeasible in small and low market-integrated regions, where free-riding problems may be large and reciprocal concessions may be obtained at high transaction costs, due to the number and power of free riders. In this case, restricted liberalization under the provisions of Article XXIV appears as the only chance ... in order to increase the degree of market integration ...
>
> (Lopez and Matutes 1998: 256–7)

The free rider issue, however, may be overcome through the introduction of the concept of voluntarism, which is the second principle of the APEC process, to open regionalism. Voluntarism is defined as leaving the implementation of every agreement among APEC members to the discretion of each member economy. In other words, the member economies are able to choose which sectors to liberalize with which players and when (Drysdale 1997: 8). Since the member economies unilaterally reduce trade barriers while taking into account the possibility of free riders, there is no room to complain about free riding.[16]

It was in 1995 that the word 'voluntary' was explicitly used in the declarations of Ministerial or Leaders Meetings for the first time (Ogita 2001: 9). The concept of voluntarism was laid down at the APEC's inception for the purpose of embracing ASEAN countries as participants of APEC. Hence, the principle of voluntarism was regarded as common sense among original members. However, prior to 1995, it became necessary to reconfirm this principle. First, because the number of members increased, bringing in new member economies that did not regard voluntarism as a given principle of APEC. Second, because APEC's overall activities rapidly progressed, and trade liberalization, which usually requires member economies to implement obligatory actions, came to the center table of APEC's activity. When Malaysia expressed reservations to the Bogor Declaration of 1994 clearly stating the target end date for liberalization, the country partly aimed to confirm once again that voluntarism was the principle of APEC. Third, the movement to give binding force to the agreements of APEC was gaining strength at that time. Post-1993, APEC annually held the Leaders Meeting, which debated the binding feature of the agreements. Even though the Meetings were informal, Leaders' agreements were somewhat directed by political commitments. The United States insisted that the OAA should be regarded as a binding agreement. Therefore, in the consultation for the Osaka Meeting process, some of developing economies asserted that the principle of voluntarism should be recognized again as a basic character of APEC. Moreover, the appellation the EVSL consultation adopted a 'V' for voluntary at the Vancouver Meeting in 1997. This showed the necessity to emphasize the voluntary nature of this consultation even though the EVSL initiative would be adopted as a declaration of 'Leaders.'

The spirit of voluntarism is reflected in the general principles in the OAA under the section on 'flexibility.'

<FLEXIBILITY>

Considering the different levels of economic development among the APEC economies and the diverse circumstances in each economy, flexibility will be available in dealing with issues arising from such circumstances in the liberalization and facilitation process.

(APEC Leaders Meeting 1995b: Part One, Section A, 8)

However, there is an interpretative gap concerning the concepts of voluntarism and flexibility among member states. Until now, APEC member economies have been unable to reach agreement on this issue. The United States equates voluntarism with flexibility, while South Korea and Thailand understand that each term has a different meaning, and adopt their terms to suit the occasion. Although the concepts of 'voluntarism' and 'flexibility' appear very similar, there is one significant difference. Voluntarism is applied to the decisions of a member economy itself, while flexibility is used for making implementation plans.

Objectives

Objectives of the GATT/WTO

The preamble of the GATT agreement stated that the primary objective of the GATT was 'the substantial reduction of tariffs and other barriers to trade and to the elimination of discriminatory treatment in international commerce.' It also described that these objectives would be achieved 'by entering into reciprocal and mutually advantageous arrangements.' The GATT considered itself to be responsible not only for the elimination of trade barriers but also for all fields of free trade. Therefore, in addition to tariff reduction, the GATT included the non-tariff measures (NTMs) as its main agenda at the Tokyo Round. Consequently, new trade rules regarding NTMs were agreed governing import licenses, anti-dumping duties, subsidies and countervailing duties, government procurement procedure, and customs valuation and standards. The scope of negotiations expanded again at the Uruguay Round, and member countries struggled to make rules on liberalization of services, intellectual property rights and trade-related investment measures (TRIMs).

Essentially inheriting these objectives from the GATT, the WTO set two main objectives: reduction or elimination of trade barriers and making trade rules. In addition, the WTO also covers areas related to trade facilitation such as standardization and harmonization.

Objectives of APEC

APEC did not have any concrete objectives at the beginning. Rather, it aimed to eschew building bloc economies and to promote the development of its members through economic cooperation. Accordingly, Ministers assembled in Canberra in 1989 merely 'to discuss how to advance the process of Asia Pacific Economic Cooperation' (APEC Ministerial Meeting 1989a). The Joint Statement issued at the meeting indicates that the discussions covered a variety of topics under the four agenda items:

- world and regional economic developments;
- global trade liberalisation – the role of the Asia Pacific region;

•opportunity for regional cooperation in specific areas; and
•future steps for Asia Pacific economic cooperation.

(APEC Ministerial Meeting 1989a)

Two years later, however, APEC clearly regarded its aim as being 'to reduce barriers to trade in goods and services and investment among participants' (APEC Ministerial Meeting 1991: Annex B, Seoul APEC Declaration, paragraph 1). The details of the process through which regional liberalization became a key objective of APEC are as follows.

Though the chairman's summary at the first Ministerial Meeting mentioned trade liberalization, APEC did not intend to create a free trade area in the region at that time. For APEC, the most important concern was how to strengthen and further liberalize the multilateral trading system (APEC Ministerial Meeting 1989b: paragraph 8). This would require consideration of how to remove 'any obstacles to a comprehensive and ambitious MTN result' (APEC Ministerial Meeting 1989b: paragraph 9). As such, the statement of the first Ministerial Meeting indicates that APEC should encourage an open multilateral trading system and should avoid becoming an inward-looking trading bloc (APEC Ministerial Meeting 1989a).

At the second Ministerial Meeting held in Singapore, Ministers still recognized that a continuing central theme of APEC would be the promotion of a more open world trading system. On the other hand, they also agreed that 'it was desirable to reduce barriers to trade in goods and services *among participants*' (APEC Ministerial Meeting 1990: paragraph 19, italics by the author), and even though it was restrictive in nature, Ministers regarded such a new issue as a tool for realizing APEC's fundamental objective. In order further to explore this issue, the Informal Group on Regional Trade Liberalization (RTL) was established in March 1991. At the third Ministerial Meeting in Seoul, Ministers adopted the Seoul APEC Declaration, representing the principles, objectives and understandings of APEC, in which trade liberalization among participants was one of four objectives.

With the emergence of regional trade liberalization as a key issue, the scope of APEC activities has rapidly expanded to overlap with those of the WTO. Following the Seattle Meeting of 1993, liberalization in the region was promoted to the main topic for discussion. At last APEC economies committed to 'complete the achievement of our goal of free and open trade and investment in the Asia-Pacific ... with the industrialized economies no later than the year 2010 and developing economies no later than the year 2020' (APEC Leaders Meeting 1994: paragraph 6). Developing member economies objected to such a trend in APEC, claiming that the original role of APEC was to promote not only liberalization but also economic cooperation in all fields related to liberalization. Quite clearly, the APEC goal of creating an open and liberal economic system complements the objectives of

GATT/WTO. However, they emphasized that APEC should be distinguished from the WTO in the field of trade 'negotiations.'[17] As a result of adopting demands from both sides, APEC activity is based on three central pillars: trade and investment liberalization, trade and investment facilitation, and economic and technical cooperation.

Differences at the operational level

Binding force of agreement

Binding force of the GATT/WTO agreements

The agreements at the GATT/WTO are generally adopted as agreements in a treaty sense, and have legally binding force when they meet necessary conditions for coming into effect such as signature and ratification. Four reasons explain why this is the case: the origin of the GATT, the principle of reciprocity, economic sovereignty, and the constitution of original members.

First, as discussed above, a series of bilateral commercial 'treaties' were enacted prior to the GATT establishment. It was natural that the participants in the conference, which sought an appropriate international trade system after World War II, selected the existing framework of bilateral treaties as the basis of the GATT. Second, as the principle of reciprocity is merely a basis for negotiation process, reciprocal commitments to liberalization do not have the legal backing to enforce the agreement. Thus, the GATT requires cooperative action among the member countries to ensure the legally binding power of an agreement by adopting that agreement in the form of a treaty. Third, each country had the sovereign right to impose tariffs and regulations on imports unilaterally. Therefore it was necessary for the GATT agreement to lay obligations upon contracting parties to reduce tariffs and non-tariff impediments by means of binding force. In other words, there exists 'the irony that to reduce regulation of one kind it takes regulation of another kind' (Winham 1992: 21). Finally, it was the United States which proposed the ITO Charter, which predated the GATT agreement, and the original contracting parties to the agreement were mainly composed of the developed states. These factors permitted the straightforward adoption of the Western-style legalistic approach to the decision making procedures.

Binding force of APEC agreements

In contrast to the GATT, the declarations/joint statements made by Ministers and Leaders of APEC do not have any binding force. Most are mere recommendations or policy statements indicating the direction that APEC activities should take. This was the understanding among member economies at the very beginning of APEC.

When the agreements merely declared necessity of cooperation, it did not matter if the agreements had legally binding power. However, conflicting views regarding the binding force have become apparent as APEC activities increasingly deal with concrete issues and require member economies to act specifically. After the Seattle Meeting in 1993, when the United States altered its position so as to increase its level of involvement, the United States began to exert pressure in an attempt to make the agreements legally binding. However, the Asian members were keen to retain the historical non-binding forms of agreement. The Non-Binding Investment Principles[18] declared at the Jakarta Ministerial Meeting in 1994 illustrate this tension between the two opposing views. Although members adopted the Principles in non-binding form, every provision was carefully drawn up as if a treaty was being drafted so that the document could serve as the groundwork for binding principles in the future (Kikuchi 1995: 251).

Moreover, the Osaka Meeting in 1995 represented a new phase in the vision and goals of APEC. Leaders declared that '[they] have ... entered the action phase in translating this vision and these goals into reality,' agreeing to 'adopt the Osaka Action Agenda ... to carry through [their] commitment at Bogor.' They also declared that they 'will implement the Action Agenda with unwavering resolve' (APEC Leaders Meeting 1995a: paragraph 2). This progression of APEC activities rendered the binding force problem even more controversial. In order to proceed towards trade liberalization, more specific actions towards achievement should be taken. Some industrialized member economies, especially the United States, attempted to lay the groundwork for the formation of a legally binding framework at the Osaka Meeting. During this meeting, in the light of their steadily improving economies, developing economies seemed to be less hesitant to accept the need for specific actions such as reducing export subsidies and harmonization of administrative procedures governing certification. Despite this, there is no alteration to the traditional recognition that APEC agreements have no binding force.

More attention should be paid to APEC since it suggests a unique liberalization measure, under which each member economy would liberalize unilaterally and simultaneously without being legally bound to do so. In APEC, 'peer pressure' is expected to play a role in securing implementation of agreements. If agreements are put into practice as they are in the current APEC system, a stronger or more formal organization might not be required (Kahler 1995: 35). The effect of this 'peer pressure,' however, is hard to guarantee. Moreover, each action of trade liberalization in APEC is not reciprocal but mutual.[19] This means that a member economy that commits to a sharp unilateral reduction in tariffs cannot expect or require other economies to liberalize to the same level. Liberalization measures in APEC are weak compared to those of the GATT/WTO, which are defined as a 'propulsive power to liberalization' based on the principle of reciprocity.

Such characteristics of APEC are another reason that APEC would be regarded as simply a 'consultative meeting' of leaders and ministers.

Decision making process

Decision making process in the GATT/WTO

In practice, the decision making process of the GATT was based on consensus building, even though Article XXV provided that decisions should be based on the majority vote except where otherwise determined.[20] The consensus procedure developed throughout the lifetime of the GATT and became well established despite being an unwritten rule. The WTO adopted this practice as Paragraph 1 of Article IX of the Marrakesh Agreement, which states 'the WTO shall continue the practice of decision-making by consensus followed under GATT 1947.'[21] Thus decision making by consensus became formalized under the WTO. In a footnote to that provision, the meaning of consensus is defined as follows: 'The body concerned shall be deemed to have decided by consensus on a matter submitted for its consideration, if no Member, present at the meeting when the decision is taken, formally objects to the proposed decision.' This means that consensus in the WTO, as well as majority voting and unanimity, is a formal procedure for making legally binding decisions.

In many international organizations, which have procedural provisions in their constitutional documents, participants make decisions mainly by formal voting arrangements such as majority voting and unanimous voting. Recently, however, there seems to be a trend towards an increased use of consensus as a mode of decision making in international practice. This may be explained by changes in the international society, which has grown more diverse as well as more interdependent, and as a result, unanimity and majority voting have become less suitable as modes of decision making (Van Hoof 1983: 225–6).

Decision making process in APEC

Some principal trade countries played leading roles in negotiations when the main issue of the trade round of the GATT was tariff reduction (Winham 1992: 56). Therefore, it was difficult for developing countries to participate in the round negotiation. Even if they were able to take places at the negotiation table, their affiliation with established international institutions meant that they did not have any chance to object to the existing decision making system. However, APEC developed along different lines from traditional international institutions. Participation of ASEAN members in APEC from its inception is reflected in the influence of these countries over the initial design of the APEC operating principles. In APEC, the diversity of member economies requires special consideration regarding methods of decision making. The ASEAN countries accordingly stressed that sufficient discussion should be guaranteed before reaching an agreement among all APEC members.

At the first Ministerial Meeting, APEC adopted consensus-based procedures for its decision making process (APEC Ministerial Meeting 1989b: Paragraph 16). The APEC procedures, however, differ from those of the GATT/WTO. The consensus-technique in the GATT/WTO provides for the continuation of negotiations until an agreement is reached without any special objection. After such negotiation, participants adopt agreements not by voting but 'by consensus.' In contrast, in the APEC process, consensus procedures are based on step-by-step consultations rather than voting. If there is any dissent on issues among member economies, such issues are left out of the acceptable contents. Then, at the end of the meeting, APEC Ministers or Leaders declare the common assent of all members as 'consensus.' In this sense, consensus in the APEC process is not a formal decision making procedure that can put legally binding power on the agreements. This APEC process may represent a co-option of the ASEAN consensus procedure.

Round no.	Place/name	Year	Subjects covered	Participating members
First	Geneva	1947	tariffs	23
Second	Annecy	1949	tariffs	13
Third	Torquay	1951	tariffs	38
Fourth	Geneva	1956	tariffs	26
Fifth	Dillon Round	1960 –61	tariffs	26
Sixth	Kennedy Round	1964 –67	tariffs, anti-dumping measures	62
Seventh	Tokyo Round	1973 –79	tariffs, non-tariff measures, framework ' agreements	102
Eighth	Uruguay Round	1986 –94	tariffs, non-tariff measures, rules, services, intellectual property, dispute settlement, textiles, agriculture, creation of the WTO, etc.	123
Ninth	Doha Development Agenda	2001–	tariffs, non-tariff measures	146

Source: WTO (2001).

The problem with APEC-style consensus is that each member economy is likely to have different interpretations of one issue, even though they have reached a consensus on it.[22] This is one of the reasons why APEC agreements are often criticized as ambiguous and superficial, lacking specific provisions, sometimes no more than empty slogans. On the other hand, it is likely that consensus in APEC could be reached because members have discretion to make interpretations of agreements freely and independently. Nothing seems to be agreed within the framework of APEC that requires common interpretation among member economies. APEC has never purported to play an executive role similar to the GATT/WTO and hence has been able to develop a unique style of consensus building.

Liberalization approach

Liberalization approach of the GATT/WTO

The principal mechanism of the GATT for addressing the reduction of tariff levels and other trade impediments is the multilateral tariff/trade negotiations (MTNs), referred to as 'trade rounds.' Over the fifty years of its history, the GATT/WTO had nine trade rounds (Table 1.1). The first five were called 'multilateral *tariff* negotiations,' while the subsequent rounds were known as 'multilateral *trade* negotiations.' This change in the name reflects the GATT's development. The GATT gradually evolved through the series of rounds in terms of increasing its size, broadening the scope of issues covered and improving the negotiation process. However, at the Kennedy Round, the characteristics and function of the rounds underwent dramatic change. Prior to the Kennedy Round, the reduction of tariffs on imports was the major item on the agenda. However, after the Kennedy Round, the scope of negotiations rapidly expanded to include non-tariff measures.

It was also following the Kennedy Round that 'package deal' measures were incorporated into the decision making process. As previously mentioned, the GATT simply transformed the bilateral negotiation process of the prewar period into a multilateral process. However, in order to protect itself from the possibility of free riders, it contrived a new procedure that effectively excluded them (Winham 1992: 53). This operational technique developed into a 'single undertaking' procedure at the Uruguay Round.

While member countries recognized that MTNs still have much significance in promoting freer trade, it is a fact that MTNs have been facing some obstacles. This is attributable mainly to structural problems such as the increase in the number of participants in round negotiations and the expansion of the negotiating area. Numerous participants and various agendas make negotiations much more complicated, and also make conflicts of interest much more acute. As a result, MTNs based on a single undertaking procedure tend to be protracted.

Liberalization approach of APEC

Faced with possible deadlock during the Uruguay Round, which was negotiated through a traditional rule-based approach, APEC offered a different option for liberalization. The OAA of 1995 prescribed a unique mechanism, referred to as 'concerted unilateral action (CUA).' CUA is essentially a combination of two different definitions of actions: actions by individual member economies and actions agreed by APEC, referred to as 'collective action.' According to the CUA mechanism, the Manila Action Plan for APEC (MAPA) in 1996 consisted of two parts: the Individual Action Plan (IAP) and the Collective Action Plan (CAP). The former is the action list for liberalization, which member economies would pursue respectively and unilaterally. The latter is one that all members would undertake commonly and uniformly. Retention of these contrastive views in the liberalization approach has resulted from differences in the understanding of how to realize trade liberalization in the region between the Asian member economies and the United States. Asian countries emphasized measures based on voluntarism, which led to a concept of IAP according to which members would take the initiative in implementing liberalization at their own speed.[23] In contrast, the United States proposed an idea of CAP, which requires that all members should make efforts to achieve common goals under a single schedule.[24] The United States most likely thought that IAP put too much weight on voluntarism to secure implementation of liberalization.

It is basically recognized that the commitment of the APEC members is legally non-binding. In this sense, CUA is totally different from the bargaining model and the give-and-take processes that typify the GATT/WTO. Unlike the WTO approach, CUA suggests that member economies should act independently, each laying out plans for liberalization. What a member receives from the other members on the way to liberalization is encouragement and criticism in the form of so-called 'peer pressure' only. Several APEC members, however, oppose the idea of CUA, feeling that liberalization under this approach may fail to be fully realized. Nevertheless, based on the assumption that members are more likely to reach long-term goals through 'peer pressure' than strictly legalistic and detailed trade agreements, CUA was finally chosen as the primary measure for implementing the OAA. This is a new tactic to promote the reduction of barriers to trade and investment. However, questions have been raised as to whether CUA can truly liberalize trade in the absence of legally binding requirements.

The development of correlation

Consistency with Article XXIV of the GATT agreements

Today, in addition to the WTO, which promotes trade liberalization on the global level, there are many regional trade agreements (RTAs). The significance of RTAs is highly regarded under the GATT/WTO system with the phrase that '[they] have greatly increased in number and importance since the establishment of GATT 1947 and today cover a significant proportion of world trade.'[25] Article XXIV of the GATT agreement permits the formation of preferential trading arrangements as exceptions to the non-discrimination principle in the form of customs unions (CUs) and free trade areas with the following requirements. First, countries establishing free trade areas should not increase external tariffs. In CUs, the common tariffs for third countries should not be higher or more restrictive than the general incidence of these duties before the CUs were formed. Second, participants should eliminate duties of 'substantially all the trade' between the constituent territories. Third, CUs or free trade areas should be implemented 'within a reasonable length of time'.[26]

Some critics have argued that the 'free and open trade and investment in the Asia-Pacific' aimed at by APEC is not the same as the common RTAs regarded as complements to the GATT/WTO liberalization process. Dieter explains the situation as follows:

> [A]n APEC free-trade area granting preferences on a basis other than that of most-favored-nation treatment is in striking contradiction with the spirit of the GATT. APEC includes so great a part of the global economy that Asia-Pacific integration within this framework could develop into an alternative to liberalization in the WTO context. Precisely because some APEC countries are economically so potent, successful integration in the Pacific region could weaken the process of multilateral liberalization under the GATT or in the WTO context.
>
> (Dieter 1997: 20)

However this criticism is not necessarily relevant from the legal point of view, given that APEC is not categorized as a free trade area under Article XXIV, mainly because it does not discriminate against third parties with its fundamental concept of 'open regionalism.' As former Director General of the WTO, Renato Ruggiero elucidates:

> The second interpretation of open regionalism is ... that the gradual elimination of internal barriers to trade within a regional grouping will be implemented at more or less the same rate and on the same timetable as the [elimination] of barriers towards non-members. This would be generally consistent not only with the rules of the WTO but also – and this is very important – with the MFN principle.
>
> (Ruggiero, quoted in Drysdale 1997: 3)

APEC is neither an RTA as an exception from MFN obligations nor a violation of them. It is hard to establish a legal place for APEC in the regulations of the WTO. The reasons are as follows. First, APEC is just a consulting forum, which is not required to inform the WTO as an RTA under Article

XXIV. Second, regional trade liberalization in APEC is based on 'open regionalism,' which means APEC does not offend the non-discrimination principle. In other words, APEC is not at issue to be examined regarding its consistency with Article XXIV.[27] In addition, most APEC members themselves did not want APEC liberalization to be part of a formal arrangement requiring WTO notification under Article XXIV. In particular, they were concerned that consistency with the WTO rules depended on the examination result, and in such case, that there was a possibility that APEC's regional trade liberalization would be deemed a violation of Article I (Saxonhouse 1996: 206). This thinking on behalf of APEC members is apparent in the wording of official statements, which refer to 'free and open trade and investment in the region' rather than 'a free trade area.'

The WTO plays a key role in managing the international free trade system. At the same time, various RTAs work complementarily toward the WTO's mission. In the sense of the traditional framework of multilateralism and regionalism, which generally implies that the former is superior to the latter, APEC is peculiar and unique: it does not exist completely under the umbrella of the WTO system, nor yet is it against the WTO. In reality, APEC seems comfortable managing the two somewhat contradictory roles as an independent body which is part of the WTO system.

Attitude of APEC toward the WTO

The WTO does not pay much attention to the position of APEC in the WTO system. On the other hand, how does APEC conceive of its position in the WTO system? APEC declarations and statements repeatedly recognize the superiority of the GATT/WTO system and emphasize that regional liberalization should be implemented in accordance with the framework of the GATT/WTO. However, the role and its position in the WTO system, which APEC itself recognize, seem to be changing slightly as time goes on.

In fact, APEC has itself made a significant role change from a venue for consultation on trade liberalization to an institution for implementing liberalization. APEC's initial objective, as mentioned above, was to ensure a successful conclusion of the Uruguay Round. From the second to the fifth meeting, APEC Ministers repeatedly issued declarations concerning the Uruguay Round in a bid for a constructive outcome. It is widely recognized that this continual pressure from APEC contributed to the successful conclusion of the Round. At that time, APEC played an 'effective cheerleader role' encouraging and supporting MTNs (Petri 1999: 15).

At the Seattle Meeting in 1993, however, APEC's contribution to the Uruguay Round subtly changed. Up to the Seattle Meeting, APEC acted as a cheerleader/supporter, encouraging MTNs from beyond the round table on which GATT members had been bargaining on tariff reduction and other agenda items. In Seattle, however, fear of the possible failure of the Uruguay Round negotiations forced APEC to adopt a more active role, attempting to ensure an alternative route to multilateral liberalization through liberalization at the regional level. This new role is amplified in the Joint Statement (APEC Ministerial Meeting 1993) as follows:

> Ministers ... demonstrated their commitment to this [early and successful conclusion to the Uruguay Round] goal *by expressing their preparedness to take additional specific trade liberalizing measures... .*',
>
> (paragraph 17. Italics added by the author)

> Ministers noted in particular the effective role played by APEC in maintaining the momentum for a satisfactory outcome to the Uruguay Round ...
>
> (paragraph 19)

The challenge to APEC to lead multilateral trade liberalization by shifting from a mere cheerleader to an executing institution persisted after the conclusion of the Uruguay Round. The results of this challenge were the Bogor Declaration in 1994 and the OAA in 1995. It was mainly a change in US attitude toward the APEC process, a step up in its level of participation, which proved the catalyst for this change in the nature of APEC. From 1994 to 1995, APEC recognized the primacy of the WTO and the need to strengthen the multilateral trading system in conformity with the GATT/WTO provisions. This means that in effect APEC still placed itself under the WTO system at this time.

> APEC economies will take the lead in strengthening the open multilateral trading system and enhancing global liberalization momentum by participating actively and positively in multilateral negotiations and *exploring the possibility of taking joint initiatives under the WTO*, including initiatives for the first WTO Ministerial Meeting in Singapore. APEC economies will take fully into account the outcome of such multilateral activities.
>
> (APEC Leaders Meeting 1995b: Section B. Italics added by the author)

After 1996, APEC took a further change of direction, pursuing a partnership with the WTO while calling for cooperation on trade liberalization at the regional and multilateral levels. At this stage, APEC appeared self-confident and, as an implementing body of the regional trade framework, was keen to emphasize its differences from the WTO. This attitude is encapsulated in the following statements:

> APEC's voluntary framework and the WTO's legal one can mutually reinforce liberalization and the process of analysis and consensus

building in one forum can contribute to progressing negotiations in the other.

(APEC Trade Ministers Meeting 1996: paragraph 12)

Ministers agreed to work to ensure that regional and multilateral trade and investment initiatives complement and support each other.

(APEC Ministerial Meeting 1997b: paragraph 6)

Although it is not clear from these excerpts whether APEC intends to significantly change its role, from its statements and declarations it can be seen to be cultivating a role as an independent executive body, while utilizing the WTO as a means to resolve contentious issues. The presence of APEC in the free trading system would become greater than before. These are the circumstances in which the EVSL consultation began.

Concluding remarks

The distinctive feature of APEC is not only diversity of its member economies, which is a far from unique phenomenon given that Asian and other developing countries take part in many international institutions. For example, both NAFTA and the EU are composed of various members whose levels of development are different. One of the factors that makes APEC different and contrasts with the situation in many other institutions is the participation of developing countries in APEC from the very beginning and their influence in the decision making process. APEC has adopted distinctive principles such as voluntarism and open regionalism. It also developed differently from ordinary international intergovernmental institutions. In general, given that they developed out of the Western states tradition, such institutions gave non-Western countries little chance to participate in institution building.

The GATT, on the other hand, was established in order to substantially reduce tariffs and other trade barriers and to eliminate discriminatory treatments in international trade that were brought into the bloc economy in the 1930s. The GATT was based on a series of bilateral trade agreements, concluded mainly among Western countries which, until the late 1930s, comprised a fairly elaborate network. Accordingly, it took reciprocity and the rule of law as guiding principles of its institutional operation.

These inherent differences become most apparent with respect to the controversial issue of binding force. The WTO regards binding force as an essential element of the agreements in respect to advancement of liberalization. Western states consider binding force the only secure measure for the full implementation of agreements. APEC, however, recognizes that liberalization under its framework can be achieved only through the voluntary actions of individual members. Since the economic development levels of member states are diverse, forcing a single rule on all the members is thought unlikely to be effective. Furthermore, the GATT/WTO and APEC contain different interpretations of the decision making process. At first glance, the decision making processes of these institutions look similar, as both regard consensus as the most significant part of the process. However, deeper examination reveals crucial differences. Consensus in the GATT/WTO is a formal procedure for making legally binding decisions, as majority voting and unanimity are. On the other hand, consensus in the APEC process means not the legal procedure for decision making, but the scope of assent which can be shared among all member economies.

In this way, despite the fact that the two institutions share the common objective of realizing a freer world trading system, they differ in many fundamental aspects. Hence it is natural that APEC and the WTO implement different measures for trade liberalization. It makes sense that APEC seeks a mutual and unilateral approach as opposed to GATT/WTO's style. Consequently, the WTO can be regarded as a locus of negotiations and rule making whereas APEC functions as a consultative body.

Even though the two institutions share a common objective, no close correlation or mutual cooperation has been shaped between APEC and the GATT/WTO. APEC, which advocates open regionalism and operates as an independent consulting body, is not in the position of intergovernmental institutions like the IMF and the World Bank nor is it in the same category as RTAs like the EU and NAFTA. Under the WTO system, the former are expected to cooperate with the WTO in its aim of achieving greater coherence in global economic policy making (Marrakesh Agreement, Article III-5), and the latter are formally allowed under the Article XXIV of the GATT agreement as exceptions to the non-discrimination principle. It is hard to classify APEC under the current regulations of the WTO. On the other hand, APEC members insist on the consistency of APEC with the WTO, viewing both as instruments for the maintenance and strengthening of the global free trade system.

This gap between the self-recognition of APEC and the recognition by the WTO of APEC in relation to the WTO is reflected in the one-way relationship between the two. In every Ministerial Meeting from 1990 to 1994, APEC made declarations calling for the successful conclusion of the Uruguay Round, demonstrating the possibilities of trade liberalization in the APEC region. These connected movements indisputably brought a conclusion to the Uruguay Round. However, APEC merely unilaterally 'cheered' multilateral negotiations. In this respect, a close two-way correlation failed to emerge between them. The unilateral nature of the relationship between APEC and the WTO persisted after the Uruguay Round. As APEC transposed its role from consulting to independent executive body, however, it seems to have shifted from its position under the umbrella of the WTO, securing its presence in the free trade system for two-way cooperation with the WTO despite its recognition of the GATT/WTO's superiority.

Notes

1 According to Jackson (1989: 31), this was because the conference was sponsored by and under the jurisdiction of ministries of finance, while trade was under the jurisdiction of different ministries. In addition to this, Winham (1992: 26) says that the initial emphasis for Second World War reconstruction was to re-establish a payment mechanism, for without monetary exchange trade was impossible. Therefore, less attention was given to trade issues.

2 The ITO Preparatory Conference consisted of nineteen members: Australia, Belgium, Luxembourg, Brazil, Canada, Chile, China, Cuba, Czechoslovakia, France, India, Lebanon, Netherlands, New Zealand, Norway, South Africa, Syria, the United Kingdom and the United States.

3 Although fifty-three states signed the ITO Charter, only Australia and Liberia ratified it.

4 Participants of this trade round were the members of the ITO Preparatory Conference (see note 2) plus Burma, Ceylon, Southern Rhodesia and Pakistan.

5 The reason why the United States concentrated on tariff reduction was 'to take advantage of the president's negotiating powers before the Trade Agreements Act had to be renewed in 1948' (Diebold 1996: 157).

6 APEC inherits several concepts of economic cooperation in the Asia-Pacific region designed by international non-governmental institutions in the second half of the twentieth century. In the 1960s, two such institutions were inaugurated. One is the Pacific Trade and Development Conference (PAFTAD), in which professional economists discuss and analyze economic problems relating to the region; the other is the Pacific Basin Economic Council (PBEC) that provides a forum for exchanging information among business people from the region. The Pacific Economic Cooperation Conference (PECC), founded in 1980, also actively furthers regional collaboration by linking academics, private business and governmental officials. See Beeson (1996: 39).

7 As to the position of ASEAN in APEC, the significant role of ASEAN was declared both in the Joint Statement and the Chairman's Summary Statement of the First Ministerial Meeting in 1989 (APEC Ministerial Meeting 1989a; 1989b: Paragraph 16). Regarding how the APEC process should be conducted, the Kuching Consensus declared in February 1990 showed clearly ASEAN's basic attitude at that time.

8 Interview with APEC-related officials, the Ministry of International Trade and Industry (MITI), Japan, August 1995. Moreover, Sandra Kristoff, the then United States Ambassador for APEC affairs, proposed that APEC should become a formal economic cooperation association or 'a GATT for Asia-Pacific.' Fred Bergsten, the US representative and chairman of the Eminent Persons Group, stated that 'leaders in Seattle began the process of converting APEC from a purely consultative body into a substantive international institution' (Soesastro 1994: 46–9).

9 Interview with APEC-related officials of MITI (Japan), August 1995; Soesastro (1994: 46–); *Asahi Shimbun*, 10 November 1995 and *Nihon Keizai Shimbun*, 16, 17, 18 November 1995.

10 *Yomiuri Shimbun*, 18 November 1995; *Mainichi Shimbun*, 18 November 1995; interview with APEC-related officials of MITI (Japan), November 1995.

11 Reciprocity is often regarded as synonymous with 'mutual relationship.' Yet they are different. First, in a reciprocal relationship, a voluntary action belongs only to the giving side because a contingent action is obligatory in return. In contrast, a 'mutual' relationship occurs when both participants give to each other of their own free will. Second, reciprocity includes balance and symmetry in the sense of a bilateral relationship where one gives and the other returns. By comparison, a mutual relationship does not necessarily require such a balance between participants (Kuwahara, 1975: 416).

12 The free-rider issue originates from the contradiction between two core principles of the GATT: non-discrimination and reciprocity. Concessions such as reducing tariffs and elimination of NTMs given unconditionally by MFN obligation are not reciprocal but unilateral. The side that gives concessions cannot necessarily expect returns from the other side. In this point, the principle of non-discrimination embodied in the unconditional MFN clause contradicts the principle of reciprocity, which is explained as one side giving to the other and the other returning with equivalency.

13 For details of 'diffuse reciprocity,' see Keohane (1986) and Krasner (1987).

14 Developing countries originally understood the meaning of this provision as the need not to pay for concessions from industrialized nations. Later, however, contracting parties agreed the official interpretation of this provision to be that each developing country should provide a return concession proportional to its stage of development (Takase and Akasaka 1993: 46–7). The interpretative note of this provision says that 'it is understood that the phrase "do not expect reciprocity" means, in accordance with the objectives set forth in this Article, that the less-developed contracting parties should not be expected, in the course of trade negotiations, to make contributions which are inconsistent with their individual development, financial and trade needs, taking into consideration past trade developments'.

15 The concept 'open regionalism' that emerged from the practice of economic cooperation in the Asia-Pacific continued from the 1970s. It was at the first PECC meeting in Canberra in 1980 that the concept was initially articulated (Garnaut 1994: 273).

16 However, such criticism could be deemed appropriate: the progress of the APEC process could be prevented by members' reluctance towards active liberalization due to their disgust with free-riders.

17 *Yomiuri Shimbun*, 12 July 1995.

18 It states twelve principles such as national treatment and minimizing the use of performance requirements for the improvement and further liberalization of member economies' investment regimes.

19 See note 11.

20 There were only a few cases in which voting was necessary in the entire history of the GATT. Details on cases decided by voting were not made available despite obtaining interviews with officials for legal affairs of the WTO (22, 25 November 2000).

21 Article IX of the Marrakesh Agreement also states that 'where a decision cannot be arrived at by consensus, the matter at issue shall be decided by voting.' In the voting, each member country has one vote.

22 For instance, although consensus was reached concerning the promotion of liberalization on the basis of the voluntarism principle in the EVSL consultation, the Japanese and United States' conceptual interpretation of voluntarism differ in the extreme.

23 Most of the Asian members (China, Indonesia, Hong Kong, South Korea, Malaysia, The Philippines and Japan) emphasized the efficiency of this idea (interview with an APEC-related official of MITI (Japan), July 1995).

24 Besides the United States, the supporters of the CAP were Australia and New Zealand (interview with an APEC-related official of MITI (Japan), July 1995).

25 The Preamble of the Understanding on the Interpretation of Article XXIV of the GATT 1994.

26 Article XXIV of the original GATT agreement contained a non-specific provision on the time-scale for implementing integration projects. At the Uruguay Round, member countries discussed clarifying the criteria and, as a result defined 'a reasonable length of time' as generally within ten years.

27 Interview with officials of the WTO Secretariat, 22, 25 September 2000.

2   The development of EVSL consultations and setting the research questions

Jiro Okamoto

Early Voluntary Sectoral Liberalization (EVSL)[1] was an attempt to liberalize certain sectors before the general goal of 'free and open trade and investment' by 2010 for developed members and by 2020 for others. The idea of liberalizing certain sectors earlier than others originated in the *Osaka Action Agenda* (OAA), which was endorsed by the Leaders Meeting in 1995. The idea gained momentum in 1996. At the Subic Leaders Meeting in 1996, they agreed to support the Information Technology Agreement (ITA) at the WTO Ministerial Conference that was to be held within a month in Singapore. The subsequent success of ITA at the WTO was believed to indicate the possibility of conducting similar liberalization initiatives in other sectors.

In this chapter, how the international consultations on EVSL started and developed, and what result they produced, will be explained first in some detail. The purpose of this work is to construct common understandings of EVSL and its consultation process. The first section will deal with the origin and the early stage of EVSL, the second section will take up the period of building the basis for consultations, and the third will describe what happened in the period of more concrete consultations on what EVSL could and should deliver.

After clarifying the development of EVSL consultations, tangible research questions will be set in the fourth section. The issue that this book tries to analyze ultimately (why EVSL failed) is too general, and it is difficult for case studies in Part II to tackle them as it is. Thus, by organizing points of contention that have been brought out in the previous sections, concrete and manageable research questions are presented for Part II case studies.

The origins of EVSL and the impact of the success of ITA (1995–6)

The idea of liberalizing specific sectors earlier than others originated in the process of making the OAA in 1995. The OAA (APEC Leaders Meeting 1995b) stated that APEC economies will:

identify industries in which the progressive reduction of tariffs may have positive impact on trade and on economic growth in the Asia-Pacific region or for which there is regional industry support for early liberalization.

(Part One, Section C, 1. Tariffs, Collective Actions-b)

identify industries in which the progressive reduction of non-tariff measures may have positive impact on trade and on economic growth in the Asia-Pacific region or there is regional support for early liberalization.

(Part One, Section C, 2. Non-Tariff Measures, Collective Actions-b)

At this stage, the emphasis was put just on the study to identify industries that were thought to be desirable for early liberalization. No member economies raised opposition to the inclusion of the above phrases in the OAA, as the concept of EVSL was still vague.[2] Moreover, there was no specific time limit set in the OAA to finish the study. In a multilateral forum such as APEC, if there is no explicit opposition from participants to any agenda, it will be resolved that they reached consensus.

In 1996, APEC members concentrated on their first Individual Action Plans (IAPs) and Collective Action Plan (CAP). These efforts eventually culminated in the *Manila Action Plan for APEC*, which was adopted by the Manila Ministerial Meeting and endorsed by the Subic Leaders Meeting in November.[3] At the same time, the idea of EVSL gained momentum in 1996. By the time APEC Leaders met in November, the direction was firmly set. In the Leaders' Declaration, they announced,

We further *instruct our ministers to identify sectors where early voluntary liberalization would have a positive impact* on trade, investment, and economic growth in the individual APEC economies as well as in the region, *and submit to us their recommendation on how this can be achieved.*
(APEC Leaders Meeting 1996: paragraph 8. Italics added by the author)

The Leaders' instruction to Ministers to identify and report sectors for early liberalization made the EVSL process within APEC formal. In other words, as Leaders committed themselves in EVSL in this way, the APEC activities in 1997 had to pursue the issue.[4]

The main factor that drove the idea of EVSL during 1996 and after was the successful conclusion of the ITA at the WTO. It is important to note that the modality of tariff reduction under the ITA framework seems to have had a strong influence on EVSL. Thus, it is useful to review the ITA process in 1996 and its characteristics before going on to explore the development of EVSL.

The initiator of the ITA process was the United States, which already had international competitiveness in products such as computer hardware and software, semiconductors and telecommunication equipment. Japan soon followed suit. In April, the Quadrilateral Trade Ministers Meeting (Quad Meeting) between the United States, Japan, the European Union (EU) and Canada, held in Kobe, declared that they strongly supported the negotiation of an ITA (Quad Meeting 1996a). This statement, however, was not without reservation from participants. The EU Trade Commissioner imposed a condition to support an ITA, which was to include the EU in any agreement on semiconductors and other information products between Japan and the United States. The Japan–US Semiconductor Agreement was to terminate at the end of July and the US government was adamantly demanding the continuation of the Agreement, though the Japanese counterpart rejected the US claim.[5] The EU was wary of being excluded again from a possible arrangement between the two largest IT producers, and tried to link the two agendas.[6]

In July, Japan and the United States agreed to bring the bilateral agreement to an end and, instead, resolved to give private industries responsibility for monitoring foreign access to their respective markets by creating a regular meeting. Furthermore, they agreed to establish a 'Global Governmental Forum' for semiconductor trade by inviting both developed and developing economies.[7] Following the Japan–US decision, the EU softened its stance on ITA. The *Chairperson's Summary* of the Quad Meeting in Seattle in September stated:

> The Quad countries are determined to provide the leadership necessary to complete the Information Technology Agreement and to work together urgently to conclude the ITA by the Singapore Conference ... We intend to vigorously pursue an intensive work program on all relevant issues so as to ensure that broad participation from countries can be agreed at Singapore.
>
> (Quad Meeting 1996b)

Thus, by September, a basic alliance for the ITA among the United States, Japan, the EU and Canada was established. The combined value of the IT trade of the alliance was around two-thirds of the world total.

How did APEC respond to the development of the ITA initiative? The *Statement of the Chair* released after the APEC Trade Ministers Meeting (Meeting of Ministers Responsible for Trade) in July 1996 in Christchurch stated,

> We [Trade Ministers] discussed the possibility of undertaking more limited sectoral initiatives, perhaps in the shorter term. In this context, we listened with interest to explanation of the proposal for an Information Technology Agreement, which would contribute to APEC

liberalisation objectives, and determined that we would consider this
further in the lead up to the [WTO] Singapore Ministerial Conference.
(APEC Trade Ministers Meeting 1996: paragraph 10)

The Statement clearly illustrated that the Ministers' interest in EVSL was
encouraged by the development of ITA. Following the September Quad
Meeting that declared its commitment to seeking an early conclusion to the
ITA, APEC members started talks on the issue in October in Geneva, where
WTO headquarters are located. It was reported, however, that, after
listening to the explanation from the United States, Japan and Canada on
the ITA, various members, all of them developing economies, expressed
concerns. Malaysia argued that it was necessary to ensure flexibility in the
areas of product coverage and timeframes for tariff elimination.[8] The
Philippines claimed that it would be impossible to reduce its tariffs on
computers and semiconductors from the current minimum rate of 3 per
cent.[9] Taiwanese manufacturers of IT products articulated their concerns
about joining the ITA and eliminating the IT tariffs without making sure
that their immediate competitors from Korea, Malaysia, Thailand and the
Philippines were to do the same.[10]

The differences in attitudes towards the ITA between developed and
developing members of APEC were brought into the Manila Ministerial
Meeting in November. Regarding the ITA, the *Joint Statement* of the
Meeting read,

> In recognizing the importance of the information technology sector in
> world trade, Ministers endorsed the efforts at WTO to conclude an
> information technology agreement by the Singapore Ministerial
> Conference and urged other members of the WTO to work to that end.
> (APEC Ministerial Meeting 1996: paragraph 31)

In general, the APEC Ministers agreed to support the ITA to be concluded
at the inaugural WTO Ministerial Conference in Singapore. However, the
agreement was basically made on the concept of the ITA, not on details of
how and when the tariffs should be reduced. For instance, it was reported
that the Trade Minister of Malaysia commented after the Meeting, 'you
cannot expect every country to undertake market-opening measures at the
same time, at the same pace and over the same product sectors.'[11]

Nevertheless, the APEC Leaders Meeting, held two days after the
Ministerial, made a big step forward towards the ITA. The Leaders'
Declaration stated,

> Recognizing the importance of information technology in the twenty-
> first century, APEC Leaders call for the conclusion of an information
> technology agreement by the WTO Ministerial Conference that would

substantially eliminate tariffs by the year 2000, recognizing need for flexibility
as negotiations in Geneva proceed.
(APEC Leaders Meeting 1996: paragraph 13. Italics added by the author)

Leaders approved the degree of tariff reduction (substantial elimination) and
the deadline for tariff reduction (the year 2000), which the Ministerial
Meeting could not agree on, in exchange for some concessions (recognizing
need for flexibility). Though the meaning of the words 'substantially' and
'flexibility' remained ambiguous, it was clear that the Leaders' accord had a
driving effect on the conclusion of ITA at the coming WTO Ministerial
Conference.

The Singapore Ministerial Conference of the WTO in December 1996,
held less than a month after the APEC Ministerial and Leaders Meetings,
successfully concluded the ITA. At the Conference, the ITA was signed by
twenty-nine economies, nine of them APEC members: Australia, Canada,
Hong Kong, Indonesia, Japan, Korea, Singapore, Taiwan and the United
States. By April 1997, eleven more economies notified their acceptance of
the ITA. Three of them were APEC members: Malaysia, New Zealand and
Thailand. The Philippines and China had subsequently joined the ITA by
the time the Agreement entered into force in July 1997. There were forty-
eight participating economies altogether in the ITA by September 1999.
Among APEC members, Brunei, Chile, Mexico, Papua New Guinea, Peru,
Russia and Vietnam were yet to join the Agreement.[12]

The ITA is a distinctive agreement on liberalizing a specific industrial
sector and is solely a tariff elimination mechanism.[13] From the development
of ITA before and after the Singapore Ministerial Conference, several characteristics that influenced the modality of EVSL can be pointed out.

1 Supporters of the ITA tried to form a 'critical mass' and succeeded.
   Critical mass is a relative concept. If the *mass* of participants of an agreement reached a critical level, the motivation for non-participants to join
   the agreement would get considerably stronger, because the cost of not
   joining would surpass that of joining. Critical mass is not necessarily a
   function of the number of participants. For instance, the ITA stated in
   Paragraph 3 of the Annex that participants would start cutting tariffs
   once their total trade in IT products covered approximately 90 per cent
   of the world total (WTO 1996). Obviously, critical mass for the ITA
   was thought to be the number of participants whose IT trade comprised
   90 per cent of the world total.

2 'Product coverage' of the ITA is shown in the Attachments to Annex.
   Attachment A (a list of headings according to the Harmonized System
   1996) and B (a list of products) which cover a wide range of information-related products,[14] and participants must reduce tariffs on *all*
   products covered without exception.

3   The ITA employs a 'staging' process for tariff elimination, which means participants must reduce tariffs in equal rates and at equal times in principle. After the fourth stage in January 2000, tariff elimination for all the products covered must be complete. In certain cases, however, the ITA allows extended staging on a product-by-product basis, if a participant so requests and others agree.[15] In other words, flexibility in tariff reduction under the ITA framework is only allowed in extended implementation periods. Nevertheless, the staging period cannot be extended beyond 2005 in any case.

Building foundations for EVSL (1997)

APEC Ministers were assigned to two EVSL-related tasks in 1997. One was to select sectors for EVSL and the other was to recommend the procedure by which EVSL should be implemented. Both assignments were to be reported to the Vancouver Leaders Meeting in November for endorsement.

Setting the modality

Most of the first half of 1997 was used for discussion on how EVSL should be undertaken. At the very first stage of discussion, the pro-liberalization members of APEC, such as the United States, Canada, Australia and New Zealand, were considering EVSL as just a trade liberalization mechanism like the ITA. Their basic intention was to make the EVSL process a tariff reduction/elimination mechanism with due attention to NTBs. However, strong requests from developing members such as China and ASEAN countries to include trade facilitation and Ecotech elements in EVSL, were made as early as January, when the APEC Senior Official Meeting (SOM) and the Committee for Trade and Investment (CTI) met in Victoria for the first time that year. The SOM and CTI recommended that EVSL comprise all three 'pillars' of APEC activities: trade liberalization, trade facilitation and Ecotech. The United States and other pro-liberalization members did not object to the inclusion of trade facilitation and Ecotech in the EVSL process, as they resolved that this would secure developing members' participation in EVSL.[16]

At the Montreal Trade Ministers Meeting in May 1997, the basis of the modality for EVSL began to emerge. The *Statement of the Chair* held that:

Acting on this [Leaders'] instruction [in Subic, November 1996], Ministers reviewed ways in which *early voluntary liberalization, complemented by trade facilitation and economic and technical cooperation*, in APEC could achieve these objectives and contribute to multilateral liberaliza-

tion of trade and investment in a manner consistent with and complementary to the WTO.

Ministers confirmed their willingness to consider favourably opportunities for *voluntary liberalisation through Individual Action Plans ...*

Ministers agreed to direct officials to examine the merits of pursuing
comprehensive liberalization in such sectors having regard to defining scope
and coverage, including those that support enhanced infrastructure and
sustainable development ...

Ministers instructed officials, undertaking this work, to have full
regard to:

• encompassing, to the extent possible, *tariff and non-tariff dimensions and
   elements of facilitation and economic and technical cooperation*;
• *the fullest possible private sector input*, consultation and support, including
   through ABAC;
• *critical mass, by developing initiatives supported by significant groups of APEC
   members*, taking into account the different levels of economic development and diverse circumstances of APEC member economies ...
   (APEC Trade Ministers Meeting 1997. Italics added by the author)

Though the final decision was to be made at the Ministerial Meeting in
December, the inclusion of trade facilitation and Ecotech elements in EVSL
became certain. The Statement above shows some other important points
made by the Trade Ministers regarding EVSL. First, Ministers planned
EVSL to be conducted *through* IAPs. Considering the characteristics of IAPs,
it meant that EVSL would be implemented on a voluntary basis, albeit
subject to 'peer pressure.'[17] At the same time, however, Trade Ministers
directed officials to examine the merits of pursuing comprehensive liberalization of EVSL sectors that were to be selected. The concept of *comprehensive
early sectoral liberalization through voluntary actions*, which became the focal
point of disagreements in EVSL consultations in the following years, came
to the surface. Second, unlike other APEC activities, Ministers seemed to
accept that full participation by APEC members was unnecessary (or maybe
impossible) for EVSL. Their instruction to officials was to build a critical
mass for EVSL. Subsequent withdrawal by Chile and Mexico from EVSL in
late 1997 did not affect the formation of critical mass, and the consultations
kept on going. Third, the Ministers invited active involvement of the
private sector, especially the APEC Business Advisory Council (ABAC), in
the EVSL process. In response to the invitation, ABAC involved itself deeply
in EVSL for the rest of 1997 and 1998.

Sector selection

At the Montreal Meeting in May, Trade Ministers were already discussing
sectors that might be candidates for EVSL (APEC Trade Ministers Meeting

1996). The discussion was inconclusive and Ministers directed officials to study sectors appropriate for early liberalization by the end of August. Sector nomination for EVSL by each member and the sector selection process at the senior officials and ministerial levels intensified until just before the Ministerial Meeting in November. By mid-July, thirteen out of eighteen APEC members had submitted their nominations to the SOM. The total number of nominations was sixty-two, covering over thirteen sectors including overlaps.[18] The number of nominations, details of nominated product coverage, proposed measures and timeframe varied greatly from member to member.[19]

The CTI and SOM started work on consolidation of these nominations. During the consolidation process, officials did basically two things. First, they invited each nominating economy to make a presentation of its proposals so that duplications among nominations could be clearly identified. Following this process, SOM reduced the number of nominations from sixty-two to forty-one by the end of October. Second, they gauged the extent of support from member economies for each nomination. This calculation was then used as a numerical indicator that made the comparison among nominations possible.

The SOM produced a report specifically on EVSL just before the Vancouver Ministerial Meeting in November and submitted it to Ministers for the final decision on EVSL sector selection (APEC Ministerial Meeting 1997a). The report set guidelines for Ministers to consider when selecting sectors, which included 'levels of support' and 'mutual benefit/balance' among members. To provide information on the levels of support, a worksheet that specified sponsors and supporters of all forty-one nominations was attached. The report explained that 'balance' could refer to internal balance among liberalization, facilitation and Ecotech elements within a sector, or balance within a group of selected sectors. Finally, among the forty-one nominations listed in the worksheet, SOM recommended that Ministers select the fifteen sectors that enjoyed the most support.

While the official intergovernmental consultations were going on, ABAC was also having intense consultations on sectors which ABAC, as a whole, should recommend to APEC Ministers and Leaders as the private sector's input. ABAC's vigorous commitment to the sector selection process came from its deep dissatisfaction with MAPA. In their report to APEC Leaders in 1997, finalized in September in Santiago (ABAC 1997), they argued that MAPA lacked clear expression of plans and milestones to measure progress toward the Bogor liberalization goal of 2010/2020, and urged the need for transparency and specificity in all aspects of IAPs. Thus, for ABAC, EVSL was an apt vehicle to complement the IAPs. The report stated, '[t]o facilitate the APEC process, ABAC believes that prioritization of certain sectors is necessary to test the applicability of APEC's objectives and principles' (ABAC 1997: 9).

At the ABAC Meeting in Santiago, after a long discussion among representatives, ABAC selected eight priority sectors (industries and subcomponents) to recommend to the official sector selection process.[20] They were: chemicals, environmental products and services, food, oilseeds, pharmaceuticals, pulp and wood products, toys, and transport and automotive products (ABAC 1997: 9–26). Of the sectors that ABAC recommended to Ministers, all but pharmaceuticals were eventually selected for EVSL.[21]

The Vancouver Ministerial and Leaders Meetings, November 1997

Following prior intergovernmental discussions and consultations, with private sector input, the foundations for EVSL in the next two years were formally adopted at the Vancouver Ministerial Meeting in November 1997. In a *Joint Statement*,[22] Ministers declared that they agreed to pursue the initiatives, acknowledging and welcoming the fact that proposals included measures that would promote trade facilitation and Ecotech as well (APEC Ministerial Meeting 1997b: paragraph 4).

The details of the EVSL plan were provided as an Annex to the *Joint Statement*. According to the Annex, Ministers accepted most of the recommendations of the SOM (APEC Ministerial Meeting 1997b: Annex). Table 2.1 shows the final fifteen sectors identified, with their nominators and general objectives.[23]

Among the fifteen sectors, Ministers called for the development of arrangements for trade liberalization, facilitation and Ecotech in nine sectors (the Front Nine) in the first half of 1998, with a view to commencing implementation in 1999. The Ministers resolved that six other sectors (the Back Six) needed 'further work' and directed Senior Officials to develop the study by June 1998 for their assessment.

It is interesting to note that, in Table 2.1, the width and depth of general objectives for the EVSL sectors varied even within the Front Nine. While most sectors referred to tariff and NTB liberalization or elimination, some sectors' objectives were more modest. On the one hand, for instance, the environmental sector's objective was to identify goods, services and NTBs for liberalization, while the energy sector aimed to outline the coverage and set tariff reduction and NTB discussion schedules. On the other, the forest sector's objectives indicated a liberalization schedule of specific products to be completed within specified time limits. It can be seen that, at this stage, the fifteen sectors' goals for EVSL, and even those for the Front Nine, were hardly uniform and comparable.

As for the modality of EVSL, Ministers stated that the EVSL initiative was an attempt to *complement* the IAP process, whereas the Trade Ministers' chair statement had described the process as 'voluntary liberalization *through* IAPs' six months ago in Montreal. This difference is important because, first, it clearly illustrated that there was a need to complement IAPs.

Table 2.1   *Final fifteen EVSL sectors (November 1997)*

	Sectors	Nominated by*	General objectives**
Front 9	Toys	China, HK, (Singapore), (US)	- To eliminate all tariffs on toys. - To set up a schedule to identify all NTBs and eliminate them by 2000.
	Fish & fish products	Brunei, Canada, (Indonesia), NZ, Thailand	- To support the fisheries schedule for liberalization measures as set out in APEC.
	Environmental goods & services	Canada, Japan, Taiwan, US	- To identify goods and services covered to liberalize tariffs. - To identify and set up work plans to deal with NTBs.
	Chemicals	(Australia), (HK), Singapore, US	- To support region-wide acceptance of tariffs in the Chemical Tariff Harmonization Agreement. - To align regulatory systems within the region in hazard assessment, material safety data sheets, and notification of new chemicals.
	Forest products	Canada, (Indonesia), NZ, US	- To eliminate paper tariffs by the start of 2000/2002 with wood tariffs eliminated by the start of 2002/2004 based on a NTB study to be completed by mid-1999. - APEC to adopt performance-based building codes for wood products in construction applications.
	Gems & jewelry	(Taiwan), Thailand	- To support a study of the sector and a work plan for identifying and negotiating removal of NTBs, as well as applicable tariffs and quotas.
	Energy equipment & services	Australia, Thailand, US	- To outline the coverage and set tariff reduction schedules and NTB discussions.
	Medical equipment & instruments	Singapore, Thailand, US	- To set the schedule for tariff elimination. - To address NTBs, specific to payment, and regulatory and trade matters.
	Telecommunications MRA	US	- To finalize the APEC MRA, implement provisions over the course of the year.

Back 6	*Food*	Australia, Thailand***	- To define the scope of product coverage under the APEC Australia proposal. - To begin a work plan for a rigorous discussion of the benefits and needs of an open food system that includes a strong economic and technical focus.
	Oilseeds & oilseed products	Canada, Malaysia, US	- To continue discussions among relevant trade associations in the region with a view toward establishing a work plan in 1998.
	Fertilizers	Canada, Japan	- To work among interested member economies to solidify consensus for tariff elimination and to collectively address NTBs by the year 2004.
	Automotive	Japan****, US	- To advance the work underway to harmonize automotive standards and regulation and their respective approval processes. - To simplify and harmonize customs procedures. - To coordinate and expand Ecotech project, and to establish an automotive dialogue on automotive trade.
	Natural & synthetic rubber	Japan, Thailand	- To support the general liberalization of rubber markets by lowering tariffs and eliminating NTBs.
	Civil aircraft	Canada	- To build consensus among APEC economies on the elimination of all customs duties and other charges levied on, or in connection with the importation of products identified in the Annex to the Agreement on Civil Aircraft and in connection with the repair of civil aircraft.

Notes: HK = Hong Kong, NZ = New Zealand, PNG = Papua New Guinea.

* members in brackets did not nominate respective sectors as at 16 July 1997 but did later.

*** nominated the sector as "canned and processed vegetables and fruit" and "rice and rice products" as at 16 July 1997.

**** nominated the sector as "transport equipment" as at 16 July 1997.

Source: * APEC Ministerial Meeting (1997a), *Inside U.S. Trade* (15 August 1997: 17 - 20).

** ABAC (1998).

ABAC's dissatisfaction with MAPA seemed to be shared by Ministers. Second, logically, if EVSL were to be conducted under the normal APEC liberalization process, the norm and modality of the IAP process would automatically apply to EVSL. If not, however, there would be a chance for another modality to be applied, to complement the 'disappointing' IAP process.[24]

Nevertheless, Ministers reconfirmed that the process would proceed in accordance with the nine general principles[25] set out in the OAA in 1995. Problems for the coming EVSL consultations, again even before it started, were that some OAA principles were products of compromise among members.[26] They were ambiguous in meanings and could be interpreted differently by each member. The focal point was the interpretation of the relations between the 'comprehensiveness' and 'flexibility' principles by EVSL participants.

In addition, a section in the OAA that indicated the framework of APEC liberalization and facilitation stated:

> APEC economies that are ready to initiate and implement cooperative arrangements may proceed to do so while *those that are not ready to parti cipate may join at a later date* ...
> (APEC Leaders Meeting 1995b: Part One, Section B; italics added by the author).

In accordance with the above guideline, Ministers declared in Vancouver that

> *the process of early liberalization is conducted on the basis of the APEC principle of voluntarism whereby each economy remains free to determine the sectoral initiatives in which it will participate* ...
> (APEC Ministerial Meeting 1997b: Annex; italics added by the author).

From this statement, it looked very clear that the EVSL process was to be conducted by *voluntary actions* from each member, in the same way as for any other APEC activities. With that in mind, Ministers asked the Leaders Meeting to instruct members to begin consultations on 'product coverage, flexible phasing measures covered and implementation schedule' (APEC Ministerial Meeting 1997b: Annex).

The Leaders Meeting in Vancouver welcomed and endorsed the Ministers' decision on EVSL sector selection and instructed Trade Ministers to finalize the detailed targets and timetables for the Front Nine sectors by June 1998. At the same time, though, the Leaders stated:

> *APEC liberalization proceeds on a voluntary basis, propelled by commitments taken at the highest level.*
> (APEC Leaders Meeting 1997: paragraph 6; italics added by the author).

What this statement might imply was that, once the highest level of each-member government committed to APEC initiatives (including EVSL) by endorsing them at the Leaders Meeting, the voluntary nature of APEC activities should deliver on the commitments. In other words, once Leaders committed to certain APEC initiatives, members might not be totally free in taking *voluntary* action. In retrospect, the interpretations of 'voluntarism with the highest level of commitment,' again, differed from member to member, and became another focus of heated debate in 1998.

In summary, though it cannot be seen as a failure, what the foundation building process for EVSL in 1997 did was just to select sectors roughly. Much remained to be done in 1998 in deciding product coverage in each selected sector, what measures were to be implemented by when, and how those measures were to be implemented.

The development and results of EVSL consultations (1998–9)

Two years after the first sign of sectoral liberalization appeared in the OAA, the EVSL process finally entered into concrete consultations on what, how and when. This section closely follows the development of the consultations which were to effectively 'collapse' a year later, and summarizes the results of the consultations.

The packaging attempt and resistance

After the Ministerial and Leaders Meetings in Vancouver, the CTI started to work on defining programs for the Front Nine sectors. CTI formed 'Specialist Groups' for all nine sectors under its jurisdiction and let them concentrate on working on respective sectors. The first 'status reports' for nine sectors were submitted by CTI to the first SOM in 1998, held in February in Penang. After studying the reports, Senior Officials asked the CTI to progress proposals for each sector further and get revised reports ready for their reconsideration at the next meeting. CTI held a special meeting on EVSL in Kuala Lumpur in April to arrange the schedule for its tentative sectoral proposals. After the special meeting, the CTI asked each member economy to provide comments on those proposals so that the CTI could submit revised reports to the SOM Chair by late May.[27]

The revised reports by Specialist Groups, gathered by the CTI, were presented at the second SOM in June in Kuching. The proposals of the reports were in matrix form, providing information on product description, product coverage in HS six-digit form, measures of actions and the implementation schedule in each sector. At this meeting, Senior Officials already recognized that 'flexibility was a critical issue' to address (APEC SOM 1998a). The meeting revealed that some proposals provoked opposition, or reservation, from some members as, in the APEC process, applying 'flexibility' usually implied that members requested extension of liberalization timetables and/or non-participation in liberalization in some sectors or products.

Figure 2.1 **Areas for EVSL consultations (1998)**

Sectors		Liberalization	Facilitation	Ecotech
Front 9	Toys			
	Fish & fish products			
	Environmental goods & services			
	Chemicals			
	Forest products			
	Gems & jewellery			
	Energy			
	Medical equipment & instruments			
	Telecommunications MRA			

Note: ▭ 'EVSL package'. ▩ The 'core target' of pro-liberalization members.

The main reason for opposition/reservations seems to have arisen at this stage because much stronger emphasis was put on the liberalization element in some sectors compared with others, and the difference came from which members were the chairs of CTI Specialist Groups. The most assertive nominator of each sector was appointed as the chair of the respective Group and held the responsibility of finalizing a report on that sector. The pro-liberalization members – Australia, Canada, New Zealand and the United States – occupied five of the eight posts.[28] According to an APEC-related MITI official, the reports produced by these members asserted their pro-liberalization stance without mentioning the fact that there was opposition/reservation even at the CTI Specialist Groups' discussion level.[29]

Another important development was that the SOM also proposed that the final agreements on EVSL, comprising liberalization, facilitation and Ecotech in each sector, should be endorsed 'in their entirety' (APEC SOM 1998a). This was the first signal in a formal document of proposals to make

EVSL a 'package deal.' Making EVSL a package meant, of course, that members could not 'remain free to determine the sectoral initiatives in which they will participate.' In the normal sense, it was inconsistent with the EVSL modality of voluntarism set out at the Vancouver Ministerial Meeting, and in the OAA in general. However, it may be argued that to conduct EVSL as a package was consistent with the 'comprehensive' commitment also set out in Vancouver and the OAA.

Logically, as there were nine sectors and three elements, twenty-seven areas were to be addressed for EVSL in 1998. In fact, because the telecommunications sector did not aim for liberalization under EVSL, the areas for consultation in 1998 can be shown in matrix form in Figure 2.1. Each column under Liberalization, Facilitation and Ecotech represents an area for consultation in each sector. Thus, undertaking EVSL as a package meant making commitments to all measures set for all columns inside the dark outline.

In fact, the pro-liberalization members had already been keeping in close contact with one another after the Vancouver Ministerial Meeting, and had consulted with the purpose of making the EVSL process comprehensive. In other words, they had agreed to packaging EVSL well before the status reports submitted to the SOM in June.[30] As they were all strong advocates of liberalization, especially in primary commodities, and given the fact that they had only the liberalization element in mind in the initial stages of EVSL, their intention clearly was prevent members from avoiding the liberalization element in any EVSL sector. Thus, for them, the 'core target' of the EVSL package was to make sure that the liberalization element of each sector, which is shown by the shaded area in Figure 2.1, would be undertaken by all participants. It should be remembered that, when and if packaged along the lines advocated by the SOM *Chair's Summary* (APEC SOM 1998a), the modality of the EVSL process would become very similar to the ITA model. It can be seen that, at this stage, the direction of the EVSL process was set to become a 'clone' of the ITA.

Japan, which had problems with liberalizing the fishery and forest sectors, came to understand the intention of the move to package EVSL at this point. Prior to the meeting, the Japanese government had believed that each member could pick, or leave, any columns in Figure 2.1 at will. China and Taiwan, which were potentially against the idea of an EVSL package deal, did not make their positions very clear. Korea, another potential ally of Japan on EVSL, changed its attitude during the course of the 1998 process, due to the liberalization policies adopted by the new President Kim Dae-Jung.[31]

The report of the second SOM, which included status reports by CTI Specialist Groups, was passed on to the Kuching Trade Ministers Meeting in June. The Chair of the Meeting summarized the discussion on EVSL as follows (APEC Trade Ministers Meeting 1998):

Ministers recognised that *specific concerns have been raised by individual economies in each sector.*

(Paragraph 3. Italics added)

There is *emerging consensus on product coverage, target end rates and target end dates* ...

(Paragraph 4)

Participation in the 9 sectors and all three measures (trade liberalisation, facilitation, and ecotech) in each sector will be essential to maintain the mutual benefits and balance of interests. ...

(Paragraph 5)

Ministers agreed that flexibility would be required to deal with product-specific concerns raised by individual economies in each sector. Such flexibility would generally be in the form of longer implementation periods. In principle *developing economies should be allowed greater flexibility.*

(Paragraph 6)

Ministers agreed that all consideration of *other forms of flexibility should take into account the broader goal of maximising mutual benefits, and the need to maintain the balance of interests.*

(Paragraph 7)

Ministers also noted the significant work done on NTMs, facilitation and ecotech, and endorsed the existing implementation schedule, and the related work programme in these areas.

(Paragraph 8)

Ministers will consider the final agreements/arrangements of each sector in its entirety at the Ministerial Meeting in November, with a view to commencing implementation in 1999.

(Paragraph 11)

At first glance, it is unclear what the *Statement* was trying to say. On the one hand, recognizing that problems had been raised by some members in each sector's liberalization proposal, it said that Ministers agreed on the need for flexibility. On the other, it acknowledged emerging consensus on product coverage and tariff reducing schedules in each sector's proposal, and reported that Ministers endorsed the SOM's idea of packaging by saying the final arrangements were to be considered in their entirety. Considering all EVSL-related paragraphs, however, the *Statement*'s emphasis was, in principle, that the EVSL process should be a comprehensive undertaking (package deal) with equal commitments from each member in each sector. Flexibility in actions would be allowed basically for developing economies and as a form of extended time schedule. Strong verification seemed to be needed for insisting on other forms of flexibility, especially on the part of developed members.

At Kuching, the usual pro-liberalization members of Australia, Canada, New Zealand and the United States, plus Hong Kong and Singapore, who had no problems with liberalization (the 'package deal' group), were ready to push the EVSL packaging at the Ministerial level. The package deal group argued that, as the commitments taken at the highest level for EVSL should not be treated lightly, participants should undertake EVSL as a package. They also insisted that 'a big and influential member like Japan' must participate to give a good example.[32] On the other hand, other members did not expect the process to proceed that fast. The Japanese MITI Minister and his staff attended the Meeting, thinking that they had insisted on the voluntary principle of APEC enough to ensure members' freedom to participate (or not participate) at Vancouver and also at other available opportunities. In addition, they thought that 'a big and influential member like Japan' should clearly state its opposition towards the EVSL package for other members who were potentially against the idea but not 'influential.'[33]

Though the Japanese government opposed the packaging of EVSL, the outcomes of the Kuching Trade Ministers Meeting were not favorable to Japan. According to usual APEC practice, when opposition was raised to an issue, as it was by Japan in Kuching, the process would have stopped. However, in the case of EVSL, the process went on.[34] Trade Ministers instructed Senior Officials to continue working on the sectoral arrangements in order to finalize them by September.

The subsequent process of finalizing EVSL arrangements became difficult and confrontational as neither the 'package deal' group nor the 'voluntarism' group (Japan, conspicuously, and its allies) would compromise. A summary record of the discussion at the CTI meeting in September clearly illustrated what the problems were. According to the summary, members' information on their reservations was not detailed and some opted for product exclusions, rather than proposing alternative end rates and/or end dates (APEC CTI 1998). The third SOM in 1998, held in September in Kuantan, further confirmed these problems. The Chair admitted that significant work on EVSL arrangements in all three elements (liberalization, facilitation and Ecotech) was still needed to achieve a more substantive and credible 'package' before it could be submitted to the Ministerial Meeting in November (APEC SOM 1998b). The packaging procedure did not proceed as the 'package group' had hoped.

On the 'private' front, ABAC's activities on EVSL in 1998 also produced conflict as time went on, reflecting the debate at the official level.[35] At the Mexico City Meeting in February, ABAC set up an EVSL Task Force, along with others, and appointed the US and New Zealand representatives as co-chairs of the Task Force. By these appointments, a basic structure of the

ABAC discussion on EVSL (pro-liberalization members to drive, and Japan and others to oppose) was effectively established. The ABAC Chair's letter, dated 31 March and addressed to the Chair of the Trade Ministers Meeting in 1998 (the Malaysian MITI Minister), insisted that the EVSL initiative should be *inclusive, comprehensive* and *credible*[36] (ABAC 1998: 19–21), already showing strong support for the EVSL package.

At the Sydney Meeting in May, fifteen shepherds were appointed to co-ordinate the discussion for each EVSL sector, and substantive talks were started. The nationality of the shepherd for each sector was almost identical to that of the chair of the CTI Specialist Group, thus the debate for each sector also became almost identical to that occurring at the official level.

The Taipei Meeting in September was to conclude the annual ABAC report to Leaders, and the discussion on EVSL became intense. Prior to the Meeting, the Japanese government (MITI) produced a 'position paper' on EVSL and handed it to Japanese ABAC representatives.[37] The main points of the paper were: Japan could not agree with a comprehensive undertaking to implement an EVSL package as the process was started with the under-standing that each member was able to choose sectors to participate voluntarily; and Japan would not participate at all in the tariff reduction process in the forestry, fishery, food and oilseed sectors. The Japanese ABAC representative in charge of the EVSL Task Force asserted his position at the Taipei Meeting along with the MITI position paper, and the Meeting was stopped for 40 minutes.[38] However, finally he had to concede and sign the original report to avoid the collapse of the whole ABAC process.[39]

Kuala Lumpur, November 1998: the breakdown

The Ministerial Meeting in December 1998 in Kuala Lumpur finally arrived. The latest proposals on arrangement (status reports) for the Front Nine sectors were submitted to the Meeting by the SOM. The result, in short, was failure to reach an agreement on packaging EVSL as had been earlier intended. Moreover, they resolved not to seek agreement on the liber-alization element even on a sector-by-sector basis. The EVSL process could not mobilize a *critical mass*.

In the *Joint Statement* of the Meeting, EVSL was defined as an 'integrated approach to liberalization through the incorporation of facilitation and Ecotech measures, undertaken through the APEC principle of *voluntarism*' (APEC Ministerial Meeting 1998: paragraph 11). At the same time, Ministers agreed that members *might* implement the tariff commitments immediately on a voluntary basis (APEC Ministerial Meeting 1998: paragraph 13). Thus, in effect, they allowed members to choose the option of not carrying out liber-alization in the Front Nine sectors under the EVSL framework.

Instead of pursuing the liberalization of the nine sectors within the EVSL framework further, Ministers decided to refer the initiative to the WTO. The *Joint Statement* indicated,

Ministers ... also agreed to improve and build on this progress in 1999 by *broadening the participation in the tariff element beyond APEC*, to maximize the benefit of liberalisation. *In this regard, the WTO process would be initiated immediately on the basis of the framework established in Kuching and subsequent information provided by economies*, having regard to the flexibility approaches as contained in the status reports with a view towards further improving their participation and endeavouring *to conclude agreement in the WTO in 1999 ...*
(APEC Ministerial Meeting 1998: paragraph 15. Italics added by the author)

In the next paragraph, however, Ministers added,

This process of expanding participation beyond APEC will not prejudice the position of APEC members with respect to the agenda and modalities to be agreed at the Third WTO Ministerial Conference.
(APEC Ministerial Meeting 1998: paragraph 16. Italics added by the author)

What Ministers implied was that APEC, as a whole, would invite as many WTO members as possible to support its early sectoral liberalization initiative at the WTO level, while APEC members themselves were not necessarily bound to the initiative. In any normal sense, the credibility of the initiative was hardly strong.

Although the Ministers could not agree on the liberalization element of the Front Nine, the *Joint Statement* declared that they reached consensus in implementing the facilitation and Ecotech elements. Though the Statement did not outline the measures to be undertaken, they were set to commence in accordance with work programs in each sector (APEC Ministerial Meeting 1998: paragraphs 14 and 18).

Recognizing the result of EVSL in the Front Nine sectors, the Leaders' Declaration just stated that Leaders welcomed the 'progress' achieved on the EVSL package, which was no longer the package intended earlier. In addition, Leaders instructed Ministers to implement the agreement reached for the Front Nine, and to advance work on the remaining six sectors in 1999 (APEC Leaders Meeting 1998: paragraph 19).

It will be useful, here, to check each member's actual stance on the liberalization element of the Front Nine sectors that the Ministers decided to refer to the WTO, by utilizing Appendix 4 (reservations in product coverage, target end dates and target end rates of the Front Nine sectors). The Appendix shows the divergence between the SOM proposals of liberalization measures in the Front Nine (Appendix 3) and measures acceptable to every member, at the time of the Kuala Lumpur Ministerial Meeting. In checking every member's stance, it is important to remember the three points which were announced in the Statement of the Chair of the Kuching Trade Ministers Meeting in June 1998: that there was emerging consensus on product coverage, target end rates and target end dates; that participation in the nine sectors and all three measures (trade liberalization, facilitation and Ecotech) in each sector would be essential; and that flexibility would be in the form of longer implementation periods while developing economies should be allowed greater flexibility.

First, look closely at the reservations in product coverage (the column under 'Exclusions') and the end tariff rate (the column under 'End rate proposal') in each sector since these were not to be applied as measures to assure flexibility. What attracts attention is the fact that several (or sometimes many) members made demands to exclude certain products in all nine sectors, and Japan was the only developed economy among them. The proportion of the products that members asked to be excluded from the SOM proposals in each sector varied, but in some cases, the proportion was higher than 50 per cent: China in chemicals (63 per cent) and environmental products/services (84 per cent); Thailand in forestry (50 per cent) and environmental products/services (95 per cent); and Japan and Taiwan in fishery (100 per cent). Demanding a 100 per cent exclusion meant the rejection of tariff reduction in the sectors in question, and, as we have said, that was the case for Japan and Taiwan in fishery. In other words, the members that rejected the EVSL package were Japan and Taiwan. According to Appendix 4, Japan asked to exclude 31 per cent of products from the forestry sector's coverage, though it was widely believed that Japan maintained the stance of totally rejecting liberalization in this sector. One the other hand, Korea, which changed its policy direction to support liberalization in early 1998 (see Chapter 7), still demanded that 17 per cent of fishery, 12 per cent of forestry and 7 per cent of environmental products/services be excluded from its tariff reduction plan.

On the ultimate levels of tariff reduction in each sector, there were several (sometimes many) members who insisted they should be higher than the rates proposed by SOM. From those who wanted higher end rates than the SOM proposals but not more than 5 per cent, the following members were noticeable: The Philippines (86 per cent of the product coverage) and Thailand (67 per cent) in the toys sector; Indonesia (80 per cent), The Philippines (100 per cent) and Thailand (79 per cent) in the medical equipments/instruments sector; China (87 per cent) and The Philippines (100 per cent) in the fishery sector; The Philippines in the forestry sector (97 per cent); The Philippines (99 per cent) and Thailand (62 per cent) in the energy sector; and Malaysia (59 per cent) and The Philippines (94 per cent) in the environmental goods/services sector. In all sectors except for gems and jewelry, there were members that claimed the end rates should be more than 5 per cent higher than the SOM proposals. Among them, Papua New Guinea asked 96 per cent of the product coverage in the fishery sector and 53 per cent of those in the forestry sector to be placed in this category. China wanted 40 per cent of the forestry sector products to have end rates in this category, and Indonesia, 48 per cent of the energy sector products.

Second, what was the stance of each member on the implementation period of the tariff reduction in the Front Nine sectors? The longer period of implementation was accepted by the SOM and Trade Ministers Meeting levels as a means of securing flexibility and, in principle, it was to be applied to developing members. However, considering that EVSL was an 'early' liberalization initiative, if many developing members requested very long periods of implementation compared with the SOM proposals, the very concept of EVSL would be undermined. Provided that the Bogor target is 2010/2020 and all the target end dates proposed by SOM fell in the first half of the 2000s, it is reasonable to assume that the longest extension acceptable was around five years. According to Appendix 4, however, there were many members who requested an extension of from six to ten years. For instance, China asked for such an extension for 31 per cent of product coverage in the chemicals sector. Thailand insisted that 57 per cent of products in the same sector should be given a six- to ten-year extension. Brunei wanted such an extension for 50 per cent of the products in the medical equipments/instruments sector, and Korea, which tried to be more active in its liberalization policy, asked for such an extension in 17 per cent of the products in the environmental goods/services sector. Only Malaysia and Thailand requested extension of eleven years or more. Both of them asked for these extensions in chemicals (22 per cent of the product coverage for Malaysia and 32 per cent for Thailand), forestry (1 per cent and 2 per cent respectively), energy (34 per cent and 15 per cent) and environmental goods/services (17 per cent and 5 per cent).

True to their reputation, the United States, Australia, New Zealand, Singapore and Hong Kong do not appear in the columns under 'Exclusions' and 'End rate proposal' in Appendix 4. However, the United States' and Australia's requests for extended phasing, which was supposed to be allowed for developing members in principle, draw attention. The United States asked for extension of two years or fewer in the tariff reduction schedule on 1 per cent of the products in the environmental goods/services sector, and on 2 per cent of energy products and 3 per cent of fishery it demanded extension of three to five years. On the other hand, Australia requested two years or fewer extensions for 1 per cent of fishery products, 3 per cent of forest products, 9 per cent of energy products and 5 per cent of environmental goods/services products. Australia also asked for three- to five-year extensions for 2 per cent of forest products and 54 per cent of energy products. However, obviously these two members' reservations did not become focal points of the EVSL consultations.

Three important points can be raised from the above analysis. First, in contrast to what the Trade Ministers Meeting had expected, it was hard to evaluate that consensus on product coverage, target end rates and target end dates was emerging, even in the APEC sense of consensus which meant 'areas of agreement without legal binding power' (Chapter 1). Second, of the sixteen participants in EVSL, only four (Canada, New Zealand, Singapore and Hong Kong) were ready to accept the SOM proposals as they were. Third, among the members that could not accept the SOM proposals as they were, it was Japan and Taiwan that totally rejected the EVSL package, while other developing members might have attempted to postpone, or eviscerate, the EVSL initiative as a whole by demanding various measures of flexibility no matter whether or not they were acceptable in the international consultations.

Damage control in 1999

In January 1999, New Zealand, as the host member of APEC in the year, submitted the arrangements for the early sectoral liberalization initiative to the WTO. The report included detailed product coverage, end rates and end dates with flexibility proposals, which had been prepared by the SOM for the APEC Ministerial Meeting in Kuala Lumpur in the previous year.[40] The APEC initiative was now called 'Accelerated Tariff Liberalization' (ATL), and communication with WTO officials started in Geneva. It is doubtful, however, whether all APEC members seriously thought about pursuing the ATL initiative at WTO level. In addition to the non-binding character of the initiative, it was already obvious that the WTO Ministerial Conference in Seattle, which was to be held in November/December that year to agree on the commencement of the new round of negotiations, involved several issues such as anti-dumping, liberalization of agricultural markets and trade–labor standard relations that would divide APEC members. These circumstances hardly made it ideal for APEC members to act as a unit on ATL.[41]

At the second SOM in May, however, though efforts had been made by the CTI to set a framework for tariff reduction in the remaining six sectors except for automobiles (which did not include a tariff element from the beginning), a consensus emerged among Senior Officials to propose to Trade Ministers that the tariff element of the Back Six sectors be referred to the WTO as well (APEC SOM 1999b: paragraph 19) to avoid further confusion and confrontation among members. The Trade Ministers Meeting, held in Auckland in June, agreed on passing the tariff element of those sectors on to the WTO as the SOM had recommended (APEC Trade Ministers Meeting 1999: paragraph 15 and 17). Thus, tariff reduction in all fifteen sectors was left out of the EVSL framework altogether.

As the decision was made to refer the tariff reduction element to the WTO, the important task for EVSL in 1999 was to gather measures for reducing NTMs and for promoting facilitation and Ecotech for the EVSL sectors. The first SOM in 1999, held in February, understood that it was vital to develop a number of 'deliverables' in those elements to restore APEC's credibility (APEC SOM 1999a: paragraph 18). In June, Trade Ministers specified eight 'deliverables' in Annex A of the *Statement of the Chair*. They were:

(1) a study on the full range of non tariff measures and their impact in the forest products sector;
(2) a study on the consistency of global fisheries' subsidy practices with the WTO rules;
(3) an Automotive Dialogue involving the auto industry and government across APEC to map out strategies for increasing integration and development of the auto sector;[42]
(4) a seminar on implementation of ISO safety standards for the toy sector;
(5) implementation of training programmes for Jewellery Testing, Assaying and Hallmarking;
(6) a survey of environmental goods and services markets in APEC;
(7) a programme of training and development of designers and sample makers in the toy and novelties industry, and;
(8) an APEC Gems and Jewellery Conference.

(APEC Trade Ministers Meeting 1999: Annex A)

Further work on NTMs, facilitation and Ecotech for all fifteen EVSL sectors continued within respective Specialist Groups which submitted an eighty-page report to the CTI. The CTI then presented it, with a summary, to the third SOM in August. The summary itself consisted of thirteen pages of numerous 'deliverables,' though the number of deliverables differed from sector to sector (APEC CTI 1999).

Discussion on EVSL at the Ministerial Meeting in September 1999 in Auckland was uncontroversial because there was no longer a tariff element. In regard to tariffs, how APEC should deal with the WTO Ministerial Conference in November became the focus. In general, Ministers resolved that APEC should contribute to the launch of the new WTO round which should be broad based and include industrial tariffs.[43] They declared that the ATL added impetus to this cause and APEC members would pursue ATL 'earnestly' (APEC Ministerial Meeting 1999: paragraph 16–21, 26). Ministers also agreed that they would 'actively and constructively' participate in the new round on tariffs and NTMs on agriculture (APEC Ministerial Meeting 1999: paragraph 24), which they could not do in the EVSL framework.

As for the facilitation and Ecotech elements, Ministers tidied up the measures identified by Trade Ministers in June and added four projects in Annex B to the *Joint Statement*. The added measures were:

(1) Food: seminar on reduction of antibiotic residues in the domestic animal products;
(2) Medical equipment: seminar for government regulators/harmonization of regulation monitoring system;
(3) Energy: seminar/workshop on 'Promoting Trade and Investment in the Energy Sector among APEC Economies through EVSL', and;
(4) Telecommunications: Mutual Recognition Arrangement.

(APEC Ministerial Meeting 1999: Annex B)

Figure 2.2 Results of EVSL consultations, 1998 - 9

Sectors		Liberalization	NTMs	Facilitation	Ecotech
Front 9 (1998)	**Toys**	To WTO as ATL			OO
	Fish & fish products	To WTO as ATL	O		
	Environmental goods & services	To WTO as ATL			O
	Chemicals	To WTO as ATL			
	Forest products	To WTO as ATL	O		
	Gems & jewellery	To WTO as ATL			OO
	Energy	To WTO as ATL		◎	
	Medical equipment & instruments	To WTO as ATL			◎
	Telecommunications MRA			◎	
Back 6 (1999)	**Food**	To WTO			◎
	Oilseeds & oilseed products	To WTO			
	Fertilizers	To WTO			
	Automotive			O	
	Natural & synthetic rubber	To WTO			
	Civil aircraft	To WTO			

Notes: O identified at 1999 Trade Ministers Meeting.   ◎   Added at 1999 Ministerial Meeting.

[shaded box] "Agreeable" areas for NTMs, facilitation and Ecotech.

Source: made by the author according to APEC Trade Ministers Meeting (1999) and APEC Ministerial Meeting

Summary of the results

Figure 2.2 summarizes the results of the EVSL consultations that became the center of APEC members' attention in the late 1990s.

After the intense debate and collapse in 1998 and the damage control attempt in 1999, what the EVSL consultations produced was much less than expected, particularly by the pro-liberalization members. As explained earlier, the tariff element of the Front Nine sectors was passed on to the WTO as the ATL initiative. The decision to refer the tariff element of the Back Six sectors to the WTO as well in 1999 was made without even detailed proposals such as ATL. In retrospect, the EVSL process revealed, or reconfirmed, that any non-voluntary tariff reduction measures could not proceed within the APEC framework. Vigorous efforts made by the 'package deal' group to apply binding force to a part of the APEC liberalization process were, in the end, rejected.

For NTMs, trade facilitation and Ecotech, twelve measures were agreed to by the end of 1999. As there were many 'agreeable' areas for these elements in logic (illustrated by shaded areas in Figure 2.2), and considering that these were the areas where members sought 'deliverables' to restore APEC's credibility, twelve agreements look less than impressive. For chemicals, oilseed, fertilizers, rubber and civil aircraft sectors, no concrete measures were set out in 1999.[44] In addition to the small number of agreements, the substance of each agreement did not seem to have immediate effects on intra-regional trade flows. Nine measures out of twelve agreed were related to Ecotech and, by the very nature of Ecotech, would take time to generate effects on trade. Measures for NTMs, which could have quicker effects, were not immediately aimed at reducing NTMs but at studying their impact on trade and consistency with the WTO rules.

Regarding the bottom line of EVSL, which was to produce more 'concrete' and 'earlier' effects on intra-regional trade of EVSL sectors, the results cannot help but be called a 'failure.' It might have been inevitable for EVSL to fail as both governments and private sectors of some pro-liberalization members visibly and quickly lost their interest in the process after the decision on the tariff elements of the Front Nine sectors in November 1998.[45]

Setting the concrete research questions

As indicated in the introductory section of this chapter, the general question of the research project is 'why EVSL resulted as it did?' Since the detailed development and results of the EVSL process have been explained in the previous three sections, the general question can now be broken down into more concrete ones, reflecting stages of the EVSL process. In this section, those questions will be pointed out. The case study chapters will then enquire into these concrete questions to illustrate respective members' actions (or inactions) and reactions on EVSL and factors behind those activities. In addition, of course, specific factors that affected certain members', but not others', EVSL policies will be covered in the case studies where necessary. Enquiries by case studies, when put together, should be able to indicate clearly why EVSL had to 'fail.'

Questions on policy making processes in members

First of all, *how each member formulated its EVSL policy* must be examined. The examination should include institutional settings for trade policy making, political and bureaucratic actors involved in the process and influential players from outside the government (i.e. interest groups). Of course, it is of great importance for case study chapters not only to identify those involved in the EVSL policy making, but also to pay careful attention to how they interacted within the institutional settings of the process. This analysis would construct the basis for examining other questions which will be laid down subsequently in this section, as any actions and/or reactions to the EVSL process by any members were made via their respective EVSL policy making processes.

Questions on sector selection and selected sectors

It might have been unavoidable for members, even for those in the 'voluntarism' group such as Japan, China, Taiwan and some ASEAN countries, to accept the EVSL concept before the process actually started, because the concept, and thus the initiative itself, was hardly clear-cut at the initial stage in 1995 and 1996. However, as the EVSL process proceeded, there must have been strong motivation for each member to make its opinions heard to secure its 'national interest.' As indicated in the previous sections, one of the most important issues was the sector selection for EVSL in 1997. In retrospect, this is where the 'disappointing' results of EVSL originated as the final fifteen sectors included four (fishery, forestry, food and oilseeds) in which Japan rejected liberalization under the EVSL framework.

Then, the questions which must be answered are: *how did members perceive the way in which EVSL sectors were selected and what did they do, if anything, to secure the inclusion of their nominations?*; and *were members satisfied or dissatisfied with the selected sectors?* In particular, it is very interesting and important to study why Japan allowed the inclusion of the controversial four sectors in the final fifteen, as well as analyzing other members' perceptions and attitudes. The examination of these questions should also demonstrate the differences in attitudes (positive/negative) among members even before consultations on details started.

Questions on the modality

The proposal to include the trade facilitation and Ecotech elements in EVSL in early 1997 did not provoke any opposition. It was adopted and endorsed at the subsequent Ministerial and Leaders Meetings that year. After the EVSL sectors were selected, the focus of consultations in 1998 was shifted to the complicated agenda of 'how to implement what on which products in the Front Nine sectors by when.' The most important issue became the 'how' factor as it could make consultations on 'what' and 'when' worthwhile or effectively kill them (and it did kill those on the tariff element).

Before going into the questions on the EVSL modality, two related questions should be addressed. They are: how did each member understand the 'voluntary' nature of APEC activities in general?; and how did they interpret the ambiguous, and sometimes incompatible, principles for the APEC liberalization and facilitation set out in the OAA? As 'voluntary' actions were the norm for all APEC activities and the OAA principles were meant to apply to any liberalization and facilitation processes under the APEC framework, EVSL was not an exception. The differences in understanding these conceptions must have influenced the EVSL process and each member's policy making.

The heated debate on EVSL in 1998 that eventually led to the 'collapse' of the process developed around the packaging attempt of EVSL and resistance to this. The intentions of the pro-liberalization members such as the United States, Canada, Australia, New Zealand, Singapore and Hong Kong in driving the EVSL package deal, and that of Japan which stubbornly rejected the move, were obvious. But *how did other members react to the packaging of EVSL?* In other words, who else supported the package? Or was it only Japan which rejected the attempt? The stance of members other than those mentioned above was not clear, as the attention of the media was concentrated on the US–Japan confrontation. In relation to this question, *whether or not members perceived the EVSL packaging as an attempt to alter the APEC modality* is another important question. The conventional modality characterized by voluntary and flexible undertakings was adopted by the APEC forum because developing members such as the ASEAN countries insisted on the need to avoid domination and compulsion of the APEC agenda by bigger and more powerful developed members. Developed members accepted it to secure wider participation in the forum. If most of the developing members experienced a sense of danger in altering the APEC modality, there was a possibility that EVSL could have failed even without the 'Japan factor.' If that was the case, an additional question of 'why they did not explicitly oppose moves to alter the modality' can be raised.

The next question is: why did the packaging attempt proceed until the Kuala Lumpur Ministerial Meeting in 1998, even though it was clear that it did not have unanimous support from members? It must have been obvious that demonstrating the disappointing results of EVSL in Kuala Lumpur to the world would seriously affect APEC's credibility, and was to no member's advantage. In the normal procedure of the APEC process, 'consensus' is an important guarantee against domination by any member(s) and APEC activities are not supposed to continue without it.[46]

The United States and others argued that, as the highest level of each government had committed to the initiative (i.e. EVSL was initiated and the subsequent process endorsed by the annual Leaders Meetings), all members must participate in all elements of all sectors. In accordance with this argument, they developed the packaging attempt. It is true that the APEC liberalization process as a whole had been encouraged and driven by Leaders' commitments such as the Bogor Declaration (1994), the OAA (1995) and the MAPA endorsement (1996), and EVSL can be seen as the same. Nonetheless, *how each member interpreted the importance of 'the commitment made at the highest level of the government' particularly for EVSL* seems to have been hardly uniform, and became one of the vital factors for the failure of EVSL.

Questions on the members' liberalization strategies

General trade liberalization strategies of members should be brought into the analysis. To be more precise, a question that should be asked is: *how did members' strategies toward WTO liberalization affect their policies for EVSL?* In relation to that, *how did they understand the differences between APEC and WTO liberalization?* The enquiry into these questions will ultimately lead to another question of *how much does APEC and its liberalization process weigh in members' respective foreign (economic) policy agendas?*

At the completion of the WTO Uruguay Round of trade negotiations in 1993, it was already decided as a 'built-in-agenda' that negotiation on liberalization in the agricultural and services sectors were set to start in 2000, and as time passed, the WTO 'Millennium Round' was planned to be formally launched at the Seattle Ministerial Conference in late 1999. APEC members supposed that the commencement of the new round was coming close; thus, they must have participated in the EVSL consultations while considering how they should act at the WTO level to secure their 'national interests.'

For instance, and in general, the positions of the United States and Japan towards the new round were quite opposite. The United States wanted the new round to be conducted on a sector-to-sector basis and, as a result, to produce 'frequent harvests.' The concept of the United States seemed to be to make the new round a series of negotiations along the ITA model. Japan, on the other hand, argued that the new round should include as many sectors as possible, including tariffs on industrial products, and be a 'single undertaking.' Japan's intention was to make the agricultural sector just one part of the liberalization agenda, thus avoiding too much attention being paid to it during the negotiations. The US and Japanese positions towards the new WTO round were reflected in their EVSL, and were illustrated by their confrontation in the EVSL 'package deal' issue. What about other members, then, and how did their liberalization strategies affect the EVSL process? Analysis of this question will be important in studying the issue of 'what kind of liberalization is possible in the APEC framework.'

Questions on the impact of the 'Asian economic crisis'

The Asian 'economic crisis,' which broke out first as disastrous currency depreciation in Thailand in mid-1997 and consequently plunged many Asian APEC members into economic turmoil, occurred at the same time as the EVSL consultations. Though the explanation of the development of the EVSL process earlier in this chapter did not touch upon the crisis because this is an exogenous factor, it should be brought into consideration for case studies as the impacts of the crisis on some members were so severe.

From the latter half of the 1980s to the mid-1990s, Asian members, especially those in ASEAN, had enjoyed dramatic growth of their GDPs through foreign direct investment inflows and increased exports. As a result, they were more ready to participate in trade liberalization negotiations than ever before. In fact, they even started unilateral trade liberalization to underpin their transnational economic activities.[47] The initial stage of EVSL in 1995 and 1996 overlapped with the final phase of their economic 'boom' period. The EVSL sector selection process in 1997, however, coincided with the outbreak of the crisis and the ensuing EVSL consultations developed alongside it. Then, *how did the Asian 'currency/economic crisis' influence members' EVSL policies?* As the crisis caused chaos not only in economies but also in politics, and, directly or indirectly, led to changes of government in members such as Indonesia, Korea and Thailand, it is more likely than not to have affected EVSL policies. Moreover, those who were not directly affected by the crisis could have felt the impact. It is possible that members like the United States and Australia, who already had meaningful trade and investment relations with the crisis-hit economies, might have changed their attitudes towards (or expectations for) EVSL as they saw the prospect of those markets diminishing. The possibility that the crisis influenced EVSL consultations cannot be ignored.

Notes

1 It seems that the term EVSL (Early Voluntary Sectoral Liberalization) was formally adopted by the APEC forum in late 1997. In this chapter, however, to avoid confusion, the whole continuous process of early sectoral liberalization within the APEC framework (1995–9) will be called the 'EVSL' process.

2 In addition, 'it was hard to say no to just studying and identifying sectors for early liberalization, even if members had some concerns about the idea itself.' Interview with an APEC-related official, the Ministry of International Trade and Industry (MITI), Japan, 17 December 1999.

3 MAPA set the framework for the method of how the APEC trade and investment liberalization and facilitation process should proceed from January 1997. MAPA consisted of

IAPs from each member, and the CAP agreed by all members. Each member is to revise and resubmit respective IAP every year to indicate its liberalization plan for the next year. CAP is also to be revised every year. This process continues until regional free trade and investment is realized by the Bogor target years of 2010/2020.

4 'Selecting sectors' implied that concrete discussions/consultations for early liberalization would start on those selected sectors. That made some members cautious, but again, there was no explicit objection raised at the Subic Meeting because no one yet knew how those sectors would be selected. Interview by Tatsushi Ogita with APEC-related officials, the Ministry of Foreign Affairs, Japan, 20 December 1999.

5 The original agreement was signed in 1986 to reduce Japan's surplus in semiconductor trade with the United States. The agreement was renewed in August 1991 and then included a 'numerical objective' that 'foreign' imported products should occupy 20 per cent or more of Japan's semiconductor market. The United States insisted that 20 percent of market share by foreign products was a promise made by the Japanese government, but the Japanese government firmly kept the stance that it was just a guideline as the government could and should not intervene in private sector activities. Japan also argued in 1996 that the share of foreign semiconductors in the domestic market was almost 30 per cent by 1995, thus there was no need to retain the Agreement.

6 *Mainichi Shimbun*, 24 April 1996.

7 *Reuters News Service*, 24 and 26 September 1996.

8 *Jiji Press Newswire*, 22 October 1996, and *Reuters News Service*, 22 November 1996.

9 *Jiji Press Newswire*, 22 October 1996.

10 *Taiwan Business News*, 21 November 1996.

11 *South China Morning Post*, 24 November 1996.

12 Peru, Russia and Vietnam were not yet APEC members in 1996 when the APEC Leaders agreed to support and promote the ITA initiative.

13 ITA provides for the review of non-tariff barriers (NTBs), but there is no binding commitment concerning NTBs.

14 For details of the product coverage of ITA, see Attachments to Annex, WTO (1996).

15 In fact, many participants, mainly developing ones, have requested the extension of staging and this has been agreed by others. For detail, see participants 'schedule of commitments' at ⟨http://www.wto.org/wto/goods/itscheds.htm⟩.

16 Interview with an APEC-related official of MITI, 17 December 1999.

17 As mentioned earlier, each APEC member is to submit its IAP every year for improvement. The re-submitting process is to be monitored by all other members at the Senior Officials Meetings. In fact, the voluntary nature of EVSL had been confirmed as early as the Subic Leaders Meeting.

18 APEC Ministerial Meeting (1997a).

19 For instance, Canada nominated nine sectors (or product categories) and the United States eight, while Malaysia and Taiwan nominated only one each. Chile, Indonesia, Mexico, Papua New Guinea and the Philippines did not nominate any at this stage (Chile and Mexico eventually pulled out of EVSL). Some members nominated sectors with HS two-to four-digit classifications, but some others equalise first noted 'details to be advised.' The same can be said on measures and timeframe for liberalization. See *Inside US Trade* (15 August 1997: 17–20).

20 A staff member of a Japanese ABAC representative said, 'ABAC's sector selection process became intense because of participants' understanding that it was certain that their recommendations would be accepted by Ministers.' Interview, 13 January 2000.

21 The fact that seven out of eight ABAC recommendations were officially selected for EVSL could be seen as an indication of the EVSL process attaching importance to private sector inputs. However, domestic business organizations' involvement in and initiatives towards the CTI-SOM process were heavy and influential from the initial stage of EVSL, particularly for pro-liberalization members such as the United States and Canada. (Interview with an APEC-related official of MITI, 23 February 2000.) It is hard to

imagine that those organizations' lobbying towards respective governments and their activities within ABAC were different in substance and timing. It seems more rational to consider that the official sector selection process and the ABAC recommendation process were closely related and that the high success rate of ABAC recommendations was not an accident.

22 It seems that the term 'Early Voluntary Sectoral Liberalization' was formally adopted at this Meeting, too. See APEC Ministerial Meeting (1997b: paragraph 4).

23 These objectives were not provided in the Annex to the *Joint Statement*. However, as early as at the first ABAC meeting in February 1998 in Mexico City, they were given for discussion. Interview with staff member of a Japanese ABAC representative, December 1999.

24 An APEC-related official of MITI described has, at this stage, pro-liberalization members already had the intention to make EVSL bear different modality from the IAP process. Interview, 23 February 2000.

25 Nine general principles for APEC liberalization and facilitation are: (1) comprehensiveness; (2) WTO-consistency; (3) comparability; (4) non-discrimination; (5) transparency; (6) standstill; (7) simultaneous start, continuous process and differentiated timetables; (8) flexibility; and (9) cooperation. See APEC Ministerial Meeting (1995: Part One, Section A).

26 For the details of the making of the OAA principles, see Ogita and Takoh (1997: 1–5; 15–23).

27 The submission was actually made on 4 June.

28 The chairs of Specialist Groups for the Front Nine sectors, excluding the telecommunications MRA which did not include the liberalization element because of its nature, were as follows: toys – Hong Kong; fish and fish products – Canada; environmental products – Canada; chemicals – the United States; forest products – New Zealand; gems and jewelry – Thailand; energy equipment and services – Australia; and medical equipment and services – Singapore.

29 Interview, 23 February 2000.

30 Interview with staff of a Japanese ABAC representative, 2 December 1999.

31 Interview with staff member of a Japanese ABAC representative, 2 December 1999.

32 Interview with an APEC-related official of MITI, 17 December 1999.

33 Interview with an APEC-related official of MITI, 17 December 1999.

34 Interview with an APEC-related official of MITI, 17 December 1999. The interviewee explained that he felt the WTO modality was brought into the APEC process.

35 The following episode, again, shows the close relations between the official EVSL process and the 'private' input by ABAC. Moreover, several support staff of different Japanese ABAC representatives admitted that they had MITI and Foreign Affairs officials within their team in 1998, and that other economies, including the United States, were more or less the same. Furthermore, staff members claimed that most ABAC representatives from member economies, including Japanese representatives, were in close communication with their respective governments even when ABAC meetings were going on (interview, 1 December 1999 and 5 January 2000).

36 Letters from ABAC Chair to the Malaysian MITI Minister on EVSL were released after every ABAC Meeting. Other letters were dated 21 May and 12 October and the basic messages in the letters were the same: the emphasis was on the need for inclusiveness, comprehensiveness and credibility. See ABAC (1998).

37 Interview with staff members of a Japanese ABAC representative, 1 December 1999.

38 Interview with staff members of a Japanese ABAC representative, 1 December 1999.

39 Interview with staff members of a Japanese ABAC representative, 1 December 1999.

40 See WTO (1999a). In April, New Zealand submitted more detailed proposals. See WTO (1999b).

41 In retrospect, the Seattle WTO Conference could not agree on the new round as a whole, so the split among APEC members on ATL did not surface.

42 The first Automotive Dialogue was held a month later in Bali, 26–7 July 1999.

43 Tariffs on industrial products were not included as 'built-in-agenda' for the Seattle WTO Conference, while liberalization on agricultural products and services were set to be included for the new round of trade negotiations at the conclusion of the Uruguay Round.

44 MITI's 'official' stance on the results of EVSL seems that members 'agreed' on every one of the areas in Figure 2.2 including the liberalization element. For liberalization, members 'agreed' to pursue it at the WTO, and for other elements, members 'agreed' to do at least 'something' in all shaded areas in Figure 2.2, though measures identified in 1999 did not cover all areas. Interview with an APEC-related official of MITI, 17 December 1999.

45 Interview with a support staff member of a Japanese ABAC representative, 1 December 1999.

46 As a matter of fact, there had not before been a case like EVSL that directly touched upon the sensitive consensus issue. In other words, 'consensus' has been gained among members only in 'general' principles, 'long term' objectives and the like. For instance, as mentioned several times in this chapter, the OAA principles are general and members can interpret some of them almost completely freely. Moreover, no one has ever clearly defined what the 'free and open regional trade and investment,' which APEC members are to achieve by 2010/2020, means.

47 For a detailed discussion, see Okamoto (1995).

3   Analytical framework

Jiro Okamoto and Michael Wesley

Following the detailed explanation of general development and the results of EVSL and more concrete research questions raised in Chapter 2, this chapter sets an analytical framework for studying the EVSL process. The framework will be based on the well known 'two-level game' model by Putnam (1988) that includes both the multilateral consultation aspect and the domestic policy making aspect. The analytical framework set here will be shared by the case studies in Part II.

First, in this chapter, literature on foreign policy making processes will be reviewed briefly. It will be pointed out that the analysis on linkages of domestic and international politics is essential to understanding the development and outcomes of international negotiations (consultations, in APEC's case) including EVSL. Second, it will be argued that the Putnam model is most suitable for analyzing the EVSL process, and the original 'two-level game' model will be explained in some detail. However, it is not necessarily the case that the original model can be applied to EVSL as it is. Thus, third, with reference to the preceding discussions on the model in the 1990s, possible modification of, or extensions to, the Putnam model will be considered in order to make it more robust for analyzing the specific EVSL case.

Brief review of literature

The 'agent–structure problem,' the controversy over whether individual volition or circumstantial constraints are the primary locus of explanation of social phenomena, has plagued political science as much as most other branches of the social sciences (Wendt 1987). Following these other branches of social science, international relations theorists tended to rely either on structure or on agency as the ontological basis on which to build their theories.

Structural-level theories of international relations became influential in the 1970s, as the international system was characterized and looked to as the main influence on the foreign policy actions of states. Perhaps the most famous structural theory is that developed by Waltz in *Theory of International*

Politics (1979), which, in the interests of theoretical parsimony and elegance, argues that since states are functionally similar units, the internal nature of the state 'drops out' as a variable explaining international outcomes, in favor of the ordering of the system and the distribution of capabilities among states. Most modern attempts to theorize international–domestic linkages try to retain the parsimony and scientific rigor of the neo-realist model, while escaping the straitjacket of Waltz's rejection of the explanatory rich-ness of the domestic sources of international politics. Keohane and Nye (1977) argued that the international system consisted of not only military/political power but also economic power, which was the distribu-tion of economic activities and wealth. According to their argument, economic 'interdependence' sets limits on what states can do in terms of foreign relations because the destruction of interdependence would be too costly for any state.

Though these arguments on the international system restricting what states can do sound reasonable, they do not necessarily mean that the inter-national system forces states to take one particular approach towards their respective policy agenda. Rather, it can be seen that the international system provides a certain range of policy options. Gourevitch (1978: 911) asserted that '[h]owever compelling external pressure may be, they are unlikely to be fully determining ... The choice of response therefore requires explanation. Such an explanation necessarily entails an examination of politics: the struggle among competing responses.'

Other international relations theories have concentrated on agency-level explanations. For instance, Morgenthau (1949) described well-trained leaders and diplomats as independent variables for foreign policy making, and the rationality and human nature of those people were taken as the most important factors behind their respective policies. However, by the end of the 1950s, close interactions between the governmental policy making process and domestic society was receiving greater recognition. Waltz (1959) argued that a state's functions were determined by the needs of domestic society. It was more so in the economic policy arena as it was real-ized that foreign economic policy had significant and direct consequences for the material interests of domestic society by influencing trade and domestic flows. Katzenstein (1978: 19) specified domestic actors as consisting of political groups (primarily the state bureaucracy and political parties) and major interest groups which represented various arms of production including industry, finance, commerce, labor and agriculture.

The development of arguments on state–society relations saw the emer-gence of the 'state-centric' approach, including Katzenstein (1978) and Krasner (1978a) among others. The state as a whole was taken as an actor in foreign policy making, and political leaders and bureaucratic officials were viewed as individual participants in the process. In this case, these 'policy makers' were assumed to represent the concept of 'national interest' and participate in the policy making process not so much as agents of any particular groups in the society or governmental institutions. Rather, they were considered to be taking actions to achieve their policy objectives (national interests) by pursuing public policies. In other words, state policy makers had relative autonomy in foreign policy making. Ikenberry (1988: 167–71) argued that the policy preferences of a state could differ from the demands of interest groups because private interests tended to be narrow without considering the state's economic strategy, and rarely took economic policies of other states into account. Moreover, 'policy makers' were in a position that enabled them to link the foreign economic policy of their own state with that of others and to tie certain policy issues to a larger set of international issues. By doing so, they could bargain for their state's overall interests.

On the other hand, it is undeniable that policy makers have their own bases of political support, such as electoral constituencies, interest groups and the bureaucratic organizations they direct. As they depend on those bases to maintain their current status, policy makers' interests, priorities and responsibilities in policy making can be influenced by their support bases. In fact, the state-centric approach too admits the importance of the demands of society on foreign policy making. Katzenstein (1978: 4, 308) states that '[g]overmnent officials do not define foreign policy objectives single-handedly but in conjunction with business and financial leaders' and 'the main purpose of all strategies of foreign economic policy is to make domestic policies compatible with the international political economy.' The ability to influence government decisions is not necessarily confined to business and financial sectors, and the amount of influence that those interest groups can exert on the government depends upon the policy issues at hand and each state's institutional settings for dealing with those issues. In other words, whether a state (policy makers) is 'strong' or 'weak' in insisting on its policy objectives towards its society differs from state to state and issue to issue.[1]

A class of international relations theorists has tried to go beyond the agent–structure controversy by theorizing on the mutual influence of agency and structure, or how domestic political processes influence those at the international level, and vice versa. This has largely been a response to dissatisfaction with the explanatory power of international relations models that concentrate solely on international factors or assume state interests to be exogenous. Such attempts can be grouped into four, based on their characterization of the international and the domestic, and the lines of causality they draw between these political arenas.

The first group sees domestic politics and international politics as separate but linked policy arenas, connected by governments able to pursue their interests in each arena. Ikenberry (1986), and later Mastanduno *et al.* (1989), see state policy makers as able to respond to policy challenges in the most appropriate arena, whether domestic or international. The domestic and international domains each possess different and distinct incentives and limitations on state action; thus domestic goals may be most effectively pursued with international strategies, or vice versa. Barnett (1990) theorizes along similar lines, arguing that the domestic and the international each set different limits on the state's ability to mobilize its resources.

A second group of theorists are those that use domestic structures to generalize states' foreign policies as ideal types. This is a diverse group, ranging from classical realists such as Kissinger (1966) and Waltz (1959) to liberal theorists of the link between democratic politics and peace between states (Doyle 1986, 1997; Schweller 1992). Other variants within this group contend that domestic institutions, networks and social structures have a determining effect on foreign policy (Risse-Kappen 1991, 1994), or that differences in foreign policy type arise from states as either state-centered or society-centered polities (Katzenstein 1978). Still others suggest that foreign policy is at times the externalization of internal policy and ideology of states, particularly hegemons, or that foreign policy attempts to make international structures compatible with domestic imperatives (Ruggie 1982).

A third group reverses this causality, and examines the effects of international forces on domestic politics. Its members construct various models to chart how changes in international economic conditions can drive domestic political changes and alignments (Gourevitch 1978; Milner 1988; Rogowski 1989; Zakaria 1992; Garrett and Lange 1995; Keohane and Milner 1996; Verdier 1998).

Finally, a fourth group attempts a synthesis of elements of the first three, to develop models of how domestic preferences converge to determine, and are in turn influenced by, international politics. Gourevitch's (1996) attempt to plumb the domestic sources of international cooperation leads him to explain regime formation and persistence by reference to the convergence of domestic preferences towards cooperation and the maintenance of a credible commitment to these institutions within and among states. Moravcsik's (1997) liberal theory also assembles domestic preferences, their aggregation through state structures, and their patterns of interdependence and intensity between states as a model for explaining international politics.

By reviewing literature, it is clear now that an analytical framework for case studies of the EVSL process needs to provide two interrelated viewpoints at the same time: international–domestic political linkages, and domestic state–society relations in foreign policy making. Furthermore, it should offer flexibility for each case, as APEC members differ in many ways, including their levels of economic development, political regimes and culture.

Though it was formulated by referring to the US foreign policy making process, Putnam's 'two-level game' model aims to fulfill these requirements. The model has been widely accepted in the study of international negotiations. Many case studies have adopted the model[2] and numerous attempts have been made to modify, or extend, the model.[3] Putnam's characterization of the domestic and international as each establishing the bargaining parameters, or 'win-sets', available to diplomats in the other arena, makes it a member of the class of theories in the first group, which see domestic politics and international politics as separate but linked policy arenas. However, Putnam's concepts of 'synergistic linkage' and 'reverberation' also take his model beyond this group by pointing the way towards models with closer causative links between national societies and across the domestic–international politics divide. This model possesses greater explanatory power than the others reviewed above by describing a process of constant consideration of both international and domestic factors, the causes of voluntary and involuntary non-compliance (defection), and the importance of issue linkages for the achievability of agreements.

The 'two-level game' model and its applicability to the EVSL process

The basic concept of Putnam's model (Putnam 1988) is to divide a state's foreign policy making into two levels, as the title of the model suggests: the international negotiations to seek agreements are called 'Level I' and the domestic discussions within each group of constituencies to decide whether international agreements can be 'ratified' are called 'Level II.' At the connecting point of both levels, there are 'political leaders,' or 'negotiators,' who represent a state at the international negotiations table, and, simultaneously, seek to achieve international agreements that will be attractive to their domestic constituencies.

Tentative agreements as a result of Level I bargaining are to be discussed at Level II. As Putnam's original literature made clear, the 'ratification' process does not necessarily take a formal procedure in legislative bodies. The point is that Level I agreements must be accepted by Level II constituencies. 'Final ratification must simply be voted up or down' (Putnam 1988: 437). In other words, if they are decided as not acceptable as a whole, or even in part, the Level I agreements need to be discarded unless negotiations can be reopened and new or amended agreements approved by all other parties at Level I. No state is able to amend Level I agreements by themselves.

The concept of the win-set

Other important and basic concepts of the model are the 'win-set' for a given Level II constituency and the size of the win-set. The win-set is defined as the set of all possible Level I agreements that would generate enough support to be ratified at Level II. Thus, successful Level I agreements must fall within the win-set of each participating state in the negotiation. In other words, international cooperation via agreements is only possible where those win-sets overlap with each other. While not strictly quantifiable, relative restrictions can be discussed when talking about larger or smaller win-sets. This is a particularly useful concept when comparing between states, between issues, or with the same issue over time. Putnam assumed that the larger each state's win-set, the better the chance for them to overlap, therefore the more than likely an international agreement will be successful. On the other hand, a smaller Level II win-set can be an advantage at Level I negotiations. Negotiators from a state with a small win-set can argue that there is not much room to compromise if they are to secure their domestic ratification.

It should be noted that there have been attempts to modify Putnam's original assumptions on this point. For instance, Iida (1993) argued that the information on policy preferences of domestic constituencies is not necessarily available, and developed an imperfect information model by assuming uncertainty of domestic preferences. According to his analysis, under the condition of uncertainty in negotiation partners' win-sets, negotiators can be in an advantageous position only if the counterparts perceived their partners' domestic restraints were significant, but agreements are still achievable. If negotiators do not have enough information on both domestic and counterparts' win-sets, however, they cannot attain negotiation advantages. In these cases, agreements become hard to reach. Downs and Rocke (1995) indicated the possibility of political leaders (negotiators) manipulating information, and emphasized that relations between political leaders and constituencies in Level II would have influence on international cooperation in general.

Even if an agreement is reached at Level I, there are possibilities for states to defect. Putnam added the importance of distinguishing *voluntary* and *involuntary* defections. The former implies that states may purposefully not implement measures agreed at Level I with or without Level II ratification, because of their egoistic but 'rational' interests under the circumstance of the absence of binding power of the agreement. Involuntary defection, on the other hand, means failed ratification of a Level I agreement at Level II, no matter how sincere the intention of negotiators. Thus, the smaller the win-sets, the more likely involuntary defection will take place, as the probability of the Level I agreement falling within the Level II win-set decreases.

Putnam suggested that there are three factors that affect the size of the win-set: Level II preferences and coalitions; Level II institutions; and Level I negotiators' strategies. First, the size of the win-set depends on the distribution of power among, as well as the preferences and coalitions of, domestic actors. In other words, the 'domestic politics' of each negotiating party influence the fate of Level I negotiations via influencing the size of the win-sets. Though Putnam did not nominate any particular theories of domestic policy making as the most appropriate for the two-level game model, and this is where the model is flexible and inclusive, he proposed several principles of domestic politics that would decide the size of the win-set.

1   If the cost of 'no-agreement' at Level I is perceived to be low by Level II constituents, the win-set would be small. Since the low cost means there is not much to lose by no-agreement, constituents can be 'choosy,' and

so can negotiators at Level I. The perception of the cost of no-agreement has close relations with the level of satisfaction of constituents with the status quo. The lower level of satisfaction with the status quo suggests that more energy will be channeled into negotiating an alternative state of affairs, and that there will be more flexibility in assessing the acceptability of negotiated accords or initiatives. The higher the present satisfaction, the more exacting will be assessments of proposed alternatives, and the less energy will be devoted to finding alternatives.

2   Whether the negotiated issue at Level I provokes *homogeneous* or *heterogeneous* interests among Level II constituents is an important matter in terms of the size of the win-set. If the interests of Level II constituents are relatively homogeneous, the more negotiators can win at the Level I negotiation, the better the chance for the agreement to be ratified at Level II, while not leaving too much room for negotiators to compromise at Level I. In this situation, the perception of the cost of no-agreement would generate cleavage within constituencies. The power balance between 'hawks' (who want the Level I negotiator to go all the way) and 'doves' (who are more concerned about possible no-agreement and want the negotiator to go as far as a Level I agreement can hold) on the issue will ultimately decide the size of the win-set. On the other hand, if the interests of Level II constituents are diversified, the size of the win-set is potentially large. However, the size cannot be defined easily and the Level I negotiator needs to do complicated calculations to strike a Level I agreement.

3   *Issue linkage* at Level I is another factor that influences the domestic politics, and thus, the size of the win-set. As it is impossible for political leaders to stand for interests of all constituents in each issue simultaneously, multi-issue negotiations at Level I make them face tradeoffs for each constituent's interests in each issue. Moreover, the issue linkages at Level I can be transnational. If a transnational agreement is reached on tradeoffs with other negotiators at Level I, political leaders can enlarge the domestic win-set without changing the preferences of constituents.[4]

These principles of domestic politics look to have particular importance for the EVSL case. APEC members' failure to achieve an agreement on the liberalization element of EVSL seems to imply that the majority of Level II constituents in each member perceived the cost of no-agreement on EVSL to be relatively low, thus effectively reducing the size of the respective win-sets. Members' Level II constituents might have been thinking EVSL was unnecessary because either: they had to liberalize anyway by the Bogor target of 2010/2020, or they did not have to commit to liberalization under APEC because there was a new WTO round scheduled to start soon. Both the United States' and other pro-liberalization members' enthusiastic push for the EVSL package deal and Japan's total rejection of it indicate that they had small win-sets, and may suggest that their perceptions on the cost of no-agreement were somewhat low. The homogeneous/heterogeneous interest principle seems to have substantial implications for how members saw the results of the EVSL sector selections and their subsequent attitudes towards EVSL. It must be fair to say that the more nominated and supported sectors were included in the final fifteen, the more homogeneous interests of Level II constituents could be expected. For instance, political leaders of the United States, which nominated nine sectors of the final fifteen and supported five others, can expect more homogeneous Level II interests in EVSL than their Japanese counterparts, only three of whose nominations were included in the final fifteen (see Table 2.1 and Appendix 2). The rule of 'the more, the better' seems to be relevant for the US EVSL policy. The assumption of issue linkages is surely to apply to EVSL by its nature, as there were fifteen sectors and three elements (liberalization, facilitation and Ecotech) to be negotiated upon. Members with high rates of success in the sector nominations can be assumed to face fewer domestic tradeoffs than those with low success rates (and fewer nominations in the first place). Moreover, the concept of transnational issue linkages appears to explain some incidents quite well, such as the inclusion of trade facilitation and Ecotech elements in the EVSL agenda and dismal results on the NTMs, facilitation and Ecotech elements after the tariff element was referred to the WTO.

Second, Putnam argued that the institutional settings for domestic decision making affect the size of the win-set. It is rather obvious that if 'ratification' procedures at Level II, whether formal or informal, differ, the probability of Level I agreements being ratified also varies. The two-level game framework does not touch upon the domestic process and lets empirical studies describe it. This is another area where the model is flexible and inclusive, which is important when applied to the EVSL process. In EVSL case studies, for instance, the effects on the US government of not being given trade negotiation authority by Congress and drastic changes of government in Indonesia can be covered by this assumption.

Third, the negotiators at Level I themselves are able to change the size of the win-set. If negotiators are to increase the possibility of a Level I agreement to be ratified by Level II constituents, they may use 'side-payments.' For example, the Japanese government promised to provide a huge amount of subsidies to the domestic agricultural sector as a 'countermeasure to the Uruguay Round commitments,' when they decided in 1993 to allow 'minimum access' rice imports every year. This side-payment somewhat weakened the traditional and vigorous opposition of agricultural cooperatives towards the opening of the domestic rice market, hence enlarged the win-set, and enabled Japanese policy makers to sign the Marrakesh Treaty. Side-payments, or concessions, can also be made internationally. Since ratification by all participants at Level II is required for an international agreement to be successful, Level I negotiators are assumed to be ready to give concessions to their counterparts, if they want the agreement. The

inclusion of elements other than liberalization in EVSL can also be understood as a cost-effective concession from pro-liberalization members to get
wider participation in the process. Pro-liberalization members doubtless
preferred more participation than less in EVSL. The additional cost of the
inclusion of trade facilitation must have been almost nothing, as their
product standards, customs measures and other areas of facilitation were
perceived to be 'global standards.' The inclusion of the Ecotech elements
could provoke domestic opposition depending on the amount of additional
budget expenditure they were to spend, but it was already one of the 'pillars'
of APEC activities anyway. Moreover, concrete measures for trade facilitation
and Ecotech were to be discussed and decided through consultations yet to
begin; thus they could see opportunities to reject huge budget expenditure
on them, or give more concessions if they believed them necessary.

External factors affecting the structure of win-sets

Though the two-level game model does not touch upon the direct relations
between Level I negotiators and Level II win-sets of other states, Putnam
acknowledged that Level I negotiators could seek to influence each other's
win-set to maximize the possibility of ratification by 'ambassadorial,' or
diplomatic, activities, such as wooing opinion leaders and offering foreign
aid. Also, so-called 'external pressure' such as the US insistence on market
access may directly, or indirectly via their political leaders' practice, have
effects on restructuring the win-sets of states. These external influences do
not necessarily enlarge the win-sets. For instance, financial or any other
support may be given to counterparts' Level II constituents in covertly
expecting them to oppose or reject a certain Level I agreement, and too
much pressure on other states' opening their domestic market may create a
political backlash.

The assumptions in this section may prove valuable when applied to
EVSL case studies especially for *other members* than the 'big guns' such as the
United States and Japan, which may think they have potential to go their
own ways. To be more precise, the external factors perspective can be useful
in analyzing the decision making processes of Australia, Indonesia, Korea
and Thailand, all of which were watching the US–Japan confrontation over
the EVSL package deal.

Preferences and priorities of Level I negotiators

Lastly, if Level I negotiators are not regarded as mere agents of their
domestic constituents, their policy preferences and priorities must be
brought into the analytical model. As, by definition of the model, Level I
negotiators are the persons who ultimately decide whether to make agreements, they are able to reject the agreements even if those agreements fall
within their respective Level II win-sets. In other words, Level I negotiators

hold 'veto' power. Putnam gave three motives that can affect political leaders' preferences. Political leaders seek Level I agreements that would: (1) improve their standings in domestic politics; (2) shift to a Level II power balance in which they are able to implement their favored policies; and (3) be consistent with their own concepts of 'national interest.' Moravcsik (1993: 30–1) called the preference of a Level I negotiator according to these factors an 'acceptability-set' and argued that the relation between the acceptability-set and the win-set would influence the outcome of international negotiations. Evans (1993: 405–8) classified Level I negotiators into three categories – 'hawks,' 'doves' and 'agents (of domestic constituencies)' – and explained the implications of each case.

Since it is reasonable to assume that the support bases and political beliefs of political leaders differ from each other, who represents states at Level I can be crucial for the outcome of international negotiations. Careful attention should be paid to policy preferences, priorities and their changes, particularly when governments have changed during the negotiation process (in the case of EVSL, Korea, Thailand and Indonesia). In addition, Evans's assertion (Evans 1993: 406) that it is almost inevitable that a Level I negotiator would 'win' if he/she was a hawk and preferred the status quo, because he/she sets the negotiation agenda, is noteworthy in the EVSL context.

Possible extensions to the 'two-level game' model

So far, the two-level model has been explained in some detail, and the model appears to be very applicable to the EVSL case studies. If we remember how the EVSL consultation process developed, however, the original model seems to be insufficient to explain several points. In this section, these points will be raised first, and, by adding some conceptions, an attempt will be made to extend the model for the purpose of improving it to make it suitable for the analysis of the EVSL process.

Nature of choices: binary or continuous

A binary choice is one where the alternatives are yes or no, acceptance or decline; a continuous choice is one between a number of differently preferred alternatives (Schelling 1978: 213–14). The dynamics of binary decisions differ profoundly from those of continuous decisions. While the latter permits of the negotiation among alternatives, compromise between preferences and possibilities, the weighing of combinations of attributes, the former forces a choice between the status quo, or a deteriorating status quo (Putnam 1988: 442), and the proposed change. It is in this context that the reserve position, or the acceptability of the status quo, becomes important. While a continuous choice allows the selection from a range of degrees of variation from the original position, a binary choice may impose the selection between a large change and no change at all. For actors making a binary choice, the balance among the costs and benefits of both the reserve position and the proposed change will be crucial; where the consequences of the choice made also affect others, the number and identity of the actors who choose one way or the other have important cumulative effects (Schelling 1978: 214).

Distinguishing between binary and continuous choices has crucial consequences for Putnam's model. Putnam develops his argument based on a certain chronological order of negotiations: first, an agreement is hammered out between states at Level I (continuous choice); then it is submitted to domestic political processes for ratification (binary choice).[5] Even where small domestic win-sets are used to manipulate perceptions in international negotiations (Putnam 1988: 440), the directionality is the same. However, in reality, it is possible that the continuous choice occurs at Level II first, and is submitted to Level I for a binary choice. Moreover, the nature of choices can be altered over time on the same level – from continuous to binary or vice versa. Such circumstances will have important effects and ramifications on the nature of the cooperation.

In the context of EVSL, considering the facts that there were frequent communications between Level I and II, that one of the most debated issues was the nature of choice that Level I required Level II to accept (EVSL package (binary choice) or voluntary action (continuous choices)), and that the pro-liberalization members virtually insisted on changing the traditional APEC modality (changing the nature of choices), to add the issue of the nature of choices to the original two-level game model is necessary in analysis of the EVSL process. Once again, the costs and benefits of the reserve position versus the proposed change will be important.

The importance of the negotiated issue: issue depth

A distribution of the costs of the reserve position versus the proposed change will occur between states. The 'depth' of an issue – its importance to political actors in the other arena – at both the domestic and international levels, will vary from state to state.[6]

Domestically, the depth of a foreign policy issue depends on the nature of the state and its society and economy, and how these are affected by the issue in question. Different issues will entail different levels of political costs and potential benefits for different states. Internationally, the depth of domestic issues depends on differences in state power and influence, both generally and with respect to the issue in question. Differences in power also affect the types of choices and the range of alternatives within a regime that some states can impose on others (Krasner 1991).

An important aspect of this type of power is the degree to which the state is dependent on the regime or interdependent relationship: 'If states that derive greatest economic gains from a preferential trade area are more vulnerable to disruptions of commercial relations within the arrangement than other participants, the political leverage of the latter is likely to grow' (Mansfield and Milner 1999: 611). These types of power are crucial within the APEC context, particularly to the outcomes of binary choices. As will be explored, these types of power can enable some states to structure the binary choices of others in such a way that the reserve position risks damaging the organization and its stock of 'cooperative capital,' as a way of forcing the choice of a costly or unpalatable proposed change. The package attempt of EVSL explained in Chapter 2 may be understood in this context.

The effects of numerous negotiators at Level I

The original Putnam model was built by focusing, *basically*, on games played by two negotiators at the Level I table; in other words, 'one-to-one' negotiations.[7] Expanding the number of negotiators who represent respective states at Level I and including the ensuing implications in the analysis are not only necessary for EVSL case studies but also fruitful for exploring perspectives not covered by the original model.

Coalition building and critical mass at Level I

The situation of many negotiators at the Level I table would induce coalition building at Level I, especially at multilateral and standing forums such as the WTO and APEC.[8] If a member (or a sub-set of members) of a forum intends to start negotiations on a certain agreement in its favor, it may attempt to build a coalition of like-minded members to get enough drive to push the initiative. Other members outside of the coalition would probably be pushed to accept starting talks on the initiative simply because they do not know what is in it and/or just because they are members of the forum. In response to the original coalition's initiative, however, if a member (or a sub-set of members) outside of the coalition finds the initiative unfavorable, then it may form another coalition within the forum to oppose the initiative, thus giving Level I negotiations a chance to become a more complicated multi-level game.

This dynamic to build coalitions at Level I because of the existence of numerous negotiators leads directly to the concept of critical mass formation, which is important in understanding the nature of both APEC and EVSL. As explained in Chapters 1 and 2, the central conception of APEC, as a regional organization designed to build support for initiatives in the wider WTO organization, is based on the concept of critical mass. '[Critical mass involves] some activity that is self-sustaining once the measure of that activity passes a certain minimum level' (Schelling 1978: 95), otherwise termed 'minilateralism' (Kahler 1992) or 'tiering' (Wesley 1997). This process involves a number of states smaller than the total desired number of cooperating states that undertake collective action in the expectation that the non-cooperating states will eventually join them. In effect, the cooperation of the sub-set is intended to act as an attraction to the non-cooperating members. The self-sustaining attraction to non-members usually exists in perceived benefits of belonging to the collaborating group, and/or the perceived costs of not joining.

If the initiative is successful, and 'goes critical,' the trend to involve non-cooperating states automatically continues towards complete desired membership. However, as Schelling (1978: 102–10) observes, critical mass dynamics have two stable equilibria: full membership and no adherents at all. The latter situation will occur if the situation fails to 'go critical,' that is if it fails to attract enough members and generate enough benefits of membership to attract other members. Often, progressive defections from the original group will occur, usually because membership has failed to deliver the benefits expected, or because the persisting number of non-members is free-riding on the collective goods provided by the collaborators. Each defection in this case increases the incentives for others to defect, until the number of collaborators reaches zero.

This logic is inherent in APEC, thus in EVSL. Its ability to serve as a catalyst for action within the WTO depends on its ability to achieve liberalization in certain sectors among economies representing a significant proportion of the global economy. In this situation, the incentive is for other WTO members to support the measure, in order to benefit also from the increased market access. However, when APEC is unable to reach agreement, or when APEC agreement does not deliver collaboration among a significant enough sector of the global economy, members of APEC are likely to begin worrying about non-members gaining unreciprocated market access. Such worries naturally encourage defection from the original collaboration.

Abilities of Level I negotiators and Level II constituencies

Another aspect that the two-player, two-level game cannot clearly conceive by its nature is the effect of the diversity in abilities of both Level I negotiators and Level II constituents to negotiate and respond. This includes the diversity in the amount of resources (human and time) that Level I negotiators and Level II constituencies are able to allocate to given issues. When a coalition is formed at a Level I forum to promote a certain potential agreement, members of the coalition are likely to allocate more resources than others into the Level I negotiation. On the other hand, Level I negotiators who do not share the enthusiasm either to support or to reject the potential agreement and those who are unable, for any reason, to mobilize resources for the matter are more likely to stay passive for the initiative. Therefore, the Level I negotiation would likely proceed at a (fast) pace set by the promoters of the initiative, and members outside the coalition with inferior negotiation abilities and resource mobilization might find themselves unable to keep up with it. In these circumstances, the potential agreement may be destroyed at the very last stage even if the prospect of agreement looked fine during most of the Level I negotiation period, since it is unlikely that negotiators who cannot really recognize what influence the agreement would have on their Level II constituents would ultimately accept it.[9]

EVSL seems to reveal this point. For instance, during the period of sector selection for EVSL in the latter half of 1997 (in around four months in effect), members had to undertake a lot of tasks, all of which were time consuming. Members were asked to nominate sectors and explain their rationales in respect to the intra-APEC trade context. Then, they needed to analyze the domestic effects of liberalization in sectors nominated by all other members to judge whether to support or oppose them. The analysis must include not only the economic effects on respective domestic sectors, but also the political ones – whether the liberalization in certain sectors would incur overall Level II support, and thus strengthen the political status of negotiators. To conduct the analysis, Level I negotiators needed to have close talks with each constituent, and it is not hard to imagine that some members might just have been unable to find the time and resources to cover all the original sixty-two nominations. On top of that, the Asian economic crisis hit some members severely while sector selection was going on. In this sense, the crisis may be understood to have affected the Level I negotiators' abilities to conduct domestic politics.

Summary

In this chapter, we attempted to set an analytical framework for the case studies. We showed that the 'two-level game' model was best suited of the existing frameworks for the analysis of the EVSL process because the model can explain the causal links between international negotiation and domestic politics by introducing concepts such as the 'negotiator' and 'win-set,' and because the model has the flexibility to allow for various circumstances in regard to domestic policy making processes. However, the model may not be sufficient to explain all the phenomena of the development of the EVSL consultations detailed in Chapter 2. Thus, to make it more robust in explaining the EVSL process, we have tried to extend the original model by introducing the conceptions of the 'nature of choices' (binary or continuous), 'depth of the negotiated issue,' 'coalition building (critical mass formation) at Level I' and 'the abilities of Level I negotiators and Level II constituencies.'

The case studies on Japan, the United States, Australia, Korea, Thailand and Indonesia in Part II will use the viewpoint of the analytical framework and try to answer the concrete questions set out in Chapter 2. Though all authors share the framework, it is not necessarily the case that all of them will discuss it in detail in their respective case studies. Comparative analysis of case studies from several different perspectives using the analytical framework will be conducted in the concluding chapter in Part III.

Notes

1 The strong/weak state argument is developed in Krasner (1978a), especially in chapter 3. Krasner (1978b) showed that it was easier for the US government to assert its policy objectives in monetary policy than in commercial (trade) policy mainly because the beneficiaries and victims of commercial policy in society were relatively easy to detect while the impact of monetary policy tended to spread widely in society.

2 For instance, see Evans *et al.* (1993), Nagao (1994) and Schoppa (1997).

3 For examples, see Mayer (1992), Iida (1993), Downs and Rocke (1995) and Milner (1997).

4 Putnam (1988: 447) called this particular case a 'synergistic linkage.'

5 In fact, Putnam (1988: 445) indicated that potential agreements might well be sent back and forth between Level I and II, since it is highly possible that the domestic coordination for setting a position in Level I negotiation and the international coordination to ensure Level II ratification would take place. Putnam, however, did not touch upon the issue of the nature of choices.

6 Putnam (1988: 445) argued that when a negotiated issue is domestically 'politicized,' the number of actors who participate in the Level II process would increase, thus the size of the win-set would shrink. Putnam, however, did not discuss the influence of actors from the other issue arena clearly.

7 Though Putnam did give several 'more-than-two-players' games in his literature, such as the Kennedy Round, the Bonn Summit and the USSR 'double-zero' proposal on arms control, he did not elaborate the effects of multiple players at Level I in his model.

8 Kahler (1992: 697–700) explained the multiple coalition building attempts at the Uruguay Round. See also Higgott and Cooper (1990), who analyzed the formation of the Cairns Group.

9 Technically, the situation explained here can occur in the two-player game. However in reality, because there is only one negotiating partner, the conditions under which the partner is negotiating may be recognized by the other partner much more easily than in multilateral negotiations. In the two-player game, negative attitudes of the partner towards a potential agreement would be detected during the negotiation process, and it is likely that some kind of response (side-payments or concessions) would be made. Certainly, it is hard to imagine that the partner's negative attitude would be left unnoticed to the very last stage of the negotiation.

Part II
The case studies

4 Japan

The structure of complete objection[1]

Tatsushi Ogita

Introduction

The EVSL initiative was significant for Japan, one of APEC's core member economies, as well as the regional institution itself. The modality of EVSL, which was an unprecedentedly aggressive trade liberalization initiative for APEC, was incompatible with what Japan had believed was the institution's principle or philosophy – *voluntarism* – and it was the first and only thing regarding APEC that the country objected to and invalidated.

Japan's stance in the EVSL consultation was impressive and interesting because, as widely recognized, the country did co-initiate the foundation of APEC in 1989, and has been leading its activities and development since. APEC has been important for Japan as the counter force to the European and North American economic blocs, and as the only regional body that the country is a member of. In spite of such a principal position in APEC and its importance to the country, Japan nevertheless thoroughly resisted certain areas of the institution's ambitious project and fiercely confronted Australia, the other initiator of APEC, and the United States, the largest economy in the region.

Why did Japan act in a way that would cost APEC a foreseeable loss of momentum, and a deterioration in international relations? This chapter tries to examine the nature, background and structure of Japan's 'complete objection' in the APEC EVSL consultation.

The actors

In principle, the APEC policy making process in Japan has been relatively closed. Only limited actors participate in the process, and most are bureaucratic organizations. This is not only the case for APEC affairs, but is also true for most foreign policy making in this country. This tendency is the result of the simple and internationally common situation that those outside the bureaucracy, even politicians, are more concerned about domestic affairs than foreign issues.

On the other hand, more are interested and participate in the making of foreign policies which have major domestic influence. Among these are trade liberalization affairs, including EVSL. Although the number did not exceed that of the GATT Uruguay Round, EVSL attracted more actors in its policy making process than any other APEC affair. This was because, as mentioned, EVSL was an unprecedentedly aggressive trade liberalization initiative brought about by APEC.

In the EVSL policy making process, the primary players were still the bureaucratic organizations: the Ministry of International Trade and Industry (MITI, now the Ministry of Economy, Trade and Industry), the Ministry of Foreign Affairs (MOFA) and the Ministry of Agriculture, Forestry and Fisheries (MAFF). Additional major actors participating in and/or influencing the process were the Prime Minister and other relevant Ministers, politicians, political parties and interest groups.

Ministry of International Trade and Industry (MITI)

APEC policy making was considered unusual in the Japanese government in that MITI officially took the lead, together with the diplomacy-oriented MOFA. MITI sent its Minister and Official, as co-representatives of Japan, to the APEC Ministerial and Senior Officials Meetings. The ministry also shared the Japanese subscription to the institution of 40 per cent, which was almost as great as MOFA's 45 per cent.

The exceptional position of MITI in APEC affairs can be explained by the fact that the ministry was the co-proposer of this regional body, along with the Australian Department of Foreign Affairs and Trade, and Robert Hawke, Australian Prime Minister at the time. APEC originated in a report by MITI's 1988 study group, which advocated the promotion of a new Asia-Pacific cooperation, although this might not have developed into a ministerial-level forum had it not been for Hawke's proposal in 1989 (Hosokawa 1999: 139–44).

Hence, MITI was playing a bigger part in APEC affairs than one might expect given that it shared representation of the government and contribution to the government's funding for APEC with MOFA. Particularly in the early years of APEC, MITI was virtually the only organ for APEC policy making in Japan. Even after MOFA and other ministries/agencies had become involved as APEC developed institutionally and gained a higher profile with the establishment of the informal Leaders Meeting, MITI was still considered the most enthusiastic and substantial player.

MITI's framework for APEC policy making was always within the International Trade Policy Bureau. Though the lead office for APEC affairs within MITI has been changed several times in the past (originally from the Southeast Asia-Pacific Division to the Office for the Promotion of Asia Pacific Economic Cooperation, then to the APEC Preparation Office – functional only while Japan chaired APEC in 1995 – and now the Regional Cooperation Division), they are all under the jurisdiction of the Bureau.

Supporting sections such as the International Economic Affairs Division were also in the Bureau. This could be interpreted as a demonstration of the ministry's consistent commitment to APEC. In the present Ministry of Economy, Trade and Industry (METI), reorganized in January 2001, the Regional Cooperation Division and its sub-division, Office for the Promotion of APEC, still take the lead.

The International Trade Policy Bureau was known as a hard-core advocate of free trade in Japanese bureaucracy. Its attitude has, in principle, been reflected naturally in MITI's stance in APEC policy making. When Japan, chairing APEC in 1995, drafted the Osaka Action Agenda (OAA), MITI initially looked forward to making a clear-cut APEC liberalization guideline advocating comprehensiveness and withstanding flexibility.

However, despite being the Ministry of *International Trade* and Industry, it is also true that the industrial concerns of the ministry sometimes got the better of it. For example, the Japanese government finally inserted the so-called Flexibility Principle into OAA at the request not only of MAFF and concerned with agriculture parties but also of intra-MITI sections overseeing domestic (and less competitive) industries. In 1996, MITI, along with MAFF, tried to make some portions of Japan's Individual Action Plan purposefully insignificant, in an effort to conceal that it had little in its jurisdiction to offer for APEC liberalization because it had already sacrificed what it had in the 'initial actions' liberalization package presented at the Osaka Meetings.

In spite of such occasional exceptions, however, MITI was nevertheless regarded as an internationalist in general (Kusano 1997: 85).

Ministry of Foreign Affairs (MOFA)

MOFA had been sharing the Japanese delegation to APEC with MITI since the institution's establishment in 1989. In the preparatory and early days of APEC, however, MOFA was not only indifferent, but also sometimes even backward in its response to the Japanese government's (i.e. MITI's) efforts on APEC issues. This attitude can be explained by MOFA's standpoint in relation to other international concerns, such as trying to deter any suspicion of a rehabilitation of the Great East Asia Co-Prosperity Sphere, and attempting to prevent Europe from becoming excessively self-protective. Another explanatory factor to be observed in MOFA was that of antipathy towards MITI's intrusion into MOFA's sanctuary of Asian diplomacy.

It was in 1993 that MOFA began to play a substantial part in APEC affairs. The impetus was the necessity to coordinate a growing number of ministries/agencies in relation to APEC, and to manage the Prime Minister's participation in the newly established APEC Leaders Meeting. Japan's chairing of APEC in 1995 was another obvious reason for the emergence of MOFA, the prime diplomatic organ in the government. During the two years before the Osaka Meetings, MOFA played an important role in APEC policy making. The ministry even proposed a new initiative for APEC economic and technical cooperation (Ecotech) called 'The Partner for Progress' (Funabashi 1995a: 194–5, 214). At this time it also had an unusually cooperative relationship with MITI.

With the duty of the chair gone, however, MOFA's commitment to APEC affairs lessened. For example, in the making of the 1996 Individual Action Plan – a bundle of commitments for APEC liberalization – MOFA literally *bundled* together the commitments presented by several ministries/agencies and did not actually *coordinate* the process. Its once cooperative relations with MITI also deteriorated.

Within MOFA, the Developing Economies Division of the Economic Affairs Bureau took principal charge of APEC affairs from late 1993/early 1994. This change coincided almost exactly with the ministry's positive change in attitude towards APEC. The former lead section had been the Regional Policy Division in the Asian Affairs Bureau, which meant that MOFA had transferred its base for APEC policy making from one bureau to another.

The current lead section, the Developing Economies Division, is not regarded as being as large or as powerful a body in the ministry or the bureau. When making OAA, the division was substantially supported by the same bureau's First International Organization Division, made up of experts in trade negotiations and in charge of GATT/WTO affairs. However, this support ceased formally after the Osaka Meetings as APEC affairs were withdrawn from the GATT/WTO division's jurisdiction. The Developing Economies Division seems to play only the role of a coordinator, not that of a substantial policy maker. This in turn seems to be reflected in the current function of MOFA as a whole.

MOFA is basically a pro-liberalization ministry because, according to wide belief, its foremost concern is to promote and maintain good relations with the United States, which is always advocating free trade (with the exception of some industries). Following a rule in Japanese bureaucracy, however, the ministry has no mandate, power or will to overrule other ministries' anti-liberalization positions if they fall within the other ministries' jurisdictions. As far as APEC policy making is concerned, MOFA has mostly been a modest coordinator.

Ministry of Agriculture, Forestry and Fisheries (MAFF)

In APEC affairs, MAFF is the most active of all the Japanese ministries after MITI and MOFA, and may actually be considered more active than MOFA. Until APEC focused on its liberalization agenda in around 1993–4, however, MAFF's relevance to APEC had been almost completely confined to the activities of the Fisheries Working Group and the Marine Resource Conservation Working Groups, with which the ministry's affiliated Fisheries Agency had close ties.

MAFF first embarked substantially on APEC affairs when the OAA started to be elaborated. After MITI and MOFA had presented the agenda's basic outline at the Special SOM in April 1995, MAFF was wary of the APEC liberalization. The ministry suggested the danger of the MITI-MOFA pro-liberalization viewpoint to politicians concerned with agriculture (the so-called *norin-zoku*) and agriculture interest groups. With their support, MAFF succeeded in inserting the Flexibility Principle as one of the General Principles of the APEC liberalization and facilitation; it declared 'flexibility will be available in dealing with issues arising from such circumstances in the liberalization and facilitation process' (APEC Leaders Meeting 1995b: Part One, Section A, paragraph 8).

While MOFA is unable to overrule other ministries' positions in their jurisdictions, MAFF has veto power in agriculture-related domains, and was therefore able to overrule MITI-MOFA's initial position. MAFF's veto power seems to have been stronger than any other ministry ruling, particularly following the GATT Uruguay Round conclusion. Since then, the ministry's consistent and absolute rule regarding liberalization issues has simply been that 'no more concession beyond the Uruguay Round commitments' can be made.

Ministry of Finance (MOF)

Along with the three ministries introduced above, the Ministry of Finance (MOF) completes the group of the so-called *four APEC-relevant ministries*. It had been regarded as the *third* APEC-relevant ministry in the Japanese government until MAFF became active in liberalization affairs. The ministry bears the remaining 15 per cent of the Japanese subscription to APEC, and is in charge of the affairs of the APEC Custom Procedure Sub-Committee in the Committee on Trade and Investment, the Trade and Investment Data Review Working Group, and the Finance Ministers Meeting.

However, MOF's relatively influential appearance in APEC policy making has little basis; it might be a reflection of its traditional identity as *the ministry of ministries*. As far as liberalization affairs including EVSL were concerned, the ministry's involvement was necessary simply because these issues were connected with customs and tariffs, which fell within its juris-diction. It seems that the ministry played only a marginal and symbolic role, and that its position concerning liberalization was irrelevant.

Inter-ministry meetings

The four APEC-relevant ministries, namely MITI, MOFA, MAFF and MOF, had frequently held informal meetings at various levels, from Division Director up to Bureau Deputy Director-General. The meetings were some-times held just to coordinate the ministries' requests and interests; on other occasions, they were held to formulate and solidify the APEC policies of the Japanese government.

In addition to the four-ministry meetings, before each APEC Senior Officials, Ministers, and Ministerial/Leaders Meeting, other meetings are also held which summon the participation of all APEC-related ministries/agencies: the Ministry of Education; the Ministry of Labor; the Ministry of Post and Telecommunications; the Ministry of Transportation; the Economic Planning Agency affiliated to the Prime Minister's Office; and others.[2] However, EVSL affairs were mainly discussed at the four-ministry meetings. The Cabinet Secretariat, which is formally (and, in fact, only as a formality) superior to all the ministries, coordinated inter-ministry meetings in drafting OAA in 1995 (Hosokawa 1999: 148–9). Since then, however, it has not played any role in APEC policy making.

Ministers

Since APEC has the annual Ministerial and Leaders Meetings as its basic and topmost organs, along with a variety of Sectoral Ministerial Meetings, Ministers are required to participate in APEC policy making. Their roles have, however, usually been insignificant and marginal. This is to be expected, as most policies of the Japanese government are made from the bottom upward in terms of bureaucracy.

The first example of unusual Ministers' activities concerning APEC was observed during 1994–5. As early as the APEC Bogor Leaders Meeting in November, 1994, the then Minister of International Trade and Industry, Ryutaro Hashimoto, discussed with officials how to chair APEC 1995, and decided to make an agenda for APEC liberalization to be adopted at Osaka. In 1995, he led the domestic coordination of interests with the Minister of Agriculture, Forestry and Fisheries, Hosei Norota (Hosokawa 1999: 148–9). Bilateral negotiations with other APEC members were also conducted by Hashimoto himself, as well as Norota and the then Minister for Foreign Affairs, Yohei Kono. The then Prime Minister, Tomiichi Murayama, was also said to be active, although he did not play as important a role as Hashimoto and Kono, who were also his Deputy Prime Ministers at that time.

The second example was seen at the climax of the EVSL controversy in 1998, when Trade Minister, Kaoru Yosano, Foreign Minister, Masahiko Komura, and Agriculture Minister, Shoichi Nakagawa, were active in establishing Japan's position against EVSL. With Prime Minister Keizo Obuchi and Chief Cabinet Secretary Hiromu Nonaka, they came together at the APEC-relevant ministers' meetings, which were held three times between the Kuching Trade Ministers Meeting in June and the Kuala Lumpur Ministerial/Leaders Meeting in November 1998. Their roles will be discussed later.

Politicians and political parties

In principle, politicians and political parties are indifferent to APEC unless its liberalization initiative threatens Japan's agricultural market. In other words, they become active when a liberalization agenda emerges, and, need-less to say, they act against it.

Politicians involved in APEC liberalization affairs are mostly the *norin-zoku*. A *zoku* (tribe) is an individual or a group of legislators who have strong formal/informal influence in specific policy areas corresponding to ministries' jurisdictions. Its existence is due to each ministry's need for its own political 'supporters' to protect and magnify its jurisdictional interests in the power struggle with other ministries. At the same time, it is a corol-lary of politicians' utilization of each ministry's substantial policy making capacity to *pork-barrel* their constituencies or industries that support them. The *norin-zoku* is influential over agricultural and forestry policies, and is recognized as one of the most powerful *zoku* (Inoguchi and Iwai 1987: 19–29, 185–8). They are objects of MAFF's policy consultation, or *nemawashi*, and their goals and actions are naturally identical to those of the ministry. They objected to comprehensive APEC liberalization regarding the OAA, as well as to EVSL, by anchoring themselves to the golden rule, 'no more concession beyond the Uruguay Round commitments.' They headed a united front with MAFF and agricultural interest groups.

Among political parties, the only party that has played any truly mean-ingful role in APEC liberalization affairs is the Liberal Democratic Party (LDP). The LDP has been in power both as a single ruling party and as a coalition government since 1994, and the main APEC-relevant ministers since 1996 have all been from the LDP. Most *norin-zoku* are also LDP politi-cians. They act within or in close cooperation with the Agriculture and Forestry Division, the Fisheries Division, or with the Special Committee on Agricultural Trade, all of which are subject to the Party's Policy Research Council. It has been said that the Special Committee virtually directed MAFF's operation in the EVSL consultation.

Interest groups

Agricultural, fisheries and forestry interest groups are the remaining piece of the united anti-liberalization front in Japan's APEC policy making.

The most influential among them is the Central Union of Agricultural Co-operatives of Japan (*JA Zenchu*), known for its fierce resistance to freeing Japan's rice market discussed at the GATT Uruguay Round. It was the Bogor Declaration of 1994 which made *JA Zenchu* wary of APEC liber-alization. In 1995, it – with MAFF and the *norin-zoku* – maneuvered for and finally succeeded in hindering a comprehensive APEC liberalization with the injection of the Flexibility Principle in OAA. *JA Zenchu* was concerned mainly with the 'food sector' and 'oilseeds and oilseed products' of the so-called Back Six sectors in the EVSL process to be discussed in 1999, but also with 'fish and fish products' and 'forest products' in the Front Nine products negotiated in 1998.

EVSL also got other interest groups involved in the process. Among them, the National Federation of Fisheries Co-operative Associations (*Zengyoren*), the Japan Forestry Association and the Japan Plywood Manufactures' Association (JPMA) were relevant to the two sensitive sectors in the Front Nine. Their call was also simply, 'no more concession beyond the Uruguay Round commitments.'

Other actors

The Diet as an organization has never made any decision on APEC matters because relevant policies have never required any enactment or amendment of laws, or ratification of treaties. Only a few discussions have taken place in plenary sessions and in committees.

Non-governmental organizations (NGOs) were greatly powerful and influential at the WTO Third Ministerial Conference at Seattle in November 1999, but not in APEC affairs in Japan. It is true that they have occasionally appeared in APEC affairs, but they have not had any actual impact on policy making. In the EVSL process, some environmental NGOs sent appeals and met with MITI regarding liberalization of forest products. They did not cooperate with anti-liberalization interest groups such as *Zengyoren* and JPMA, but they did at the WTO Seattle Conference.

The process

This section begins the chronology of Japan's actions concerning the EVSL process at the year 1995. This is because, firstly, EVSL should be 'in accordance with the general principles set out in the Osaka Action Agenda,' adopted at the year's Leaders Meeting (APEC Ministerial Meeting 1997b). Secondly, how Japan drafted and elaborated the agenda suggested the nation's attitude towards APEC liberalization. Thirdly, the preliminary idea of EVSL emerged at Osaka, and it was interestingly different from that which was discussed at Subic.

November 1995: Osaka, Japan

It was the Flexibility Principle that was the most controversial among the nine General Principles of liberalization and facilitation in OAA. The controversy clarified Japan's reluctance to make APEC liberalization bold and aggressive.

In addition, the Comprehensiveness Principle also caused friction and revealed of the country's position, or strategy, towards liberalization. The Principle in the finalized agenda read as follows: 'The APEC liberalization and facilitation process will be comprehensive, addressing all impediments to achieving the long-term goal of free and open trade and investment' (APEC Leaders Meeting 1995b: Part One, Section A, paragraph 1).

In the first draft presented to the Special SOM four months prior to the Osaka Meetings, however, Japan, as the chair, proposed the following paragraph:

> APEC actions toward liberalization and facilitation will cover areas related to trade and investment i.e., tariff / non-tariff measures affecting trade and investment / technical barriers to trade / sanitary and phytosanitary measures / standards and conformance / custom procedures / intellectual property rights / subsidies / safeguard / rules of origin / anti-dumping and countervailing duties / government procurement / competition policy / deregulation, etc.[3]

This suggested that Japan wanted to interpret 'comprehensiveness' in the APEC liberalization as covering all *areas of liberalization-related measures*, not all *industries*. Such a strategy of interpretation would appear again in the following year's discussion, in Paragraph 8 of the Subic Leaders' Declaration that initiated EVSL, and in the succeeding EVSL controversy. It should be noted that the first draft of the agenda was drawn up after MAFF and the *norin-zoku* had successfully altered their government's (i.e. MITI-MOFA's) earlier pro-liberalization orbit, and therefore that such a strategy possibly reflected their intentions.

The other focus of interest in the OAA was the paragraphs which marked the first appearance of the founding idea that eventually led to EVSL. One of the two relevant paragraphs was as follows: 'APEC economies will identify industries in which the progressive reduction of tariff may have positive impact on trade and on economic growth in the Asia-Pacific region or for which there is regional industry support for early liberalization' (APEC Leaders Meeting 1995b: Part One, Section C, paragraph 1). This paragraph was supposedly included under the initiative of the United States and other pro-liberalization members. The other members – including the chair country Japan – had no reason to oppose it.

What is interesting in this paragraph is, firstly, that the object of the verb 'identify' is 'industries,' and, secondly, the non-usage of the word 'voluntary,' which later became the focal point in the EVSL controversy. How would these two change a year later?

November 1996: Subic, The Philippines

The idea of early liberalization in specific industries developed in 1996 and appeared again in the Subic Leaders' Declaration. Paragraph 8 of the Declaration was as follows:

We further instruct our ministers to identify *sectors* where early *voluntary* liberalization would have a positive impact on trade, investment, and economic growth in the individual APEC economies as well as in the region, and submit to us their recommendations on how this can be achieved.

(APEC Leaders Meeting 1996. Italics added by the author)

Japanese officials today say that it was only natural for Japan to have felt wary of the initiative as it was a new idea whose character and modality were still ambiguous. In spite of the current excuse that Japan was not strongly against the initiative, another credible story existed at the time that confirms the country's reluctance.

According to an official, it was Japan that converted the word 'industries,' which had appeared in the OAA, into 'sectors.' Moreover, the country had earlier proposed 'areas of APEC works' as a substitute, but in the end, settled with the compromise of 'sectors.' This clearly suggests that Japan had had the intention of avoiding the new early liberalization initiative addressed to specific industries, and wanted to interpret its comprehensiveness – if it were to be comprehensive – as covering all the liberalization-related areas or measures. As easily understood is that this maneuver was analogous to what Japan had done with the Comprehensive Principle in the OAA.

The other difference between the Subic and Osaka texts was the insertion of 'voluntary.' This adjective in the paragraph seems somewhat strange, as how positive an impact early liberalization would have has nothing to do with whether it is voluntary or not. The word was supposedly forcibly added afterwards. By whom, when and how the insertion was made is unknown. Considering Japan's later assertion on the voluntarism of EVSL, however, it is not unreasonable to guess that the country supported the addition.

In the 1996 process, MITI and MAFF worked in close cooperation in the Japanese government. Thus, the two ministries may have maneuvered to alter the paragraph as mentioned above. If so, some degree of wariness concerning EVSL was shared by the two active APEC-relevant ministries at the time, and it began as early as the initiative's official time of origin.

January 1997: Victoria, Canada

When it originated at Subic, EVSL was considered as an initiative relevant to the single area of liberalization on the subject of tariff and non-tariff measures. At 1997's first SOM held at Victoria in January, however, APEC member economies from ASEAN and China demanded that the initiative address not only liberalization, but also facilitation and Ecotech, which composed the entire *areas of APEC works*. This requirement was officially included in the Statement of the Chair at the Meeting of Ministers Responsible for Trade, held at Montreal four months later.

Japan probably supported the ASEAN and Chinese position at that time, as it complied with Japan's conventional strategy of interpreting APEC liberalization as being comprehensive in addressing all the *areas of APEC works*, not necessarily all *industries*. This extension of the scope of EVSL gave the country a basis on which it could later criticize EVSL as being excessively focused on the tariff element, in order to sidestep the calls for Japan to liberalize its own forestry and fisheries markets.

November 1997: Vancouver, Canada

In spite of taking such early and substantial precautions, at the Vancouver Ministerial Meeting in November 1997, Japan accepted the commencement of the EVSL initiative in fifteen sectors, including 'fish and fish products,' 'forest products,' the 'food sector' and 'oilseeds and oilseed products.' The country seemed far less reluctant than it would be in the following year, although it was reported that it unofficially expressed its objection to liberalizing agriculture and forestry sectors under EVSL.[4]

Japan probably considered itself as being able to ensure a free hand in not participating in the liberalization aspect (i.e. only participating in facilitation and Ecotech) of some sensitive sectors of EVSL, such as those given above. This seemed feasible, following the given paragraph in the Annex to the Ministers' Joint Statement for EVSL:

> the process of early liberalization is conducted *on the basis of the APEC principle of voluntarism, whereby each economy remains free to determine the sectoral initiatives* in which it will participate, we [APEC ministers] therefore call for the development of appropriate agreements or arrangements for market-opening and facilitation and economic and technical cooperation measures ...[5]
>
> (APEC Ministerial Meeting 1997b: Annex. Italics added by the author)

This might make up the basic excuse for Japan to believe that it would 'remain free to determine' not to make any more concessions beyond the Uruguay Round commitments in the agriculture, forestry and fisheries sectors.

Such interpretation of the voluntary EVSL modality seemed to be shared by the relevant actors in Japan. Officials of MITI, MAFF and MOFA spoke in unison of voluntarism in EVSL. In fact, the acceptance of EVSL was agreed at the four APEC-relevant ministries meeting before the Vancouver Meetings. Among interest groups, for example, *Zengyoren* received a document dated 20 November (the day before the opening of the Ministerial Meeting) from the Fisheries Agency, which explained that EVSL would not affect the sensitive sectors due to its voluntary mode of operation, even though *Zengyoren* was supposedly not fully aware of the initiative itself. It appears that the *norin-zoku* was also still unfamiliar with EVSL, and that Ministers played a small role as well.

June 1998: Kuching, Malaysia

The APEC Meeting of Ministers Responsible for Trade at Kuching in June 1998 was 'to finalize detailed targets and timelines' (APEC Leaders Meeting 1997: paragraph 6) for the EVSL Front Nine sectors, including 'fish and fish products' and 'forest products.' Up until then, EVSL had already headed for comprehensive liberalization as a *package deal*. This was probably pressed forward by the United States, Australia, Canada and New Zealand, and was clearly different from Japan's understanding and expectation of EVSL. The *package deal* would require each member economy to take action in all three areas (i.e. liberalization, facilitation and Ecotech) in each of the nine sectors, and its advocators' goal was liberalization (not facilitation or Ecotech) by every member in all the sectors. It hindered Japan's conventional strategy of putting *area-axis* comprehensiveness ahead of *sector-axis*, according to which all the three areas should be collectively covered in all (and not necessarily in each of) the nine sectors, but all the nine sectors need not be covered in an (or in each) area (see Figure 4.1).

Figure 4.1 The package deal vs. Japan's strategy in EVSL

Element (Area)-Axis →

		The package deal			Japan's strategy*		
		Lib.	Fac.	Ecotech	Lib.	Fac.	Ecotech
	Toys	◎	○	○	○	○	○
	Fish & fish products	◎	○	○	○	○	○
	Environmental ...	◎	○	○	○	○	○
Sector	Chemicals	◎	○	○	○	○	○
Axis	Forest products	◎	○	○	○	○	○
	Gems and jewellery	◎	○	○	○	○	○
	Energy	◎	○	○	○	○	
	Medical ...	◎	○	○	○	○	
	Telecom. MRA	/	○	○	/	○	

Note: * The figure for 'Japan's strategy' is a model and does not necessarily reflect Japan's actual position. ◎ indicates special focus.

While the *package deal* drive was progressing, the Japanese anti-liberalization united front also became active. MAFF and its affiliated Fisheries Agency and Forestry Agency began to consult closely with the relevant interest groups, such as *Zengyoren*, the Forestry Association and JPMA, and with the *norin-zoku*. In the fisheries industry, *Zengyoren* and the All Japan Seafood Import Consultative Group – which belongs to the Fisheries Policy Department of *Zengyoren* – appealed against EVSL liberalization on 'fish and fish products' to MAFF, MITI, MOFA, the *norin-zoku* and the Prime Minister in December 1997 and May and June 1998. In May, they, along with the Japan Forestry Association and JPMA, also petitioned the office of one of Japan's members at the APEC Business Advisory Council (ABAC).[6]

Shortly before the Kuching Meeting, the relevant ministers also aggressively embarked on the EVSL problem. The Trade Minister, Mitsuso Horiuchi, and Agriculture Minister, Yoshinobu Shimamura, both expressed Japan's opposition to the EVSL liberalization in the forestry and fisheries sectors. Horiuchi stated at a press conference that Japan had already announced its principle of voluntary action on EVSL, and would clarify it at Kuching.[7] Shimamura met US Agriculture Secretary Dan Glickman in Washington, D.C. to say that Japan would reject any EVSL liberalization in the forestry and other sectors.[8]

At the meeting, Japan maintained its position in postponing the conclusion, in the belief that the Vancouver agreement had been arbitrarily changed in its interpretation. Trade Minister Horiuchi made no compromise with US Trade Representative (USTR) Charlene Barshefsky and other ministers, who fiercely criticized his position; he once even suggested leaving the negotiation table.[9] On the one hand, the 'Statement of the Chair' (APEC Trade Ministers Meeting 1998) noted in Japan's favor that '*specific concerns have been raised by individual economies in each sector*' (paragraph 3; italics by the author). However, on the other hand, it also stated '[t]here is *emerging consensus* on product coverage, target end rates and target end dates' (paragraph 4), on which Japan registered reservation. Horiuchi could not brush off the Statement itself because of its being 'of the Chair' and not 'of the Ministers,' did not attend the joint press conference.[10]

September 1998: Kuantan, Malaysia

At the next official opportunity to discuss EVSL at SOM held at Kuantan in September, Japan again defended its position, sending in as many as sixty officials.[11] Before the meeting, the then Agriculture Minister Shoichi Nakagawa – newly appointed at the end of July – stated at a press conference that Japan should keep its voluntary principle. The Administrative Vice-Minister of International Trade and Industry, Osamu Watanabe, also added that the APEC liberalization had begun with the principle of voluntarism.[12] The conclusion to the problem was again postponed until the final stage of the 1998 process, at the Kuala Lumpur Meetings in November, although an agreement on all the Front Nine sectors had reportedly become an expected possibility.[13]

Shortly before the Kuantan SOM, an ABAC meeting was held at Taipei. MITI communicated closely with Japan's ABAC member there and worked simultaneously from Tokyo, in an effort to defend Japan's position by considering each word included in the Council's Report to the APEC Economic Leaders. *JA Zenchu* also sent its staff to the meeting to check the discussion and conclusion there. After the ABAC member was obliged to endorse the report advocating a comprehensive EVSL, some *norin-zoku* tried to summon him to the Diet for an inquiry (but did not).

After the SOM, the relevant ministers met USTR Barshefsky, who was visiting Tokyo, to insist on APEC's principle of voluntarism, and that APEC not be used for tariff negotiation.[14] The then Trade Minister Kaoru Yosano, who was also newly appointed at the end of July, toured Southeast Asia to meet Indonesian Minister of Industry and Trade Rahardi Ramelan, and Malaysian Prime Minister Mahathir Mohamad. He asked for their understanding of his country's predicament, but only got negative responses.[15]

November 1998: Kuala Lumpur, Malaysia

If Japan had sought a compromise in the EVSL controversy, it was during the last three weeks before the Kuala Lumpur Meetings.

At the APEC-relevant ministers' meeting on 23 October, Trade Minister Yosano proposed to assess the effects of liberalization on each fish product. Opinions on this proposal were divided. On one hand, as Yosano himself said, 'It is just a study for negotiation.' A MITI official also explained that it was to make the other APEC members understand Japan's position better. On the other hand, most newspapers reported that the proposal suggested the country was seeking a compromise, admitting tariff elimination on certain products. It was also reported that Prime Minister Obuchi had called upon ministers to make as much effort as they could for adjustment, and the then Chief Cabinet Secretary Nonaka commented at a press conference that Japan could not avoid addressing the EVSL issue as an official APEC agenda.[16] In contrast, Agriculture Minister Nakagawa reportedly repudiated the Trade Minister's proposal, saying that 'Assessment is okay, but it is separate to the acceptance of forestry/fisheries liberalization in EVSL,' and criticized MOFA officials for stirring up Japan's anxiety over isolation.[17]

The anti-liberalization united front, consisting of MAFF, the *norin-zoku* and the relevant interest groups, soon began to strike back. In late October, Agriculture State Secretary Tadahiro Matsushita and Forestry Agency's Director-General Toru Yamamoto toured Malaysia, Indonesia and Thailand, while the other State Secretary, Hiroaki Kameya, visited China and Korea with Shoji Miyamoto, the Director-General of the Fisheries Policy Planning Department, the Fisheries Agency.[18] Agriculture Minister Nakagawa also traveled at the beginning of November to the United States to meet

Assistant to the President for Economic Policy (Director of the National Economic Council) Gene Sperling, USTR Barshefsky and Agriculture Secretary Glickman, in an effort to make the United States recognize Japan's difficult situation.[19] In the same period, the LDP's Special Committee on Agricultural Trade requested Prime Minister Obuchi not to compromise,[20] and reaffirmed to MOFA that EVSL should be on the basis of voluntarism.[21] *Zengyoren* and the Forestry Association held anti-EVSL conventions on the same day, 4 November, with the participation of *norin-zoku*.[22]

MOFA reportedly then showed inclination towards a compromise. It seemed that the ministry did not have a strong policy preference, but wished only to avoid Japan's isolation. At the same time as Nakagawa, Foreign Minister Komura visited Indonesia, Australia and New Zealand to request their understanding of Japan's partial rejection of EVSL, but was unable to consolidate any support. MITI, the other reported compromise-seeker, kept relatively silent during this period.

Prime Minister Obuchi's leadership did not seem strong or coherent. Some say that at the first APEC-relevant ministers' meeting on 8 September, Obuchi confirmed with Ministers that Japan could not admit any liberalization beyond the Uruguay Round Commitment in the agriculture, forestry and fisheries sectors.[23] As mentioned above, however, he reportedly showed an inclination towards a compromise at the second APEC-relevant ministers' meeting on 23 October. Furthermore, when requested not to compromise by the LDP's Special Committee on Agricultural Trade five days later, he is said to have suggested the possibility of a concession, saying that 'It is also necessary to cooperate with other APEC member economies.'[24] Nevertheless, at the meeting with Indonesian Coordinating Minister for Economics, Finance and Industry, Ginandjar Kartasasmita, on 29 October, Obuchi reiterated Japan's principle of not accepting tariff elimination in the two sensitive EVSL sectors.[25] Additionally, Chief Cabinet Secretary Nonaka, a close assistant of the Prime Minister, began to emphasize Asian financial and economic problems, drawing away from EVSL as a top priority at Kuala Lumpur.[26]

It was finally reported that the Japanese government had, by around 5 November, consolidated its position to decline EVSL in the two subject sectors.[27] The third APEC-relevant ministers' meeting on 10 November confirmed this decision,[28] and also endorsed Foreign Minister Komura's proposal to offer approximately 27 billion yen in aid to Asian forestry and fisheries industries over the following five years.[29] However, Trade Minister Yosano still suggested a possible concession at the last moment at Kuala Lumpur, saying 'Instructions from Tokyo may be necessary [depending on the developments (there)].'[30] His Administrative Vice-Minister Watanabe also forecast various turns of events until the final stage, and stated that Japan's attitude would depend on the response of the other Asian members.[31]

In the latter days leading up to the Kuala Lumpur Meetings, while Asian member economies such as China, The Philippines, Thailand, newcomer

Vietnam and Malaysia (in the chair) began to assume a position more or less on Japan's side, the anti-EVSL actors tried to make sure that Japan would reject liberalization in the forestry and fisheries sectors. On 11 November, *JA Zenchu*, the Forestry Association and *Zengyoren* held a joint conference at the LDP's headquarters.[32] After this, the LDP *norin-zoku* left for Malaysia, to get confirmation from Prime Minster Mahathir that his government would accept Japan's position.[33] Obuchi also sent Mahathir a letter asking for his support.[34]

What the Japanese ministers did at the Kuala Lumpur Meetings was simply to keep their position and to decline any concession. In spite of the reported possibility of a political settlement taking place at the Leaders Meeting on 17–18 November, the EVSL controversy came to a conclusion at the Ministerial Meeting held on 14–15 November. Ministers first recognized the following, satisfying Japan's conventional assertion: 'The EVSL initiative, undertaken through the APEC principle of *voluntarism*, is an *integrated* approach to liberalisation through the *incorporation of facilitation and economic and technical cooperation measures*' (APEC Ministerial Meeting 1998: paragraph 11. Italics added by the author). Afterwards, they declared in favour of sending the EVSL tariff element to the WTO agenda.

On the same day of the ministers' statement, MAFF immediately released the following comment to welcome the conclusion at Kuala Lumpur:

> At the current APEC Ministerial Meeting, as a result of much effort of the Minister for Foreign Affairs and Minister of International Trade and Industry, our nation's assertion regarding forest and fish products was sustained.
>
> (1) Based on the principle of voluntarism, our nation will not participate in the tariff measures of EVSL in forest and fish products.
> (2) It will not be negotiated at APEC, which is originally not for negotiation, but at WTO. In such case, our nation's positions, which are that the next WTO round should be a comprehensive negotiation, and so on, will not change.
>
> (MAFF in Zengyoren 1999: 11)

In line with MAFF, *Zengyoren* released a welcoming comment, and Agriculture Minister Nakagawa said at a press conference that he appreciated the result.[35] A MAFF senior official reportedly depicted it as 'an overwhelming victory.'[36]

September 1999: Auckland, New Zealand

The tariff element of EVSL virtually ended in 1998. Set on course at Kuala Lumpur, the Ministerial Meeting at Auckland in September 1999 decided that the EVSL tariff element in the Back Six sectors would also be sent to WTO. Although the Back Six included the 'food sector' and 'oilseeds and oilseed products,' which were the sensitive sectors for Japan, the country's anti-liberalization actors – namely, MAFF, the *norin-zoku* and relevant interest groups – kept generally quiet in 1999.

The interpretations

For Japan, at least in the APEC process, the stubborn objection observed in the EVSL consultation was unprecedented. Although what the nation did was out of character, why or how it acted in that manner is fairly straightforward but can nonetheless be analyzed from different angles.

Invoking Robert Putnam's 'two-level game' theory and its core analytical tool called 'win-set,' Japan's Level II win-set was basically *constricted*, as the country could not finally agree to the commencement of the EVSL tariff element in the specific sectors at Level I. There were observations of some *constant* factors that had been constricting Japan's Level II win-set in foreign policy making generally or in the APEC liberalization affairs especially. It is also believed that the *size* of the win-set, however, was not constant but instead had been *shrinking* from 1997 to 1998. Therefore, Japan accepted EVSL in the first year but did not in the second. This is possible at least in a relative sense, although the Japanese government might insist that not Japan's win-set but the nature of EVSL changed.

Constant factors constricting the win-set

It is obvious who was constantly constricting the win-set in Japan. The reason why MAFF, *norin-zoku* and relevant interest groups rejected the EVSL tariff element is also clear. The question is how their position bound the one of Japan as a whole nation, and constricted its Level II win-set.

Consensus seeking in the bureaucracy

Putnam takes Japan as an example in which 'propensity for seeking the broadest possible domestic consensus before acting constricts the ... win-set, as contrasted with majoritarian political culture' (Putnam 1988: 449). Such a political or policy making culture, in a broad sense, would be a primary constant in constricting the Japanese Level II win-set on EVSL consultation. It can be observed in both bureaucratic and political strata.

Consensus seeking among the actors may imply that each of them has veto power. In fact, 'the different sectors of Japan's bureaucracy seem to exercise veto power against each other' (Funabashi 1995a: 217). As a rule in Japanese bureaucracy, while no ministry has any authority to make any decision free from the jurisdiction of others, it has the power to avoid the interference of others in its area of jurisdiction.

It was this institution (rather than culture) that made the Japanese government insert the Flexibility Principle into the OAA in 1995. The insertion 'just occurred, rather than [being] consciously judged, at the equilibrium point ... among the three ministries' intentions,' at the point where MITI and MOFA's inclination towards comprehensive liberalization and MAFF's rejection of liberalization beyond the Uruguay Round commitments met (Ogita and Takoh 1997: 28).[37]

Also, in the EVSL process, neither MITI nor MOFA had authority, power or will to say anything about liberalization in the forestry and fisheries sectors. They had to comply with MAFF's assertion to reject the tariff element in the two sectors, regardless of foreseeable conflict in their respective regional forum. At the bureaucratic stratum, MAFF limited the win-set to 'EVSL without tariff element in the forestry and fisheries sectors.'

Consensus seeking and the lack of discipline at the political level

Although bureaucracy is a substantial machine in policy making, in principle, it should be politicians or political leaders who make the final policy decision of a nation. The mutual veto power of bureaucratic organizations is exercised 'especially when they lack strong direction from the political leadership' (Funabashi 1995a: 217). Political leaders ought to be able to make decisions regardless of bottom-up policy output from the bureaucracy, and should be able to overrule the decisions of a ministry.

Consensus seeking and mutual veto power, however, can be seen among Ministers in the Cabinet as well as in bureaucracy. Strong leadership is rare in Japanese politics, where even the Prime Minister has difficulty overruling other Ministers' calls, despite his/her authority. As the President of the ruling LDP, he/she can scarcely discipline the party powerfully either. Although there have been exceptions such as Yasuhiro Nakasone, Keizo Obuchi did not seem to be a strong Prime Minister or Party President during the final phase of the EVSL controversy in the latter half of 1998. He did not, or could not, persuade the Agriculture Minister or his party's *norin-zoku*, although he supposedly worried about the negative fallout of Japan's resistance to the EVSL tariff element. He could do nothing but let them constrict the win-set. The veto power of the Agriculture Minister or the *norin-zoku* is known to be especially strong because the LDP itself and many of its powerful members depend on the constituency of rural, agricultural areas.

As Putnam writes, 'a weakening party discipline ... reduce[d] the scope for international cooperation' (Putnam 1988: 449). Ultimately, the Trade and Foreign Ministers were at Kuala Lumpur with virtually no bargaining leeway.[38]

The positions of APEC and WTO towards agricultural liberalization

Whereas the consensus seeking discussed above is a general factor originating in Japanese political culture, the positions of APEC and the WTO towards agricultural liberalization were factors specific to APEC liberalization which strongly and continuously constricted Japan's win-set.

Even the Japanese agriculture-related actors, who thoroughly rejected the EVSL tariff elements in the forestry and fishery sectors, *had not refused*, and *could not*, refuse agricultural liberalization at every opportunity. Since the GATT/WTO regime has been vitally important for trade-dependent Japan, at its multilateral trade negotiations, the country had to make concessions in the agricultural sector for the success of the rounds as a whole. However, Japan has never committed itself to agricultural liberalization at any other opportunity.

APEC liberalization had played the role of driving multilateral trade liberalization in the period between the Uruguay Round and the Doha Development Agenda. Moreover, the APEC membership includes the United States, Canada, Australia and New Zealand, which had been asking Japan to free its agricultural market. Therefore it was impossible and dangerous for Japan to commit to agricultural liberalization partly because it was unacceptable in itself and partly because it could lead to more requests of concessions in the forthcoming round.

Japan's golden rule is 'no concession at any other or earlier opportunity than the forthcoming WTO round.' This constantly constricted Japan's win-set in all the opportunities for APEC liberalization from the OAA to EVSL.

Small win-set as a bargaining strategy at Level I

It should be additionally noted that, in a certain respect, its small win-set as leverage enabled Japan to maintain its objection and to get a favorable conclusion at the Level I negotiation. For example, at Kuala Lumpur, Foreign Minister Komura explained to USTR Barshefsky that if Japan were to accept the tariff element in the two sensitive sectors, the Obuchi Administration would surely be destabilized by the hawkish *norin-zoku*.[39] This can be interpreted as a strategy which Putnam describes as the way 'the negotiator may use the implicit threat from his own hawks to maximize his gains (minimize his losses) at Level I' (Putnam 1988: 444). A senior Malaysian official said that he had felt that Japan was indeed using its own small win-set as such a bargaining strategy.

Factors affecting the win-set in 1997

A criticism against Japan – arising from the EVSL controversy – was a complaint which said that the nation should not have agreed to the commencement of the initiative at Vancouver in November 1997, if it was going to object the next year. Setting aside the many probable counter-arguments to that criticism, there is the consideration that Japan's win-set was larger at that time than in 1998. There are some factors which can be pointed out in a hypothetical explanation of the expansion of the Level II win-set, or a reduction of the Level I negotiators' toughness in 1997, in comparison to the 1998 situation.

Smaller active constituency at Level II

The most fundamental factor of the larger win-set in 1997 was the smaller number of actors who participated in the EVSL policy making process. Putnam points out that 'participation rates [of constituents in the ratification process] vary across groups and across issues, and this variation often has implications for the size of the win-set' (Putnam 1988: 445). Although he does not clarify the relation between the participation rate and the size of the win-set, in the EVSL case of 1997, it was considered the smaller the participation, the larger the win-set.

A smaller, active constituency existed at Level II, firstly and mainly for the simple reason that EVSL was less well known. In general, 'APEC ... has been limitedly known by too few, understood by even less, and has interested a minimal number of participants in its policy making process' (Ogita and Takoh 1997: 5). A *fortiori*, so was EVSL.

Secondly, it is possible that most actors, who might even include Ministers, were distracted by the serious economic and financial crisis in Japan at the time. It is significant that the Vancouver Meetings were held in the same month as the Hokkaido Takushoku Bank and Yamaichi Securities went bankrupt.

Thus, whether or not to agree to the commencement of EVSL was supposedly decided solely by substantial discussions among the relevant bureaucratic organizations. Few *norin-zoku* or interest groups actively participated in the decision making. This would have expanded, or at least not constricted, the Level II win-set in 1997.

MITI's role at Level II

It is true that all four APEC-relevant ministries agreed to accept the commencement of EVSL in the name of voluntarism. Considering its long-term commitment to APEC, however, it may be reasonable to suppose that of the four ministries, MITI played the leading part in Level II ratification. The role the ministry played was probably proportionally much larger in 1997 than in 1998.

MITI's position as such could expand (not constrict) the Level II win-set, because of its enthusiasm for APEC, which the ministry itself had proposed, and also because the ministry had infused the philosophy of voluntarism into APEC during its development process.

News negotiators at Level I

Japan's last Cabinet reshuffle before the Vancouver Meetings was in September 1997. This meant that Japan's Level I negotiators at Vancouver (except for Prime Minister Hashimoto) had been APEC-relevant ministers for just two months. It is difficult to judge whether two months was long enough or too short a period, but they were possibly *less tough* than other APEC members' negotiators who had held their positions longer. Trade Minister Horiuchi, too, might not have been as tough a negotiator at Vancouver in November 1997 as he was at Kuching in June 1998.

It is somewhat doubtful, however, that Japanese Trade and Foreign Ministers played substantial roles in the EVSL consultations in 1997. This factor could be considered marginal.

Factors affecting the win-set in 1998

As mentioned above, Japan's Level II win-set would shrink between 1997 and 1998. In addition to the constant factors discussed above, the ones constricting the win-set in 1998 exclusively can clearly explain the nation's stubborn objection.

Larger active constituency at Level II

In comparison with the situation in 1997, the constituents in the Level II ratification of EVSL were greater both in number and activeness. More and more actors were involved, such as the *norin-zoku* and relevant interest groups. Even MAFF seemingly became more concerned and more cautious than when it had agreed to the commencement of EVSL.

This larger, active constituency was brought about by the EVSL consultations' clarification of scope, goals and mode of operation. The shorter period until the commencement of the WTO Millennium Round was obviously another stimulant. Needless to say, it constricted the Level II win-set considerably.

MITI and Trade Minister's stance at Level I and II

MITI was still an important player in the 1998 APEC and EVSL process, in spite of MAFF's increasing influence. MITI reportedly sought a compromise at the final phase of the EVSL controversy, even though it then seemed less pro-liberalization than usual.

This was supposedly because MITI was uncomfortable with the idea that some of the other APEC member economies were ignoring the APEC principle of voluntarism. The ministry had nurtured this principle and was proud of it as the foremost necessary philosophy/modality in involving Asian countries as members, who had been wary of Western member superiority and domination in APEC. In this regard, as the co-founder of APEC, MITI seemed particularly uncomfortable with the other founder, Australia, as well as the aggressive United States.

It was also rumored that MITI had to take responsibility for its leading role in accepting EVSL at Vancouver. This is hypothetically possible, but contradicts the fact that all four relevant ministries had agreed on acceptance beforehand. As MITI had taken the lead in accepting the commencement of EVSL in the name of voluntarism in 1997, however, it was natural that MITI should lead objection to the package deal in 1998.

Trade Minister Horiuchi supposedly suffered the same malaise that MITI did. It would have been magnified by the fact that he had agreed, as Japanese co-negotiator, to commence EVSL at the Level I negotiation at Vancouver. This would explain his aggressive attitude at the Kuching Meeting in June 1998, and MITI's leaning towards a compromise after his resignation as the head of the ministry in July.

In any case, the backwardness of the leading ministry, MITI, and the Trade Minister surely constricted the Level II win-set, and made Japan take a hard-line attitude at Level I.

New administration and its unstableness

As mentioned earlier, weak discipline within the ruling party and the administration constricts the win-set, and the Obuchi administration was an example of this. It came to power in July 1998, when Obuchi won the election for the LDP presidency. However, its foundation was fragile because of the party's pounding in the national election for the House of Councilors – which actually brought the end of the former Hashimoto Administration – and because of criticism of the LDP's unchanged modality in choosing the premier of the nation. In fact, the new administration's approval rate was far lower than the disapproval rate, which was higher than 50 per cent in the last four months of 1998. Moreover, the gap between approval and disapproval was biggest in November, when the Kuala Lumpur Meetings were being held (see Figure 4.2).

This situation constricted the Level II win-set, and deprived the Level I negotiators of any room for concession.

Effects of the Asian economic crisis on Japan's Level I position

The Asian economic crisis coincided with the EVSL process, and its various effects on the initiative could not be avoided. The crisis had both positive and negative impacts on Japan's Level I strategy in the EVSL consultation.

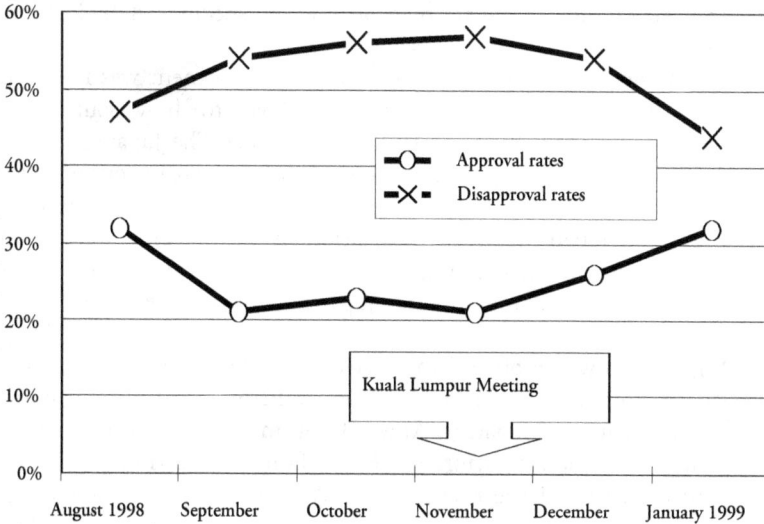

Figure 4.2 Results of opinion polls testing support for the Obuchi administration in its first six months

Source: *Asahi Shimbun,* 23 March 2000.

On the one hand, the crisis made it difficult for some Asian member economies to voice their objection to the United States driven packaged EVSL, as they vitally needed financial assistance from the America-influenced IMF. Otherwise, they would probably have more or less supported Japan because they had been advocating voluntarism, and were wary of the dominating US presence in APEC. This Asian silence seemed to weaken Japan's position in the Level I negotiation, but at the same time, it may have been this isolation that conversely pushed Japan to a more resolute position.

On the other hand, the crisis gave Japan an excuse to insist that the restoration of the Asian economy was a more critical agenda for APEC's 1998 process. The country could also maneuver the so-called New Miyazawa Initiative and other monetary aid as leverage to reactivate Asian support. This is what Putnam called 'international side-payment' (Putnam 1988: 450). In fact, in the final phase of the EVSL controversy, Japan succeeded in getting some Asian support, although it can hardly be said that the nation's commitment to making large loans to Asia had nothing to do with gaining it. This possibly strengthened Japan's Level I position.

Other factors affecting Japan's Level I position

A few other observations were made that hypothetically improved Japan's Level I position in bilateral relations with specific APEC member economies.

Firstly, the new Japan–South Korea Fisheries Agreement was finalized in September 1998, and could have acted as a lever to draw South Korean support for Japan's position in the EVSL controversy. The Japanese Fisheries Agency's Shoji Miyamoto reportedly asked his South Korean counterpart not to criticize Japan at APEC, suggesting that a move otherwise might negatively affect the Japanese Diet's ratification of the fisheries agreement.[40] Although the outcome of the suggestion remains unclear, it was undoubtedly a move aimed at magnifying Japan's odds at the EVSL Level I negotiation.

Second, the 'Anwar problem' may have given Japan an edge in gaining Malaysian support. Former Malaysian Deputy Prime Minister and political rival of Prime Minister Mahathir, Anwar Ibrahim was arrested on 'homosexuality' charges two months before the Kuala Lumpur Meetings. The United States fiercely criticized the events as a serious violation of human rights, and the relationship between the two countries soured. It was reported to be a situation favorable to Japan to form a united front with the year's chair of APEC against the United States, in which 'the two isolated countries appreciate[d] each other's presence in order to avoid blame placed on them.'[41] With a commitment for financial aid added, Japan obtained Malaysia's promise to back it at Kuala Lumpur.[42]

Factor expanding the win-set

It should be noted that another, exceptional hypothetical factor was found, one that could have expanded the Japanese Level II win-set in 1998. It was the Trade Minister change at the end of July, from Horiuchi to Yosano. As mentioned earlier, Horiuchi was a 'hawk' in objecting to the EVSL tariff element, but Yosano seemed to be a compromise seeker. The appearance of Yosano might have expanded the win-set, but it was not enough to counteract other constricting factors.

The simultaneous Foreign Minister change, from Obuchi to Komura, did not seem to have any impact on the size of the win-set.

Concluding remarks

Although a variety of analyses are possible, as discussed above, the determinants in Japan's EVSL policy making were neither many nor complicated. The two interconnecting fundamental determinants were, firstly, the thorough rejection of liberalization in the agriculture, forestry and fisheries sectors beyond the Uruguay Round commitment by the triad of MAFF, *norin-zoku* and relevant interest groups. Secondly, political leadership and discipline in policy making was, as usual, lacking, which in turn made the stubborn protection of agricultural interests possible. The win-set shrinkage in 1998 compared to 1997 was also due more to the entry of the agricultural triad in the policy making process than to any other factor.

If the position Japan carried throughout the EVSL controversy had been based on sound reasoning and had been a positive, voluntary choice made by the political leadership, it would have been less problematic. However, Japan's position was more one of 'involuntary defection,' the negative outcome of the two determinants noted above, since 'the smaller the win-sets, the greater risk of involuntary defection' (Putnam 1988: 439). In which case, Japan's policies on international trade negotiations addressing agricultural liberalization are usually made in a 'diminishing equilibrium' at Level II. Within such an environment, there can exist only limited scope for international cooperation.

In the past, however, Japan has made some agreements to open up its agricultural market based on political decisions. Internationalist policy makers, including members of the *norin-zoku*, have played important roles in these processes to reach a compromise. Why did they not function in the EVSL process? A possible factor was the *norin-zoku*'s lack of self-discipline, caused by political realignment throughout the 1990s. Another was the weakness of the Prime Minister's leadership at the time. It could also have been affected by the forthcoming bureaucratic reorganization. These should be investigated in the context of structural change in Japanese politics, and remain to be discussed.

Notes

1 This chapter is based on a great deal of information obtained from many interviews that the author has conducted since 1995. Endnoting for quotations from the interviews and words of thanks are omitted not just for editorial reasons, but also because some interviewees wished to remain unidentified.
2 All these organizations' names are in the forms used before the bureaucratic restructuring.
3 This text was personally obtained by the author.
4 *Nihon Keizai Shimbun*, 23 November 1997.
5 It should be noted that such a principle of voluntarism had never appeared in APEC's official documents before this. Even the Seoul APEC Declaration (APEC Ministerial Meeting 1991: Annex), which 'represents the principles, objectives and understandings of APEC ... and provides a firm foundation on which to base APEC's work' (APEC Ministerial Meeting 1991: paragraph 8), contains no mention of 'voluntarism' or 'voluntary.' The same goes for the OAA's general principles for liberalization and facilitation (APEC Leaders Meeting 1995b: Part One, Section A). The first appearance of the word 'voluntary' in the context of liberalization was in the Osaka Ministerial Meeting's Joint Statement in 1995 (APEC Ministerial Meeting 1995: paragraph 6). The word 'voluntarism' was, as mentioned above, first used at Vancouver in 1997. Refer to Ogita (2001).
6 In August *Zengyoren* also petitioned the Matsushita Electric Industrial Corporation, which provided another Japanese ABAC member.
7 *Nihon Keizai Shimbun*, 19 June 1998.
8 *Nihon Keizai Shimbun*, 20 June 1998.
9 *Asahi Shimbun*, 26 June 1998.

10 *Nihon Keizai Shimbun*, 24 June 1998; *Asahi Shimbun*, 24 June 1998.
11 *Nihon Keizai Shimbun*, 19 October 1998.
12 *Asahi Shimbun*, 13 September 1998.
13 *Sankei Shimbun*, 15 September 1998.
14 *Yomiuri Shimbun*, 18 September 1998; *Mainichi Shimbun*, 18 September 1998.
15 *Asahi Shimbun*, 23 September 1998; *Yomiuri Shimbun*, 24 September 1998.
16 *Nihon Keizai Shimbun*, 23 October 1998; *Asahi Shimbun*, 27 October 1998; *Yomiuri Shimbun*, 30 October 1998.
17 *Nihon Keizai Shimbun*, 24 October 1998; *Asahi Shimbun*, 27 October 1998.
18 *Asahi Shimbun*, 27 October 1998.
19 *Nihon Keizai Shimbun*, 4 November 1998; *Asahi Shimbun*, 6 November 1998.
20 *Yomiuri Shimbun*, 29 October 1998.
21 *Mainichi Shimbun*, 6 November 1998.
22 *Asahi Shimbun*, 5 November 1998.
23 http://www2.justnet.ne.jp/%7Easia/apec/apec02.htm.
24 *Yomiuri Shimbun*, 29 October 1998.
25 *Asahi Shimbun*, 6 November 1998.
26 *Nihon Keizai Shimbun*, 5 November 1998; *Asahi Shimbun*, 6 November 1998.
27 *Asahi Shimbun*, 6 November 1998; *Nihon Keizai Shimbun*, 8 November 1998.
28 *Nihon Keizai Shimbun*, 10 November 1998.
29 *Asahi Shimbun*, 11 and 14 November 1998.
30 *Asahi Shimbun*, 10 November 1998.
31 *Asahi Shimbun*, 10 November 1998.
32 *Asahi Shimbun*, 12 November 1998.
33 *Sankei Shimbun*, 14 November 1998.
34 *Mainichi Shimbun*, 14 November 1998.
35 *Asahi Shimbun*, 18 November 1998.
36 *Asahi Shimbun*, 19 November 1998.
37 This observation is analogous with Theodore J. Lowi's criticism of pluralist politics: 'One of the major Keynesian criticisms of market theory is that even if pure competition among factors of supply and demand did yield an equilibrium, the equilibrium could be at something far less than the ideal of full employment at reasonable prices. Pure pluralist competition, similarly, might produce political equilibrium, but the experience of recent years shows that it occurs at something far below an acceptable level of legitimacy, or access, or equality, or innovation, or any other valued political commodity' (Lowi 1979: 57–8). The insertion of the Flexibility Principle in the OAA, as well as its complete rejection in the EVSL consultation, might occur at something below the level of diplomatic rationality or democratic legitimacy.
38 *Sankei Shimbun*, 16 November 1998.
39 *Nihon Keizai Shimbun*, 14 November 1998; *Sankei Shimbun*, 15 November 1998.
40 *Asahi Shimbun*, 14 November 1998.
41 *Sankei Shimbun*, 14 November 1998.
42 *Nihon Keizai Shimbun*, 13 November 1998.

5 The United States

Linkage between domestic agreement and foreign disagreement

Satoshi Oyane

Introduction

This chapter studies the approach taken by the United States in the APEC Early Voluntary Sectoral Liberalization (EVSL) initiative in relation to its domestic politics. The trade policy of the US government is generally speaking strongly influenced by domestic politics. But the US government adopted a consistently positive stance in the EVSL initiative and therefore took a hardline posture against the negative position of Japan (specifically the refusal to liberalize in regard to forest products and fish and fish products). The biggest reason for the failure of the EVSL initiative was this discord between the United States and Japan. How did this external stance of the United States tie in with the domestic politics unfolding behind the negotiators? What kind of causal relationship was there with the failure of the EVSL initiative?

The linkage between the international negotiations and domestic politics may be analyzed by the 'two-level game' model proposed by Robert D. Putnam (Putnam 1988; Evans *et al.* 1993; Milner 1997). This model was constructed with US international negotiations in mind – so much so that it is criticized as being biased – and, as such, could be considered suitable for this chapter.

In the past, the following pattern was seen in US trade negotiations: (1) the negotiating posture taken by the US government lacked continuity and changed, strongly reflecting domestic division; (2) in the face of this, the US government tried to meet domestic needs by soliciting international concessions. US domestic industry is divided and Congress tends to oppose actions of the Executive Branch. When this endangers the international cooperation of the US government, other countries are forced to yield. For example, in the economic friction between the United States and Japan, the US government frequently hinted at the possibility of Congress adopting a harder line against Tokyo, and thereby obtained concessions from Japan. Further, (3) the US government uses the concessions obtained from other countries to quell domestic opposition. The international agreement is then realized.

This pattern is predicated on two assumptions. First, there are remarkable divisions in the United States, which cannot be easily closed. Second, the US government fully recognizes international demands and is oriented toward international cooperation. These two points are considered natural in US trade politics and are treated as *a priori* in analyses. In the EVSL initiative, however, these two assumptions were not met. The US government actively and successfully involved itself in domestic coordination, but failed in achieving an international agreement. Does this imply the emergence of a negative domestic–international linkage that the original two-level game model did not assume? This chapter will deal with this question too.

Analytical framework

The 'two-level game' model

As pointed out by Richard Higgott, multilateral cooperation in APEC cannot be fully understood by theories such as neo-realism or neo-liberalism, which put focus on international structures (Higgott 1993). In particular, when analyzing the political process behind the EVSL initiative, structural theories tend to be too macroscopic in nature and are liable to oversimplify the phenomena. In general, international trade has direct effects on the domestic economy and domestic policy. Therefore, especially in developed nations, industrial and labor organizations do not remain passive over international negotiations, but actively and strategically lobby the government (Krauss 1993). Further, the government steers domestic politics in pursuit of suitable international agreements (Moravcsik 1993: 24–7). The 'two-level game' model should be effective in detecting this political dynamic in the EVSL initiative.

This is because the 'two-level game' model explains international negotiations from the perspective of the domestic political process – how domestic consensus (according to Putnam's concept, 'ratification') is achieved to enable international cooperation. Therefore, the core concept of the two-level game model lies in the 'win-set,' that is, the range of international agreements that can be ratified domestically. If the win-set is large, there is a good possibility of an international agreement being ratified. In US trade policy, however, the win-set has traditionally been small. In the face of this, the actions for realizing international cooperation had crystallized into the pattern seen above. The small size of the win-set was due to several factors.

According to Putnam, the size of the win-set is governed by: (1) the distribution of power preferences and possible coalition among domestic constituents; (2) domestic political institutions; and (3) the strategies of the international negotiators (Putnam 1988: 442–56). First, in domestic institutions, the United States has a pluralistic political system where individual interests are openly expressed and easily reflected in policies. What is particularly important to note in US trade policy is that the authority over trade rests not with the Executive Branch, but with Congress (Constitution, Article 1, Section 8). The Executive Branch is delegated authority over international negotiations, but the results of the negotiations must be ratified by Congress. Ratification of individual aspects of individual negotiations would be impractical, so the 'fast track' procedure is used. Note that in the past decade or so, Congress and the Executive Branch have mostly been controlled by different political parties. At the time of the EVSL initiative, the White House was in the hands of the Democrats, while Congress was controlled by the Republicans. Given such 'divided government,' Congress usually criticizes and obstructs Executive Branch policies (O'Halloran 1994).

Further, the domestic actors tend to be strongly divided and fluid in the United States. The US government harbors various interest groups, which press different claims on the White House through Congress. Members of Congress are elected to office, so tend to bend to the demands of their constituents and their interest groups (Verdier 1994). The Executive Branch is also divided as a result of such pressure. The Commerce Department, the Labor Department, the Office of the USTR (United States Trade Representative) and other parts of the government sensitive to industry interests tend to adopt positions against the free-trade Treasury Department, Presidential Council of Economic Advisors, State Department and National Security Council.

In this way, the US government is hampered by opposing interests domestically and internally, and finds it hard to pursue 'rational' policies. The United States is a 'weak state' in the sense that the government cannot pursue policies separate from domestic interests. Therefore, domestic needs and dissatisfactions are projected externally and other countries tend to be pressed to solve the dilemma (Krasner 1978b). This is reflected in negotiation strategies. The US government hints at domestic divisions and an uncompromising stance to the foreign side or uses the same as positive outside pressure to win concessions.[1] Of course, the US government quite often prepares intricate international proposals so as to cleverly bridge the gap between domestic and international demands (Oyane 1992).

The 'two-level game' pattern in the United States

In this political composition, US foreign trade policy has swung between managed trade and free trade, and between a hardline international stance and moderate persuasion of domestic interests. Robert A. Pastor proposes the term 'cry and sigh paradox' to describe this (Pastor 1981). In other words, when interest groups first raise a 'cry' in order to secure trade interests, Congress presses the Executive Branch for action through public hearings, legislation and resolutions. As opposed to this, the free traders voice opposition to managed trade. In the midst of this, the government seeks steps from other countries to settle the issue within the framework of its free trade policy. Here, all the related parties 'sigh.' I. M. Destler describes this standoff between Congress and the Executive Branch as a kind of inter-approval system. Congress delegates its authority over negotiations to the Executive Branch to protect itself from the pressure of its constituents and involvement in a managed trade policy. At the same time, it has sought moderate managed trade measures (such as voluntary export restraints) from the Executive Branch (Destler 1995). This swing, however, has largely tilted toward managed trade since 1985. With the ballooning US trade deficit, Congress has moved more toward the side of the interest groups. The Executive Branch in turn has shifted its position toward Congress. In this way, US trade policy has become more one-sided and hardline, to the extent of being called 'aggressive unilateralism.' This said, the pattern of international negotiations continues to be structured in basically the same way (Martin 1994; Kusano 1991: Chapters 3 and 4). The trade policy of the Clinton Administration may also be understood as an extension of this.

Seen from this pattern of international negotiations, it was thought that in the EVSL initiative, the US government would fail to put forth any consistent policies, lean toward a hardline stance in the process to seek concessions, but in the end compromise and reach international agreement. In fact, however, the US government remained consistent in policy. Further, while adopting a hardline stance toward Japan, it displayed certain flexibility toward the other APEC members. Despite this, no international agreement was achieved.

This may be considered to have been due, first, to the lack of much of a domestic division and therefore the absence of any policy swings. According to Putnam's hypothesis, if consensus can be achieved domestically and the win-set becomes larger, the possibility of an international agreement becomes greater, but other countries can take advantage of this to force concessions (Putnam 1988: 460). In the EVSL initiative, however, no international agreement was achieved. Further, the United States did not make any concessions. This may have had something to do with the approach taken in building the domestic consensus.

Second, domestic consensus probably failed to lead to an international agreement due to problems in the government's understanding of international negotiations. APEC is characterized by a stress on Asian-like voluntarism, non-binding accords and consensus. Under the US initiative, however, the negotiations changed to Western-style horse-trading and legally binding force. Faced with this, there was a backlash in the Asian countries (Nesadurai 1996; Elek 1995; Kikuchi 1995: Chapters 6, 8 and Conclusion). The United States may have failed to tie in its domestic consensus with an international agreement due to its disparate understanding of the situation from the Asian countries. This being said, the 'two-level game' model also lacks this perspective. Even if focusing on negotiating tactics in international negotiations, understanding of the international situation behind them is assumed as a given premise. The suitability of negotiating skills is largely governed by this understanding. This chapter focuses on this point.

Below, an overview will be given of the policy of the Clinton Administration toward APEC and the decision making process behind it. The case of the EVSL initiative will then be analyzed.

Policies and policy making process of the Clinton Administration

APEC policy

The Clinton Administration arose calling for reconstruction of the domestic economy. In rebuilding the domestic economy, trade policy came under review. As pointed out by Deputy Secretary of Commerce Jeffrey Garten, one-third of the economic growth of the United States stems from exports. Growth, employment and savings cannot be achieved in the United States with just the domestic economy alone (Garten 1997: 69–70). One of the most promising regions for US exports is the Asia-Pacific. The Commerce Department designated ten markets where future growth in demand was particularly expected as 'Big Emerging Markets' (US Department of Commerce, International Trade Administration 1995). Among these, four (the Chinese Economic Area – China, Hong Kong and Taiwan – South Korea, ASEAN and India) were located in the Asia-Pacific region. According to the fact sheet of the Bureau of East Asian and Pacific Affairs of the State Department, the biggest rationale for US involvement in APEC is the economic success of APEC members. US trade with APEC members accounts for two-thirds of its global trade (US Department of State 1998: 1). Therefore, President Clinton, in speaking at Waseda University in July 1993, called for the creation of a 'Pacific Community.' He argued that the Pacific region was a wellspring of employment, income and growth for the United States and that it was not enough just to change the United States – that it was necessary to change other countries in the Asia-Pacific region (US President 1994a: 1020).

The US government considered APEC as a tool for liberalization of trade and investment. Therefore, it tried to institutionalize commitments and negotiations toward liberalization. Specifically, it pushed for and achieved the first Leaders Meeting in Seattle in 1993. Further, upon receipt of the report of the APEC Eminent Persons Group, it pressed for establishment of a standing Trade and Investment Committee. In his speech at the Seattle Meeting, President Clinton concisely expressed these policy objectives of the United States. The President spoke of the need for domestic economic growth, launching initiatives to the fast-growing Asia-Pacific and new arrangement for international relations for the United States to take leadership in the international economy (US President 1994b: 2016).

The attempted institutionalization of liberalization was a reflection of the 'result-oriented approach' of the Clinton Administration. The new Administration negatively assessed previous negotiations to open up foreign markets as securing the procedures for market access, but as failing to produce any practical results. Therefore, to secure results in market access, it adopted the policy of wielding Section 301 of the Trade Act for hardline negotiations to obtain firm commitments (USTR 1994: 61–2; Lincoln 1999: Chapter 4). In the 1994 APEC Bogor Meeting, the Clinton Administration pressed for deadlines for liberalization and secured the Bogor Declaration.

Of course, this APEC policy of the United States invited a backlash in Asia. APEC had traditionally adopted an 'Asia-like unofficial approach.' Cooperation had been promoted in broad fields through negotiations stressing each country's voluntarism and flexibility. The United States applied a 'Western-type official approach' to this and pressed for binding liberalization through barter-type negotiations (Kikuchi 1998: 190–3). Therefore, Malaysia, China and others raised opposition to the Bogor Declaration, the Leaders Meetings and the Trade and Investment Committee. The Asian countries were even worried about US domination of APEC. These fears appear to have been heard by the US government. The February 1994 Economic Report of the President pointed out the interdependence of the Asia-Pacific and indicated a policy of adopting a cooperative approach rather than hardline measures (US Council of Economic Advisers 1994: 231).

The United States, however, caused relations with Japan, South Korea, China and others to deteriorate due to its bilateral negotiations for greater market access. At the same time, it felt the difficulty of its 'result-oriented approach' (Lincoln 1999: Chapter 4). This reverberated among its main policy makers as well. The well-known 'Lord Memo' was written in the middle of this and pointed to the need for a more moderate, stable Asian policy.[2]

In response, APEC was reevaluated as an alternative to bilateral negotiations. The 1995 Economic Report of the President stressed the significance of 'plurilateral' free trade accords (US Council of Economic Advisers 1995: 214–20). The idea was to promote market liberalization among several countries of certain sizes and thereby make up for deficiencies in the WTO. The previous Reagan and Bush Administrations had also linked bilateral negotiations to promoting trade liberalization beneficial to the US. 'Plurilateralism' represented a new version of this practice.

The policy making process

The Clinton Administration tried to make innovative institutional reforms in the process of formulation of trade policy. This was through the establishment of the National Economic Council (NEC). The NEC was aimed at smooth, top-level coordination to sweep away the internal disagreements endemic to earlier government, and the resulting inefficiency in decision making and negotiations. Further, it attempted to take a comprehensive approach in domestic economic policy and international economic policy. The NEC was established inside the White House and was frequently joined by the President himself. It aimed at in-depth debate and consensus building (Destler 1996).

The hosting of the APEC Leaders Meeting was proposed by the Assistant to the President, Robert Fauver, and decided on at the NEC with the support of the Assistant to the President, Robert Rubin (Chairman of the NEC) and the Deputy Assistant to the President, Bowman W. Cutter (Chairman of the NEC Deputies Committee). The policy of APEC Leaders Meetings on a yearly basis was also decided here (Funabashi 1995b: 119–20).[3]

More detailed studies and routine policy matters were handled at the NEC Deputies Committee. As a working level interdepartmental coordinating organization under it, there was the Trade Policy Staff Committee (TPSC). When agreement could not be reached there or more important issues arose, the Trade Policy Review Group would take over (USTR 1995: 111–12).

The role of the NEC, however, declined around 1995 before the start of the EVSL initiative. This was due to the failure of US policy towards Japan, the mid-term elections, and personnel changes (the transfer of the Assistant to the President, Robert Rubin, to the post of the Secretary of Treasury; the resignation of Deputy Advisor Bowman Cutter; and the failure of their successors to display the same leadership as Rubin and Cutter). Therefore, for a time, disagreements again arose inside the government. There was unavoidably a subsequent decline in the role of the NEC (Destler 1996: 43–59; Destler 1998: 100–5).

Further, the Clinton Administration made positive use of the Trade Promotion Coordination Committee (TPCC) established by the previous Bush Administration. This was chaired by the Commerce Secretary and enabled the related departments to coordinate their efforts in national export strategies. Then government and industry were also able to exchange information and opinions to an unprecedented depth. The TPCC tried to link export strategies with trade policy, but reportedly did not conflict in authority with the NEC (TPCC 1995: 14; Destler 1996: 97).

The NEC and TPCC were significant in promoting the formation of a consensus within the government, in having the government as a whole stress domestic industry and in ensuring a dialogue between the public and private sectors, and thereby in stressing consensus and formalizing emphasis on dialogue between government and industry. The question is how this affected the APEC EVSL initiative.

Under such policy-coordinating organizations, APEC policy is the responsibility of the Office of the USTR and the State Department. The former plays a leadership role. This small office is assisted in staff, information and diplomatic channels by the State Department. While there was the possibility of diplomatic concerns separate from economics being reflected in policy depending on the involvement of the State Department, there was reportedly none of this at the EVSL initiative. The USTR and the Secretary of State attend APEC Ministerial Meetings. The State Department also has an ambassador class APEC coordinator. Senior Official Meetings (SOM) of APEC are attended mainly by the Deputies of the Office of the USTR and State Department, while working-level meetings are attended not only by representatives of the Office of the USTR and State Department, but also by those of the Commerce Department, the Agriculture Department and the Transport Department, depending on the issue.[4]

The Commerce Department, the Agriculture Department, the Transport Department, the Treasury Department and other related departments put together the arguments of the industries under their purview, and policy related information and recommendations in background papers or position papers, which are then submitted to the Office of the USTR and the State Department. The related departments coordinate at the TPSC or the NEC Deputies Committee and routinely contact each other individually. The Office of the USTR, the State Department and the Commerce Department appoint APEC coordinators for coordination of domestic and foreign policies and exchanging information.

Generally, the results of Executive Branch negotiations, as explained earlier, have to be ratified by Congress. Congress fell under the control of the Republicans as a result of the 1994 mid-term elections, so the country ended up with a 'divided government.' Therefore, while the Clinton Administration repeatedly submitted fast track authorization bills to Congress, these failed to pass. Since no fast track authorization was obtained, even if agreement had been reached on lowering tariffs at the EVSL initiative, it would have been unclear if legal authority could have been obtained for implementation domestically. The refusal of Congress, however, did not reflect particular interest in APEC. Congress submitted very few draft laws or draft resolutions regarding APEC. Public hearings were only held once a year timed to the Leaders Meetings. Congress had only a superficial concern. The points of contention in the fast track proposals were the expansion of NAFTA and related issues of the environment, labor and human rights.

Finally, what about industry? As already alluded to, US industry benefits tremendously from trade with the Asia-Pacific basin. Greater market access could be expected to lead to greater benefits. Industry, however, failed to take any initiative in opening up the Asia-Pacific markets. The initiative was taken by the Clinton Administration. President Clinton thought that the Seattle Meeting was the perfect opportunity for showcasing the possibilities of APEC to the public, so took positive steps such as starting the Leaders Meetings.[5] Industry interests rose, guided by the Administration's APEC policy.

The question is how to feed back such rising industry interests into government policy. In the past, the public and private sectors basically maintained their distance from each other – or more accurately, pretty much ignored each other. The biggest reason for this was the ideology of *laissez-faire*. The government refrained from intervening in the market while industry had an aversion to the constraints accompanying government assistance. The fluidity of personnel in government and industry also inhibited the establishment of any stable personal or mental ties. Therefore, government only intervened in industry as an exception after the fact when industry had suffered damage due to trade and sought relief, and when massive support was obtained at Congress (Fukushima 1994: 118–19; Vogel 1987). However, this situation changed drastically under the Clinton Administration.

Contacts between the public and private sectors were held at industrial advisory organizations. Starting from the Tokyo Round of the GATT negotiations, the government established private sector advisory committees (1974 Trade Act, Section 135). These were elevated to advisory organizations for trade policy as a whole in the Omnibus Trade and Competitiveness Act of 1988 as a result of the growing trade deficit and loss of international competitiveness. They went into full mode operation after the start of the Clinton Administration.

The advisory organizations include seven committees such as, at the top, the President's Advisor Committee for Trade Policy and Negotiation, as well as the Industry Advisory Committee and the Agricultural Policy Advisory Committee and thirty sectoral, functional and technical advisory committees. These are run by the Office of the USTR, the Commerce Department, the Agriculture Department and others, and serve as effective forums for the exchange of information and opinions between government and related industrial organizations (USTR 1994: 110–11).

Under the Clinton Administration, there was not only increased closeness between government and industry, but also a weakening of ideological opposition to this. Close ties between government and industry were no longer roundly criticized and even won certain legitimacy. This being the case, the need for industry to call upon Congress declined. Congress formerly was the only remaining recourse of industry to wield influence over the 'untouchable' government. According to a source at the American Electronics Association (AEA), while industry was maintaining contacts with Congress, it shifted to a pattern of action of 'first going to the Executive Branch and then, if not receiving satisfaction, going to Congress.'[6]

In view of this, there was a contrastive possibility in domestic consensus and the United States' understanding of international negotiations. That is, there was a possibility of domestic consensus being smoothly formed first (function of the consensus building system of NEC on down, lack of interest of Congress, and closer relations between government and industry) and, on the other hand, the possibility of the consensus building system not functioning fully (swings in the role of the NEC, relative decline in role, adverse effects of 'divided government,' limited effect of private advisor organizations). Further, the effects on international negotiations probably differ between consensus mainly achieved by the government and consensus mainly achieved by industry and Congress.

The United States' understanding of international negotiations is influenced by whether the effect of institutionalization of APEC, or the backlash of the Asian countries against it, is stressed. Further, it is influenced by the degree to which 'plurilateralism' is respected. How did these factors affect the APEC EVSL initiative and how do they relate to the 'two-level game'?

The case analysis

The EVSL initiative may be divided into three phases. The first phase started from the November 1996 Manila Ministerial Meeting and Subic Bay Leaders Meeting to October of the following 1997. During this phase, the EVSL scheme was floated and the participating countries proposed sectors for liberalization.

The second phase was from the November 1997 Vancouver Ministerial Meeting and Leaders Meeting to the June 1998 Kuching Trade Ministers Meeting. During this period, the APEC members decided on fifteen sectors for EVSL and started negotiations. The negotiations, however, ran aground and no decision was made before the agreed deadline.

The third phase was after this period. The negotiations stalled even after the extension of the deadline and the matter was left to the WTO.

How did US domestic politics interact with international negotiations in each of these phases? As already explained, this chapter focuses on the domestic consensus building and understanding of international negotiations. Particular attention will be paid to the forestry product sector – a point of contention between the United States and Japan.

The first phase: orientation towards EVSL

Excessive lesson of ITA

In the summer of 1995, the United States and the EU commenced negotiations on an Information Technology Agreement (ITA) aiming at the elimination of tariffs on information-related products. The APEC Ministerial Meeting held in Manila in November 1996 debated whether to support and implement this in APEC. The Ministerial Meeting failed to draw adequate conclusions, but the Leaders Meeting decided to support it definitely and agreed to aim at an ITA at the WTO. Here, a bilateral (United States and EU) agreement was expanded to a plurilateral (APEC) agreement and further to a multilateral (WTO) agreement. Simultaneously, voluntary liberalization efforts of the countries concerned evolved into measures with internationally legal binding force. Expecting that events would follow a similar path, the Leaders Meeting demanded that the ministers select similar sectors for early liberalization. This was the start of the EVSL initiative.

This evolution of the ITA dovetailed perfectly with the United States' APEC policy. First, a promising US industry could benefit from trade with the Asia-Pacific region. That is, the semiconductors, cellular phones, communications equipment, etc. covered by the ITA constitute, borrowing the words of President Clinton himself, the 'core of America's competitiveness' and 'a big part of that bridge we have to build to the future.'[7] Eighty per cent of the trade of that US industry was with APEC members. The trade was worth as much as one million US dollars a year. Second, the ITA provided a deadline for reduction of tariffs in line with the 'result-oriented approach.' APEC members were allowed 'flexibility' and agreed to 'substantially eliminate' tariffs by January 2000. Third, the ITA was raised to a liberalization measure of the WTO through APEC as envisioned by 'plurilateralism.'

This was a result of leadership by the US government, in particular the commitment of President Clinton. The ITA was supported by Japan, Singapore, Indonesia and other countries, but was opposed by Thailand, Malaysia and China. Therefore, the discussions at the Ministerial Meetings reached an impasse. President Clinton then turned his persuasive skills on the individual heads of state while coordinating with Prime Ministers Howard of Australia and Hashimoto of Japan and other leaders, and secured agreement (though with flexibility and 'substantial' reduction of tariffs). No deadline for reduction of tariffs was incorporated in the initial draft agreement, but incorporation was realized through the arguments of President Clinton and others.[8] Therefore, it was only natural for President Clinton to boast that the ITA was the result of 'determined, consistent diplomacy.'[9] John Wolf, the APEC coordinator, also stressed that the ITA was the 'biggest result' of the APEC meeting and constituted a 'dramatic step' in world trade.[10]

The lesson of the ITA was a tremendous one. That is, it confirmed the suitability and possibilities of the APEC policy of the United States. The US government treated APEC as a 'catalyst' or 'building block' and settled on a policy of pursuing trade liberalization at the WTO using APEC as a lever. From the viewpoint of the US government, APEC was a perfect 'catalyst' due to the following three points: First, the plurilateral APEC lessened the costs and risks of bilateral negotiations. The US government had run into difficulties with its market access negotiations with Japan and China (Lincoln 1999; Ohashi 1998). Further, APEC included countries with lesser relations with the United States and countries harboring other delicate problems. Second, APEC included both industrialized and developing countries and studied international agreements able to be approved by both, that is models of WTO agreement. Third, APEC was suited for building consensus. APEC called for a sense of unity as a community and was able to smooth over differing interests through broad economic and technical cooperation.[11] Therefore, the US government took the lead in the discussions at Manila and Subic Bay for the early liberalization of other sectors aiming at a 'second ITA.'

Optimism in international negotiations

Due to the sheer magnitude of its earlier success, however, the US government underestimated opposition within APEC. There was a potential clash with other APEC members in its perception of international negotiations. As already seen, a conflict surfaced in APEC over the 'Western-style official approach' and 'Asian-style unofficial approach' over the Bogor Declaration and the Osaka Action Agenda. Several APEC members harbored concern over the United States dominating APEC and utilizing it for tough trade liberalization over the ITA as well. Malaysia even declared that it might not always follow the agreements of the Leaders Meeting. The officials in charge of APEC in the US government, however, did not believe that the US policy differed that much from APEC traditions.

They considered the stress on voluntarism, non-binding commitments and consensus in APEC to be less of an inherent practice due to the history and diversity of the Asian nations, and more of a resistance to liberalization as tends to be seen in developing countries. Fred Bergsten of the Institute for International Economics also expressed this view. This may have been the general understanding in Washington. Bergsten even claimed that the arguments for voluntarism of the Asian countries were akin to the protectionism of the textile industry in the United States (Bergsten 1996: 76–7). One US government official explained away criticism that the United States was changing the nature of APEC by saying that APEC was not being 'shifted' by the United States, but 'progressing.' The use of the term 'progress' can also be seen throughout reports of the Office of the USTR and the Department of State.[12]

The massive success of the ITA also had an effect on consensus building in the United States. The ITA whetted the expectations of domestic industry. Further, due to the optimistic perception of the government regarding APEC negotiations, these expectations swelled excessively. For example, the Telecommunications Industry Association (TIA) began full-scale activities for liberalization in APEC on the occasion of the ITA. The American Forest and Paper Association (AF&PA) also believed that elimination of tariffs, which had not been achieved at the Uruguay Round of the GATT negotiations, could be immediately realized.[13] The ITA, however, as explained earlier, came with the reservations of 'flexibility' and 'substantial reductions' of tariffs. These reservations and the orientation of the Asian nations toward voluntarism behind them, however, failed to interest industry. For example, typically, a trade advisor and attorney of Digital Equipment Co. publicly dismissed these issues: 'I'm not concerned about one or two wrinkles in the wording.'[14]

Domestic coordination by industry advisory organizations

After the Subic Bay Leaders Meeting, the US government began preparation of a proposal for new sectors for liberalization.

At that time, the government listened to the expectations of industry. The dialogue between government and industry was mainly held through the previously mentioned Industry Policy Advisory Committee and Industry Sector Advisory Committee, under them or the Agricultural Policy Advisory Committee. 'Mainly' is used in the sense that there were unofficial contacts and exchanges of information accompanying them at a frequency never seen in previous administrations from the top level to the working level.

These advisory committees were run by the Office of the USTR, the State Department, the Commerce Department, the Agriculture Department and others, and were attended by representatives of large and small industrial organizations and export organizations. The consensus building was typically of the following pattern. First, the Office of the USTR laid out its basic policy. The industry side then presented those of its demands which were in line with that policy. The related departments then sought corrections in view of the need for a realistic approach and balance with other sectors. Industry brought these back and resubmitted their demands. The Office of the USTR called this an 'open process' and reportedly considered all industry proposals. Contacts between the public and private sectors were essential not only for industry but also for government. This was because preparation of proposals and international negotiations requires expert technical information and knowledge and this had to be supplied by the private sector. In particular, telecommunications was a highly technical field, so the Office of the USTR repeatedly solicited information and opinions from certain veteran industry representatives.[15]

While striving for an 'open process,' the influence of industry is affected by its involvement in the advisory committees, and its financial organizational strength. According to one government official, the powerful industries were chemicals, forestry products and telecommunications, while the relatively weak industries were toys and jewelry.[16]

The industrial advisory committee for forestry products was the Wood and Wood Product Committee. The Committee was chaired by the Vice-President of the AF&PA, Stephen M. Lovett. In this regard, the AF&PA secured an advantageous position for itself and was making positive use of it. As opposed to this, the biggest agricultural organization, the American Farm Bureau Federation, also expressed interest in liberalization of wood in respect to afforestation, but was not engaged in any notable activities toward that end. In general, US agricultural, forestry and fishery organizations are too diverse and numerous, and argue for different interests. There used to be diversity in the forestry and paper sector as well, with the National Forest Products Association, the American Paper Institute and the America Forest Council. These three organizations, however, merged into the AF&PA in 1993 and therefore eliminated most problems of diversity of organization. The AF&PA consists of 200 affiliated organizations and 1.6 million members, and has secured legitimacy for its arguments in view of its scale and interests (the US forest industry is the world's largest and exports as much as 380 billion US dollars a year; the biggest export destination is Japan) and its representative nature for the industry.[17]

The government counterparts to the AF&PA are the Office of the USTR which is handling APEC (Asia & Pacific – APEC Affairs), the State Department (Bureau of East Asian and Pacific Affairs, Office of Bilateral Trade Affairs, APEC coordinator, etc.), plus the Commerce Department (Forest Products & Building Materials Division of International Trade Administration, Office of Japan Trade Policy and APEC coordinator). The related departments coordinated their activities through policy discussions at the NEC Deputies Committee and TPSC, and did not exhibit any particular disagreements. Even if the role of the NEC fell in relative terms, its influence could not be observed in the EVSL initiative. These government organizations maintained close relations with industry. In its annual report, the AF&PA called for 'the achievement of fair and equitable market access' and stated that the 'AF&PA worked closely with the US government' in the EVSL initiative (AF&PA 1998: 21).

Therefore, industrial organizations did not rely on Congress to the previous extent. There was reportedly not that much pressure from Congress in the drafting of proposals for sectors for liberalization.[18] Even so, Congress had a serious indirect impact. Around that time, Congress was debating the government's fast track authorization bill. Numerous oppositions arose. What the members of Congress were concerned about, of course, was not APEC, but the expansion of NAFTA and the environmental and labor issues accompanying it (Destler and Balint 1999). Even so, since fast track authorization meant comprehensive ratification procedures, APEC was similarly adversely affected. Therefore, the Executive Branch, in selecting the sectors for liberalization, considered remaining sectors covered by its trade negotiating authority already received for the Uruguay Round. These included wood, paper, nonferrous metals, fish products, processed fish products, oilseeds and others. The forestry products and fish products causing a problem between the United States and Japan were included in that group.

The government also considered the proposals and situations of other countries. For example, it anticipated extremely strong resistance to liberalization of agricultural products from Japan and South Korea, so excluded these products. Conversely, it believed it was certain that Canada would propose forestry products and New Zealand fish products, so decided to leave them to these members[19] (in the end, the US government proposed forestry products).

In this way, the US government submitted proposals for liberalization of nine sectors to APEC on 15 July 1997. These were: forestry products, chemicals, telecommunications equipment (for mutual recognition agreement), environmental goods and services, automobiles, energy goods, medical equipment, toys and oilseeds. It expected other APEC members to propose several other sectors of interest. All the expectations of US industry were therefore covered.[20]

As seen above, in the first phase, the US government prepared its proposals for sectors for early liberalization seeking a repeat of the ITA. At that time, based on the wishes of industry, an unexpectedly smooth domestic consensus was achieved. This domestic consensus was aided in part by the government's optimistic perception of international consultations. While this was different from the perceptions of the Asian countries, it did not prove a problem at this stage. Therefore, from the viewpoint of the US government, the 'win-set' was large and the possibility of an international agreement was extremely high.

The second phase: rise of discord between the United States and Japan

Limited effect of fast track

The proposals of the APEC members covered as many as sixty-two sectors. At the time of the September and October meetings of the Trade and Investment Committee, SOM studied these, primarily sectors that had large support, and narrowed the list down first to forty-one and finally to fifteen sectors. At that time, the United States stressed the realization of an agreement and persuaded Australia to withdraw its proposal for processed foods, considering that it would overly irritate APEC members. This was despite the fact that it would have been beneficial to US industry as well. Conversely, there were no sectors which would have been detrimental to US industry. This was truly the selection hoped for by the United States. Reflecting this, the US government came out as the sponsor or supporter for fourteen of the fifteen sectors, that is all except for natural and synthetic rubber.

A Ministerial Meeting was held in Vancouver on 21 and 22 November 1997. It was agreed that liberalization would be based on the APEC principle of voluntarism, and that it would be treated as a package with facilitation and economic and technical cooperation. The Leaders Meeting of 25 November instructed the trade ministers to prepare detailed targets and schedules before June 1998.

Before the Meeting, a problem arose in the United States which cast a shadow over the international negotiations. Congress voted down the fast track authorization bill. Right before the vote, APEC Coordinator John Wolf testified in a public hearing of the Asia-Pacific Subcommittee of the International Relations Committee of the House of Representatives, where he stressed the importance of the passage of the fast track bill (US House of Representatives 1998: 3–7). This failed to have an effect. USTR Charlene Barshefsky criticized the vote, stating that 'foreign governments are completely perplexed' by the politics of US trade.[21] What merits attention here is that what Barshefsky was concerned about was not the difficulties of the US government in the international negotiations, but the commotion among APEC members.

As the government saw it, the EVSL initiative was designed to consider what to bring forward for negotiations at the WTO, and trade negotiating authority (ratification by Congress) was not an issue. Authorization would become an issue at the stage of establishment and implementation of a liberalization agreement at the WTO. The government officials took the optimistic view that when this occurred, the chances for ratification were high, judging from the advantages to be gained from liberalization and the expectations of domestic industry. Therefore, USTR Barshefsky and Presidential Advisor Dan Tarullo (in charge of international economic policy and chairman of the NEC) argued that the failure to achieve fast track authorization had no direct impact on the EVSL (US White House 1997). The problem was the possibility that the other APEC members would doubt US commitment and lose their enthusiasm in the negotiations.

Accordingly, in the Vancouver Leaders Meeting, President Clinton made no reference at all to the fast track and instead called for the need for sustained effort to open up markets. This was designed to prevent the Asian countries, then facing financial crisis, from turning inward and, in doing so, demonstrate the reliability of Asia to the market (US Department of Commerce 1998).[22] In his State of the Union address at the beginning of the following year, the President declared his intention to resubmit his fast track proposal.

In this way, the Clinton Administration refrained from using domestic divisions (here the opposition of Congress) for international purposes so as to win concessions. This probably had a reverse effect in a phase where it was necessary to give some incentive to the members of APEC for the EVSL initiative.

Similar concerns to those of the government arose in industry as well. On 4 November, the APEC Business Advisory Council (ABAC), an organization for the support of APEC, sent letters to major members of Congress in which it stressed that the failure of approval for fast track authorization would threaten the efforts of the members of APEC. The ABAC representatives included large corporations such as General Motors, Goldman Sachs and Cargill (US Department of Commerce 1998).[23]

Package or voluntarism

The EVSL consultations began. The US representatives for the consultations were led by the Office of the USTR. In addition, the Commerce Department handled forestry products and fish products, the Agriculture Department handled food and oilseeds, and the State Department and Transport Department, air transport. In the beginning of the consultations, neither the US government nor industry anticipated running into any problems. Each sector was based on a proposal from an APEC member, and agricultural products and other sensitive sectors were excluded. While they realized that Japan and South Korea were negative about forestry and fish products, Japan had conditionally agreed to talk about forestry products. At the start, the problems faced by the US government were mainly technical in nature, for example, specific measures for liberalization of telecommunications and their relation to the reliability of communications and social stability.[24]

Even after the start of the consultations, domestic consensus continued. No special demands or disagreements arose either inside the government or in Congress or industry over the policy or tactics in the consultations. This was because the government held briefings on the nature of the consultations for Congress and industry and a consensus continued to be maintained inside the government through the permanent TPSC, the APEC coordinators and routine contacts. Further, USTR Barshefsky, though previously criticized for her lack of negotiating skills, had by now earned broad-based trust. The USTR staff led by her had adopted a generally aggressive stance. There was no dissatisfaction on this point domestically either.[25]

In the forestry product consultations, however, criticism arose from a completely different source. The NGOs began to claim that liberalization would increase logging operations in forests and that lumbering would ruin the global environment (this later bloomed into a major issue). The NGOs lobbied Congress as well. Even a leading member of Congress like Richard Gephart wrote a letter to Barshefsky calling upon her to pay attention to environmental issues.[26] On the other hand, workers increased their support of the forestry product consultations. The Association of Western Pulp and Paper Workers, the United Brotherhood of Carpenters and Joiners of America, and other groups reversed their previous opposition to the Clinton Administration and declared their support, claiming that trade liberalization would increase employment. These organizations further asked the President to convey his concerns personally to the heads of Japan and China.[27] This was because Japan, China and others had taken a negative posture toward reduction of tariffs for forestry products.

The disagreements in the international negotiations, in particular the disagreement between the United States and Japan, cast a shadow over the EVSL initiative as a whole. The Japanese government completely rejected any reductions in tariffs of forestry and fish products and legitimized this stance from the perspective of the APEC principle of voluntarism. In proclaiming the principle, this opposition by Japan went beyond resistance by a mere single country and bloomed into an issue affecting the initiative as a whole. This was because other APEC members might also express their concerns over rapid liberalization and follow Japan. In the negotiations from February to June 1998, the amount of flexibility that should be allowed in liberalization became a major point of discussion.

Viewing this, the US government believed that it could persuade the developing countries by flexibly dealing with the question of the deadline for elimination of tariffs. At SOM, extended tariff phase out periods and refusal to reduce tariffs to zero were debated. Japan, however, flatly rejected a reduction of tariffs and could not be dealt with by these means. The US officials refrained from responding frontally to the argument over the principles of APEC, but repeatedly argued that voluntarism 'doesn't mean countries can do whatever they want.' Further, they emphasized that the previous Vancouver Ministerial Meeting and Leaders Meeting had pointed to the importance of a package agreement (Hosokawa 1999: 90–1).[28] As already seen, this was because the US government tended to think of the principle of voluntarism of APEC as a cover for protectionism and, in particular, viewed Japan's arguments as a typical case of this. While not responding to the debate over principles, the US government considered the possibility of this Japanese argument over principles leading to a negative stance by other members to be a serious problem. According to a member of the USTR, the disagreement between the United States and Japan was less about 'package or voluntarism' and more 'package or nothing.'[29] Therefore, the US government began to lean toward a hardline stance toward Japan.

While it did not look like the disagreement between the United States and Japan would be resolved, some progress was seen in the initiative. Basic agreement was forming over product coverage, end rates and end dates for tariff liberalization. In the forestry product sector, it was agreed that tariffs would be abolished for wood and furniture from January 2002 to January 2004, and for pulp, paper and printed products from January 2000 to January 2002. The remaining points of contention were the end date for environmental equipment, the end rate for jewelry and flexibility in all sectors, in other words, extension of end dates.[30]

When the Trade Ministers Meeting opened in Kuching on 22 and 23 June 1998, the expert committees of each sector submitted 'status reports' in the names of their chairmen. Japan and several other members, however, expressed opposition or attached reservations to these. The Trade Ministers Meeting unofficially discussed the pending issue of flexibility, set different extended dates for each sector and compromised on the point of extending dates by three years in some sectors. Even so, agreement was not reached.[31]

The Chair's Statement of the Trade Ministers Meeting reflected the discussions over flexibility and the US–Japan discord. That is, on the one hand, the Chair's Statement indicated that important progress had been made 'based on APEC's principle of voluntarism,' and pointed out that flexibility was necessary to obtain maximum participation. On the other hand, it stated that participation in all nine sectors was important in maintaining the 'mutual benefit and balance of interest' and that a consensus was being formed over product coverage, end rates and end dates – thereby reflecting the arguments of the United States and others. The references to greater flexibility allowed for developing countries and to consideration of the mutual benefit and balance of interests in other modes of flexibility were both in response to the US position. The USTR report mentioned only the latter point of the Chair's Statement (APEC Trade Ministers Meeting 1998; USTR 1999: 168).

In the second phase, the international negotiations began to run into difficulties. The clash in governments' perceptions of international negotiations started to surface. In particular, Japan's emphasis on the traditional principle of voluntarism of APEC could only aggravate this. Domestic consensus in the United States, however, was firm. The dialogue between government and industry and, further, Congress, continued to function effectively. Almost all industrial organizations and members of Congress easily understood the degree of stubbornness the posture of Japan conveyed. The hardline stance of the US government was therefore judged to be appropriate. Accordingly, there was no incentive domestically to change the negotiating policy. The 'win-set' for the US government shrank as the international consultations grew more distant, despite the continuing domestic consensus.

The third phase: failure of agreement

Hardline policy against Japan

The argument didn't develop very much in the Ministerial Meeting and Leaders Meeting of November 1997 either. In the Trade Ministers Meeting of June 1998, progress was made in the discussions of flexibility. Specifically, delays for implementing the tariff cuts or backloading the cuts toward the end of the target dates were studied (USTR 1998a).[32] The US government opposed further delays, but gave priority to agreement and therefore exhibited a certain degree of flexibility.

Even so, the US soft line was predicated on Japan's policy not leading to negative stances of other members. Therefore, the United States became even more hardline in its attitude toward Japan. In the US–Japan Summit Conference of 22 September 1998, President Clinton specifically discussed deregulation and the EVSL initiative and asked for cooperation from the Japanese side.[33] Around that time, the US government took the hardline policy of applying pressure on Japan and simultaneously isolating Japan in APEC. Needless to say, this reflected its strong frustration with Japan. At the same time, members of the US government judged that pressure and isolation were the only way to override bureaucratic resistance and get the Japanese Ministers and heavyweights of the Liberal Democratic Party to act. This was confirmed at the NEC. It was decided that the related Secretaries would take joint action.[34]

That is, on 2 November, USTR Barshefsky argued to visiting Agriculture, Forestry and Fisheries Minister Shoichi Nakagawa that the success of the EVSL initiative depended on Japan, and that success in the initiative was important in dealing with the Asian financial crisis. The Assistant to the President, Gene Sparling (in charge of the NEC) and the Agriculture Secretary Glickman also made similar statements. Further, on 13 November, Barshefsky met with the MITI Minister Kaoru Yosano and sharply criticized Japan's stance. She went so far as to describe Japan's approach as 'terribly disturbing and destructive.' Further, she pointed out that liberalization of forestry products, refused by Japan, was 'very, very important.'[35]

At SOM on 13 November, while an attempt was made to finally coordinate on flexibility, no agreement was reached. The proposal considered was that the industrialized countries would liberalize 95 per cent of the products in each sector and the developing countries 80 per cent, that liberalization of the remainder could be delayed for a certain period, and that the delay could be from one to five years.[36] Even with this, the Kuala Lumpur Ministerial Meeting held on 14 and 15 November failed to reach an agreement on the EVSL initiative. The US government then sought to hand over the incomplete EVSL initiative to the WTO. The US government had originally considered the EVSL as a 'catalyst' for the WTO and this idea therefore followed naturally from its APEC policy. It was also necessary in linking the expectations of domestic industry. This idea received broad-based support from members including Japan. Along with this, the EVSL changed in name to the ATL (Accelerated Tariff Liberalization). In this way, the Ministerial Meeting agreed that broad participation of the APEC members should be sought for reduction of tariffs in nine sectors and that the start of the WTO process should be requested. At that time, the joint declaration of the Ministerial Meeting described the EVSL as follows: 'the EVSL initiative, undertaken through the APEC principle of voluntarism, is an integrated approach,' and thereby incorporated both the concepts of voluntarism and a package approach (APEC Ministerial Meeting 1998). The subsequent Leaders Meeting welcomed this development in EVSL and expressed support for the initiative in the remaining six sectors. At this time, the Clinton Administration did not attempt any special leadership or persuasion, in stark contrast to the ITA of two years before. In this way, the US officials were able to press ahead without reassessing their previous policy, as there was no intervention from top leaders or policy reversals, and domestic consensus was continuing.

After the conference, Barshefsky severely criticized Japan. She argued that 'Japan refused to exercise any leadership and that is inexcusable' and that this was a 'failure for Tokyo.'[37]

A 'success' of EVSL scheme?

On the other hand, Barshefsky emphasized the appropriateness and results of the EVSL concept. This was because the failure of the EVSL initiative did not generate any dissatisfaction domestically and it did not harm future WTO negotiations. In fact, some people in the AF&PA and AEA began saying that if a package agreement had not been prioritized, partial agreement could have been achieved. After the Asian financial crisis, the Asian countries sharply increased their exports of lumber to the United States.

Some members of the AF&PA began leaning toward protectionism and calling for a hardline stance in opening up the Asian markets. In the midst of all of this, Barshefsky defended the effectiveness and legitimacy of the administration's policy: 'We have successfully applied the approach we employed with the Information Technology Agreement and expanded it to cover these nine sectors' and 'APEC had again shown itself to be a catalyst for broader agreement in the WTO' (USTR 1998b).[38]

In June 1999, the Trade Ministers Meeting emphasized the importance of ATL in the nine EVSL sectors and concurred on working toward agreement at the WTO. The US government hoped that the ATL would also lead to greater exports and employment. The International Trade Bureau of the Commerce Department calculated that the ATL would cover 29 per cent of US exports and support employment of 2.2 million workers (US Department of Commerce, Trade Compliance Center, Market Access and Compliance, International Trade Administration 1999). On 28 July, the Senate Foreign Relations Committee approved a resolution recognizing the importance of APEC and asking the Administration to deal positively with it in the future as well (US Senate 1999).

The much-anticipated WTO Ministerial Conference was held in November 1999. The US government approached the conference without being able to coordinate with Japan. The Ministerial Conference, however, was suspended without this US–Japan discord ever having surfaced. NGOs staged violent demonstrations against the WTO, making the conference itself impossible. The NGOs aimed their criticism at the deterioration of the global environment which would result from trade liberalization. The forestry product sector was one of the major points of contention. In the US government, the Office of the USTR and the White House Council on Environmental Quality had already prepared detailed reports to allay the concerns of the NGOs, but these failed to have any effect (USTR and White House Council on Environmental Quality 1999). Greenpeace USA, Friends of the Earth, the Global Forest Policy Project, the Pacific Environment and Resource Center, and other organizations continued, and even grew stronger in, their opposition. This being the case, the AF&PA was forced to argue that, in the United States, lumber and paper were produced with the greatest consideration to the environment and that trade liberalization, through the international spread of those products, would lighten the burden on the resources of environmentally fragile countries (AF&PA 1999).

Japan continued to argue over the principle of voluntarism. From the US perspective on international consultations, while some concessions had been possible, it had gone beyond the limits of tolerance in its dealings with Japan. Inside the United States, the previous consensus was basically maintained. No one called for a change in consulting policy. As stated by an official in the Commerce Department, the US government did not share a common image of the agreement with the Japanese government.[39] The US government, rather, became harder in its policy toward Japan. The 'win-set' would no longer be expanded. The EVSL initiative thereby failed.

Conclusion

The political process in the United States over the EVSL initiative departed from the traditional pattern. In the United States, domestic consensus was achieved unexpectedly smoothly and remained firm. In particular, the increasingly close relations between government and industry had great significance in this. Therefore, the government was able to adopt a consistent consulting policy and did not even have to make any mid-term corrections. Accordingly, the US government did not press other APEC members for concessions using domestic divisions as an excuse, and did not use the international consultations as a vehicle for achieving domestic consensus. If this domestic consensus had been backed up by better comprehension of the negotiating environment, the possibility for success in the EVSL initiative might have been higher. The US government, however, underestimated the APEC tradition of voluntarism and non-binding commitments. Therefore, when Japan rejected liberalization of forestry and fish products. the US government did not view this as a legitimate argument of principle, but took it as protectionism having a detrimental influence on other APEC members. The domestic consensus and excessive expectations made the government's hardline stance even more rigid. The fact that the domestic consensus was founded on industry interests also made it harder for the government to be more international and broader in its judgments.

The 'two-level game' model particularly stresses how domestic divisions make international agreement more difficult. The former US pattern of international negotiations fit this perfectly. In the case studied in this chapter, however, domestic consensus became a factor behind a failed international agreement. This domestic consensus was aided by excessive international expectations and a disparate perception of international consultations from other APEC members. Further, the consensus was solid and led by industry, so was lacking in flexibility. In the political process discussed in this chapter as well, the 'two-level game' possibly manifested itself in the clash and linkage between the domestic and international levels. This however was different from what was envisioned in the original model and different from the previous US pattern of diplomacy.

The political process in the EVSL initiative can perhaps be said to show a typical case of current US 'trade politics.' This political process in one respect reveals structural changes in 'trade politics.' In particular, there is a big difference from the past in the increasingly close relations between government and industry and in their entrenchment and legitimization. This fact has been pointed out previously here and there, but its importance and repercussions must be again underlined. In another respect, the political process of the EVSL was accidental and situational in aspect. While the closer relations between government and industry resulted in a relative decline in the role of Congress, Congress still holds power over trade and can increase its involvement depending on the issue or situation. For example, Congress has become increasingly distrustful of the WTO, and is even debating withdrawing from it. Further, the EVSL initiative was not an issue harming domestic industry. The country may well become divided over issues where harm to domestic industry is projected, or where there would be major differences in interests among domestic industries.

Notes

1 The effect of external pressure depends on the two-level game in the negotiation counter-part (Schoppa 1997).
2 *Washington Post*, 5 May 1994.
3 Interview with two APEC-related officials of the USTR (9 November 1999) and the Department of State (19 November 1999).
4 Interview with several APEC-related officials of the USTR (1 November 1999), the Department of State (4 and 10 November 1999), the Department of Commerce (5 November 1999) and the Department of Agriculture (12 November 1999).
5 *Washington Post*, 20 November 1993.
6 Interview with an international trade policy related official of the American Electronics Association (AEA) (1 November 1999).
7 *New York Times*, 26 November 1996.
8 *New York Times*, 26 November 1996; *Washington Post*, 26 November 1996; *Asahi Shimbun*, 20 and 26 November 1996.
9 *Washington Post*, 26 November 1996.
10 *Inside US Trade*, 15 November 1996, p. 10; *Asahi Shimbun*, 15 November 1996.
11 Interview with two APEC-related officials of the USTR (9 November 1999) and the Department of Commerce (5 November 1999).
12 Interview with an APEC-related official of the Department of Commerce (5 November 1999) For the use of the term 'progress' in government reports in this context, see, for examples, US Department of State (1997: 1) and USTR, *Trade Policy Agenda and Annual Report*, every year.
13 Interview with an international trade policy related official of the Telecommunications Industry Association (TIA) (8 November 1999) and the American Forest and Paper Association (2 November 1999).
14 *Washington Post*, 26 November 1996.
15 Interview with an official of the TIA (8 November 1999), the AEA (1 November 1999), an APEC-related official of USTR (9 November 1999) and an industry policy related official of USTR (12 November 1999).
16 Interview with an APEC-related official of the Department of Commerce (5 November 1999).
17 Interview with officials of International Trade Administration in the Department of Commerce (5 November 1999) and the American Farm Bureau Federation (2 November 1999).
18 Interview with a senior advisor of a Senator (9 November 1999), and with APEC-related officials of USTR.
19 *Inside US Trade*, 18 July 1997, p. 10 and 21 November 1997, p. 5.
20 Interview with two APEC-related officials of the USTR (9 November 1999) and the Department of State (19 November 1999).
21 *Washington Post*, 12 November 1997.

22 *Washington Post*, 23, 24 November 1997.
23 *Washington Post*, 23, 24 November 1997.
24 Interview with two APEC-related officials of the USTR (1 November 1999) and the Department of Commerce (5 November 1999).
25 Interview with two officials of the Foreign Agriculture Service in the Department of Agriculture (11 November 1999) and an official of the International Trade Administration in the Department of Commerce (5 November 1999).
26 *Inside US Trade*, 26 June 1998, p. 19.
27 *Inside US Trade*, 3 July 1998, p. 16.
28 *International Trade Reporter*, vol. 15, no. 41, 21 November (1998), p. 1737; *Inside US Trade*, 15 May 1998, p. 22.
29 Interview with an APEC-related official of USTR (1 November 1999).
30 *International Trade Reporter*, vol. 15, no. 25, 24 June (1998), pp. 1080–1.
31 Interview by Jiro Okamoto with an APEC-related official of the Ministry of International Trade and Industry, Japan; *Inside US Trade*, 29 May 1998, p. 7.
32 *Inside US Trade*, 26 June 1998, p. 18.
33 *Asahi Shimbun*, 24 September 1998.
34 Interview with APEC-related officials of the USTR (1 November 1999) and the Agriculture Department (12 November 1999).
35 *Asahi Shimbun*, 4, 16 November 1998; *Inside US Trade*, 6 November 1998, p. 3; *International Trade Reporter*, vol. 15, no. 45, 18 November (1998), pp. 1912–13.
36 *Asahi Shimbun*, 14 November 1998.
37 *Washington Post*, 19 November 1998.
38 *International Trade Reporter*, vol. 15, no. 45, 18 November (1998), p. 1913.
39 Interview with an official of the International Trade Administration in the Department of Commerce (5 November 1999).

6 Australia
The loss of regional vision

Michael Wesley

Introduction: Australia and APEC

Arguably, APEC is more important to the foreign and trade policy of Australia than to that of any of its other member states. In foreign policy terms, APEC's institutional confirmation of an 'Asia-Pacific' region resolves the ongoing uncertainty in Australia over whether its European cultural heritage creates enduring commitments to Europe and North America or whether its trade complementarities and geographic proximity make it a member of the Asian region. By including the United States and Northeast Asia, the APEC framework encompasses Australia's main strategic ally and its major trading partners.

In trade policy terms, APEC is a culmination and expression of a revolution in Australian economic ideas, from a protectionist, inward-looking, conservatism, to a vigorous, creative, external focus. For much of the twentieth century, Australia instituted one of the highest tariff regimes in the world. Under pressure from an economic crisis beginning in 1974 that struck Australia proportionately harder than most other OECD economies, these structures of protection began to be dismantled in the 1980s. Strict, racially based immigration controls were phased out by 1972; in 1983 an Accord with the trade union movement was signed to address both unemployment and inflation; the currency was floated; and financial markets were deregulated (Kelly 1992: 54–94). Sweeping, across-the-board tariff cuts were enacted in 1988 and again in 1991. Microeconomic reform followed with the launching of National Competition Policy in 1995. As the EC's Common Agricultural Policy and the US Export Enhancement Program excluded Australian primary producers from their traditional markets, Australia helped found the Cairns Group of Fair Agricultural Traders to place agricultural trade on the GATT agenda. A Closer Economic Relations (CER) agreement was signed in 1983, instituting free trade with New Zealand.

When Australian Prime Minister Bob Hawke proposed the creation of a body that was eventually to become APEC in Seoul in January 1989, it was consistent with the revolution in Australia's thinking about economic and trade policy. Several other domestic, regional and international imperatives also informed this proposal. First, trade figures began to emerge in the late 1980s suggesting that while its exports to East Asia were expanding, Australia's market share in the region was declining, especially, and most disturbingly, in agriculture (Drysdale and Lu 1996). Partly this was the result of a unique development in Asia-Pacific trade: while most economies were unilaterally liberalizing barriers to trade, most were maintaining high tariffs in sectors where other Asia-Pacific economies' comparative advantage lay. The rapid economic development of the region and the growth of sectoral protection were not unrelated: it was regional growth and rapidly shifting comparative advantage that most threatened 'traditional industries' in the region's economies. Second, by the late 1980s, the global trading system appeared to be in trouble. The Uruguay Round negotiations were experiencing great difficulties, while regionalism seemed on the rise with the signing of the Single European Act and the North American Free Trade Agreement. Australian policy makers became concerned about the rise of blocs – none of which it was a natural member of – as well as the enduring acrimony between the United States and Japan on trade matters. A permanent break between these powers – one Australia's most important military ally, the other its most important trade partner – was an unpalatable choice. A regional structure would help mitigate these conflicts and trends: 'the original motive for Asia Pacific economic cooperation was essentially conservative: to conserve and extend a process of market integration amongst rapidly growing economies and their major regional partners' (Garnaut 1999: 3). Third, a regional free trade structure would allow the Australian government to address rural demands, stabilize expectations and moderate domestic perceptions of the risks of trade liberalization (Garnaut 1999: 15).

As APEC developed, Australia invested a large amount of diplomatic resources in the organization, placing great store in its tangible and intangible benefits. Australia and its Prime Minister of the time, Paul Keating, were closely involved in the next major development in APEC, the addition of the Leaders Meetings from the first Summit at Seattle in 1993. Policy makers in Australia had become uncomfortable with the fact that Australia had no regular opportunity to consult with the heads of state or government in their own region of the world. Keating first proposed the Leaders Meetings when US President George Bush visited Australia in December 1992; Bush's successor Clinton eagerly adopted the suggestion. Australian diplomacy worked hard to convince other Asia-Pacific states to attend a Leaders Summit. The inauguration of the annual APEC Leaders Meetings at Seattle in 1993 satisfied this requirement of Australia, as well as broader objectives of those with greater ambitions for APEC: 'When I wrote to other APEC leaders in 1992 suggesting that we strengthen APEC's institutional structures by adding an informal leaders meeting, I had strategic as well as economic, purposes in mind' (Keating 1998).

By the launch of the Australian Foreign and Trade Policy White Paper in September 1997, APEC had come to occupy a central and crucial position in

Australia's diplomacy: 'APEC is the most significant regional forum in which Australia participates, and will remain a key element in Australia's regional strategies over the next fifteen years' (DFAT 1997a: 42). Furthermore, the government was strongly committed to maintaining APEC's momentum and viability, in the face of public criticism of economic reform and liberalization, the One Nation Party's anti-Asian engagement rhetoric,[1] and the onset of the Asian financial crisis. Australia's trade policy makers were also aware of the need to keep the major Asia-Pacific economies and their leaders engaged in the organization, by ensuring APEC delivered ongoing benefits to its member-states (DFAT 1997a: 43).

The Early Voluntary Sectoral Liberalization (EVSL) scheme promised to meet most of these requirements. As a system of accelerated, targeted, reciprocal tariff cuts, EVSL was a proposal designed to address both international and domestic cynicism about the diffuse APEC process and its economic benefits. Australia became an enthusiastic EVSL supporter and campaigner. This chapter traces Australian policy making on the EVSL initiative chronologically, examining the interaction of its domestic and international imperatives and stimuli. In doing so, it uses the two-level game framework developed in Chapter 3 to search for the vital determinants of Australia's EVSL policy.

The emergence of the EVSL initiative: Australian responses

The EVSL initiative drew its inspiration from the negotiation of the Information Technology Agreement (ITA), signed at the Singapore WTO Ministerial Meeting in December 1996. The ITA had been an unresolved initiative of the Uruguay Round which particularly US private information technology companies had continued to lobby for. Agreement was reached between the EU, the United States, Japan and Canada in April 1996 to support the negotiation of an international trade agreement which would eliminate customs tariffs on a broad range of information technology and telecommunications products by the end of the century. The latter three then took the ITA to APEC, which had by July 1996 agreed to consider the ITA proposal further in the lead-up to the WTO Ministerial Conference, scheduled for Singapore in December 1996. The result in Singapore was the Ministerial Declaration on Trade in Information Technology Products, signed by twenty-eight WTO members, and economies acceding to the WTO, on 13 December 1996. By mid-1998, ITA signatories had risen to forty-five participants accounting for over 93 per cent of IT trade.

The ITA, along with APEC's role in the success of the WTO Financial Services Agreement, suggested a new and exciting role for APEC within the WTO system (Hannah 1999). Advocates of liberalization in other sectors immediately began advocating the use of the 'ITA model' through APEC to the WTO. Representatives of agricultural and food industry associations who had attended the Singapore WTO Ministerial Conference began lobbying for an initiative to liberalize aspects of the food and agriculture sectors on the model of the ITA following the Singapore meeting (Hooke 1998).

The earliest reference to the EVSL initiative occurred at Osaka in 1995, when senior officials were asked to 'identify industries in which the progressive reduction of tariffs may have positive impact on trade and on economic growth in the Asia-Pacific region or for which there is regional industry support for early liberalization' (APEC Leaders Meeting 1995b). By the time of the Subic Bay Leaders Meeting the next year, leaders' instructions had further developed, directing Ministers to:

> identify sectors where early voluntary liberalization would have a posi-
> tive impact on trade, investment, and economic growth in the
> individual APEC economies as well as in the region, and submit to us
> their recommendations on how this can be achieved.
>
> (APEC Leaders Meeting 1996)

Australian policy makers and trade diplomats had followed carefully the development of the 'ITA model,' the confluence of the necessary conditions for EVSL's launch, and the push for EVSL by the Americans and the Canadians. Australian considerations of the effect of EVSL on Australia were based on a number of factors. One was concrete experience with the ITA. Generally the conclusion among policy makers was that the ITA was a positive development for Australia. While at the time of the ITA Australia's information technology sector trade deficit accounted for approximately one-quarter of the total trade deficit in elaborately transformed manufactures (ETMs), information technology exports were growing at 21.8 per cent, much higher than the rate of ETMs export growth. Australia's simple average Most-Favored-Nation tariffs on ITA products stood at 2.7 per cent, with none greater than 5 per cent and half at zero (Gibbons 1997: 5–6). It was felt that Australia would benefit from this agreement; consequently Australia was one of the first to sign.

The debate within the Department of Foreign Affairs and Trade (DFAT) was not only over the prospects and implications of APEC sectoral liberalization measures in themselves. Australian trade policy makers were also focused on the possibility of another round of multilateral trade negotiations through the WTO. While the Uruguay Round outcomes had inbuilt commitments to further multilateral talks on agriculture and services, Australian policy makers had a number of reasons for favoring a comprehensive round at or around the turn of the millennium. By late 1997, Prime Minister John Howard was publicly promoting a 'millennium round' to international business groups. One reason for this desire was Australia's growing manufactures trade with developing countries, and the persistence of high manufactures tariffs in these countries. There was little prospect of addressing these trade barriers outside of a comprehensive round. Another reason was the calculation made by many policy makers that the most obdurate agricultural trade barriers would not be dislodged outside of the context of a comprehensive round, where trade concessions and side payments could be linked across and among sectors.

Australian trade policy makers also realized that the prospects for a multilateral round were slim without the commitment of the large economic players – the United States, the European Union and Japan – to a comprehensive round. A debate developed within DFAT partly influenced by these calculations. One group of trade policy makers argued that if the United States were able to secure its trade objectives through sectoral initiatives, it would be uninterested in a multilateral round. For this school of thought, the ITA contained a worrying precedent, of allowing US trade objectives to be secured sectorally through APEC and WTO Ministerial Meetings, and thus removing any incentive to engage in the protracted process of a WTO round. The counter-argument was made by those who argued that opposing EVSL in APEC would jeopardize US commitment to that institution. Denying the United States its major objective with regard to the organization could well prompt a loss of US interest or even a withdrawal from APEC.

Later in 1997, as the Asian financial crisis unfolded across the region, trade officials began to think of EVSL as a way of demonstrating the continuing viability of APEC during times of economic distress. Although Australia remained largely unaffected by the Asian crisis,[2] concern grew among policy makers and exporters that Asian economies in distress would retreat towards autarkic solutions to the downturn. The ongoing EVSL initiative provided an opportunity to shore up regional economies' commitment to trade liberalization:

> We have a number of objectives [within the APEC process]. The primary one is to try to pursue the early voluntary sectoral liberalisation agenda to maximise the outcome to the benefit of Australia. In doing so, that is part of a broader desire to shore up the momentum for trade liberalisation in the region in what is a very difficult year.
>
> (Fayle 1998: 116)

Debate also continued within government about the merits of sectoral versus comprehensive liberalization, an issue that became the subject of a study by the Productivity Commission,[3] discussed below. However, at this early stage, as these various debates worked towards resolution, the argument tended towards those supportive of the sectoral experiment, based on continuing disappointment at the Uruguay Round's lack of a systemic approach to liberalizing industrial and agricultural tariffs, and some disappointment at the modest achievements of the APEC Individual Action Plans. A decision was made to support the initiative in late 1996, and early work was commissioned on sectors which Australia would nominate for early liberalization.

The development of Australian policy and nominations

Actors and policy coordination

The Leaders' instructions at Subic Bay in November 1996 were followed by more specific instructions by APEC Trade Ministers to senior officials to undertake studies and report back to them by August 1997 on possible sectors for early liberalization (APEC Trade Ministers Meeting 1997). These instructions established the parameters for the initial development of the EVSL initiatives at the domestic level within APEC economies. First, the Montreal plan instructed officials to include as much as possible in their proposals the three 'pillars' of APEC action: liberalization in both its tariff and non-tariff dimensions; trade facilitation; and economic and technical cooperation. Second, EVSL nominations were to include the fullest possible private sector input: 'Since the early stages of the EVSL exercise, Ministers have emphasized the importance of taking into account private sector interests. Member economies have consulted with business in developing the liberalization initiatives for each sector.'[4] The third instruction to senior officials was to prepare EVSL nominations with a view to creating critical mass for stimulating broader sectoral action through the WTO. This required nominations to include those sectors where a large proportion of world trade was conducted within the Asia-Pacific.

Within Australia, a number of different government Departments were likely to be or would come to be affected by the EVSL initiative as it developed. Traditionally, DFAT was charged with the carriage of trade policy and the management of APEC affairs. The Department merged the portfolio of Foreign Affairs with that of Trade in 1987, partly to reflect the centrality of trade policy to Australia's diplomacy. Over time, DFAT has developed into a strong advocate for free trade within the Australian federal bureaucracy. Within the Department, a number of different sections became involved in APEC EVSL at different times: in addition to area sections, such as the Northeast Asia Division, the Market Development Division and Trade Negotiations Division, which contained much of the Department's expertise on liberalization negotiations, were heavily involved. The latter Division was given responsibility for the assessment and formulation of Australia's sectoral nominations, as well as being charged with the process of gauging the impact of the accelerated liberalization of the fifteen sectors finally nominated on the Australian economy. Coordination, liaison and management of Australia's responses to EVSL were the responsibility of Australia's Ambassador to APEC and his/her staff within the Department. These, along with the Minister for Trade, took responsibility for presenting Australia's nominations and policy as the EVSL process developed through a succession of APEC Senior Officials Meetings (SOMs) and Ministerial Meetings.

As EVSL was likely to require tariff cuts from Australia, other aspects of the federal bureaucracy were also involved. Perhaps the next most crucially affected Department was the Department of Industry, Science and Resources (DISR). Its general portfolio responsibility for Australian industry, and its recent experience with the bruising debate over further tariff cuts to the textiles, clothing and footwear (TCF) and passenger motor vehicles (PMV) industries,[5] made DISR wary of new liberalization proposals generated from outside of Australia. The motive for DISR was to work closely with DFAT to ensure Australia's more sensitive sectors were not nominated for EVSL, but that Australia should nominate sectors for which it had been trying to expand export markets for some time (Wright 1997). Other government Departments with specific responsibility for industry sectors likely to be affected by or benefit from EVSL included the Department of Agriculture, Fisheries and Forestry, and the Department of Communications, Information Technology and the Arts. These Departments shared similar motivations to DISR in relation to EVSL.

The Treasury, the Department of Finance, the Department of the Prime Minister and Cabinet and the Department of Environment and Heritage also had interests in the development of the EVSL program. Most of these interests, however, were concerned with managerial, coordination or financial aspects of the policy, rather than substantive policy matters. Because of the large spread of affected bureaucratic interests, DFAT organized an intensive program of consultation on the coordination and impact of the EVSL initiative in early 1997. The consultations in effect registered with DFAT the interests and concerns of the other Departments, to be taken into account as DFAT developed the EVSL policy. The relative lack of domestic controversy raised by EVSL among other Departments or industry groups in part reflects this comprehensive early process of consultation and DFAT's continuing discussion of the EVSL initiative with other Departments as the process developed.

Within DFAT, the debate had already occurred on the costs and benefits of EVSL, and it had been decided that EVSL was consistent with Australian APEC policy and trade goals, that EVSL was generally consistent with the original philosophy of APEC, and that progress on EVSL would represent progress towards the Bogor goals:

> we saw it in the national interest to try to ginger up the liberalisation process ... there is no doubt that the individual action plans were not delivering us everything that we wanted. We saw a need to put some type of focus in the liberalisation agenda that would get us some concrete outcomes and push the envelope out. So we drove early voluntary sectoral liberalisation because of that.
>
> (Fayle 1998)

Econometric research was done tabulating various sectors which could have been nominated, and their trade impacts across the Asia Pacific. These were published and circulated as a way of demonstrating to other economies the pros and cons of various early sectoral liberalizations (DFAT 1997b).

Responses from business and decision on nominations

DFAT actively sought and encouraged industry and business input into the formulation of the Australian EVSL nominations (Fayle 1998). Industry reactions to this encouragement ranged from enthusiastic support to lack of interest. The most enthusiastic supporters were the agricultural and food exporters associations, which were largely dissatisfied with the persistence of trade barriers and subsidies after the conclusion of the Uruguay Round. They were also underwhelmed by the progress of the APEC IAPs: 'the IAPs, in relation to food, have not really gone much further than what the countries committed to under the WTO and the long-term objectives of the Bogor declaration' (Hooke 1998).

There was early acknowledgement of the sensitivity of agricultural liberalization in many APEC economies. This in itself meant that these industry associations had to battle against other industry associations in Australia, representing sectors that were not so sensitive in other APEC economies, that claimed that including food and agricultural products in the EVSL nominations would jeopardize the whole proposal. Food and agricultural industries acknowledged that 'the toughest negotiation was at home,'

> in terms of how far to push the liberalisation of some sensitive sectors without spiking the whole deal. The solution for us was to push food as a processed product – more acceptable to many other [APEC] members, and rely on the 'pull factor' to eventually carry the more sensitive sectors along.[6]

Much attention was paid to the sensitivity of various parts of the food sector. Each suggested part was researched thoroughly across all APEC economies, and bracketed if significant political resistance was likely to come to liberalizing that sector from within APEC. The resulting list of less sensitive parts of the food sector was 'very narrow indeed.'

Other industry associations, while not as enthusiastic, participated in the DFAT consultations. At the other end of the spectrum, some peak bodies were skeptical of the value of the initiative, having observed that the IAPs' process was already stretching some economies, making their agreement to accelerated liberalization unlikely. Some became disillusioned at the inclusion of food and agriculture in the EVSL package (despite the careful preparation of these proposals), and convinced that the EVSL initiative would ultimately fail because of the inclusion of these difficult sectors, which neither the GATT/WTO nor APEC had been able to resolve. Others claimed to have seen from an early stage that EVSL was a 'cynical diplomatic public relations exercise.'[7]

By July 1997, DFAT had consulted and prepared sectoral nominations for four sectors (food, energy, chemicals and non-ferrous metals), three of which were ultimately included in the final fifteen. From an early stage, DFAT was careful to cull from its package of proposed sectors any that were controversial or sensitive. In this way, DFAT negotiators were also prepared early to oppose any nominations made by other APEC economies of sectors that were sensitive for Australia.

Nominations were made initially by most APEC economies; by July 1997, sixty-two nominations covering thirteen sectors for early liberalization had been received by the SOM Chair. At the SOM in St John's, trade officials began to consolidate overlapping nominations. The number of nominations was reduced to forty-one as the result of a round of consolidation, rather than culling. To assist in further culling, officials developed a measure for comparing levels of support for different sectors among all APEC economies. Using these measures, officials were polled, and each nomination was given a certain level of support in comparison with the others. The polling produced a list of fifteen sectors which were announced by Ministers and Leaders at Vancouver in November 1997.

Within Australia, industry watched the EVSL process as it accelerated towards the package of fifteen sectors to be announced by leaders at Vancouver. There were three types of industry reaction. One was no reaction at all, from those sectors of the economy untouched by the entire EVSL episode as it had thus far developed. Another was from sectors of the economy that would be affected by sectoral nominations made by other countries. Expressions of concern were raised by some of the sectors experiencing trade deficits, such as the furniture trade and certain sections of the chemicals industry. Parts of the forestry industry worried that Australian phytosanitary standards on timber imports would be targeted as a non-trade measure as part of the EVSL proposal. Others, such as telecommunications and the automotive sector were reassured by guarantees from the outset that EVSL in their sectors would not contain a liberalization component.

The final group was those industries that had succeeded in persuading the Australian government to propose their sector for EVSL. Those industries that had been nominated as Australia's EVSL proposals, on the other hand, waited to see if they would survive the culling process and make the final package. They remained in close consultation with DFAT as the process continued. Some engaged in their own process of international lobbying in support of getting their sectors to the final round. For example, the Australian Food and Grocery Council used its membership of the International Alliance of Food Product Associations to lobby its counterparts in each of the APEC member economies in that alliance (Hooke 1998). In the end, Australia's energy, chemicals, and processed food sector nominations were all successful (the former two in the Front Nine), while non-ferrous metals was unsuccessful.

The establishment of 'full' support for EVSL

During this culling process at the international level, further calculations were made by DFAT economists as the EVSL package began to be narrowed down towards the fifteen sectors announced at Vancouver. These calculations showed that Australia stood to make substantial gains if the fifteen-sector package was implemented. As a result Australian policy makers further resolved to support the EVSL process enthusiastically, and to sell it to the Australian public as an example of APEC's continuing viability and vitality. Ministers took advantage of the issue to shore up support for APEC and to demonstrate the effectiveness of the government internationally. For example, Minister for Trade Tim Fischer used the EVSL issue as an example of government activism in two separate speeches in early 1998: one to the Silver Perch Industry Association, and another to a Liquid Natural Gas Conference (Fischer 1998a, 1998b). Both sectors were included in the EVSL package. These examples show a government both using an international issue for domestic electoral advantage, and at the same time maintaining the size of its domestic win-set for the international-level agreement.

Australian policy makers, calculating net gains from the EVSL package, prepared to invest a large amount of diplomatic resources behind seeing it through to its conclusion. In the federal budget of May 1998, the government committed an extra ten million Australian dollars over four years for 'market development and promotion in the Asia Pacific and elsewhere.' In a joint statement, the Ministers for Foreign Affairs and Trade emphasized that a significant proportion of this would be used for 'funding to support Australia's effort towards the early voluntary sectoral liberalization agenda in APEC where Australia has significant commercial interests in the liberalization of fifteen sectors worth over 800 billion US dollars in intra-APEC trade' (Downer and Fischer 1998).

The government faced no serious objections from the Parliamentary Opposition on the EVSL initiative. The Australian Labor Party (ALP), in opposition since March 1996, regards the creation of APEC as one of the great achievements of the ALP in government (1983–96). Generally, then, the Opposition's criticisms of government policy on APEC were couched in terms of asserting that more should be done on APEC in general, in order to maintain an active Australian role in the organization, and to prevent the organization from falling into decay. This line of argument emerged with regards to the EVSL initiative from Senator Peter Cook, formerly Australian Minister for Trade, and now the Opposition Spokesman for Trade, who criticized the parsimony of the additional announced government funding for EVSL:

> This measure will also include the provision of funding to support the Early Voluntary Sectoral Liberalisation agenda in APEC ... This is an incredibly small funding measure considering that one of the aims of

the program is to 'help offset the effects of the current Asian economic instability on the Australian economy' ...

(Cook 1998a)

Given the generally benign response of the public and the Parliament to EVSL, the government naturally was taken by surprise at the emergence of criticisms of EVSL from a Productivity Commission Staff Research Paper produced by a team headed by one of the most respected government economists in Australia, Philippa Dee. The paper expressed support for the general principle of EVSL:

There is a strong argument in favour of negotiated EVSL outcomes that recognise the characteristics of different regions, so that all APEC members continue to be involved in the process and to ensure that APEC captures the benefits associated with the diversity of the region.

(Dee *et al.* 1998: 21)

The concern of the paper writers, however, had been raised by the flexibility with which the EVSL sectors had been chosen. The tendency of the nominations process to schedule less politically contentious sectors for liberalization was leaving a pattern where peak tariffs in the region were left untouched. This led to a further tendency of the EVSL process to reinforce 'cascading protection,' where sectors that are upstream in the production chain are liberalized first, so that tariffs are progressively higher at stages further down the production chain towards more elaborately transformed manufactures. The Report warned that partial liberalization of 'easy' sectors, as proposed by EVSL, could result in resources being moved further away from liberalized sectors towards downstream protected sectors, resulting in the potential for EVSL to allocate resources further away from a pattern than in a world free of trade distortions, leading to possible allocative efficiency losses: 'A danger with liberalizing only part of a production process is that inputs may be made cheaper for highly protected downstream industries, resulting in losses of efficiency and overall economic welfare' (Dee *et al.* 1998: 13–14).

These assertions were tested by feeding the data for some of the nominated sectors into an econometric model. The results were interpreted to show that 'wide coverage is required for all [economies] to gain and none to lose' (Dee *et al.* 1998: 21). The Report recommended that any EVSL initiative should consider and allow for linkages in the production chain, ideally addressing protection at all stages; that every EVSL proposal nominate moderate to highly protected sectors, perhaps by twinning these with nominations of more lightly protected sectors; and that EVSL needed to target both tariffs and subsidies (Dee *et al.* 1998: 22). Generally, the Report recommended that 'the EVSL process could consider adopting guidelines that ensure APEC economies are genuine in their commitment to realizing gains from sectoral liberalization' (Dee *et al.* 1998: 21).

For the government, these arguments were easy for economists to make, but would not long survive the realities of APEC negotiations. The criticisms in the Productivity Commission paper recalled earlier criticisms of APEC, which ignored the general progress of liberalization in APEC to concentrate on specific instances of peak tariffs in other APEC economies.[8] The paper also raised the sensitive issue of the tariffs debates of 1997: 'liberalizing chemicals will tend to encourage resources out of domestic chemicals production and also out of domestic coal and gas production, while encouraging an expansion of domestic textiles, clothing, and other manufacturing' (Dee *et al.* 1998: 14). The government and DFAT expressed skepticism about the paper, raising, among other things, the possibility of selection bias in the sectors fed into the model; by its own admission, the paper tested five of the fifteen sectors which 'tend[ed] to involve liberalization at the upstream end of the processing chain' (Dee *et al.* 1998: 14). In the end, however, the criticisms of EVSL failed to gain much media coverage or any political momentum that would have complicated the issue of EVSL for the government. Industry remained largely aware of, but unmoved by the paper. After some anxious weeks, DFAT was able to look past the paper and begin to concentrate on the upcoming round of international negotiations.

The emergence of divisions over EVSL and Australian responses

By early 1998, APEC officials had begun to publicize the initiative as a major positive undertaking by the organization in the midst of the Asian financial crisis: EVSL would cover 'goods estimated at 1.5 trillion US dollars with tariff reductions to 0 to 5 per cent' (Adlan 1998). An ABAC meeting in Sydney in May 1998 endorsed the EVSL initiative and urged all APEC member economies to participate in comprehensive and credible sectoral packages. In June, a meeting of APEC Telecommunications Ministers at their third APEC Ministerial Meeting in Singapore issued the Singapore Declaration endorsing the EVSL telecommunications MRA for conformity assessment of telecommunications equipment.

However, there were four crucial aspects of EVSL that were yet to gain agreement of all member economies. First, although a package of fifteen sectors for EVSL had been agreed, the actual product coverage on the basis of GATT harmonized system (HS) tariff codes had not yet been finalized. Second, the 'end rates,' or tariff levels to which the EVSL process would eventually lead, had yet to be agreed. Third, the 'end dates' of the EVSL project had not been hammered out. Finally, the vexed question of 'flexibility' had yet to be resolved. This was essentially represented by the 'voluntary' aspect of the whole package. Earlier discussions had revealed that 'flexibility' meant a range of different things to different APEC economies. For some, flexibility signified that an economy could participate in some of the fifteen sectoral initiatives but not others; for others it meant that economies could choose their own dates for commencement. Yet others argued that it referred to the free choice of modalities open to economies on how they would cut their tariffs: either gradually according to a timetable designed to bring them to the agreed end dates and rates; or all at once before the arrival of the end dates. Significantly, there were economies within APEC that objected to all three interpretations, insisting that EVSL be undertaken by all economies implementing equal tariff cuts at the same time.

These differences developed into open rupture by the time of the Trade Ministers Meeting at Kuching in June 1998, where a major disagreement occurred over the concepts of flexibility and voluntarism. As early as the Vancouver meetings, and certainly by the time of the Kuching Ministerial, the EVSL initiative had hardened into a single package, with the Statement of the Chair at the end of the meeting recommending that the APEC economies should be endorsed 'in their entirety.' The 'bundling' together of the fifteen sectors had been argued for on the basis that there was a diverse group of sectors that had been agreed to, and that each of the sectors in the final fifteen was necessary in order to achieve an internal balance within the whole package. At Kuching Japan began to insist on voluntarism, particularly regarding its right to opt out of the liberalization of forestry and fisheries products. Despite heavy pressure from the Chair and other APEC members, the issue remained unresolved.

The escalating dispute over EVSL, as an initiative that Australia enthusiastically supported and the subject of a deepening dispute between Japan and the United States, stimulated a vigorous diplomatic response from Australia. Shortly after the Kuching Meeting, the Foreign and Defense Ministers of Australia and the United States met for annual consultations in Sydney, where 'The two governments agreed on the imperative for APEC to conclude in November the early voluntary sectoral liberalization initiative approved by APEC leaders in November 1997 and to press ahead with further improvements in Individual Action Plans' (Australia–US Ministerial Consultations 1998). Australia was joined by Canada, Hong Kong, New Zealand, Singapore and the United States in the diplomatic effort to persuade Japan to agree to accept the EVSL package. A variety of persuasive gambits was brought into play. One line of argument was to assert that Japan's refusal to support the initiative would damage the region in a time of crisis. A diplomat from one of the mediating countries commented, 'If the second-biggest economy says it cannot join, how can we ask deeply troubled economies like Indonesia to join in?'[9] The United States also weighed in with this line of argument, with US Trade Representative Charlene Barshefsky arguing that Japan would be playing a destructive role in APEC if it failed to endorse the whole EVSL process.[10] At a bilateral meeting with Japanese Foreign Minister Masahiko Komura in early November, Foreign Minister Alexander Downer warned that Japan's failure to support EVSL because of sensitivities of its own economy could result in other Asia-Pacific countries raising problems with sensitive areas in their own economies. Japan vigorously rejected these interpretations, countering rather that repeated suggestions that APEC was a failure were themselves more likely to contribute to the failure of the group.[11]

Intensive efforts to find a compromise solution between June and the November Leaders Meeting failed. In early November, Japan offered to accelerate its tariff cuts in other areas to compensate for its refusal to do so on forestry and fisheries products, but this offer was rejected by the other APEC economies. Gradually, under the duress of the Asian financial crisis, other economies began to support greater voluntarism in the EVSL process. Japan's position on the fisheries and forestry sectors remained non-negot iable: later, in November, a solution floated by the United States that Japan could 'differentiate' the timing of cuts to these areas, was rejected by Japan.[12] The compromise reached at the Kuala Lumpur Ministerial and Leaders Meeting was to refer the liberalization components of the Front Nine sectors to the WTO, while continuing work on their other aspects, as well as the development of the 'Back Six.'

Predictably in an economy that had supported the EVSL concept strongly, the general reaction in Australia to the Kuala Lumpur outcome was one of disappointment. Trade Minister Tim Fischer referred to the decision to refer the liberalization sectors of the Front Nine to the WTO as 'the second best outcome,' but argued that 'the EVSL process is not dead, but rather it will be pursued through the WTO' (Fischer 1998c). Prime Minister John Howard dismissed suggestions that the outcome reflected badly on APEC's viability, or was disastrous in the midst of the Asian finance crisis:

> Now I don't want that to be seen as in any way signalling a serious setback to APEC. I don't think it is. Given the nature of the downturn in the Asian economies over the last couple of years it was inevitable that there would be, as I said, a dropping back from top to third gear in the APEC car. And that is what happened. But other aspects of the APEC meeting were highly successful.
>
> (Howard 1998)

The media reaction to the outcomes at Kuala Lumpur was largely negative. Many editorials did, in fact, draw the conclusion that the fate of EVSL had demonstrated APEC's malaise.[13] The Parliamentary Opposition blamed shortcomings in Australia's leadership and diplomacy for the outcome:

> the performance by Australia at APEC last week was nothing short of a national disgrace. The outcome of the forum last week was disastrous not just for Australia but for the economies in this region ... [The

government] puts no effort into APEC and it stands back, shocked and horrified, when APEC collapses around its ears.

(Cook 1998b)

The fate of EVSL

Events at Kuching and Kuala Lumpur were widely interpreted as a body blow to APEC. Against a background of perceptions of APEC having failed to respond adequately to the Asian finance crisis, plus accusations of APEC's ill-conceived expansions in membership, EVSL for many had turned from an initiative that was to have restored APEC's credibility into another symbol of the forum's decline. Despite public perceptions, however, EVSL was by no means a closed book at the beginning of 1999. It was only the liberalization components of eight of the Front Nine sectors that had been passed to the WTO (the telecommunications sector had contained no liberalization component; instead an MRA was signed in Singapore in June 1998). APEC still had carriage of the facilitation and economic and technical cooperation components of the Front Nine sectors, plus an undertaking to develop further the Back Six sectors.

At a Preparatory SOM meeting in Singapore in December 1998, a Malaysian representative briefed senior officials on the first steps of a process of taking the first nine EVSL sectors into the WTO. The meeting agreed to develop the economic and technical cooperation and facilitation elements of the Front Nine sectors further, and to do additional work on the Back Six at meetings in Wellington in February. Between Singapore and Wellington, a variety of perspectives developed within APEC economies on what should be done on EVSL in 1999. In the first place, the disagreement between the advocates of flexibility and the supporters of the package approach had not been resolved. The former continued to insist that the liberalization components of the Back Six should be subject to flexibility provisions within APEC.

At the other end of the spectrum were the enthusiasts for the package approach on liberalization for the Back Six. Led by the United States, these economies insisted that the attempt should be made in 1999 to see the Back Six through to completion, thereby salvaging the EVSL process after the disasters of 1998. This thinking was echoed from within Australia by those industry groups that had been the most enthusiastic supporters of EVSL. Following the Kuala Lumpur meetings, National Farmers' Federation Trade Committee Chairman Brendan Stewart lamented that the Kuala Lumpur outcome would harm Australian exporters. He urged the Australian government to redouble its efforts within APEC to ensure regional markets remain open and send a strong signal to the WTO round. These sentiments were echoed by Australian Industry Group Director Leigh Purnell, who said the decision to refer the liberalization components of the Front Nine EVSL sectors to the WTO would be damaging for Australian industry, especially if it signaled a pause in APEC liberalization.[14]

Between these two groups were a number of economies concerned about further damage being done to APEC if acrimony were to plague the remainder of the EVSL negotiations. For these, the broader organization, its aims, and its store of cooperative capital were more important than the fate of the EVSL initiative. EVSL had already been widely interpreted as a failure; a sacrifice of the remainder of the initiative in favor of preserving the cooperative spirit of APEC seemed to be the least damaging outcome. Despite pressure from Australian agricultural and industry peak groups, this was the position increasingly adopted by the Australian government. Given the centrality of APEC to Australian foreign policy, it was inevitable that concern for APEC would eventually trump enthusiasm for EVSL, which was plainly crippled by an enduring dispute between the organization's two biggest economies. An obvious precedent had been established in Kuala Lumpur to refer the liberalization components of the Back Six to the WTO, just as had happened with the Front Nine. Australia's Ambassador to APEC acknowledged these and other difficulties plaguing the upcoming negotiations to a Parliamentary Committee in early 1999:

> [Involved in the carriage of work on the Back Six] will be very difficult issues ... In some respects, having come to that understanding at a top political level in Kuala Lumpur, the logical thing to do with the remaining six sectors is to think how they can be progressed to a stage where you have something useful to transfer to the WTO at an appropriate moment.
>
> (Hewitt 1999)

Much of the solution to the problem of what to do with the Back Six was hammered out in early 1999, prior to the APEC Trade Ministers Meeting in Auckland in June. There, Trade Ministers agreed that the atmosphere within the WTO was now positive for the negotiation in the WTO of the tariff elements of the remaining six EVSL sectors. They took the decision to refer the tariff elements of the remaining six EVSL sectors to the WTO for negotiation during the upcoming Millennium Round. Referral of the Front Nine to the WTO had entailed a name change for EVSL to 'Accelerated Tariff Liberalization' (ATL). Determined to salvage some of the EVSL initiative within APEC, officials and Ministers developed a table of non-tariff measures, facilitation and economic and technical cooperation measures for the fifteen EVSL sectors, and compiled a list of 'deliverables' based on the EVSL sectors.

The reasons for admitting defeat on EVSL and passing the liberalization component of the initiative to the WTO were many. One was the desire to avoid further damaging disputes during the organization's tenth anniversary year; another was a sensitivity to further 'airing APEC's dirty linen' in the lead up to WTO talks. However, a major price for passing on EVSL was to clear the air for a major initiative in 1999: to press for negotiations on industrial (non-agricultural) tariffs to be launched at the third WTO Ministerial Meeting in Seattle in November 1999. The immediate difficulty would be convincing some of the APEC developing economies to support APEC's call for the inclusion of industrial tariffs negotiations in the Millennium Round.

But the United States was not as willing to abandon early trade liberalization in favor of a more comprehensive Round. Meeting in Auckland in September, APEC Trade Officials and Trade Ministers failed to reach consensus on a common APEC position in the WTO Millennium Round negotiations. The United States continued to push for an 'early harvest' sectoral approach to be included in the Round. This was resisted by APEC members advocating a comprehensive approach to liberalization rather than a consecutive sectoral approach. Here was one of the splits over EVSL revisited in another context. A compromise was suggested by New Zealand Trade Minister Warwick Smith, who proposed that member economies be allowed to take non-binding provisional liberalization measures ahead of final comprehensive ratification of the Millennium Round outcomes.

In this situation, it became Australia's interest to try to engineer some sort of compromise in support of the larger goals to be achieved in the upcoming WTO Round. To include industrial tariffs negotiations in the Millennium Round was a task that would require APEC working at full capacity in its role of supplying critical mass within the broader multilateral community. Allowing controversy over 'early harvest' to derail this, in a way made all too predictable by the progress of EVSL in 1998, would be to mortgage these larger goals to continuing division in APEC. In this situation, Australia began to try to persuade the United States to accept the decline of the EVSL initiative, and to accept a compromise deal on 'early harvest.' In this, Australian officials were able to call on close relations built up with US officials in the course of APEC negotiations. The United States had always been informed and consulted on Australian initiatives, and there tends to be a significant convergence of views between Australian and US trade officials, despite specific trade disputes between the two economies.[15] It was in this context that Australian officials argued to their counterparts that compromise within APEC would be conducive to securing broader WTO goals.

The decision to refer the Back Six sectors to the WTO had taken the pressure off APEC trade negotiators, and significantly improved the atmosphere of negotiations from the time of the June meeting in Auckland. Conditions were much more conducive to creative compromise. The battle on gaining APEC advocacy on including industrial tariffs in the upcoming Round had largely been won by the time of the June Trade Ministerial, which declared:

> Ministers agreed that the negotiation agenda should be broader than that already specified in the built-in agenda principally on agriculture and services, and that these areas and negotiations on industrial (non-

agricultural) tariffs should serve as an integral part of the forthcoming
[WTO] negotiations.

(APEC Trade Ministers Meeting 1999)

The fate of the Back Six thus followed that of the Front Nine on trade liberalization. Not as much work had been done on the Back Six, and further
work was discouraged by the fact that all of the Back Six sectors excluding
oils and oilseeds would be included in the industrial tariffs negotiations (the
food sector was largely processed foods, included in non-agricultural negotiations).

By the time of their meeting in September in Auckland, officials and
Trade Ministers had hammered out a common position for APEC on the
Millennium Round. They agreed that APEC would push for a speedy but
comprehensive round of negotiations, including on industrial tariffs, to be
ratified as a single package within three years. The compromise to allow the
United States position was that while APEC would advocate a fast, comprehensive package of negotiations – meaning that no single parts of the agenda
would be enacted until all of the negotiating agenda was negotiated and
resolved – some ATL sectors and measures could be completed and implemented on a provisional basis. This meant that the ATL tariff reductions
could be made early, but would not be bound until the whole package was
finalized (APEC Ministerial Meeting 1999). This was the ultimate fate of
the EVSL initiative that had been launched with so much expectation. The
Auckland APEC Leaders Declaration in September 1999 did not mention
EVSL, instead calling for 'a balanced and sufficiently broad-based agenda
and be concluded within three years as a single package which does not
preclude the possibility of early results on a provisional basis' (APEC Leaders
Meeting 1999).

The reaction of Australian APEC policy makers and officials to
widespread perceptions in Australia that EVSL had been a failure was to
stress APEC's continued viability. Responding to a question in Parliament,
Foreign Minister Alexander Downer expressed 'disappointment' about the
outcome on EVSL, but stressed the other 'low profile' successes of APEC.[16]
APEC Ambassador Joanna Hewitt characterized the decision to refer EVSL
liberalization to the WTO as a positive outcome, because it implied that the
Japanese government had agreed to consider the liberalization of the fisheries and forestry sectors within the WTO (Hewitt 1999). Furthermore,
referral to the WTO would mean that the EU would be involved in ATL
discussions and bound to any outcomes agreed (Hewitt 1999). Other officials took encouragement from the fact that the robust discussions on EVSL
had forced a number of APEC economies to 'define their positions' with
respect to a number of sensitive sectors. The statements of support of sixteen
of the APEC economies for ATL in the WTO salvaged at least on-paper
support of original objectors to the concept of EVSL, others claimed. Finally,
APEC's existence would also continue to attune the supporters of sub-

regional trade blocs to the costs of trade-diverting policies (Garnaut 1999: 23).

Despite such reassurances, criticism was inevitable from strong APEC supporters, worried about EVSL's effect on APEC more generally. Such concern generally surfaced in the deliberations of Parliamentary Committees and among academics. Senator John Hogg, an ALP member of the Foreign Affairs, Defense and Trade Legislation Committee, voiced such concerns thus:

> the impression that has been created is that APEC as a reform body has stalled ... given that difficulty of the consensus arrangements, the consensus environment, given the fact that when the first major hurdle came after all the economies had agreed to early voluntary sectoral liberalisation, when it got to the hard issues, the appearance definitely is there that it stumbled.[17]

Other questions asked by Parliamentarians in the same Committee were motivated by similar concerns over whether the EVSL episode had damaged APEC or the progress towards the Bogor deadlines.[18] Others worried over whether EVSL had reflected a weakening of Japan's interest in APEC.[19]

A variation on these concerns was questions about how the fate of EVSL would affect the perceptions of the organization in other economies. These were speculations about whether the frustration of APEC on EVSL would impair APEC's ability to deter the formation of discriminatory sub-regional trade agreements and bilateral pressures (Garnaut 1999: 23–4). Such fears were heightened by some of the developments in 1999, such as the increased discussion of a Northeast Asia Free Trade Area and the formalization of 'ASEAN plus Three' consultations. The desire to avoid such occurrences had been an original reason for Australia supporting the formation of APEC; the fear of Australian exclusion from the area of its greatest trade intensity is a constant underlying theme of Australian foreign policy. Reminders of East Asian Economic Caucus-type structures are a great cause of concern for Australian APEC supporters:

> One large risk of the current disillusionment [with APEC] is that it will encourage exclusive regional arrangements within East Asia. The East Asian Economic Caucus has enhanced credibility and new importance as a consequence of perceptions that APEC has failed. The annual meetings of ASEAN countries, Japan, China, and Korea, is the East Asian Economic Caucus at work.
>
> (Garnaut 1999: 28)

The Parliamentary Opposition in Australia interpreted the EVSL outcome as a failure of Australian trade diplomacy from the start. An ALP Policy Discussion Paper released in June 1999 regarded EVSL as having been flawed from an early point from Australia's point of view: '[When], in 1997, APEC members identified fifteen sectors in which EVSL would proceed ... None of Australia's priorities were included in the first tranche of sectors. The second tranche only tangentially addressed our interests' (Cook 1999). Contributing to this was a failure of Australia to show leadership, according to Kim Beazley, the Leader of the Opposition:

> at the 1998 meeting, the EVSL proposals failed to receive endorsement and were referred to the WTO. This means we have been marking time in APEC for three years now. Australia used to be the point-man for APEC – no-one plays that role today.
>
> (Beazley 1999)

Australian industry reacted with disappointment to the EVSL outcomes. This was greatest among EVSL's strongest original supporters in the food and agricultural sectors. The National Farmers' Federation interpreted the decision to refer liberalization to the WTO at Kuala Lumpur as potentially very harmful to Australian exporters. The Australian Industry Group agreed, stating that the inability to deliver EVSL would be damaging for Australian industry, especially if it signaled a check to APEC's momentum for liberalization.[20] Others, such as the Australian Food and Grocery Council's Mitch Hooke, were more philosophical, arguing that 'reality got hold of' the EVSL initiative. He remained optimistic about the prospects for ATL specifically and the WTO in general. Others, such as the Australian Chamber of Commerce and Industry, were unconcerned about the fate of EVSL, as long as no damage had been done to the IAPs process, on which it had concentrated at all times. More generally, the passing of EVSL went unremarked by the public and the media. The press coverage of the Auckland meetings was largely dominated by news of efforts to put together a peace-keeping force for East Timor. Reflecting its extremely limited issue depth in Australia, EVSL slipped from view with scarcely a ripple.

Conclusions

The enduring puzzle of Australia's experience with the EVSL initiative is why Australia, which had invested so much diplomatic capital and energy in building APEC and securing the commitment of regional economies to the organization, failed to play a greater role in averting the rupture over EVSL. From the beginning, Australian policy makers were aware of the potential sensitivity of proposing the accelerated liberalization of some sectors to various Asia-Pacific economies. In developing Australia's own sectoral nominations, officials had been careful to interrogate Australian sectoral nominations for areas of sensitivity for other economies, bracketing and excluding those tariff lines that were thought to be controversial. The question is why this process did not occur again at the Senior Officials' level, when the culling of the forty-eight sectors reduced them to a package of fifteen. Trade officials of all APEC economies were well aware of the various sensitivities of Asia Pacific economies; it is not clear what it was about the EVSL modality that they thought would enable economies such as Japan to overcome these traditional difficulties in this instance.

For Australia, the option of pushing forward with EVSL reflected a number of specific circumstances in its domestic and regional policy agendas. Domestically, the upheavals of the One Nation Party episode plus the debates over TCF and PMV tariff cuts (and the wisdom of economic reform generally) had upset the comfort of the elite consensus on regional engagement and economic liberalization. The ALP's landslide electoral defeat in March 1996 had been taken by some to show that Keating's 'big picture' had gone too far.[21] By 1997 there was a sense of a lack of long-term vision about Australia's interests and how they would be achieved.

Events in 1996 and 1997 were also beginning to dissipate Australia's regional momentum. A series of foreign policy blunders set the new government on the back foot: China's anger over Australian support for the US intervention in the Taiwan Straits crisis in March 1996; strong protests from several Asian countries over its sudden decision to discontinue Australia's Development Import Finance Facility aid program; and the announced 'strengthening' of the Australia–US alliance interpreted by China as part of a coordinated 'containment' policy. The underwhelming IAPs submitted at the Subic Bay APEC Ministerial Meeting brought to an end the period of APEC's energization and decisiveness that had been ushered in at Bogor in 1994.

In these contexts, it is possible to understand why Australia supported EVSL, in the hope that it would provide some of the direction and momentum that had been lost, at least in terms of Australia's regional strategy. The uncontroversial nature of EVSL in the Australian domestic context seemed to provide additional incentives to support the initiative. The domestic homogeneity of the issue furnishes one part of the answer to why Australian policy makers were so uncompromising in their promotion of the EVSL package until the Kuala Lumpur Leaders Summit, but there are other answers as well.

At this stage it is important to emphasize that APEC has always been only partly about trade liberalization for Australia. More important are its objectives of preventing the rise of exclusionary trade blocs in the region, reconciling cross-Pacific trade tensions, and maintaining US engagement with the Asia-Pacific region. These are objectives that were, and still are, potentially competing. One reason why Australia historically was so proactive in advancing the APEC process was in an attempt to develop APEC in a way that kept all of these objectives in balance. By the mid-1990s, as APEC matured, some of these incompatibilities became less and less capable of being reconciled. In particular, US impatience with the consensual, flexible nature of APEC began to eat into its commitment to the organization.

Australia's vigorous support for the EVSL process represented a loss of balance between its objectives for APEC. As Asian engagement became less of a pressing priority with the onset of the Asian economic crisis, Australia began to pursue other objectives with much greater vigor. One was Australia's tangible economic benefits from APEC. This tied in with the Coalition government's pledge in its White Paper to base Australian foreign policy on the national interest, defined as security, prosperity and jobs for the Australian population. The Liberal/National Coalition's desire also to appeal to its National Party rural heartland further led to a more vigorous targeting of agricultural trade distorting measures and barriers, particularly in Europe and Northeast Asia. The other major objective was to preserve US commitment to the Asia Pacific, and in particular Australian access to, ease of communication with, and interoperability with US policy making in the region. Both imperatives led to support for EVSL – as a way of dismantling trade barriers and keeping the US interested in APEC.

The EVSL episode, and its denouement in September 1999, represents one symptom in a much broader malaise that has beset Australia's regional policy at the turn of the century. Other symptoms included the atmospherics that attended the launching of INTERFET (peace-keeping force to East Timor), and some of the rhetoric concerning the impact of the Asian financial crisis.[22] There are strong grounds for believing, with the moribund state of APEC and the rise of ASEAN plus Three, that Australia has fallen a long way behind developments in the western Pacific. For a state whose future will be, for better or worse, tied into that of this region of the world, there is much to be learnt from a reconsideration of what happened in the EVSL episode.

Notes

1 The One Nation Party was formed in Australia in late 1996, under the leadership of Independent MP Pauline Hanson. Its policies committed it to a number of values from Australia's political past: an end to reconciliation between Aboriginal and non-indigenous Australians; a re-imposition of trade barriers; and an end to Asian engagement. After a political high-water mark when it won almost one-quarter of the vote in the Queensland state elections in late 1997, the One Nation Party saw a decline into factionalism, mutual recriminations and investigations into the fraudulent use of party finances by 1999.

2 See Wesley (2001).

3 The Productivity Commission, an independent Commonwealth agency, is the Australian Government's principal review and advisory body on microeconomic policy and regulation. It began its life as the Tariff Board, and has been through progressive incarnations as the Industry Assistance Commission and the Industry Commission before becoming the Productivity Commission.

4 APEC Secretariat Website (http://www.apecsec.org.sg/), September 1999.

5 The Industry Commission published Reports on PMV tariffs in May 1997 and on TCF tariffs in September of the same year. Both industries are highly politically sensitive in Australia: they are on average uncompetitive by world standards, but are high-volume employers of lower-skilled workers in depressed regions. PMV tariffs averaged at 25 per cent in 1996; TCF tariffs at 35 per cent; both represent significant peaks in an Australian tariff structure largely reduced to the 0–5 per cent range by two general tariff reductions,

in 1988 and 1991. The job losses involved in the tariff reductions proposed by the Industry Commission Reports aroused a wave of public sympathy and opposition to further deregulation and opening of the economy and 'economic rationalism.' Significantly, many business and political leaders chose the occasion of the debates to attack APEC for having opened up Australian markets while the markets of other APEC members remained largely closed to Australian exporters. Reacting to this criticism, the government elected to freeze PMV and TCF tariffs between 2000 and 2005, after which further reviews would be made.

6 Personal interview, 8 December 1999.

7 These comments were made in the course of confidential interviews with industry representatives. It is important to note that they were made in late 1999 – possibly with the benefit of hindsight. A number of DFAT officers involved in the industry consultations expressed surprise that these views had been voiced.

8 See, for example, Industry Commission (1997).

9 This quote from an unnamed official appeared in Geoffrey Barker, 'Japanese Refusal Seen as a Threat to APEC', *Australian Financial Review*, 15 October 1998.

10 M. Dwyer, 'APEC Trade Reform Plan Condemned,' *The Australian Financial Review*, 31 July 1998.

11 T. Boyd, 'Japan Won't Budge on Fish and Forests,' *The Australian Financial Review*, 2 November 1998.

12 M. Dwyer and J. Gray, 'Crunch Time for APEC,' *The Australian Financial Review*, 12 November 1998.

13 See, for example, Editorial, 'APEC Needs Leadership', *The Australian Financial Review*, 13 November 1998, and Editorial, 'APEC's Free Trade Retreat', *The Australian Financial Review*, 17 November 1998.

14 M. Dwyer, 'More Fast-Track Trouble at APEC Forum,' *The Australian Financial Review*, 16 September 1998.

15 These include disagreements over the US Export Enhancement Program and more recently a dispute over Australian industry subsidies paid to a leather manufacturer exporting its goods into the US market, which the US threatened to take to the WTO.

16 *Hansard*, 24 November 1998.

17 'Speech to Senate,' *Hansard*, 24 November 1999.

18 Foreign Affairs, Defence and Trade References Committee, 28 May 1999.

19 Foreign Affairs, Defence and Trade References Committee, 15 February 1999.

20 M. Dwyer, 'More Fast-Track Trouble at APEC Forum,' *The Australian Financial Review*, 16 September 1998.

21 Prime Minister Paul Keating became associated during his period of office (1991–6) with a 'big picture' vision of Australia's closer engagement with the Asia-Pacific region, along with a much more independent and self-confident approach to domestic issues and the outside world. Often the term was used disparagingly by his critics to imply that in pursuing such goals he had lost sight of the day-to-day concerns of ordinary people.

22 For details, see Wesley (2001).

7 Korea

Trade policy to draw political support

Yutaka Onishi

Introduction

In June 1998, Korea hammered out full-scale participation in EVSL for the first time at the Cabinet Minister level, surprising the members of the APEC Meeting of Ministers Responsible for Trade in Kuching, Malaysia. Furthermore, in the conferences in Kuala Lumpur in November 1998, Korea proposed trade liberalization of its most sensitive sectors, including fish and fish products and forest products. This action was so dramatic that it prompted Charlene Barshefsky, United States Trade Representative (USTR), to call it 'the proposal which couldn't be believed.'[1] Korea suddenly showed a positive movement toward liberalization, while it had had a negative position towards opening its market further since the Uruguay Round.

This position contrasted sharply with that of Japan. Particularly in the forest products and the fish and fish products sectors, Japan has consistently expressed unwillingness to participate in liberalization since the APEC Informal Leaders Meeting at Vancouver in November 1997. Japan continued in this stance until November 1998, when its traditional policy forced the negotiations to break down.

Japan and Korea have similar problems and political environments in terms of primary industries: these sectors in both countries consist of small self-employed companies (run by farmers and fishermen) whose numbers are declining; the sectors domestically enjoy the status of the most highly protected industries; and both countries suffer from a low food self-sufficiency rate. Though the numbers of farmers and fishermen are small, they have a disproportionate level of political influence. Therefore, both governments had kept insisting on protectionism for primary goods on almost all trade negotiations.

It was natural for Korea to sustain protectionist policies in line with those of Japan. Why did Korea, conversely, propose extreme trade liberalization? Further, the policy of liberalization in the first half of 1998 was modified at the end of 1998, and again changed in the Millennium Round of the World Trade Organization (WTO), shifting back to a protectionist position similar to Japan's. Why did policy conversion take place in this way?

Theories

This chapter explains why the Korean government changed its trade policy regarding EVSL, which was proposed in the APEC Informal Leaders Meeting at Subic, The Philippines in 1996. After the initial proposal at Subic, the identification of targeted sectors in EVSL was to be decided upon in the Montreal Meeting of Ministers Responsible for Trade in May 1997. Based on the experience of APEC regarding liberalization of the communication industries, which had played a positive role in the Information Technology Agreement (ITA) negotiations, EVSL was aimed at promoting the complete liberalization of trade and investment in the region, as set out in the Bogor Declaration of 1994. The Ministerial Meeting in Vancouver recognized the sectors for early voluntary liberalization, and the program was to be decided by the end of 1998, with the intention of implementing it in 1999. But some differences were evident concerning the definition of voluntarism and flexibility among the members, which halted the negotiations in the Kuala Lumpur Ministerial Meeting in 1998, and postponed them to the Millennium Round of the WTO.

Korea made a dramatic policy change in the negotiation process. The country wasn't positive toward EVSL until the Senior Official Meeting (SOM) in February 1998. At that time it declared it would not participate in the negotiations over the fish and fish products and forest products sectors, as these were sensitive fields in its political economy. However, at SOM 2 in April 1998, Korea expressed the intention of participating in the negotiations of all Front Nine sectors of early voluntary liberalization on the condition that the reserved lists of items would be attached. Subsequently, a formal expression at the Cabinet Ministers' level for full participation was made at the Meeting of Ministers Responsible for Trade in Kuching, Malaysia in June 1998. At this time, Korea explained that it was seriously grappling with liberalization on the related APEC meetings concerning the execution of conditions in the Individual Action Plans (IAPs) of the Manila Action Plan for APEC (MAPA) that it had not tackled with such attention before (Bark *et al.* 1998).

It is hard to understand immediately why Korea performed this bold shift in policy stance from protectionist to opening its market in the most politically sensitive sectors. Moreover, the Korean government modified the policy again at the end of 1998 back to a cautious line regarding liberalization. Korea then demonstrated a negative stance during the negotiations of the Back Six sectors of EVSL, and even embraced a position opposing market release of primary goods, in line with Japan, for the WTO Millennium Round.

Why did Korea shift to a liberal policy, inconsistent with its previous protectionist stance, and then move back in a cautious direction? That is the subject of this chapter. In order to fully explain the reasons behind these actions, it is necessary to discuss some valid hypotheses that have been used to explain Korean politics and administration.

Leadership hypothesis

It is easy to assume, and has often been stated, that the change in Presidents was the determinant of the dramatic policy conversion in 1998. In this year, Kim Dae-Jung took office, replacing Kim Young-Sam. Kim Dae-Jung was a fundamental believer in the market economy, and he thought that the free market mechanism would strengthen Korean competitiveness on trade. Some would argue that the change of trade policy in 1998 was a simple result of this change in Presidents.

From his speeches and public statements, it is obvious that Kim Dae-Jung promotes free market mechanisms. He has stated that he does not agree with government intervention in the economy, and thinks that it is better to open the domestic market. Many officials in the government have also emphasized the importance of his role in the policy conversion. Theoretically, because of the character of 'the delegated democracy' (Nakano and Yeom 1998), the change in Presidents may have been connected with this big conversion of policy. Indeed, in the past, policy conversions have often occurred in line with changes in President.

Logically, however, there are four problems in explaining theory. First, the former President's stance was never negative toward opening the market. He clearly promoted globalization and made Korea a member of the Organization for Economic Cooperation and Development (OECD), both of which actions were related to the release of the Korean market. And it is certain that the partial liberalization of the financial and rice markets was promoted as an outcome of the Uruguay Round agreement. Korea changed its economic structure in line with the international division of labor (Son and Han 1998). The change in 1998 does not reflect that Kim Young-Sam was a protectionist. Rather, what should be questioned is why the trade policy of the latter half of his era was protectionist in spite of his tendencies toward a policy of globalization.

Second is the President's ability to make such shifts in policy. Even if the direction of their policy trajectory had not changed, we could say that there was a difference in the abilities to make policy changes between the Kim Young-Sam and Kim Dae-Jung administrations. It could be said that Kim Dae-Jung probably had a stronger leadership than Kim Young-Sam. But at the same time the leadership of Kim Dae-Jung was more restricted. For example, while Kim Young-Sam and his ruling party almost always enjoyed a majority in the assembly, Kim Dae-Jung held a fragile political and administrative base since he never controlled a majority in the assembly. Moreover, his government consisted of two coalition parties with different policy intentions. We can hardly support the argument that the leadership of Kim Dae-Jung was stronger than that of Kim Young-Sam.

Third, the policy conversions could be explained by the change in leadership on the basis of the fact that Kim Dae-Jung must have been politically separated from the former ruling coalition. This is true because he was from the opposition party, which meant that, separated tentatively from the policy network and connections of past administrations, he could perform a bold policy conversion. Certainly, by this thesis, we can explain his economic policy, by which he fought against big business groups. However, we could not apply this theory to his market-oriented stance in the fish and fish products and forest product sectors. It may have been true that any networks associated with Kim Young-Sam were cut off for the new administration, but very important parts of the electoral foundation of Kim Dae-Jung were the districts that also held the politically powerful fisheries. If the leadership of Kim Young-Sam was restricted by his policy network, that of Kim Dae-Jung should also have experienced the same restrictions.

Last, the most significant problem of this hypothesis is that the reconversion at the end of 1998 cannot be explained at all. The theory cannot explain why basic trade policy position changed once again under the same President, for no less than one year.

Pluralization hypothesis

The pluralization or lame duck hypothesis is a modified version of the leadership hypothesis. Using this, Kwon and Onishi (1999) explained why Korean administrative reform happened only in the early days of the President's term. According to their argument, Korean bureaucrats act as faithful agents of the President in the early days of his term in order to acquire important posts. But they intend to survive by insisting on the interests of their organizations during the latter part of the President's term. This means that even if they support the President's policy in the beginning, they have a tendency not to support him during the rest of his term. The theory seems to explain the case very well. Certainly it could explain the negative position of bureaucracy on trade policy during the latter half of the Kim Young-Sam administration.

However, it cannot explain the policy shift during the Kim Dae-Jung administration if you examine the purpose of bureaucratic organization. The department in charge of trade in the Kim Young-Sam administration was the Ministry of International Trade and Industry (MITI). This ministry was protective toward weak industries, for information on domestic industries came in easily. As a result, even if Kim Young-Sam had aimed at liberalization in the beginning of his term, MITI might have become protective in the latter half of his administration. However, in 1998, the trade section was removed to the Ministry of Foreign Affairs and Trade (MOFAT). This Ministry was in favor of liberalization under the Kim Dae-Jung administration. MOFAT was the department that was in charge of foreign affairs and was pro-liberalization minded. Moreover, the Korea Institute for International Economic Policy (KIEP), the think-tank that supported MOFAT's policy formation, also promoted liberalization. It is difficult to believe that these organizations would slip into protectionist mode even if the President became a lame duck.

Statist hypothesis

The dominant view of the Korean political economy is that of the Developmental State. This theory insists upon the autonomy of the bureaucratic or state mechanism (Johnson 1987). Based on this argument, the following explanation becomes possible. In Korea, the bureaucracy has autonomy and powerful executive abilities, and forms and carries out almost all policies. To cope with the economic crisis along with the currency crisis, it had to raise foreign confidence in the Korean economy by opening the domestic market. The autonomous bureaucracy used EVSL as a means to accomplish this task.

Another explanation involving a reaction to the sudden external shock of the Asian crisis has been suggested by Peter Katzenstein, who draws upon the concept of organic corporatism (Katzenstein 1985). In this theory, a small state such as Korea tries to follow rather than to compete against the big flows within the international market. Some institutional devices exist which make a cooperative compromise between labor and management possible.

Korea, which suffered from the currency crisis as an external shock, would and did open its domestic markets to gain the confidence of international investors. In order to overcome the crisis, the sacrifice of individual interests was unavoidable to a certain extent. The above argument is made well in Korea and certainly has some persuasiveness as an unavoidable outcome of the national crisis during that period. But there are some problems with the explanations. There was no body in Korea at the time that was capable of depressing any individual interests or of producing a common interest like the autonomous bureaucracy or corporatism. The Ministry of Finance and Economy (MOFE), a body that succeeded to the role of the Economic Planning Board as the conning tower of the autonomous bureaucracy, had already been dismantled under the Kim Dae-Jung administration. Even if we presume that MOFAT, which became the central agency constructing foreign economic policy under the Kim Dae-Jung administration, was at the helm, steering bureaucracy and foreign economic policy, it is hard to argue that it had the power to implement any policies alone because it had a minimal network within the industrial world. In addition, it could hardly explain the re-conversions at the end of 1998, when the economic crisis had not been wiped away and foreign confidence had not completely recovered. The Tripartite Committee of Labor, Management and Government that resembled a device of corporatism was set up at this time by the government, but, according to Kimiya (1999), this organization was not functioning from the middle of 1998 as a corporatist device; and as for the trade problem, there was no evidence that it was discussed by the Committee.

Institutionalist hypothesis

Another analytical framework that could explain the policy conversion in 1998 is that of the new institutionalism, which has recently spread to both Japan and Korea in political science. According to this theory, the deference of decision-making institutions is decisively important for the choice of trade policy. In Korea, when MITI had the authority on trade policy, coordination with domestic industries was very important in decision making, which made it easy to become protectionist. In contrast, when a foreign affairs agency has the authority, it is easy to become liberalist, because domestic policy coordination emphasizes cooperation with foreign countries, considerations of honor in relation to diplomatic negotiations and international negotiations.

In addition, regarding the decision-making process for trade policy, we should also recognize the difference in the degrees of institutional centralization between the two administrations. As the businesses concerning APEC were dispersed among various agencies, there was little ability to integrate these activities and pursue a consistent national policy at the time of the Kim Young-Sam administration (Yang 1997). In other words, while the Ministry of Foreign Affairs (MOFA), MITI and MOFE played important roles in making Korean trade policy before 1997, the job assignments of the three agencies were so complex that no section had the authority to make any decisions about the foreign economic policies that the other agencies were against. For example, MITI had the primary role of coordinating policies domestically before 1997, but the arena for coordinating among the agencies existed in the Coordinating Committee of Foreign Economic Policy, whose Chair was the Minister of Finance and Economy, and its bureau was part of MOFE, not MITI. As for the arena of the international negotiation, on the one side, the Minister of International Trade and Industry presented at the Meeting of Ministers Responsible for Trade, and on the other side, the Second Deputy Minister of MOFA attended SOM as a head. In this way, no one agency represented the state at all negotiating stages. Because there are many veto points here and there over policy changes in such an institutional setting, powerful leadership is difficult to marshal. To a certain extent, this dispersion was dissolved by the Kim Dae-Jung administration. The Office of the Minister for Trade (OMT) in MOFAT represented the Korean government in international negotiations such as the Meeting of Ministers Responsible for Trade and SOM. As for domestic policy coordination, the Prime Minister became the chairperson of the Coordinating Committee of Foreign Economic Policy. However, the OMT coordinated single-handedly as the *de facto* bureau of this committee as the committee's role decreased markedly over time.

Korea changed the system in 1998. The change solved the dispersion of decision making on foreign economic policy. Ultimately, a foreign affairs agency, MOFAT, coordinated trade policy toward a more liberal and internationally harmonized direction. The institutional hypothesis has some persuasiveness in this case. But it faces the same problem as that of the leadership hypothesis examined above. It cannot explain the liberalistic orientation in the early days of the Kim Young-Sam administration or the re-conversion to the cautious line at the end of 1998.

'Maximizing political support' hypothesis

As mentioned above, we examined several hypotheses and found they partly explained the case, but could not explain it fully. In the above four hypotheses we see only political actors such as the bureaucracy, executives and the assembly as the objects of the argument. The interest groups, who are usually the actors appearing in the policy decision process, hardly appear in these explanations. However, Tsujinaka *et al.* (1998) suggest that interest group activities appeared in Korea at the same level as those in Japan and the United States after its democratization. It would not therefore be strange if they influenced its foreign economic policy. On the basis of many case studies by international relations researchers (Putnam 1988; Evans *et al.* 1993; Kim *et al.* 1995), interest groups may play important roles in decision making in foreign economic policy by influencing the formation of the win-set, even if they do not directly participate in international negotiations. Some studies also suggest that Putnam's two-level game can be applied to the Japanese case as well (Kim Ho-Sup 1997; Jin 1998).

However, there are few case studies insisting that any interest group played an important part in the Korean foreign policy process. As for the negotiation process of EVSL, we could say that there were few interest groups influencing its decision making. Because it has not developed sub-governments, the ties between interest groups and the bureaucracy are weak in Korea, unlike Japan (Jung and Kim 1997). As the assembly committees are not active, unlike in the United States, the ties between the assembly and interest groups are also weak. A policy network like this highlights an important characteristic of the Korean presidential system. The executive branch is very sensitive to the support of public opinion, while it can keep very powerful substantial authority over the administration.

Much research on the Korean administration shows that the bureaucrats have the incentive to carry out the executive's intentions faithfully because it has substantial personnel rights to them (Onishi and Tatebayashi 1998). As networks among the bureaucracy and interest groups have not developed, it is hard for the bureaucracy to persuade the executive using network information. As a result, it is easier for the executive's intention to govern the behavior of the bureaucrats. On the other hand, the undeveloped state of sub-government means that the government is uncertain whether its policy has the people's support, in other words whether it has legitimacy. Therefore, the Korean President becomes sensitive to the attitude of the mass media toward the government and toward his approval rating, and his polices also have a tendency to focus on maximizing the people's support. For example, Kim Young-Sam became nervous about the attitude of mass media critical of the government after he became President (Yoon 1995: 50). Kim Dae-Jung also suffered criticism as a Peronist from the opposition party, which opposed his populist policy orientation.[2]

We can therefore assume that the Korean government is a rational actor that chooses its policies to maximize political support. When we consider international negotiations in this light, important variables are the construction of the political support and the strategies of other countries. Consequently, we can compose the game under some limited conditions in order to explain the government's behavior in 1998.

Next, we examine the game regarding the political support of EVSL by using simple utility theory. If critical mass was formed, EVSL was to be decided. Therefore, the states of the worlds that Korea faces are as follows:

S1: Even if Korea does not agree with the liberalization, critical mass is formed to liberalize.

S2: If and only if Korea agrees, critical mass to liberalize is formed.

S3: Agreement fails even if Korea agrees.

Facing them, Korea could choose one of two strategies, as follows:

A1: Korea agrees to the liberalization.

A2: Korea opposes the liberalization.

Political support is divided into two categories toward these strategies. One is the support caused by the recovery of foreign confidence (T). The recovery of foreign confidence in Korea was thought to be connected to overcoming crisis directly in Korea because the financial crisis at the end of 1997 came from the flight of foreign capital. The recovery of foreign confidence generally brought good results from which the Korean government could draw support. The promotion of EVSL was used as the measure for that. The other category is the support that is received from the protection of individual interests (P). For example, the Korean government can get support from the people concerned with fisheries if it succeeds in preventing the liberalization of fish and fish products. Table 7.1 shows the expected utilities of political support in each case. From here it can be said that the Korean government can get more political support when it always insists on liberalization (A1) because A1 is the dominant strategy if it is $T \geq P$; but it can get more political support when it opposes liberalization (A2) in the case of S2 when $T < P$.

Generally, however, we cannot choose any strategy if the probabilities of S1, S2 and S3 are uncertain. In the case of EVSL, the Korean government could not guess them because the attitudes of China, Taiwan and Japan were uncertain. Though the Japanese tendency was not affirmative for liberalization, Japan might give in on the Informal Leaders Meeting.[3]

Table 7.1   *Utility*

	S1	*S2*	*S3*
A1	T	T	T+P
A2	0	P	P

Table 7.2   *Loss (T≧P)*

	S1	*S2*	*S3*
A1	0	0	0
A2	T	T-P	T

Table 7.3   *Loss (T<P)*

	S1	*S2*	*S3*
A1	0	P-T	0
A2	T	0	T

When the probabilities are uncertain, as in this case, we can guess the strategy of the player by using the MiniMax Regret strategy which is chosen to minimize the maximum loss that can take place as a result of the strategy to be adopted. Tables 7.2 and 7.3 show the degrees of maximum losses.

In the first case of T≥P, the actor who adopts the MiniMax Regret strategy should always insist on liberalization because the size of the loss is always A1≤A2. On the other hand, in the case of T<P, the maximum loss of A1 is P–T, and that of A2 is T. Therefore, it is better to take A1 in the case of T>1/2P, and it is better to take A2 in the case of T<1/2P. In sum, under the MiniMax Regret strategy, the actor should choose A1 (insisting on liberalization) when T>1/2P, and should choose A2 (opposing liberalization) when T<1/2P.

This shows that the strategy of the Korean government depends on the support resulting from the recovery of foreign confidence and that resulting from the protection of individual interests. The composition ratio changes with the political importance of foreign confidence and individual interests. As will be mentioned later, at the beginning of 1998 the sacrifice of individual interests was thought to be unavoidable in order to ride out the crisis, which could be said to be characterized by conditions of T>1/2P. Most desirable for the Korean government was a situation in which it insisted on liberalization, but the agreement was not actually concluded (see Table 7.1).

Indeed, the Korean government did not really think that it could disturb the agreement regarding liberalization alone, and thought that insisting on liberalization would contribute to drawing the people's support during the financial crisis. Therefore, it decided to insist on liberalization.

Then how do we interpret the re-conversion at the end of 1998? It is interesting that this situation appeared when EVSL had virtually ended in failure in Kuala Lumpur. The phenomenon that occurred in Kuala Lumpur was S3. The Korean government no longer needed to use EVSL to recover foreign confidence. It had only to shelve the liberalization when there was a convenient opportunity. The best opportunity was brought by the mass media. Most convenient for the government was when *Chosun Ilbo*, the biggest newspaper in Korea, insisted on protecting the economically weak. It became the best material for persuading groups such as KIEP that had insisted on free trade.

The protectionist phase

The following sections cover the negotiation process of EVSL from the Subic Declaration in 1996. During this period, Korea experienced a change in Presidents and a significant change in the administrative organizations of its international negotiating structure and domestic coordinating structure. The first point of conversion in its negotiation policy occurred simultaneously with these changes. Therefore, after observing the internationally negotiating and domestically coordinating institutions of the Korean government, these sections explain how the policy attitudes toward EVSL were formed. The description is divided, in accordance with the points of change in policy attitudes, into three periods; the days before April 1998, the intervening days, and those after December 1998. Among the concrete objects of the policy change, fish and fish products are taken as a case study.

The institution

The most important characteristic of the Kim Young-Sam administration is that the authority for decision making over foreign economic policy was not centralized in the industry agency, though it seemed to be the core of the coordinating process within the state.

Two decision-making centers existed during the domestic coordinating process. One was centered on the Deputy Vice-Minister of Regional Cooperation of MITI. MITI had jurisdiction over almost all industries except for fisheries, of which the Ministry of Maritime Affairs and Fisheries (MOMAF) was in charge, and agriculture and forestry, which the Ministry of Agriculture and Forestry (MOAF) oversaw. But MITI's ability to coordinate in this area was limited because its jurisdiction did not cover the agriculture, fishing and forestry sectors. Thus, the Coordinating Committee of Foreign Economic Policy, the second decision-making authority within the government, coordinated between the agencies. The Minister of MOFE was the chairperson of this committee, which made the final decisions on foreign economic policies. That bureau was located in the Foreign Economic Policy Division, under the Foreign Economic Bureau in MOFE. Therefore, coordinating the APEC policies among the agencies was carried out under MOFE, despite the fact that it was not in charge of trade policy. It follows that the agency with no technical ability to coordinate trade policy does not exercise the strongest leadership.

In the international negotiating process, there were different authorities at different stages. In addition to the Informal Leaders Meeting and Ministerial Meeting, the Meeting of Ministers Responsible for Trade and SOM were very important in APEC trade negotiations. On the one hand, the Deputy Second Minister of MOFA led SOM. Alongside him were bureaucrats of the director general class in MITI, MOMAF and MOFE, and a director of MOAF. On the other hand, the Minister of International Trade and Industry was represented at the Meeting of Ministers Responsible for Trade, which the director-class secretaries of the above-mentioned agencies also attended.

These relationships among the Korean actors were complex. Putnam's two-level game (Putnam 1988) presumes that the Level I player is the same as the final coordinator of Level II, which cannot be adapted to this case. MITI was not the final coordinator, nor did it even have a representative at SOM.

The process

At the beginning of the process, Korea's attitude toward the framework of APEC liberalization was not negative. An unofficial group on trade liberalization (Informal Group on Regional Trade Liberalization; RTL) started functioning in the Ministerial Meeting of Seoul in 1991, which Korea chaired. Kim Young-Sam promoted globalization after the Seattle meeting in 1993, and tried to grapple with active liberalization. After the Osaka Action Agenda (OAA), however, Korea rapidly began to demonstrate a cautious attitude towards liberalization. This attitude was also shown in the preparation of IAPs. Korea did not think that market liberalization beyond that of the Uruguay Round was intended for IAPs. In other words, Korea decided to carry out the agreement of the Uruguay Round faithfully as regards of customs and non-customs duty measures that are politically sensitive in the country. In the elements of investment and deregulation, Korea established a basic policy of pursuing internationalization and advancement of the Korean economy by faithfully carrying out a five-year plan of opening its domestic market to direct foreign investment and the economic deregulation plan (MITI 1997).

Because the Uruguay Round and the negotiations to join the OECD had already exhausted Korean economic bureaucrats, they did not want any further negotiations for liberalization. This was an important reason for their negative attitude toward any further changes.[4] Much coordination was necessary for the formation of foreign economic policy in those days, even within the bureaucracy. In addition, after the decision in the Uruguay Round to release the rice market, interest groups such as agricultural cooperative associations were activated, though general criticism against this protectionist tendency came mainly from economists (Cho 1996).

After the EVSL negotiation began, the protective attitude remained. In identifying the sectors for early voluntary liberalization, the Korean attitude was passive. Korea proposed only three sectors: government procurement, steel and steel products, and petrochemicals. It made a comparatively small number of proposals, as shown in Appendix 2. Korea held a steel specialist conference and worked to remove primary products, such as agricultural and fish products, from selection, though it supported EVSL in general.

APEC members argued mainly about the situation of support at the special SOM in Singapore. We can see from Appendix 2 that Korea only showed absolute support for the government procurement that Mexico proposed, and showed support only in the fields of gems and jewelry, the automotive industry, the telecommunications mutual recognition agreement (MRA), competition policy, intellectual property rights and investment. Almost all of these areas have no direct relation to liberalization involving customs duty measures.

In Vancouver, the Ministerial Meeting identified fifteen sectors. At this time there was antagonism between two positions on EVSL. On one side was the group of positive members who supported the liberalization of primary goods, including the United States, Canada and New Zealand. On the other side were the developing economies and Japan, who were cautious about it. Whereas the positive group insisted on including many lists of articles in the identified sectors, the cautious members insisted on limiting the articles to be liberalized (Yang 1997; Ro 1997).

The Korean government did not take the decision positively. Korea had the impression that the positive members for liberalization had expanded EVSL suddenly. Its decision makers believed that EVSL would be accomplished symbolically for one or two sectors.[5] During the Vancouver meeting, EVSL was discussed little, as 95 per cent of the discussions were related to the financial crisis Asian members faced at this time. There was no room to argue in favor of EVSL for the cautious members, including Japan, all of whom were still suffering from the financial crisis. As a result, the fish and fish products and forest products discussions pending for Korea were included as EVSL targets. Korea expressed unwillingness to participate in negotiations over these two sectors, on the basis of the voluntarism that was the principle of liberalization negotiations in APEC.

Conversion to market opening

Korea felt the currency crisis, and on 21 November 1997 formally applied to the International Monetary Fund (IMF) for a relief loan. By the end of 1997, the currency crisis had become a record-breaking economic crisis. From late November to December, the mass media across the country campaigned vehemently against the IMF. They compared it to the Japanese prewar empire. The campaign changed greatly, however, as enterprises increasingly found themselves cash strapped and bankruptcies increased. The emotion of the people who were touched by the crisis propelled them into joining social movements whose aim was to return IMF loans and restore Korea's economic sovereignty as early as possible. Gathering of gold to be exported, blood donation, self-imposed reductions on traveling abroad and the recycling movement were the concrete expressions of this phenomenon. The mass media applauded these movements and praised the patriotic behavior and self-sacrifice of the participants.

Whereas heroes were praised, those who clung to their own interests were attacked. There was an intensive media campaign to rout 'traitors' from the country. At the beginning of this campaign, it was those who retained a luxurious life who were exposed on local news pages of newspapers. But soon after, the criticisms of the mass media shifted to big industrial conglomerates, labor unions, and even to individuals and groups who pursued private interests. The policy conversion was closely associated with this social atmosphere.

International negotiations

The curtain opened on the EVSL negotiations in 1998 at the SOM and CTI in Penang, Malaysia on 14 February just before the Kim Dae-Jung administration took charge. While Korea maintained the position expressed in 1997, taking into consideration that the government was undergoing administrative reorganization and policy conversion at this time (Kim Chang-Seon 1998), it was emphasized that this attitude resulted from the ongoing change of Presidents. In February, Korea was beginning to show its policy conversion prior to the reorganization and the change of administrations.

KIEP had already insisted on policy conversion toward the EVSL negotiation in the seminar on 11 February (KIEP 1998). A succession of opinions were voiced that insisted on opening the market and embodying an active attitude toward EVSL, in order to raise foreign confidence in Korea, during a KIEP seminar that was held just before the special CTI in April. Kim Chang-Seon, APEC team manager of the MOFAT, insisted that it was vital to the Korean national interest to cope with the EVSL discussion actively by securing the flexibility by which Korea could extend the period of fulfillment for sensitive sectors (Kim Chang-Seon 1998). Nam Sang-Jeong, Director of the Regional Cooperation Division in MOFAT, also argued along the same lines. Nam (1998) insisted on getting rid of the passive conservative position that had been maintained after 1995, participating in EVSL actively, and examining how to participate in its sensitive sectors in pursuit of partial participation or liberalization at the Harmonized Commodity Description and Coding System (HS) unit level. It was in the special CTI in April that this change in attitude was brought to light.

Korea demonstrated a dramatic policy conversion in the sectoral specialist meeting held at the same time. Here Korea threw aside its position of non-participation on fish and fish products and forest products, and presented a new position on fish and fish products, saying it would participate on the condition that sensitive items were reserved. As for forest products, Korea expressed a desire to participate in the negotiation in principle, though it insisted on reserving some of the items and on extension of the fulfillment period, and to plan the presentation of a list of items to be reserved (Song 1998a).

In the meeting at Kuching, Korea changed formally from the position expressed in Vancouver and showed willingness to participate in all nine sectors on the condition that the minimum list of items to be reserved must be authorized with regard to fish and fish products and forest products. Korea appealed for more foreign investment by showing to the world that it was working toward opening its market in order to raise foreign confidence in its economy. Full-scale participation in EVSL was one of these expressions. Korea was trying to make use of APEC fully in order to emphasize that it respected market principles and that its economy was open externally. Through bilateral discussions with Trade Ministers of the United States, China, Australia, New Zealand, Hong Kong and Singapore, it tried to get them to appreciate the new Korean position toward EVSL. Korea also publicly provided transparent information on the adjustments of its economic structure, and trade and investment liberalization through the proposal of the examining conference of IAPs (MOCIE 1998).

Korean behavior was the same at the Kuantan meeting. It was eager to participate in EVSL negotiation actively, and to appeal for market openness in order to increase foreign confidence. Korea held the examining conference of IAPs and explained the movement toward economic reform and measures of liberalization, and it also made and distributed materials about its present situation of economic reform at SOM. It explained efforts to extend EVSL participation through two-party talks with important members such as the United States and Japan (Regional Cooperation Division, MOFAT 1998).

Korea expressed concrete intentions to participate in negotiations on fish and fish products and forest products, which it had previously rejected. For fish and fish products, the position of Japan, China and Taiwan was to reserve all items and all contents, whereas Korea limited the range of the list of reserved items. For forest products, Japan presented almost all items to be reserved in this sensitive sector, and China and Indonesia reserved a considerable list of articles. Korea informed all members that it would reserve twelve items for a while, for example conifer timber, lumber goods, plywood, and so on, and also expressed the intention to submit an added list of items to be reserved (Song 1998b).

Korea made a positive proposal through several conferences of related ministries, and participated actively in the argument over EVSL in the unofficial SOM and the Ministerial Meeting just before the Informal Leaders Meeting at the conference in Kuala Lumpur (International Economic Bureau, MOFAT 1999). In the proposal, it explained that it intended to open 85 per cent of the total 320 items in the fish and fish products sector and 80 per cent of the 250 items in the forest products sector by 2001. Korea was the only primary goods importing economy in APEC that expressed liberalization of this magnitude.

As mentioned above, the conversion of the Korean government to liberalism, which began about February 1998, speeded up after it had been expressed officially in June. The level of liberalization finally reached a stage that was hard to understand from a primary goods importer.

The institution

When Kim Dae-Jung took office, he completely changed the decision structure of foreign economic policy used by the Kim Young-Sam administration. The trade section was transferred from MITI to MOFAT whose predecessor was MOFA. MOFAT became the leading player for Korean international trade negotiations and was also able to effect policy coordination between the agencies. In other words, the Kim Dae-Jung administration concentrated the coordinating functions of foreign economic policy.

In the domestic situation, the OMT became the new center of foreign economic policy. Its top official had the authority to coordinate its trade policy as a Trade Minister. The APEC trade and investment team assisted him in coordinating APEC policy. Because the International Economic Bureau outside the OMT also had jurisdiction at the same time, two organizations took charge of APEC policy within MOFAT. The WTO team of the OMT took charge of WTO negotiations. This situation allowed the ministry to coordinate easily. Further, the International Economic Bureau was transferred to the OMT through reorganization in March 1999, and unified with the APEC team by June 1999.

The role of the Coordinating Committee of Foreign Economic Policy, which had played an important part under the Kim Young-Sam administration, declined in importance. The Prime Minister took charge of the committee as chairman and the Vice-Prime Minister system was abolished. The MOFAT APEC team was given substantial authority over policy coordination as there was no technical economic expertise within the Prime Minister's Office. In addition, coordination of the committee became difficult because the Prime Minister's busy schedule prevented him from holding frequent meetings. Therefore, as for APEC, the OMT became the single-handed domestic coordinating authority.

In addition, in relation to APEC, the International Trade Policy Division of the Office for Trade and Investment (until June it was called the International Cooperation Division) was in the Ministry of Commerce, Industry and Energy (MOCIE). But this Ministry had lost a trade section. And the International Economic Policy Division of the Economic Cooperation Bureau was within MOFE, which had taken charge of the office work of the Coordinating Committee of Foreign Economic Policy. In part, the Bureau is involved in APEC-related policy coordination among the agencies, and participation in international negotiations.

Concentration of internationally negotiating institutions was carried out as well. After 1998, the head of SOM was the Deputy Minister for Trade in MOFAT, and the representative of the Meeting of Ministers Responsible for Trade was also the Minister for Trade in MOFAT. As for international negotiations, the leading players were unified in MOFAT.

Domestic coordination

Concentrating the coordination system inside and outside the country within MOFAT may have made promoting a policy to open the market easier because it reduced the veto points of the groups that had protectionist tendencies. But this did not eliminate negotiations between MOFAT and these protectionist groups, who were negotiating hard. How did MOFAT persuade these opponents in this negotiation?

Let us look at the domestic coordinating process with respect to fish and fish products as a case study. In the case of forest products, only the Korea Forest Service opposed liberalization because a base of forestry could not be built up if the industry was to be liberalized soon. Coordination in the forestry sector may have been easier than in the fish and fish products sector, where there are many fishermen and fishermen's associations which are powerful pressure groups.

The main actors handling APEC matters concerned with marine products were MOFAT, MOMAF, and the fishery cooperatives. The Korean Maritime Institute (KMI), the think-tank of MOMAF, was also involved. MOFAT's attitude to this industry was strongly oriented to opening the market because the position that fisheries occupied within the entire domestic economy was small.[6] On the other side, MOMAF fundamentally opposed the liberalization of fish and fish products, because Korean fishery enterprises were small, marine resources had to be protected, and their main trading partners in this sector, Japan and China, were also opposed to the liberalization of marine products (Shin *et al.* 1998). But the fishery cooperatives, which would surely be damaged by liberalization, showed little concern toward the beginning of EVSL negotiations.

Liberalization of fish and fish products was proposed at the CTI in April with gradual abolition of customs duties from 1999 to 2005. Because Korea had already changed its position toward participation in the negotiations,

MOMAF held an explanatory meeting on the early liberalization of the marine sector at Seoul on 19 April and at Pusan and Yeosu on 21 and 22 April. It explained the direction for liberalization, collected the opinions of the relevant associations and provided them with materials relating to liberalization.[7] It appears that few fishermen responded to these activities during this period. MOMAF expressed to MOFAT that it opposed the liberalization of fish and fish products, but MOFAT induced MOMAF to concede. MOFAT insisted that there was no opinion against the liberalization of fish and fish products other than MOMAF's, and that international appeal through active participation in EVSL was important for the recovery of foreign confidence.[8]

Therefore, KMI was asked by MOMAF to investigate how much and in relation to what items Korean fisheries would suffer under liberalization, and what would be suitable to select as the reserved items (Shin *et al.* 1998). The KMI submitted a list of sixty-one items (20 per cent of the total 320 items eligible for liberalization) that would suffer from liberalization.[9] This list of items was selected as the primary reserved list. MOMAF asked the National Federation of Fisheries Cooperatives (NFFC) to order the items on the list according to the degree of expected damage from liberalization.[10]

MOMAF was disgusted by the indifference to EVSL shown by fishing groups such as fishery cooperatives. MOMAF coordinated among the agencies to slow the speed and limit the degree of liberalization of fish and fish products as much as possible. But it felt that other ministries could not understand its assertion unless the marine groups and fishermen explained the present condition of the fisheries.[11] At this time, the government was formulating a plan to reserve only thirty-two fish and fish product items (10 per cent of all items) from the liberalization process.[12] NFFC at this stage made a direct request to MOFAT that the reserved list of items include at least forty-five items (15 per cent of all items). Finally, KMI selected forty-eight articles that were to be reserved in accordance with the request of MOMAF (Shin *et al.* 1998).

We can see from the above process that MOFAT, who insisted on the recovery of foreign confidence in Korea, persuaded MOMAF, who emphasized the damage to the fisheries. Strangely, such interest groups as the fishery cooperatives did not provide support for MOMAF in the coordinating process. MOFAT rejected the assertions of MOMAF on potential damage to the fishermen's interest because there were no protests from fishery groups. While the EVSL consultations progressed, the mass media also showed scant concern with EVSL, and made no comments on the damage that fishermen would potentially sustain from liberalization. Conversely, the egoistic behavior of officials, bank clerks and labor unions was criticized for disputing administrative reform and the merger of banks, as well as for labor disputes concerned with introducing the new dismissal system, which were ongoing at the time. The mass media continued to be critical of the activities of the interest groups. In this situation, the government could get more political support by insisting upon trade liberalization for the recovery of foreign confidence than by taking the individual interests into consideration.

Modification of a line

At the end of 1998, Korea modified its intention to open its market. The mass media changed the tone of their argument toward protecting the country's weak members after the tangle of Japan–Korea fishing negotiations, which played an important role in the shift.

The concern of the Korean fishermen was directed toward the negotiations between Japan and Korea immediately after Japan decided to close the negotiations and end the Japan–Korea fishing agreement, at the beginning of 1998. Japan began capturing Korean fishing boats that had entered Japan's territorial waters by precise application of the new United Nations' Law of the Sea. From this time, therefore, the Korean government began to negotiate with the Japanese government in order to promote fishermen's interests and to avoid the absence of any agreement on fishing (Jin 1998). In the beginning, the Kim Dae-Jung administration criticized the Japanese attitude, but did not grapple with the negotiations. However, the declining catches of Korean fishermen and the successive capture of Korean fishing boats by the Japanese government forced it to reopen the negotiations. Though the negotiations started in July, the two sides remained as far apart as ever. The Korean side insisted on assuring its previous quota for several years into the future (in consideration of the present difficulties in the Korean economic situation), while Japan insisted on putting priority on reserving the fishing resources.[13]

The two governments reached a tentative agreement on 25 September. MOFAT also appreciated the importance of the fishing problem as it took on negotiations with MOMAF in this process.[14] But it was because of the territorial dispute of Takeshima Island (Dok-To Island in Korean) that there was a pending diplomatic problem behind the problem of the fishing grounds in Japan and Korea. Public opinion was also interested in the Japan–Korea fishing dispute. As for the fishing itself, the public seemed to put a little distance between themselves and it because the thinking was: 'The fishermen of our country should also go into the new fishing order that will operate in accordance with the international rule of the United Nations' Law of the Sea.'[15]

However, the government's position began to change greatly when, in order to protect the fishermen's interests, the opposition party attacked the new Japan–Korea fishing agreement through legislative inspection of the administration,[16] and *Chosun Ilbo* began an anti-liberalization campaign toward EVSL.

Chosun Ilbo claimed that the Korean government had made a misjudgment in the EVSL negotiations, proposing excessive liberalization by emphasizing Barshefsky's comment in Kuala Lumpur. According to it, a person related to the government had said,

> In the beginning of negotiations, Korea had a plan to liberate 85 per cent of the fish and fish products starting from 2005, and 42 per cent of forest products from 2001. But because the delegation mistakenly thought that Japan was to submit a very positive plan to open its market at the end, it made and submitted an amendment beyond its ability to perform.[17]

On the following day, the OMT insisted that coordination among the concerned agencies was to begin in June, and that there were no different opinions on the items, which had already been agreed upon within the government. However, a serious difference of opinion came from the Director General offices of MOCIE, MOMAF, MOAF and the Korea Forest Service during the EVSL negotiation conference on 27 November. The Report on the APEC/EVSL Countermeasure Conference stated that all agencies except for MOFAT had requested not to change the degree of liberalization on which they agreed at the related Cabinet Ministers' conference due to the difficulty of explaining the policy change domestically, and MOAF and MOMAF criticized MOFAT's inability to negotiate. In its editorial, *Chosun Ilbo* criticized the attitude of the government, which, it suggested, showed indifference to the nation's weak members.

In this series of articles in *Chosun Ilbo*, there was what could be judged as a misunderstanding which arose from the shortage of specialized knowledge about EVSL. But the important point is that this report completely changed the attitude of the government, which shifted to dealing carefully with the interests of sensitive sectors. Before this, according to the member at MOMAF, MOFAT had begun to appreciate the political importance of the fishermen's interests as a result of the reporting by the mass media on the confusion of the Japan–Korea fishing negotiations.[18]

In January 1999, a secretary-level conference started between Japan and Korea to deal with the operating conditions under the new Japan–Korea fishing agreement, and the negotiations reached agreement at one point on 5 February.[19] However, after the mass media found out that the new agreement did not permit the 'two-boat purse seine' fishing method, which would seriously damage the Korean fishermen, MOFAT began to take this domestically sensitive sector more seriously in the trade negotiation. The mass media also discovered that the defect in this agreement had resulted from a mistake of the negotiators, which threw fishermen's groups into intense protest. As a result, the Korean government asked the Japanese government for re-negotiations. After negotiation were concluded, the Minister at MOMAF, who was in charge of the process, was held personally responsible and replaced.[20]

The government clearly saw from this case how much difficulty arose when domestic political actors showed their discontent with the results of trade negotiations. After this, the Korean government completely switched its trade policy on sensitive domestic sectors to a protective one. It appeared in the statement to search the national interest for the EVSL Back Six sectors (Regional Cooperation Division, MOFAT 1999) and in adoption of the policy 'to insist on handling forest products and marine products differently from the industrial goods market in consideration of their peculiarity' on the second Coordinating Committee of Foreign Economic Policy related with the WTO Millennium Round (WTO Division, MOFAT 1999). It was decided that periodic talks with Japan at the Cabinet Minister level were to be held in the fields of agricultural products, and fish and fish products, with a joint position with Japan being taken on the importance of food security.[21]

Conclusion

This chapter explained the shift of trade policy to liberalization in 1998 and the re-shift to a protective attitude. In this process, it was confirmed that the Korean policy shift could be explained through the government's perception of whether EVSL could draw more political support. The Korean government hammered out a policy of liberalization because the recovery of foreign confidence in Korea was important at the beginning of 1998. But after EVSL virtually failed, liberalization was no longer useful to the recovery of foreign confidence and so the Korean government returned to a negative stance toward trade liberalization because it could get more political support by insisting on protecting individual interests than by insisting on liberalization.

The conclusion drawn in this chapter is very simple. Not every state's case leads to this simple conclusion. The implication we must consider from here is what this simplicity is based upon.

First, we must consider the undeveloped condition of the sub-government in the Korean decision-making process. Putnam's model is formulated on the premise that the domestic political process is pluralistic to a certain extent; as we see, it is based on the American foreign policy process. However, sub-governments do not develop in all countries. We could say instead that many developing countries have not developed sub-governments. In this case, there can be a majority coalition that forms the win-set but which does not consist of individual interests.

Second, the very special conditions of the currency crisis promoted emergence of 'the national interest' in the recovery of the foreign confidence in Korea, which exceeded any individual interest. It is usually difficult to get political support if you ignore the individual interests in Korea, where many interest groups exist, while little sub-government has developed.

Third, Korea is not a substantial veto power like Japan and the United States in trade negotiations. Korea is 'a small state' (Katzenstein 1985) that must follow the big flow in international society when critical mass is formed, even if it would rather seriously resist it.

The above points seem to suggest that we should modify the theory of the two-level game when it is applied to developing countries. This will have to be verified through various cases.

Notes

1 *Chosun Ilbo*, 2 December 1998.
2 *Digital Chosun Ilbo*, 20 January 2000.
3 KIEP, interview, 3 November 1999
4 KIEP, interview, 3 November 1999.
5 MOFAT, interview, 29 October 1999.
6 *Soo San Kyungjae Sinmoon*, 27 July 1998.
7 *Soo San Kyungjae Sinmoon*, 4 May 1998.
8 *Soo San Kyungjae Sinmoon*, 27 July 1998. MOMAF, interview, 19 January 2000.
9 *Soo San Kyungjae Sinmoon*, 1 June 1998.
10 *Soo San Kyungjae Sinmoon*, 1 June 1998.
11 *Soo San Kyungjae Sinmoon*, 20 July 1998.
12 *Soo San Kyungjae Sinmoon*, 27 July 1998.
13 *Nihon Keizai Shimbun*, 16 August 1998.
14 *Joong-An Ilbo*, 29 October 1998.
15 *Joong-An Ilbo*, 26 September 1998.
16 *Joong-An Ilbo*, 29 October 1998.
17 *Chosun Ilbo*, 2 December 1998.
18 MOMAF, interview, 19 January 2000.
19 *Joong-an Ilbo*, 6 February 1999.
20 *Nihon Keizai Shimbun*, 3 March 1999.
21 *Nihon Keizai Shimbun*, 16 May 1999.

8 Thailand

Cautious involvement as an ASEAN state

Fumio Nagai

Introduction

Thailand continuously supported trade liberalization under APEC's Early Voluntary Sectoral Liberalization (EVSL) initiative; yet, if Thailand's attitude towards the EVSL process is scrutinized in detail, it is difficult to find instances where Thailand responded positively towards EVSL. For instance, at the Trade Ministers Meeting in Montreal in May 1997, Narongchai Akrasanee, who was a member of the Eminent Persons Group (EPG) from 1993 to 1995 and was also the former Minister of Commerce under the Chavalit Administration (November 1996 to November 1997), said that Thailand, as well as some other ASEAN (Association of Southeast Asian Nations) countries, did not believe the sectoral approach could be applied universally. He also said that the criteria for selecting the sectors for liberalization should be established first in order to avoid future problems.[1] At the Montreal meeting, Thailand was joined by many other developing members in seeking a delay in voluntary sectoral liberalization.[2] Moreover, at the Senior Officials Meeting (SOM) in early September 1998, Thailand was criticized, even by other fellow ASEAN countries, for its reluctance to confirm the proposals on end-dates and end-rates in EVSL sectors except for the gems and jewelry sector.[3]

The Thai government's attitude towards the EVSL process, as shown above, might not be surprising if its past attitude towards APEC is examined. Thailand, as an ASEAN member country, was anxious about the loosening of ASEAN's unity and the domination of APEC by powers such as the United States. In fact, the ASEAN Economic Ministers Meeting (AEM) in October 1993, which was held just before the APEC Ministerial and Leaders Meetings in November, clearly demonstrated ASEAN's fear that APEC would lose its original nature of a loose consultative body. The ASEAN states wondered if APEC was becoming just another body for negotiating trade rules under the leadership of the United States, just like the General Agreement on Tariffs and Trade (GATT). Although Thailand finally agreed to attend the first Leaders Meeting at Blake Island, it took a long time to reach this decision (Kawanaka 1995: 105).

Thailand's caution on APEC was repeated during the EVSL consultation process, and its attitude towards the Montreal Trade Ministers Meeting was clearly illustrated by the comments of Vithun Tulyanond. Vithun, then Deputy Director-General of the Department of Business Economics (DBE) within the Ministry of Commerce (MOC), said that Thailand would insist strongly that investment liberalization should be completed on a voluntary basis.[4] Medhi Krongkaew, then Director of the APEC Study Center, Thammasat University, who also joined the Thai delegates attending the Auckland Ministerial Meeting in September 1999, maintained that APEC was originally managed on a voluntary basis and that member economies should not be forced to act against their own intentions (Medhi 1999: 98).

Nonetheless, it should be noted that Thailand did not oppose liberalization under the APEC framework. Instead, along with other developing members, Thailand sought to delay voluntary sectoral liberalization.[5] Those interviewed repeatedly stressed that Thailand was prepared to go with decisions made by the other members. For instance, an APEC-related official at the Ministry of Foreign Affairs (MFA) said, 'if they can do it, we can do it, too. The more open APEC economies will become, the better the results will be.'[6] Medhi said, 'we did not have any strong objections to anything. At Kuala Lumpur [Ministerial Meeting], Thailand was prepared to follow the agreements on EVSL.'[7]

How should we interpret such a cautious attitude towards APEC by the Thai government? Suthiphand Chirathivat, Professor at the Faculty of Economics, Chulalongkorn University, suggests one possible answer. Suthiphand says that APEC

> is the last, not the least, major regional agenda to come into the global picture of Thailand's international economic policy in recent years. As the last initiative, it [Thailand] is less committed because it [APEC] is a consultative forum which has turned out to be serious about unilateral trade and investment liberalization.
>
> (Suthiphand 1997: 7)

Thailand was an initiator and has been a strong advocate of the ASEAN Free Trade Area (AFTA). At the same time, Supachai Panichpakdi, the former Deputy Prime Minister and Minister of Commerce, has been Secretary-General of the WTO since 2002. Thailand's cautious attitude towards APEC stands in contrast to its strong interest in ASEAN and the WTO.[8]

The aim of this chapter is to clarify Thailand's position on EVSL in terms of which actors participated in the policy making process within the government, and which methods were used by the government to coordinate the various interests among the domestic political actors. Since research on Thailand's involvement in the APEC process has been limited, this chapter tries to identify actors who were involved in the EVSL process within the Thai government, and to provide an overview of how the EVSL process changed in both the international and domestic forums from 1997 to 1998. In the final section, the chapter will, if indirectly, answer the research questions set in Chapter 2 as they relate to the analysis of the Thai government's involvement in the EVSL process.

Major actors

The number of actors involved in EVSL policy making in Thailand was quite limited and consisted mostly of bureaucrats. Politicians, generally speaking, were not very interested in EVSL. Even ministers, such as the Minister of Commerce or Minister for Foreign Affairs, had little knowledge of APEC, and relied, therefore, on the advice of bureaucrats.

Suthiphand stated that the most important governmental actors participating in Thailand's APEC policy making were three governmental agencies, namely: MFA, MOC and the Committee for International Economic Policy (CIEP) (Suthiphand 1997: 3). These three agencies were also dominant in the EVSL policy making process.[9] However, in addition to these three, the Ministry of Finance (MOF) also played an important role in the EVSL process. It may not be surprising that MOF was involved in the process. As it is a developing state, the share of import tariffs in the state revenue has been considerable in Thailand.[10] The agency responsible for the EVSL within MOF, however, was not the Customs Department, but the Fiscal Policy Office (FPO). Deep involvement by a financial ministry in EVSL policy making was a phenomenon unique to Thailand, and could not be observed in Japan, the United States, Korea or Australia.

Apart from MFA, MOC, the CIEP and MOF, other governmental actors were also involved in the EVSL process depending on the sectors intended for liberalization. The fifteen sectors dealt with in the EVSL covered not only industrial goods but also processed and non-processed agricultural products, services and even environmental goods and services. Consequently, the Ministry of Industry (MOI), the Ministry of Agriculture and Cooperatives (MOAC), the Ministry of Transportation and Communications and the Ministry of Science, Technology and Environment (MOSTE) were also involved in EVSL at different times.

In terms of domestic policy coordination, the MOI and the MOAC are assumed to play significant roles. As illustrated by Thailand's attitude towards the inclusion of agricultural products in AFTA, the Thai government has been keen to liberalize trade in the agriculture sector. MOC expressed its high expectations for liberalization in the agricultural sector at an early stage of EVSL.[11] In contrast, Thailand often showed a cautious stance towards liberalization in the industrial sector. However, in reality, the MOI and MOAC seemed to have had a less active role in coordinating domestic interests during the EVSL process, so they are excluded from the following analysis.

Ministry of Foreign Affairs (MFA)

'From its [APEC's] beginning, the major governmental agency responsible for most APEC matters was the Ministry of Foreign Affairs' (Suthiphand 1997: 3). In short, the role of MFA has been to coordinate Thailand's overall policy towards APEC.

Within the ministry, the section in charge of APEC is the Department of Economic Affairs (DEA). This department is also responsible for SOM (University Affairs Agency 1998: 14). Within the DEA, there are three sub-sections, namely the International Economics Section, the Economic Promotion and Cooperation Section and the Economic Information Section. It is the International Economics Section that is responsible for APEC.[12]

Nonetheless, despite MFA's overall influence, it retained direct responsibility for only one element of EVSL – Ecotech. The other two elements, liberalization and facilitation, fell under the direct control of MOC.[13] As Suthiphand notes, this burden-sharing between the MFA and MOC seems to have been established before the EVSL process started:

> As the APEC agenda has become more complex, the Ministry of Foreign Affairs had felt that this [the handling of all APEC affairs] is beyond its own competency. It is shown clearly in 1996 that there was a clear split of work between the Ministry of Foreign Affairs and the Ministry of Commerce. Trade and investment liberalization and facilitation under the APEC process would be mainly under the responsibility of the Ministry of Commerce. Technical cooperation within APEC, on the other hand, will be handled by the Ministry of Foreign Affairs.
>
> (Suthiphand 1997: 4)

The Committee on Asia-Pacific Economic Cooperation was set up within the MFA by cabinet resolution on 2 December 1996, when the preceding committee was dissolved and MFA requested that a new body be established. The Committee is chaired by the Minister of Foreign Affairs, and is vice-chaired by the Minister of Commerce and the Minister of the Prime Minister's Office. The other sixteen committee members are appointed as representatives from other related ministries. These include such agencies as MOC, MOF, the University Affairs Agency, the MOSTE and the Department of Technical and Economic Cooperation. Through this committee, MFA coordinates APEC policy among governmental agencies and articulates its own policy towards APEC. The Director-General for the DEA holds the position of secretary. The committee invites non-committee members according to the related theme, if necessary, and submits a report to the Cabinet on the issue of overall policy orientation and the Thai government's position at major APEC meetings. It is entitled to coordinate policies and implementation principles under the APEC framework. Moreover, the Committee, upon Cabinet approval, is empowered to prepare for the ministerial-level APEC meetings.[14] However, although it is endowed with various powers, in reality, it is rarely convened and seems to play a fairly insignificant role.[15]

Ministry of Commerce (MOC)

In MOC, the DBE is in charge of APEC affairs. The Permanent Secretary of MOC and the Director-General of the DBE attend the ministerial-level meetings of APEC, along with the Minister of Commerce. Within MOC, it is the Director-General of the DBE who is the key figure formulating APEC policy. The Director-General also plays an important role in CIEP, which will be discussed later. The Bureau of Regional Trade, set up in the DBE, supervises the Committee on Trade and Investment (CTI) of APEC (University Affairs Agency 1998: 141). One of the seven divisions in this Bureau is responsible solely for APEC.[16]

At the international meetings on trade and investment liberalization and facilitation that require detailed knowledge and skill, it is the bureaucrats in the DBE who deal with the multilateral consultations. It was these bureaucrats who coordinated interests both with other governmental agencies and domestic business groups during the EVSL process.

Depending on the sector, working groups with MFA and MOI representation were set up in MOC. In some cases, other related ministries, agencies and business associations were also invited. Preliminary meetings seem to have been held from early 1997 to focus on sectors that the Thai government would propose for the EVSL. From January to February 1998, after fifteen sectors were identified for the EVSL at the Vancouver Ministerial Meeting in November 1997, MOC held a series of intensive hearings about each sector with business associations. 'Mostly, they were organized by MOC.'[17] For the automotive and toys sectors, hearings were organized beyond March 1998.[18] MOC announced these hearings by distributing documents that included a list of Harmonized System codes and end-dates for liberalization in each sector.[19]

The Committee for International Economic Policy (CIEP)

The CIEP is a committee composed of ministers. The Deputy Prime Minister chairs the committee and the Director-General of the DBE is secretary. Suthiphand categorizes this committee as a government agency; however, strictly speaking, unlike government agencies, this committee does not have its own permanent organization, whereas the National Economic and Social Development Board (NESDB), for example, does.

> The Thai government, especially the Ministry of Foreign Affairs, had worked consistently in 1995 in order to secure the overall plan for APEC for Thailand, then handed it over to the Committee for International Economic Policy at that time, under the responsibility of

Deputy Prime Minister Dr Amnuay Virawan who chaired the Committee and the Office together with the high officials from different ministries responsible for the APEC Action Agenda.

(Suthiphand 1997: 4)

Since November 1997, however, the Deputy Prime Minister and Minister of Commerce, Supachai Panitchpakdi, chaired this committee. Suthiphand clearly points out that, from the Seattle Leaders Meeting to the Bogor Meeting, 'apart from the Ministry of Foreign Affairs, especially the Department of Economic Affairs, [the] Committee for International Economic Policy ... has become the other major governmental agency to be involved in the APEC policy making process' (Suthiphand 1997: 3).

Various ministers, such as the Ministers of Finance and Foreign Affairs, and the Secretary-General of the NESDB and the Board of Investment attend this committee. The Director-General of the DBE, supported by the Bureau of International Economic Policy as a secretariat, acts as the secretary of the CIEP.[20] Many officials from MOC also attend the CIEP, which has the role of approving documents prepared by MOC.[21]

Besides APEC, the CIEP is in charge of overall policy towards multilateral negotiations such as the WTO and AFTA. The CIEP holds meetings approximately once a month. Before Ministerial or Leaders Meetings of APEC, the CIEP is called to endorse the important decisions of the Thai government. However, matters that require political decisions (and those decisions which the CIEP cannot make on its own) are sent to the Committee of Economic Ministers for a final decision.[22]

Ministry of Finance (MOF)

MOF plays an important role in Thailand's policy towards APEC. As for the technical side of tariff liberalization, the Customs Department assumes responsibility. The Committee on Tariff Schedules, of which the Permanent Secretary of MOF is chair and the Customs Department is secretary, handles technical questions on tariffs. In terms of policy planning, the FPO plays a significant role. The FPO also acts as a vice-secretary for the Committee on Tariff Schedules.[23] Possibly because the liberalization element of the EVSL is closely related to tariff reduction, MOF came to play an important role in designing Thailand's EVSL policy. The FPO, as a representative of MOF, participated in the workshops hosted by MOC from 1997 to early 1998 and was also in charge of the Economic Committee (EC) of APEC (University Affairs Agency 1998: 141). The FPO is considered to be one of the four pillars of Thai economic policy, along with the Bank of Thailand (BOT), the Budget Bureau and the NESDB, all of which comprise elite groups (Suehiro 2000: 62–3).

Within the FPO, there is a Bureau of International Economic Policy, which is further divided into three sections, namely, Economics, the WTO and ASEAN.[24] The Economics section directly supervised EVSL matters, and dealt with trade and investment liberalization and facilitation in cooperation with MOC. Yet the FPO did not have a working committee or group that was involved with business sectors. Therefore, representatives from business never appealed to the FPO directly.[25]

One working group called the Market Access Group (MAG), which was set up in the FPO, seems to have played an important role in EVSL policy making. MAG, which was in charge of the tariff and non-tariff elements of the EVSL,[26] might have ordinarily been put under the supervision of MOC. But, as far as the EVSL process was concerned, the CIEP was assigned to tariff-related matters, while MAG was placed in the FPO rather than in MOC. This seems to have been an exceptional case, however, as the Thai government needed to treat this issue promptly. According to an explanation from an APEC-related official in the FPO, when the Vancouver meeting was over in late 1997, the DBE proposed that the CIEP establish MAG in the FPO in order to conduct research and coordination on the tariff elements of the fifteen EVSL sectors.[27] As this statement clearly shows, the EVSL consultations pushed MAG into the FPO, a decision which was, curiously enough, an initiative from MOC following an endorsement from the CIEP. Various ministries and departments such as MFA, MOC, MOI and the Customs Department sent representatives to MAG. On some occasions, other representatives from other agencies, such as the MOAC, the Energy Agency, the Federation of Thai Industries (FTI) and the BOT, were allowed to participate as observers. The Deputy Director-General of the FPO chaired MAG, and meetings were held a few times a month.[28]

The MAG meetings seem to have involved substantial discussions on the reduction of tariff rates and coordination of interests with respect to the EVSL. In cases of important decisions, it was necessary that the Minister of Finance agree with MAG's conclusions before they could be submitted to the CIEP for endorsement. When the Auckland Ministerial and Leaders Meetings concluded in September 1999, MAG was transferred from the FPO to MOC.

Policy making elites

Suthiphand, who has analyzed the policy making process within the Thai government for the Osaka Action Agenda (1995), refers to a handful of policy making elites, namely Narongchai Akrasanee, Krirkrai Jirapet (former Director-General of the DBE), Kobsak Chutikul (then Director-General of the DEA) and Karun Kittistaporn (then Director-General of the Department of Intellectual Property Rights, MOC). On the topic of these elites, Suthiphand states:

> Strangely enough, they were given quite a free hand to form the APEC strategy for Thailand since there were few people who were keen on the APEC subject. As a result, in the Banharn Government [July 1995 to

November 1996], again they were able to form explicitly the APEC process for Thailand without much intervention from other groups of interests involved.

(Suthiphand 1997: 4)

It seems that the same arrangement applied to EVSL policy making. Naturally enough, since there were few people who were interested in EVSL matters, EVSL consultations were carried out by a limited number of key persons, namely Kobsak Chutikul, Karun, Vithun (the Deputy Director-General of DBE), Charnchai Musignisarkorn (then Deputy Director-General of the FPO, MOF) and some others.

Other than these senior bureaucrats, some politicians were also interested in international economic policy, for example Supachai Panichpakdi (then Deputy Prime Minister and Minister of Commerce), Tarrin Nimmanhaemin (then Minister of Finance) and Surin Pitswan (then Minister of Foreign Affairs). However, these politicians did not have a detailed knowledge of EVSL; nor did they perform as coordinators of domestic interests on behalf of particular business associations.[29]

Interest groups

The Thai government continued to hear opinions concerning EVSL from the business sector through the FTI and the Thai Chamber of Commerce (TCC).[30]

The FTI and the TCC, along with the Thai Bankers' Association (TBA), are summit groups in the Thai business sector, and are attendees at the Joint Public and Private Coordination Committee (JPPCC). The JPPCC is widely known for the important role it plays in the economic policy making process and, in particular, the role it played under the Prem Administration (1980–8) (Anek 1992). The importance of these groups seems to have been reflected in the composition of the APEC Business Advisory Council (ABAC) representatives in Thailand. The three Thai ABAC members were Wiphan Ruenphithya (Vice-President of the FTI), Viroj Phuutchakoon (Bunroj Company) and Twatchai Yongkittikul (Bangkok Bank and the Secretary General of the TBA).[31] Wiphan was a coordinator of APEC policies in the FTI, and was supported by the Pacific-American section (a division of foreign affairs in the FTI). The ABAC secretariat was supported by the TCC. Moreover, the FTI, the TCC and the TBA held a monthly meeting called the Joint Standing Committee on Commerce, Industry and Banking, where representatives from these three associations discussed international cooperation.

Meetings between the government and the business sector on the EVSL issue were held throughout 1997 and 1998. In particular, various business associations participated in a series of 'brain storming meetings' in early 1998. Upon receiving announcements from MOC about meetings, the FTI and TCC disseminated information to their affiliated business associations. The FTI and TCC also collected opinions from the affiliated associations on each sector, and then sent the opinions to MOC and MOI.[32] In cases where the FTI and TCC could not agree, such as when raw materials and processed products companies differed in their opinions, MOC and MOI took opinions directly from those companies.[33]

The development of EVSL consultations and Thailand's response

This section aims to outline the chronology of the Thai government's response to EVSL.

The domestic sector selection process for Thai proposals

The basic stance of the Thai government at the Montreal Trade Ministers Meeting in May 1997 was, first, to oppose the universal application of sectoral liberalization and, second, to assert the need for establishing criteria for sector selection with due consideration to trade volumes and institutions.[34] In addition to liberalization, Thailand also emphasized the necessity of human resource development and technology transfer in the implementation stage of EVSL.[35] The Thai government was unhappy about the US attempt to transform EVSL into a form of trade and investment negotiations that would include labor standards, intellectual property rights, investment and government procurement. Karun stated that 'the United States wants all issues that it could not advance for negotiations in the WTO to be handled by APEC.'[36] In the end, however, Trade Ministers directed their officials to investigate the merits of sectoral and comprehensive liberalization.

In accordance with the request made by the chair at the Montreal Trade Ministers Meeting, the Thai government conducted sector identification from May to July to decide which sectors it should propose for early liberalization. The proposal was to be sent to the CTI and SOM in August. In early June, Vithun said that

> Thailand has not completed its list [of proposals]. The Industry Ministry will try to determine in what industrial sectors Thailand has the ability to compete with APEC members while the Commerce Ministry will study the potential of the agricultural sector.[37]

The Thai government, in consultation with business associations, prepared a list of sectors that Thailand would propose for the EVSL. In early July, Vachara Pannachet, a Thai representative for ABAC, listed seven sectors that the government and business sector had agreed upon, namely medical equipment and supplies, energy, rice, canned seafood, canned fruits and vegetables, natural rubber and frozen fish. He also mentioned that Thailand might also agree to liberalize other sectors before 2020, including gems and jewelry, synthetic rubber, some chemicals and long fiber pulp.[38] APEC-related officials at MFA and MOC released statements that were almost identical to the information in the newspaper article cited above. Prime Minister Chavalit Yongchaiyudh, the chair of the CIEP, approved Thailand's proposal of seven sectors,[39] and the proposal was submitted to SOM by 15 July.

When proposals from each of the members were submitted, the Thai government, in order to clarify its attitude towards sectors proposed by other members, again organized hearings with business associations. On 16 and 17 September 1997, the DBE consulted with the FTI and other business associations concerning various sectors, including fish and fish products, food (including sugar), canned and processed vegetables and fruits, gems and jewelry, wood as well as paper and pulp, energy, medical and scientific equipment and services, fertilizers, and environmental technology and services.[40]

Selection of fifteen EVSL sectors and the Thai government's response

At the Vancouver Ministerial Meeting in November 1997, fifteen sectors were selected for the EVSL. Among these sectors, Thailand gave support to toys, forest products, chemicals, food and fertilizers. The choice of fifteen sectors at Vancouver raises two important questions concerning Thailand's EVSL stance. First, did the Thai government expect that early liberalization of the fifteen sectors would be 'comprehensive'? Second, if it did expect a 'comprehensive' liberalization of the sectors, how did it understand the word 'comprehensive'? On these questions, one APEC-related official in the Thai government said that, as a personal opinion, 'according to the voluntary principle, the Thai government understood that it should agree on liberalization in sectors where agreements were possible and leave sectors on which it could not agree.'

As pointed out earlier, officials in the Thai government consistently argued that APEC should proceed on the basis of the voluntary principle. Yet, it is not hard to imagine that the voluntary principle may contradict the notion of 'comprehensiveness', which is also a principle of APEC liberalization. Nonetheless, according to a Thai official who attended the Vancouver Ministerial Meeting, no member raised questions or argument on this point. Thus, while the issue of how the members might deal with liberalization in the fifteen sectors was left ambiguous, the domestic policy coordination process started in 1998.

Coordination with domestic business associations
(the first half of 1998)

MOC and MOI started to hold hearings with business associations through the FTI and TCC from early 1998. Nonetheless, many parts of the private sector 'could not understand EVSL very well.' As it was not easy for the private sector to understand the AFTA scheme fully though AFTA specified a tariff reduction schedule, area coverage and so on, it was even more difficult for them to understand EVSL, which did not state any end-dates for tariff reduction at the time. There were also technical problems. For instance, the preparation for hearings in the energy and civil aircraft sectors was extremely difficult, owing to the very sophisticated, complex and often overlapping technologies required in these sectors. Since most Thai industries were at the infant stage of development and used standardized technology, it was difficult for local manufacturers to understand the EVSL plan.[41] On the other hand, producers and manufacturers in the gems and jewelry sector as well as the seafood sector did oppose the liberalization proposals. No obstacles were anticipated in the medical equipment sector, as there were no import competing industries in Thailand.[42] However, business was anxious about the possible effects of early liberalization in these sectors on infant industries. As a result, many reservations were put forward in many sectors. Opposition came even from the canned food and fresh vegetable sectors, which were two of the sectors Thailand had originally proposed for early liberalization. The rubber sector also opposed.

MOC held hearings to identify which of the sectors among the fifteen EVSL sectors should be liberalized and which should be protected.[43] From 15 to 30 January 1998, MOC called hearings every day for each sector.[44] Heated debates arose and difficult questions were asked. 'Will you apply the same tariff rates of AFTA to the United States and Japan [through the EVSL]?', one delegate asked. Another raised the issue of tariff rates: 'The tariff rates [which the Thai government was considering for proposal to the CTI and SOM] should not be lower than [those of] AFTA.' Meanwhile, the Department of Fisheries within MOAC claimed that it was necessary to protect fisheries, while MOI claimed that it was necessary to protect manufacturing.[45]

The Thai government's response at the international
consultations (the second half of 1998)

One of the Thai officials who attended the Trade Ministers Meeting in Kuching (22–3 June 1998) said he understood that: 'liberalization of [the] Front Nine sectors of EVSL would not be [as] easy as expected.' Vithun Tulyanond pointed out that the EVSL process still faced three significant problems: first, the product coverage in each sector was unclear; second, the timeframe for liberalization was undecided; and third, the final tariff rate for each product still needed to be discussed, as did the issue of what would constitute an acceptably 'flexible' range of tariff rates, for example zero rates for some members but up to 5 per cent for others. An official from MOC explained that the Thai government asked that tariff rates be reduced on products in the EVSL sectors by between zero and 5 per cent in the period 2003–2005, because 'the government gave the first priority to AFTA, which would achieve intra-regional tariff rates of less than 5 per cent for 80 per cent of all goods by 2003.'[46]

The Thai government's ambiguous response to EVSL can be seen in the speech made by Surin Pitsuwan, then Foreign Minister, at Thammasat University in late August. Surin said that the problem lay not with liberalization itself, but with inadequate preparation for liberalization. He continued to say that it was time to enhance human resource development so that the benefits of liberalization could be shared by all the eighteen APEC member economies in a way that would reduce the gap in development that existed between them. He also said that, to be more balanced, APEC should not spend so much time emphasizing liberalization, but should consider other important issues amongst developing members, including social conditions and sustainable development.[47]

In mid-September, SOM was held in Kuantan, Malaysia. Thailand was severely criticized by other APEC members for its proposals relating to the liberalization element of EVSL. After the Kuantan SOM, a coordination meeting was held amongst the MFA, MOC, MOF and MOI. The purpose of this meeting was to bridge the gap between the targets set by the Thai governments and the CTI and SOM and thereby revise Thailand's sectoral liberalization program. According to a *Bangkok Post* article written at the time:

> Thailand confirmed its intention to participate in all sectors but wanted to reserve tariff rates of 0–5 per cent for a number of sensitive products in each sector. It would not start decreasing tariffs before 2005. With this plan, Thailand would meet the APEC requirement only in the gems and jewelry sector, which would be traded at the final tariff rate of 0–5 per cent in 2005.[48]

The Thai government had earlier maintained that it wanted to start tariff reduction after 2005. This was mainly because Thailand could, in the areas of manufactured goods and processed agricultural products under the AFTA scheme, enjoy similar privileges at an earlier date, because AFTA was planned to come into effect in 2003. The Thai government also wanted to maximize flexibility in terms of the time frame in EVSL to allow developing members to finish liberalization by 2020. Thai officials justified this approach as it would boost state revenue from import tariffs, but it is not hard to imagine that the Thai government aimed to delay early liberalization for as long as possible because 2020 is the year APEC planned to realize 'free and open trade and investment,' as declared at the Bogor Leaders

Meeting in 1994.[49] Such a reluctant attitude on the part of the Thai government to conform to the end-rates set by SOM and the CTI drew criticism at the Kuantan SOM, even from the ASEAN members. As the *Bangkok Post* noted, 'All countries, including our ASEAN partners, attacked us. They thought our early voluntary sectoral plan was inconsistent with our policy image for trade liberalization.'[50]

Kuala Lumpur Ministerial Meeting (November 1998)

As discussed in Chapter 2, the Ministerial Meeting at Kuala Lumpur could not achieve an agreement on the liberalization element of the Front Nine sectors, and it was therefore decided to send the negotiations to the WTO. Although the Thai government claimed that it was ready to comply with the agreement, in reality, the government maintained reservations in many sectors.

According to a matrix of Thailand's 'conformance with the Kuching product coverage, target end-rates and targeted dates,' as of 13 November 1998, the scores that Thailand achieved were mostly low. The exceptions were gems and jewelry (100 per cent) as well as fish products (74 per cent). However, Thailand scored poorly in most other sectors, including toys (8 per cent), forest products (4 per cent), energy (2 per cent) and chemicals (0.3 per cent). On medical equipment and environmental goods and services, Thailand was at zero, a score which illustrated its 'reservations on all product coverage for the tariff component and/or full or partial exclusion.'[51]

Among the Front Nine sectors, the Thai government resisted liberalization in such sectors as medical equipment and environmental and energy goods.[52] Several APEC-related officials said that Thailand tried to exclude 'armchairs' from the 'medical equipment' sector and 'steel' from the 'energy goods' sector. 'Steel' had allegedly been included in the energy goods sector on the justification that steel piping was needed for the construction of power transmission lines.[53] On the other hand, officials at MOC said that Thailand expressed many reservations over the chemical and toy sectors. Thailand also resisted liberalization on particular kinds of forest products. In terms of the toy sector, Charnchai Musignisarkorn, the Deputy Director-General of the FPO, asked: 'how can we compete with foreign products that enjoy zero tariffs?'[54]

Despite achieving little, however, Thailand maintained that some progress had been made at the Kuala Lumpur Meeting. For instance, an official argued that, although the Thai government could agree with only 75 per cent coverage of the energy sector because of doubts about its qualifications, Thailand could agree to approximately 80 per cent of the liberalization in terms of product coverage ratio, a fact which definitely showed that some progress was being made in EVSL. In answer to a question of a senior correspondent from *Asia Week* about the 'failure' of EVSL, Foreign Minister Surin replied:

APEC aspired to be a step or two ahead of the World Trade Organization. In the nine sectors [which APEC agreed to refer to the WTO], they are ahead, but there are certain things in them that need to have wider participation. So, what they are doing now is making the connection to build the critical mass there and move along. [The problem] was over-expectation because the Crisis has reduced what any country can deliver. If the economies had remained as robust as two or three years ago, this problem wouldn't be there. Maybe the early sectoral liberalization was a bit of a bite to chew, but at least they made the attempt.[55]

Why was Thailand cautious towards EVSL consultations?

Three hypotheses

As evident from above description, while the Thai government officially proclaimed that it would support trade liberalization under EVSL, it also qualified its support for liberalization in many sectors. As mentioned earlier, this attitude was severely criticized by other APEC members, including ASEAN countries. In response to this result, MOF, MOC, MFA and MOI held a meeting to consider possible remedies. However, judging from the list the Thai government delivered at the Kuala Lumpur Ministerial Meeting, it could be assumed that the government could not significantly alter its position from the original proposals.

Why did Thailand take such a cautious attitude towards EVSL? Were there any particular reasons that prevented Thailand from responding more positively? It is possible to speculate on three possible reasons for Thailand's passivity: (1) the existence of opposition from politicians; (2) conflicts among or objections from bureaucratic organizations; and (3) objections from interest groups (mainly business associations).

The first hypothesis is that politicians opposed EVSL. Since politicians did not possess detailed and concrete knowledge of EVSL, they had to depend on judgments by high-ranking officials. While there is no evidence showing that politicians promoted EVSL, there is also no evidence showing that politicians scuttled EVSL either. After the Asian economic crisis had just taken place in July 1997, the Chavalit administration was replaced by the Chuan administration in November 1997. This changeover coincided with the Vancouver Ministerial Meeting. Nonetheless, the Chuan administration still supported trade liberalization in principle, despite the turmoil of the Asian economic crisis. In fact, EVSL-related ministers, such as the Foreign Minister, Commerce Minister and Finance Minister, were all key figures in the Democrat Party, whose leader was Prime Minister Chuan himself. As Medhi points out, 'they all supported trade liberalization.'[56] It can be said that no significant differences in opinion on trade liberalization existed amongst these politicians involved in the EVSL policy making process. One MOC official said, 'I have never heard a discussion in the CIEP to slow down trade liberalization due to the [Asian] economic crisis.'[57] Judging from the above circumstances, the first hypothesis that politicians hindered EVSL cannot be supported.

The second hypothesis is that bureaucratic organizations opposed EVSL, or were in conflict with each other during the policy coordination process. From earlier examinations, it seems that some differences of opinion concerning the end-rates and end-dates for liberalization did exist among bureaucratic organizations. However, those differences were not so sharp as to prevent the government from being actively involved in the EVSL process. Only a small number of bureaucrats with considerable experience in APEC affairs were involved in EVSL. These bureaucrats tended to cooperate with rather than confront each other and, in fact, had cooperated closely in the lead-up to the EVSL negotiations. For instance, MOC asserted that certain standards should be set before selecting EVSL sectors, while MFA insisted that due consideration should be paid to an early liberalization of Ecotech in order to equalize the benefits of liberalization between developed and developing economies. Based on MOC's initiative, the CIEP showed flexibility to shift MAG, which should have been primarily under the control of MOC, to the FPO.[58] Strong opposition, like that shown by the Ministry of Agriculture, Forestry and Fisheries in Japan, was absent in Thailand. Moreover, MOI did not insist on protectionism during the entire EVSL process. In sum, Thailand's stance at the EVSL consultations was not unduly affected by bureaucratic opposition or bureaucratic conflict.[59]

The third hypothesis is that interest groups (mainly business associations) opposed EVSL. As far as the author is aware, however, business associations were generally inactive and passive during the EVSL process. The government gave opportunities to business associations to express their opinions on the EVSL at MOC- or MOI-hosted hearings. The associations could have asserted their will through those channels; however, as a person from the FTI who was responsible for APEC affairs stated, 'we [the FTI] were not really involved in EVSL.' As mentioned earlier, the DBE did conduct hearings in September 1997 before the Vancouver Ministerial Meeting and other intensive hearings for each EVSL sector in January and February 1998. Other than these occasions, however, coordination was mostly done within the bureaucratic organizations. In short, the assumption that the business sector influenced the government to take a passive position towards the EVSL cannot be conclusively substantiated.

In summary, there were no conflicts amongst politicians, relations among bureaucratic organizations were generally good, and there was no significant opposition from the business associations. These conditions offered the Thai government's policy making elites a solid basis upon which to pursue economic diplomacy in favor of Thailand's 'national interest.' The most important question, therefore, is why they perceived the cautious response towards the EVSL as being in Thailand's 'national interest.' The answer seems to be closely related to the fact that Thailand considered ASEAN as well as trade liberalization under the AFTA framework to be the most important items on its diplomatic agenda.

Thailand as a promoter of AFTA

By reducing the margin between the ASEAN preferential rates and the APEC tariff rates, EVSL had the potential to nullify AFTA. As seen earlier, the primary concern for the Thai government, while conducting domestic coordination for EVSL, was the preference of AFTA over APEC. During the period 1997–8, when policy coordination for EVSL was being conducted, the ASEAN Six (Brunei, Indonesia, Malaysia, the Philippines, Singapore and Thailand) were to reduce the intra-regional tariff rates on manufactured goods and processed agricultural products to no more than 5 per cent under AFTA's ordinary tariff reduction scheme (this was called the 'Normal Track,' although later, as a result of the ASEAN summit in December 1998, the pace of tariff reduction was accelerated to finish in 2003, rather than the original target of 2008). Charnchai, the Deputy-Director of the FPO, also in charge of MAG, said that 'liberalization under APEC should not exceed AFTA.'[60] This statement is consistent with the Thai government's claim, in reference to the AFTA scheme, that it was necessary to have flexible end-dates for EVSL.

In fact, the Thai government had been maintaining a cautious stance in relation to liberalization under APEC even before EVSL started. For instance, Deputy Prime Minister Supachai, who had played a major role in enlarging and deepening AFTA, said at the informal AEM in Phuket on 27 April 1995 that: 'cooperation within ASEAN is essential and should be deeper than the level set by the APEC forum, which includes ASEAN countries in its membership.'[61] When Naronchai Akrasanee, Supachai, Karun and Wisarn Pupphavesa (a professor at the National Institute of Development Administration) participated in a forum held at Thammasat University in August 1995, they generally agreed that it would not be in Thailand's interest for APEC to accept the US line on trade liberalization. Supachai insisted that 'APEC should not become a negotiating forum.'[62] The Banharn Administration's Deputy Prime Minister and Foreign Minister, Amnuay Virawan, also said that Thailand's liberalization offer at APEC could go beyond its commitment to the WTO, but he noted that Thailand still considered AFTA as its priority.

The importance of AFTA for the Thai government could be observed through its treatment of AFTA before the EVSL process, that is during the period 1994–6. Supachai had, at the Pacific Economic Cooperation Council (PECC) meeting held in Kuala Lumpur in March 1994, already called on ASEAN to realize AFTA more quickly. Supachai's detailed proposals included a call to complete the tariff reduction program within ten years instead of the original fifteen, and to include petrochemicals and non-processed agricultural products amongst the Fast Track items.[63] Upstream petrochemical industries that used polypropylene and polyethylene, which had been included in the fifteen Fast Track goods from the initial stage of the AFTA tariff reduction scheme, were strongly demanding governmental protection. Despite these pressures, Prime Minister Chuan, in his opening speech delivered at the AEM in Chiang Mai in September 1994, supported Supachai's policy not to include petrochemicals in the Temporary Exclusion List under the tariff reduction scheme.[64]

Another major issue at the AEM in Chiang Mai was whether AFTA should cover the agricultural sector. Though Indonesia, Malaysia and the Philippines opposed the intra-regional free trade of agricultural products, the Thai government repeatedly raised the issue and called for fellow ASEAN states to support its opinion by persistently attempting to persuade them of the merits to its argument at the AEM and the Senior Economic Officials Meetings. Finally, the fifth ASEAN summit in Bangkok in December 1995 endorsed the inclusion of non-processed agriculture products in the AFTA scheme.

Nonetheless, the Indonesian government maintained at the AFTA Council held in Jakarta (10 September 1996) that the timeframe for tariff reduction in agricultural products had never actually been agreed upon. When Philippines followed Indonesia's stance, the meeting fell into disorder. On 11 September at the AEM, the Indonesian Minister for Trade and Industry, Tunky Ariwibowo, argued that liberalization of highly sensitive products such as rice and sugar was understood to start from 2010 and conclude in 2020.[65] Yet he also softened his stance, saying that he could confirm with President Soeharto and the Minister for Agriculture whether Indonesia could agree with the 2010 deadline for such controversial items. Thus, in the early morning of 12 September, before the AEM was convened, the participants visited the President's residence to confirm the timetable for phasing rice and sugar into the AFTA reduction program along with the agreement made in the previous year.

Meanwhile, the Thai delegates feared that the extension of the AFTA timeframe would loosen ASEAN cooperation. They argued that if ASEAN members agreed to extend the completion of AFTA until 2020, there would be no difference between the AFTA scheme and APEC liberalization. Of course, it had been the Indonesian President Soeharto himself who played a decisive role in setting the APEC liberalization target in Bogor in 1994. The Thai delegates were afraid that, if AFTA had a similar time schedule for liberalization to that proposed by APEC, AFTA itself might be replaced by APEC.[66]

The Thai government had maintained its policy to give priority to liberalization under AFTA until that point. Yet this position had not, until then, contradicted the liberalization process under APEC. Rather, the Thai government thought that as long as AFTA's value and attractiveness to foreign investors remained stable, APEC could be used positively. In early 1997, Rachane Pojanasunthorn, the Deputy Director-General of the DBE, said, 'if Thailand decides that it has the potential in the agricultural sector, the government should initiate the issue at the forum.'[67] Moreover, Rachane continued in supporting APEC by stating that

> Thailand must take an aggressive position at APEC as the quad coun-
> tries [the United States, Canada, Japan and the EU] [have] pushed the
> information technology agreement and succeeded. Thailand has poten-
> tial in food and agricultural processing as well as hand-made products,
> so we should strongly push for their liberalization under APEC.[68]

At the ASEAN Summit held in Hanoi in December 1998, just after the APEC Ministerial and Leaders Meetings in Kuala Lumpur in November, the Thai government pushed for the complete elimination of tariffs, without exceptions, within ASEAN by 2002. Finance Minister Tarrin wanted Thailand to take a leading position in championing complete free trade within the region to help attract more foreign investment into the ASEAN countries.[69] This was based on the Thai government's policy to accelerate intra-regional trade and investment liberalization, regardless of the results of EVSL. It was ironic for EVSL, therefore, that the Hanoi ASEAN Summit reached an agreement to conclude AFTA in 2002, one year earlier than the proposed timeframe for EVSL.

Conclusion

Though the Thai government did not formally object to the EVSL process, it could be assumed that Thailand feared the dismantling of AFTA. This fear seemed to be strengthened by the dramatic decrease in foreign investment into Thailand owing to the Asian economic crisis in 1997. Foreign invest-ment was vital for the revival of the Thai economy, so it was crucial for Thailand to make AFTA more attractive as a tool for bringing back foreign investment.

In other words, any initiatives that did not affect Thailand's trade strategy would face no objection. However, the EVSL initiative, which covered a wide range of sectors, posed a great challenge for the Thai govern-ment. The Thai government found it extremely difficult to decide whether EVSL would be the best vehicle to advance its economic interests. Indeed, Thailand expected that non-processed agricultural products would be liber-alized through EVSL. But when EVSL sought for a timeframe that would match, or even surpass, AFTA's own timetable, Thailand could not support such a scheme. Thailand also faced another problem. As a developing country, human resources in both public and private sectors were limited. EVSL, which consisted of various sectors, was a heavy burden for the Thai administration. As one of the officials who was involved in the EVSL process stated:

It was impossible to deal with fifteen sectors at the same time. At most, two to four [sectors] were enough for a small country. In developed countries, they can allocate many people for each sector, but developing countries could not afford to do it because we did not have enough human resources. At first I was in charge of chemicals, energy and environmental goods and services, but I did not have any special knowledge at all.[70]

Nor did business associations understand EVSL very well, a situation which may have contributed to the business community not opposing the EVSL process. That the Thai government, though in favor of liberalization in principle, requested more flexibility in the timeframe could be attributed to its observation that the private sector needed more time to master the EVSL process.

While Thailand was cautious towards EVSL consultations on the whole, it seemed that the government was making strategic arrangements that would steadily lead towards trade and investment liberalization under the AFTA scheme. For Thailand, EVSL (or APEC) was, and is, not the sole framework for trade liberalization. Thailand, as a small country, was carefully watching other members' reactions to the EVSL consultations, rather than attempting to fight against powers like the United States or Japan. It may be possible for two countries with similar powers and influence to negotiate or bargain with each other. However, regional cooperation in a forum such as APEC, which includes various members with differing levels of 'national power', is beyond the capabilities of small countries. Therefore, it must have seemed more realistic for the Thai administration to prioritize steady liberalization under the AFTA framework than to invest resources in the APEC liberalization framework. Ultimately, it was this equation that most shaped Thailand's reticence towards liberalization under APEC and the EVSL.

Notes

1 *Bangkok Post*, 10 May 1997.
2 *Bangkok Post*, 13 May 1997.
3 *Bangkok Post*, 21 September 1998.
4 *The Nation*, 2 May 1997.
5 *Bangkok Post*, 13 May 1997.
6 Interview with an APEC-related official, MFA, 28 September 1999.
7 Interview with Medhi Krongkaew, conducted at the APEC Study Center, Thammasat University, 30 December 1999.
8 Charnchai, former Deputy Director-General of the FPO within MOF, who supervised the international economic policy, said that among the WTO, AFTA and APEC, the Thai government gave the most importance to AFTA. Interview at the FPO, 30 March 2000.
9 The CIEP is a ministerial committee and does not possess a permanent bureaucratic office.

10 'In terms of tax revenue (the rate of tariff income in state revenue in FY 1992 was 25 percent), the Ministry of Finance sometimes resisted the reduction of tariffs' (Itoga 1994: 254).
11 *The Nation*, 24 January 1997.
12 The International Economics Section contained several working groups, including the APEC group, the WTO/G7/G77 group, the UNCTAD group, the CODEX group, and the Aviation and Transportation group. Interview with Nipada Kheo-urai, the DEA, MFA, 30 March 2000.
13 Interview with an APEC-related official, the MFA, 28 September 1999.
14 Internal documents of the MFA.
15 The reason that this committee still existed despite its nominal role seemed to be the need to show respect to MFA as the overall coordinator. In reality, the MFA could not control the trade liberalization and facilitation agenda since these are handled by the MOF and MOC.
16 Interview with an official at Bureau of Regional Trade within the DBE, 3 April 2000. The seven divisions are ASEAN, APEC, ASEM, BIMSTEC (Bangladesh, India, Sri Lanka, Thailand Economic Cooperation),the IMTGT (Indonesia, Malaysia, Thailand Growth Triangle), the GMS (Great Mekhong Sub-region) and ASEAN Dialogue (Japan, South Korea and the EU).
17 Interview with an official in charge of APEC at Foreign Relations Section, the FTI, 7 January 2000.
18 Interview with an official in charge of APEC at Foreign Relations Section, the FTI, 7 January 2000.
19 Interview with an official in charge of APEC at Foreign Relations Section, the FTI, 7 January 2000. These documents were prepared by MOC. On some occasions, documents submitted by other APEC members were also attached.
20 Interview at the Bureau of International Economic Policy, MOC, 3 April 2000.
21 Interview with an APEC-related official, the DEA, MFA, 28 March 2000.
22 Interview at the Bureau of Regional Economic Cooperation, DBE, 15 February 2001.
23 Interview with an APEC-related official, Customs Department, MOF, 5 April 2000. Other members represent the Committee of Tariff Schedule, including those from the Board of Investment, MOC and MOI. Interview with an APEC-related official, FPO, 15 February 2001.
24 This institutional arrangement was as of March 2000 when the author conducted interviews at the FPO.
25 Interview with an APEC-related official, FPO , 4 April 2000.
26 Interview with APEC-related officials, DBE, 3 April 2000.
27 Interview with an APEC-related official, FPO, 4 April 2000; 12 February 2001.
28 Interview with an APEC-related official, FPO, 4 April 2000.
29 Supachai did play an important role in bringing forward AFTA's end-date from 2008 to 2003. He was a prominent trade liberalist and was known as an advocate for promoting linkages between AFTA and the CER (Australia New Zealand Closer Economic Relations Trade Agreement).
30 Other sources said that it was the FTI and the Board of Trade that came to be very interested in APEC among business associations in Thailand following the Bogor Declaration (1994) and the Osaka Action Agenda (1995). The TCC was placed under the Board of Trade. See Suthiphand (1997: 2).
31 Interview with an official in charge of APEC at the Foreign Relations Section, the FTI, 3 April 2000. Thus, those figures were as of early April 2000 when the author conducted the interview. Also, see *Bangkok Post*, 13 May 1997.
32 In the MOI, the Office of Industrial Economics (OIE) is in charge of APEC matters. The MOI aggregated and coordinated various domestic interests from the private sector on the EVSL issue, then transmitted these interests to MOC rather than represented them directly at the international consultations. In fact, the OIE, together with the FTI, held

several hearings from business associations on EVSL during 1998, although these hearings were irregular. (Interview with an APEC-related official, the OIE, 27 September 2000.)

33 Even in those cases, the coordination of interests was conducted under the name of the FTI.

34 *Bangkok Post*, 10 May 1997.

35 *Bangkok Post*, 13 May 1997. Thailand also proposed liberalization of the food sector at this meeting. However, the proposal did not enjoy support from some other members on the grounds that it was a politically sensitive issue. *Bangkok Post*, 11 May 1997 and *Matichon*, 12 May 1997.

36 *Bangkok Post*, 10 May 1997.

37 *The Nation*, 3 June 1997.

38 *Bangkok Post*, 4 July 1997.

39 *Bangkok Post*, 4 July 1997.

40 According to the schedule sheet prepared by the DBE, which the author acquired at the FTI on 19 February 2001.

41 Interview with an official in charge of APEC at the Foreign Relations Section, the FTI, 3 April 2000 and 13 February 2001. 'Infant' industries here refer to those industries that still need support and protection from the government for their operations, for example the pulp and paper industry, the chemical industry and others.

42 Interview with an APEC-related official, OIE, 27 September 2000.

43 Interview with an official in charge of APEC at the Foreign Relations Section, FTI, 3 April 2000.

44 Internal documents of the FTI.

45 Interview with an APEC-related official, the Customs Department, MOF, 5 April 2000. The interviewee, however, did not provide any specific sectors for which MOAC and MOI insisted on protection.

46 Interview with an APEC-related official, DBE, 3 April 2000.

47 *Bangkok Post*, 28 August 1998.

48 *Bangkok Post*, 21 September 1998.

49 *Bangkok Post*, 12 November 1998.

50 *Bangkok Post*, 21 September 1998.

51 Several APEC-related officials pointed out that this list did not reflect the latest data submitted by the Thai government. Moreover, the documents the author could obtain did not explain the method of calculating the scores. Thus, it should be stressed that the citation here is just for the purpose of comparing the levels of commitments made by APEC members towards EVSL at a specific time before the Kuala Lumpur Ministerial Meeting.

52 Interview with an APEC-related official, FPO, 6 January 2000.

53 Interview with an APEC-related official, FPO, 12 February 2001. How to treat steel products also became a much-debated issue in AFTA.

54 *Bangkok Post*, 12 November 1998.

55 'Do not dismiss APEC,' *Asiaweek*, 27 November 1998.

56 Interview with Medhi Krongkaew, 30 December 1999.

57 Interview with officials in the Bureau of Regional Economic Cooperation, DBE, 15 February 2001.

58 To supervise tariff reductions under APEC, the MFA applied the same method it had in the AFTA scheme. The reason why the Thai government could respond relatively quickly to the EVSL process might have been because the government could follow, to some degree, the same pattern of institutional arrangements and coordination process that it had for AFTA.

59 However, in some cases, MOI was determined to oppose the liberalization schemes, especially when they might affect industrial projects of its own and of a particular business sector. The inclusion of petrochemicals in the Fast Track tariff reduction list under AFTA

was a typical case. MOI strongly asserted that petrochemicals should be brought back into the Normal Track.

60 Interview with an APEC-related official, the Customs Department, MOF, 5 April 2000.
61 *The Nation*, 28 April 1995.
62 *Bangkok Post*, 9 August 1995.
63 *Bangkok Post*, 25 March 1994.
64 *The Nation*, 23 September 1994.
65 *Bangkok Post*, 11 September 1996.
66 *The Nation*, 13 September 1996.
67 *Bangkok Post*, 24 January 1997.
68 *The Nation*, 24 January 1997.
69 *Bangkok Post*, 5 December 2000. This statement came from Charnchai.
70 Comment by an APEC-related official in the Thai government.

9 Indonesia

A small fish in a big pond

Hanafi Sofyan

Introduction

The EVSL (Early Voluntary Sectoral Liberalization) initiative became a focal issue in APEC over the period of 1998–9. This chapter attempts to analyze how Indonesia responded to the initiative and what the factors of those responses were.

For these purposes, how the economic crisis since July 1997 affected Indonesia's trade liberalization policy, including APEC, will be reviewed first, as it is crucial to realize that the EVSL process coincided with the occurrence of the crisis and subsequent economic, political and social confusion in Indonesia. During the period of the EVSL consultations, Indonesia was under totally different conditions from the time when it coordinated the Bogor Declaration in 1994, which set the target years for APEC to achieve 'free and open trade and investment' in the region by 2010/2020. Second, concrete policy stances of Indonesia on each EVSL sector will be clarified. It will be pointed out that Indonesia had special interests in the fishery and forestry sectors of EVSL and prioritized them, while its enthusiasm in other sectors varied significantly. Third, how Indonesia's policy stances for each EVSL sector were formulated will be explored. The focus will be on the perspectives of business associations of some EVSL sectors and their consultations with the government. It seemed that the top-down policy-making approach of the Soeharto era had begun to change; however, due to constraints such as the shortage of human resources and time limitations, the government–business consultations were not conclusive. Lastly, how Indonesia saw the results of the EVSL consultations will be stated; in general, the results were far from satisfactory for Indonesia.

The impact of the economic crisis on Indonesia's liberalization policy and interests in APEC

Indonesia to keep its liberalization commitments

In the late 1980s and early 1990s, Indonesia reduced tariff rates consistently, either unilaterally or by following the tariff reduction schedule in conformance with Indonesian commitment to international organizations such as ASEAN. The tariff reduction policy was intended to increase efficiency in domestic producers so that they could better compete in foreign markets.

However, since July 1997, Indonesia has been facing a monetary crisis that has developed into an economic, a political and a multidimensional crisis. Almost all economic institutions have been affected and the economic contraction reached minus 15 per cent. As a result, the international community's confidence in Indonesia has also declined (Tjokroamidjojo *et al.* 1999).

Facing an extremely difficult situation, the government established policies of restructuring and deregulation, especially within the monetary sector. With the assistance of the World Bank, the Asian Development Bank and the IMF, Indonesia designed an economic recovery program called the Memorandum of Economic and Financial Policies (MEFP). MEFP described a policy to solve the economic crisis. The document was to be reviewed periodically and presented to the IMF through a Letter of Intent to inform them of progress and achievements.

Macroeconomic policy has been directed towards the restructuring of Indonesia's economic foundation, which contained many distortions which were limiting the function of market economy. A healthy fiscal policy was needed to strengthen the national budget structure in order to uphold sustainable economic growth, while in the monetary sector, the flow of foreign exchange was closely monitored so that any moves by speculators which might affect the Rupiah could be identified early. Exchange rate stability was needed for foreign trade and to create certainty in business and planning. The government also redesigned banking policy. A system of well functioning banks was fundamental to the national economy. Since the beginning of the crisis, the government has closed sixty-five unhealthy banks and fixed the management of another fifteen. Recapitalization of other banks that had assets problems under the Indonesian Banks Restructuring Agency is also on the agenda.

On the trade policy front, however, some observers have questioned the benefit of Indonesia's membership in APEC and have even suggested that Indonesia should reconsider its liberalization commitments (Syahperi 1999). Nevertheless, when discussing the trade policy of Indonesia, how deep its economy is enmeshed in the Asia-Pacific region and how APEC could trigger the rehabilitation of the economy should be carefully considered. For instance, the gradual reduction of trade barriers in the region increased

Indonesia's non-oil and gas exports and, by the end of the 1990s, around 70 per cent of all Indonesian non-oil and gas exports were to APEC markets; trade and investment liberalization and facilitation within APEC increased investment from Japan, Korea, Taiwan, Hong Kong, Singapore, Australia and the United States, and around 65 per cent of foreign investment in Indonesia came from APEC members; and around 70 per cent of tourists visiting Indonesia came from APEC members. Freer trade in goods and services in the region has the potential to increase the number of tourists visiting Indonesia even further.

The government seems to have maintained its stance on trade liberalization particularly in the regional context. In 1998, ASEAN members, including Indonesia, agreed to accelerate their intra-regional liberalization efforts and establish AFTA in 2002, one year earlier than the previous schedule. The commitment was announced at the time when all ASEAN countries were affected by the crisis. In APEC that includes both developed and developing members, however, the Indonesian government has claimed that developed members should liberalize earlier than developing ones as stated by the Bogor Declaration in 1994. The domestic business community has also supported this stance.

Indonesia's interests in APEC

One of the strengths of APEC is trade and investment liberalization and facilitation, which can have positive impacts on business communities in the region, including the ones in Indonesia. Theoretically, efforts by each APEC member according to its Individual Action Plan (IAP) would provide opportunities for exports from Indonesia as well as all other members. When APEC expands its business network and partnerships, it should have a positive impact on small and medium enterprises (SMEs), too. How much these opportunities could be beneficial for each member depends on that member's economic efficiency and trading activities.

Other important objectives for Indonesia in APEC include securing its position in the international economic system that is rapidly opening up. Indonesia sees APEC as one of the four pillars which could assist in responding to the globalization challenges, along with the United Nations, the WTO and ASEAN. Through APEC, Indonesia can stand side by side with developed economies as a partner, which could help in securing its position in the international economic system.

To forward Indonesia's interests, there are several things to be considered. First, the Indonesian government needs to keep developed and developing members in APEC as equal partners complementing each other. In this sense, efforts to turn APEC from a forum for consultation to one for negotiation must be avoided because it would weaken Indonesia's position towards developed economies. Second, efforts to enhance economic and technical cooperation (Ecotech), which reduces the gap of capabilities among APEC members, must be continued. To gain equal welfare among members, Ecotech must be combined with efforts for trade and investment liberalization and facilitation. Third, efforts to include new issues, such as democratization, human rights and environmental protection which have no direct relations with trade schemes, must be avoided.

In recent years, Indonesia has been paying a lot of attention to the economic crisis. The Indonesian IAPs have been focused more on the economic recovery issue since the outbreak of the crisis, and the government has been concentrating on domestic economic and political consolidations and has downgraded its activities in the foreign affairs area.

Nevertheless, Indonesia is still concerned with liberalization within the APEC framework because it realizes that the Bogor Declaration was initiated by Indonesia. If Indonesia were no longer committed to APEC liberalization, it would create a bad image internationally and that could be counter-productive. Though the APEC liberalization process is voluntary and non-binding in nature, the Indonesian government feels an obligation to be involved in it. Thus, recent demands by domestic businesses to reduce Indonesia's involvement in APEC liberalization have been rejected.

Indonesia's policy towards EVSL

During the EVSL sector selection period in 1997, Indonesia nominated the fishery, forestry and footwear sectors, and supported other members' nomination of the oilseeds/oilseed products, toys and natural/synthetic rubber sectors (see Appendix 2). Subsequently, five out of these six sectors, all except footwear, were successfully included in the final fifteen sectors.

Among the fifteen sectors, liberalization in the fishery and forestry sectors was perceived to be the most beneficial for Indonesia, as this might generate new sources of income from non-oil and gas exports, create employment and develop natural resources. Indonesia was behind in liberalization in these sectors compared to other APEC members. The Indonesian economy should benefit by liberalizing the fishery sector since there were good prospects for growth with the potential to catch up with other countries, such as the United States, Canada and Japan, which had a strong presence in this sector. At the time, each of these countries was imposing relatively high tariffs for downstream industries. In particular, the non-tariff barriers being imposed by Japan were remarkably high.

Thus, Indonesia made fishery and forestry priority sectors. However, what was beneficial for Indonesia might not be what other members wanted. Indonesia was most disappointed with the deadlock in the EVSL consultations faced in 1998 as members failed to reach consensus in the liberalization element of the Front Nine sectors.

The rest of this section will briefly describe Indonesia's policy stances for EVSL on a sector-by-sector basis, using mostly government documents as the main source.[1]

The government argued that the economic crisis did not change Indonesia's liberalization policy in general, but that the liberalization in the APEC framework, in particular, seemed to have been overlooked in the last few years of the 1990s. The Indonesian government put more weight on AFTA in terms of liberalization, as its tariff reduction commitment in that scheme had started even before the crisis and EVSL. This tendency was reflected in the somewhat vague nature of the Indonesian policy towards EVSL as a whole.

Among the Front Nine sectors on which discussions were conducted in 1998, Indonesia enthusiastically pursued the fishery and forestry sectors as mentioned earlier. For the *fishery* sector, Indonesia agreed with the proposed product coverage by CTI and SOM, except for Arowana fish and the like. It was ready to reduce tariffs on HS 1604 (prepared or preserved fish, caviar and caviar substitutes) and 1605 (prepared or preserved crustaceans, molluscs, etc.) to 5 per cent by the end of 2004. Indonesia entirely supported the facilitation and Ecotech measures in this sector, too, such as the elimination of NTMs, sanitary and phyto-sanitary (SPS) measures, technology transfer and human resource development (HRD).

In the *forestry* sector, Indonesia supported the liberalization of forty-nine products including printed books, newspapers, pictures and other products of the printing industry such as manuscripts and typescripts. Indonesia was ready to reduce tariffs on all above products except for HS ex 9401 (wooden seats and parts) and ex 9403 (some furniture and parts), which were subject to confirmation by the Indonesian Forestry Society. Indonesia proposed elimination of tariffs by the end of 2005, and those tariffs of 20 per cent or less to be phased out by the end of 2003 (though flexibility was asked for on a number of products). On the facilitation and Ecotech elements of the sector such as NTMs study, standards and conformance, SPS measures, customs procedure and HRD, Indonesia showed full support. Moreover, Indonesia was the coordinator of the Ecotech measures identifying process in this sector.

The level of participation in the *toys* sector was rather unclear, compared with the above two sectors. Indonesia could agree with the proposed product coverage except for HS 9504 (articles for arcade, table or parlor games and parts), but the final decision on participation in this sector was acknowledged to be subject to the overall balance of the agreement. The Association of Indonesian Toy Entrepreneurs, meanwhile, stated that the tariffs on HS 9501 (wheeled toys, dolls, parts and accessories), 9502 (dolls representing only human beings and parts) and 9505 (festive, carnival or other entertainment art and parts) could be eliminated by 2000, and for HS 9503 (toys such as scale models, puzzles and parts) by 2004. In contrast to its ambiguous stance towards tariff reduction, the government agreed to support the proposed plan to eliminate NTMs and develop a mutual recognition agreement (MRA) in the sector. The government even submitted proposals for Ecotech in the sector, including technical assistance and training programs for technology transfer, SME development, HRD, product standards and testing, with a specific timetable (by May 1999) to finalize the plan.

In the *medical equipment and instruments* sector, Indonesia agreed on the proposed product coverage but applied for flexibility in end-rates. Indonesia's intention in this sector was to eliminate tariffs of around 20 per cent of the product coverage by 2001 as proposed. For the remaining 80 per cent, Indonesia intended tariff elimination to be achieved by 2003, except for certain products with the target rate of 5 per cent by the end of 2004.

For the remaining five sectors of the Front Nine, Indonesia's stance was more passive. For example, Indonesia could not yet actively support liberalization in the *chemicals* sector. During the APEC Chemical Industry Coalition Meeting in Kuala Lumpur in February 1998, the chairman of the Cooperation Agency of the Indonesian Chemical Industry Firm Associations suggested postponing EVSL in this sector because of the economic crisis in the region. Representatives from Malaysia, the Philippines and Thailand also backed this suggestion. The liberalization of the *gems and jewelry* sector did not have strong support from the government, either. It was obvious that Indonesia could not compete with other members in this sector, especially Thailand. Indonesia could participate in the liberalization of some *energy* commodities with target tariffs of 5 per cent by 2005, the rate and date already higher and later than the original proposal. In addition, it did not intend to participate in the liberalization of energy-related services. Indonesia did not intend to participate in the liberalization of the *environmental goods and services* sector. Though the liberalization (tariff reduction) element was not included and only the mutual recognition agreement was the focus of the *telecommunications* sector, Indonesia needed more time to consolidate its stance on whether to fully participate in the MRA in this sector.

Since the atmosphere to avoid another breakdown of consultations as in the previous year prevailed in APEC in 1999, the liberalization element of the Back Six sectors did not result in a serious agenda. However, the Indonesian government set approximate objectives for those sectors.

As a supporter of the *natural and synthetic rubber* sector, Indonesia was ready to participate in the liberalization of all HS 4001 (natural rubber, balata, chicle, etc.) products. However, Indonesia's participation in synthetic rubber products was unclear and still required further consultations with relevant associations. The *fertilizers* sector in Indonesia was perceived to have relative competitiveness, and liberalization in this sector had the support of the Indonesian Fertilizers Producers Association. Indonesia was ready to reduce tariffs on HS 2814 (ammonia, anhydrous, etc.) and 3105 (mineral and chemical fertilizers) with the target rate of 5 per cent by 2004 with some exceptions. The exceptions allowed the total tariff elimination of certain products in the sector by 2004.

The *food* sector in general was (and is) very sensitive for Indonesia socially and politically, and for this reason the government decided not to participate. On the other hand, in the *oilseeds and oilseed products* sector, Indonesia was able to participate in relevant HS 15 (animal or vegetable fats, oils etc.) products. The *automotive* sector did not have a liberalization agenda in EVSL, but Indonesia's attitude towards trade liberalization and facilitation in this sector in general was rather negative as unfavorable economic conditions continued. As was the case for the automobile sector, Indonesia did not consider liberalization in the *civil aircraft* sector in the EVSL framework.

In sum, Indonesia was relatively ready for liberalization in several sectors, such as forestry, fishery, fertilizers and rubber, most of which were those it had nominated for EVSL or supported during the sector selection process. The government showed a very positive stance on the facilitation and Ecotech elements of these sectors, and sometimes could even have been defined as enthusiastic. However, even in those sectors, Indonesia did not necessarily intend to participate in full tariff reduction of all products that were proposed by SOM. The government saw other sectors, such as environmental goods and services, gems and jewelry, food and chemicals, to be hard to participate in for various reasons. For these sectors, the government's interests in the facilitation and Ecotech elements also seemed to be low, as there had been very little active involvement in these areas when compared with others such as fishery, forestry and toys.

The EVSL policy making process in Indonesia

Overview

In Indonesia, the Department of Industry and Trade (DIT) played a central role in the EVSL policy making process, especially with regard to the liberalization aspect. The Department of Foreign Affairs participated in the areas of Ecotech and other collective activities. During the Soeharto era, Indonesian policy making, including that for economic affairs, had a top-down approach. There was little correlation between business communities' and the government's interests. However, according to an official in DIT who played a major role in EVSL policy making, Indonesia's policy towards each EVSL sector was based on agreements with the representatives of relevant business associations.[2] For instance, there was consensus between the government and businesses on liberalization in some EVSL sectors such as medical equipment and instruments. Indonesia could not produce these products and depended on imports. Meanwhile, consensus that Indonesia would benefit from liberalization in the fishery and forestry sectors had also been achieved.

Nevertheless, there were constraints in the EVSL policy making process, including a lack of industrial resources and a clear vision as to what APEC should achieve, combined with limited ability to conduct comprehensive studies on the situation in the international and domestic markets.[3] The

Indonesian government was not accustomed to producing comprehensive white papers or studies.

Furthermore, there were a number of related bureaucratic institutions, business associations and entrepreneurs that it was necessary to consult with in each sector. The medical equipment sector, for example, involved the Department of Health, which made a proposal to the business associations. The associations discussed the advantages and disadvantages of the proposal including the modality and timeframe of liberalization, as well as the aspects of facilitation and Ecotech. The results of the discussion were sent back to the Department of Health. The Department of Health then amended the proposal if and where necessary and forwarded it to DIT. It should be remembered that the process of consultation was not necessarily one-off, and that the medical equipment sector was one of the better cases in terms of working towards consensus.

The government's capability for EVSL policy making was reduced even further by the dramatic depreciation of the Rupiah that began in July 1997, and the subsequent economic and political chaos. It was unfortunate that the outbreak of the crisis that led to the changes of government coincided with the whole EVSL process.[4] During that period, most human resources in the government and the private sector were concentrated in dealing with the economic and political uncertainties. This situation did nothing to assist domestic policy making for EVSL.

Though the government and the private sector tried to discuss the Front Nine sectors thoroughly, under these circumstances, it became obvious to all that Indonesia had little expertise in most sectors, and therefore that it was unavoidable for discussions to be very limited in scope. General lack of expertise saw the decision making left to DIT. Other bureaucratic institutions in the government could not become fully involved, as they generally lacked an understanding of the perception of EVSL. In the private sector, business associations felt that they were under pressure to do their part quickly in order to meet the schedule set at the international consultation table. Thus, as the process continued, they tended to leave the decision making to the government, namely DIT.

In sum, decision making on EVSL in Indonesia was not based on detailed analysis on how liberalization of each sector would affect the domestic economy. The government had discussions with business associations, but the commitments from the businesses became weaker as the process went on. It should be noted, nevertheless, that government–business consultations did take place, even though the main initiative came from the government. The question now seems to be which business associations had influence on the government's decisions (and if so, how much), as the levels of influence seemed to differ from sector to sector. The rest of this section will highlight some business associations involved with EVSL, and examine their views on liberalization and how they consulted with the government.

The business perspectives and consultations with the government

The Indonesian Chamber of Commerce and Industry (KADIN)

The Secretary-General of KADIN, which is the topmost organization in Indonesian business society, stated that the Indonesian government was too optimistic about economic liberalization and that the business community did not share its optimism. The government's communication with the business community had not always been good and it usually displayed a lack of understanding of business needs. In the case of EVSL, KADIN was not invited to join in the domestic discussion. Most of the initiatives, the Secretary-General stated, came from the government which then formulated EVSL policies without the consent of the private sector. As the representative of all business associations, KADIN considered that the government should function only as a facilitator of business activities, not as an executor. They felt the same with regard to APEC.[5]

The above statement by the Director-General of KADIN contradicted that of the senior official of DIT mentioned earlier, who explained that there were intensive meetings between the government and the business community. Though the actual intensity and/or frequency of consultations, if any, between the government and KADIN could not be identified, there were some possible explanations as to why these contradicting views emerged. First, as the EVSL policy making coincided with the economic and political crisis, there were relatively frequent changes in the personnel who were responsible for EVSL consultations both within the government and in KADIN. During the period between 1997 and 1999 when EVSL was at the top of the agenda in APEC, Indonesia had three different Presidents, and Cabinet Ministers were replaced every time a new one came into office. KADIN also saw a change in its Secretary-General in early 1998. If the government and KADIN had to rebuild the EVSL consultations each time personnel changed, and that was highly likely considering that EVSL was not a policy priority, the consultations could not be conducted efficiently.

Second, the government might have tended to bypass the umbrella association so that it could talk directly with business associations of specific EVSL sectors. By cutting down the number of parties involved in consultations, the government could avoid wasting time. Furthermore, it was a fact that the KADIN's function as a coordinator of the whole business community was sometimes limited, as some of its member associations had the power to influence KADIN's policy directions. In a situation such as that, especially when the director(s) of a powerful association had personal connections with the government, the tendency of the government to talk directly with the sectoral association(s) would increase. In fact, such direct government–business consultations did occur in certain EVSL sectors.

The Indonesian Wood Panel Association (APKINDO)

APKINDO had relatively good communication with the government and made a number of recommendations. In general, APKINDO saw EVSL as a good opportunity to benefit the forestry sector.[6]

APKINDO was prepared for early liberalization of the domestic market and stated that the faster the forestry sector was liberalized the better it was for them. From the statistics, 80 per cent of the total production of Indonesian plywood was exported. Depreciation of the Rupiah would bring more gain for the sector since their exports were valued in US dollars, though Indonesian wood entrepreneurs were also faced with the new problem of their soaring US dollar loans.

On the other hand, the problem APKINDO saw was that other APEC members had numerous barriers to this sector. For example, APKINDO considered the 'import duty' imposed by Japan as discriminative.[7] Nonetheless, APKINDO understood the reason why Japan rejected liberalization in the forestry sector, especially plywood. Japan's demand for wood products had reached 8 to 9 million cubic meters per year and the supply from domestic producers was around 4 million. If Japan's domestic market were liberalized to foreign imports, local producers would face severe competition. That was a politically sensitive issue in Japan.

Certainly APKINDO regretted the failure of EVSL in achieving consensus on the liberalization element, but as all policies must be in accordance with the willingness, capacity and situation of participating countries, this was inevitable. In EVSL, the situation did not allow liberalization of the forestry sector and APKINDO did not have enough power to alter the situation either via the Indonesian government, other members' governments or through business associations. The economic crisis might have discouraged APKIDO's willingness to push its case harder because the Indonesian economy as a whole desperately needed international financial assistance at the time, and Japan was one of its main potential donors.

The Indonesian Fishery Entrepreneurs Association (GAPPINDO)

GAPPINDO's role in the EVSL policy making process was reviewing draft proposals written by DIT and discussing them with DIT officials. The government was proactive in overseeing the process and there was a good degree of cooperation between the government and business. In the final stage, GAPPINDO presented a number of requirements to be put forward by the Indonesian government at the international consultation table. For example, a letter from GAPPINDO to Mr. Tunky Ariwibowo, the then Minister of Trade and Industry, on 5 January 1999, regarding 'the Reduction of Fishery Products Tariffs in the Framework APEC-EVSL,' read that:

[t]o continue the national efficiency and to increase Indonesian export markets within APEC as well as to make the sector more open and optimally utilized, the associations need economic and technical cooperation in fishery industry, and based on that, GAPPINDO supports the membership of Indonesia in EVSL.

The Executive Director of GAPPINDO stated that, over the last ten years, statistics showed there was a continuing increase in Indonesia's fish catches, due to the fact that a relatively small amount of investment was needed in sea exploitation. He emphasized that Indonesia was competitive in the fishery sector.[8] GAPPINDO expected that, through EVSL, the barriers against the Indonesian fishery sector, including tariffs, import quotas, non-tariff barriers (such as eco-labeling and environmental issues), would be reduced or abolished. GAPPINDO was very optimistic about EVSL in this respect because Indonesia had a competitive advantage due to the limited global supply. The recent annual growth rates of Indonesia's fish catches were between 2 and 5 per cent, making Indonesia one of the top ten world fish suppliers. Recently, the production of fish and fish products in Indonesia stood at 4.6 million metric tons, of which four million were used for domestic consumption. The global trade for this sector had reached fifty billion US dollars a year. Indonesia's export value of 0.6 million metric tons equaled two billion US dollars, or 4 per cent of the total world exports. In fact, smuggling was rife both in and around Indonesia's territorial sea, so the total catch must have been much higher than the official statistics. If the government could effectively control these illegal activities and provide more opportunity for local fishermen, who were said to number around five million at that time, their extra catches and production (processed or canned) would go to the export markets, since domestic consumption was already fulfilled.[9] Based on these observations, GAPPINDO saw that Indonesia had nothing to lose by competing in the global market.

The Indonesian Rubber Entrepreneurs Association (GAPKINDO)

Indonesian natural raw rubber exports reached 97 per cent of the total production. As the Value Added Tax imposed by the government was an obstacle to domestic sales, the rubber industry focused on the more profitable export markets. This sector has become more competitive in the world market due to the Rupiah's depreciation since mid-1997.[10]

GAPKINDO maintained good relations with the government but did not need to actively participate in EVSL policy making since the rubber sector was placed in the Back Six of EVSL. Thus thorough discussions on the sector did not take place at the international consultation table. Basically, the natural rubber sector was not to be affected by the government's EVSL policy. On the other hand, the producers of synthetic rubber would have

found the competition in the domestic (and international) market tougher, if liberalized via EVSL.

Contacts between the government and GAPKINDO regarding EVSL were simply to provide and exchange information on the progress of consultations at the international level. According to GAPKINDO, what had to be done prior to tariff reduction, including EVSL, was better implementation of the Indonesian National Standard on rubber products so that the classification of rubber products could become much clearer.[11] GAPKINDO argued that most processed rubber imports into Indonesia did not comply with the Indonesian National Standard.

Indonesia's view on the results of EVSL

As the final decision to forward the liberalization elements of all EVSL sectors to the WTO was made by September 1999, it may be concluded that EVSL was 'finished' then, though facilitation and Ecotech measures were still being discussed. EVSL failed because of sharp disagreement among members, especially between the United States and Japan. Even some developing members opposed Japan for being over-protective in the forestry and fishery sectors.

In Indonesia, two contrasting views were expressed on the results of the EVSL consultations. Some argued that it would have been better if the EVSL negotiations were held as a 'package deal'.[12] If APEC members had discussed each sector separately, interest groups within any of the members would have had the opportunity to oppose the liberalization attempts. As a package and focusing on the balanced interests, however, it was easier to restrict those interest groups' influences. In contrast, there was the opinion that, if EVSL had continued to seek a package deal, it would have been against the basic principles of APEC. The packaging of EVSL would have effectively undermined the voluntary nature of APEC activities, if achieved, and any moves to force members to act would have had the effect of dismantling APEC.[13]

Nonetheless, the Indonesian government was disappointed with the attitude of Japan with regard to EVSL. From Indonesia's point of view, by referring the liberalization element of EVSL to the WTO, the early sectoral liberalization initiative would now be pursued through strict 'negotiation', rather than 'consultation,' which was the approach commonly used in APEC. The Indonesian government perceived that this was exactly how Japan preferred to proceed. The failure of EVSL to come to agreement on liberalization denied the prospects of Indonesia's two priority sectors, fishery and forestry. The gain from liberalizing these sectors was seen to be significant for Indonesia,[14] but Japan's stubborn resistance to liberalizing the sectors under the APEC framework became a major obstacle. Japan was considered an 'evil' partner since although it did not intend to open its markets in the areas of interest to Indonesia, it intended to obtain access to the Indonesian market in other sectors. When it became clear that this situation was not going to change, Indonesia lost interest in EVSL, as there would be no advantages for Indonesia if the fishery and forestry sectors remained protected.

In Ecotech, too, Indonesia saw the way Japan evaluated the proposals as ambiguous. Most developing members had interests in Ecotech and Indonesia showed initiatives in some sector, such as forestry and toys, even though developing proposals that were acceptable to all APEC members was not an easy task. In general, the evaluation of Ecotech proposals by the Japanese government took a long time. It should be asked why it was so difficult for Japan to give approval to the proposals, when Japan was in a position to help developing members.

Although Indonesia did not like the idea of sectoral liberalization 'negotiation' at the WTO and felt discontented with Japan's attitude towards Ecotech, it could not oppose or argue against Japan strongly because of the financial assistance it was receiving from Japan. Under the severe economic conditions prevailing at the time, Indonesia considered the Miyazawa Plan (financial assistance) to be more important than EVSL.

Six months after the APEC Ministerial Meeting in Kuala Lumpur in November 1998, where it was decided to forward the liberalization element of the Front Nine sectors to the WTO, Indonesia had come to see that the decision was much better than wasting time and energy in APEC consultations.[15] However, as long as the fishery and forestry sectors continued to benefit from liberalization, Indonesia would continue to support the sectoral liberalization initiative, now called the Accelerated Tariff Liberalization in the WTO.[16]

Conclusion

The development of EVSL consultations did not show many positive signs during 1999, after the APEC Ministerial Meetings held in Kuala Lumpur in November 1998 faced an impasse. Though it was also decided to refer the liberalization elements of the Back Six sectors to the WTO by September 1999, the prospect for early liberalization in the fifteen EVSL sectors at the WTO became bleak when its Ministerial Conference in Seattle could not launch a new round of trade negotiations at the end of 1999.[17]

At the time the EVSL consultations started, Indonesia was optimistic about the results. The government held discussions with relevant business associations and came to acknowledge that, through EVSL, it was the fishery and forestry sectors that would bring most benefit to the Indonesian economy. Thus, the government set the liberalization of these sectors as top priority in the EVSL consultations.

The Indonesian business community's attitudes towards EVSL varied extensively from sector to sector. For example, APKINDO and GAPPINDO, the business associations for wood and fishery products respectively, were quite enthusiastic about early liberalization, while most other sectors' associations that would have had to face severe competition following liberalization had more negative opinions and responses.

Indonesia faced some difficulties in the domestic process of EVSL policy making. The government had neither a clear vision nor enough resources (including funding) to proceed with the domestic policy consultations efficiently. In addition, both the government and business institutions had limitations in the areas of human resources and time, meaning that a comprehensive and concrete study on how EVSL would affect the economy as a whole could not be conducted. The economic and political confusion after the sharp depreciation of the Rupiah in July 1997 only made the situation worse.

Even though coordination among related institutions was not perfect, it can be seen that the government tried to achieve the best approach in EVSL policy making. Furthermore, the government tried to keep its commitment to participating in all EVSL sectors, although the focus was more on the fishery and forestry sectors.

From Indonesia's point of view, the problems that caused the failure of EVSL occurred at the international level. Indonesia felt pressure from the pace at which the EVSL consultations were run. Also, the inflexible attitude of Japan regarding early liberalization in fishery and forestry was against Indonesia's interest. The Indonesian government expected to gain some benefits from EVSL, but the results were far from satisfactory.

Notes

1 Official documents released by the Department of Industry and Trade and the Department of Foreign Affairs, the Republic of Indonesia, dated April 1998.
2 Interview with the Director-General of the Cooperation of Industrial and International Trade Institutions, DIT, 24 June 1999.
3 Interview with the Director-General of the Cooperation of Industrial and International Trade Institutions, DIT, 24 June 1999.
4 After the sudden occurrence of the Rupiah devaluation in July 1997, the government failed to manage the situation effectively and it had to accept IMF assistance six months later in January 1998. The government was handed over from Soeharto to Habibie in May 1998, after harsh confrontations between the government and civilians. The result of the general election held in June 1999 saw a huge loss to GOLKAR, and the new President, Abdurrahman Wahid, was elected by Parliament in October 1999.
5 Interview with the Secretary-General of KADIN, 7 October 1999. This person served concurrently as a Coordinator of ABAC (APEC Business Advisory Council) Indonesia.
6 This statement contradicted that of the Secretary-General of KADIN. APKINDO seemed to be very optimistic about EVSL.
7 Interview with the Marketing Manager of APKINDO, 3 November 1999. The barrier to Japan's forestry sector included a number of other factors. For instance, Japanese firms would buy forestry imports only at CIF (cost, insurance and freight) prices while most other countries adopted policies based on FOB (free on board). In other words, Japanese firms would let exporters pay for the costs of insurance, freight, etc.
8 Interview, 18 November 1999.

9 In reality, this is easier said than done because it is widely believed that illegal fishing activities are supported by local officials and fishermen. In addition, most local fishermen are currently self-employed and lack efficient fishing methods or technology. The domestic supply chain network for fish and fish products is underdeveloped as well.

10 Interview with the Executive Director of GAPKINDO, October 1999.

11 The Indonesian National Standard was released by the National Standardization Agency. This agency has responsibility for classifying domestic and imported products in HS codes.

12 Interview with Professor Suhadi Mangkusubroto, University of Indonesia, 15 February 2000.

13 Interview with Dr. Hadi Soesastro, a member of the National Economic Council, 15 December 1999. He is also an economist from the Center for Strategic and International Studies.

14 Interview with the Indonesian Ambassador for APEC Affairs, 8 July 1999. Contrary to this view, a study by the Trade Policy Forum suggested that EVSL would not benefit any APEC members, including Indonesia, as much as expected because it focused on only some parts of all economic activities. The results of the study were presented to APEC in September 1999, but by that time, the enthusiasm to pursue EVSL had already died out in the APEC forum.

15 Interview with the Director-General of the Cooperation of Industrial and International Trade Institutions, DIT, 24 June 1999.

16 Interview with the Director of Regional Cooperation, DIT, 19 October 1999.

17 The following article provided clear information on the deadlock, which occurred in the WTO Ministerial Conference, and on the Asian perspectives. 'Battle Cry: Seattle was the First Shot in a New Kind of Trade War', *TIME* (Asia edition), 13 December 1999.

Part III
Conclusion

10 Conclusion

Jiro Okamoto

Why did EVSL consultations 'fail' to come to an agreement on the liberalization element? This chapter attempts to answer this question by examining the case studies in Part II. Before that, however, it seems necessary to review the characteristics of APEC liberalization.

The characteristics of APEC and the APEC liberalization process in comparison with the GATT/WTO as discussed in Chapter 1 are highly suggestive. The fact that the characteristics of APEC derive predominantly from the diversity of the original members of the institution from its inauguration, rather than from its members' diversity itself, is worthy of note. The promoters of the establishment of APEC, such as Australia and Japan, were very keen to include developing countries, namely ASEAN members, to make the new international economic cooperation institution more meaningful. By the late 1980s, most of ASEAN members had entered into a period of high economic growth propelled by foreign direct investment inflows and export growth. Traditionally, ASEAN members had been cautious about the formation of an international organization in the Asia-Pacific region that included powers such as the United States, Japan and China, but this time, they decided to participate in APEC as original members. To accommodate ASEAN members' participation, other members confirmed that 'voluntarism,' 'open regionalism' and 'consensus,' among others, would be set as principles for APEC activities.

For APEC liberalization conducted without the existence of legally binding sanctions (due to its principle of voluntarism) or discrimination against third countries (due to open regionalism) to have a strong influence regionally and globally, it is vital to create a critical mass of participants that support and implement the liberalization measures. Otherwise, the more positive the intention to liberalize, the more serious the risk of free riding becomes. The serious risk of free riding by third countries would inevitably reduce the motivation to liberalize voluntarily. Essentially, it does not matter for the dynamics of critical mass formation whether the participants in a liberalization initiative are APEC members or not, but it is natural for APEC initiated liberalization to concentrate on creating the dynamics within the forum first, and then try to extend it outside its membership.

Thus, in addition to the aspect that members do what they can toward the Bogor goals of 2010/2020, the APEC liberalization process has, in itself, a more positive feature to attempt to form a critical mass.

Another important conclusion from Chapter 1 is that 'consensus' is considered to be imperative both by the GATT/WTO and APEC, but what consensus means is different in each organization. Consensus under the WTO is a formal 'procedure' of decision making, and agreements reached by consensus will have as much legally binding force as decisions made by voting. On the other hand, consensus in the APEC context is not a procedure of decision making; rather it refers to a certain 'range of agreements' that members agree to participate in. In other words, the contents of Joint Statements and Declarations delivered by APEC Ministerial Meetings and Leaders Meetings are consensually agreed at their respective levels, but they do not have legally binding power.

Taking these characteristics of APEC liberalization into account, the attempt will be made in the next section to answer the research questions set out in Chapter 2 by comparing the case studies in Part II, using the analytical framework (two-level game and its extensions) explained in Chapter 3. By answering these concrete research questions, the factors that contributed to the failure of the EVSL consultations to reach agreement on the liberalization element will be identified from several different perspectives. The chapter concludes by considering briefly the influence which the result of the EVSL consultations may have on the future of the organization.

Why did the EVSL consultations 'fail'?

The EVSL policy making process and the structure of win-sets

As expected, the EVSL policy making processes described in the case studies varied from member to member. Here, those diversified policy making processes will be summarized briefly and the basic structure of each member's win-set that was derived from the policy making process will be examined.

It is noteworthy that the case study of the United States argued that the APEC (EVSL) policy was formulated differently from the regular process under the Clinton administration. Traditionally, the policy making process in the United States was almost a textbook copy of pluralism, with the policy preferences of diversified and fluid interest groups attempting to influence the decisions of the Congress and Executive Branch. The receivers of those policy preferences were divided, too. Members of the Congress tended to promote the demands of their electoral and industrial constituencies. The pressure from the Congress also divided the Executive Branch in terms of each Department's inclination toward free trade or protection of domestic industries. The Clinton administration, however, reformed and revitalized the policy coordination process within the government to achieve successful results from EVSL, just like it did from the ITA for which it created a critical mass at the WTO using APEC as a lever. The inter-departmental policy coordination for EVSL, conducted mainly by the USTR and Department of State, functioned generally smoothly. At the same time, the administration actively worked with industry groups and successfully negotiated homogeneous domestic preferences for EVSL. Through this process, both the administration and industry groups began to expect major results from EVSL. In retrospect, the level of expectation went so far as to be excessive. When the domestic preferences for a certain international negotiation issue were homogeneous, the size of the win-set would be small because the domestic constituencies would demand their negotiator win as much as possible and would refuse to allow him/her much room to compromise. For the case of the United States, this became the basic stance toward the EVSL consultations.

In terms both of its relatively smooth inter-departmental and government–industry policy coordination and of the development of homogeneous domestic preferences through the consultation process, Australia's case was similar to that of the United States. The central role was played by DFAT. For Australia, a promoter of the establishment of APEC in 1989, APEC was one of the most important issues on its foreign policy agenda. That was because APEC was perceived to coalesce the policies that the Australian government had continuously been pursuing since the beginning of the 1980s: structural economic adjustment, liberalization/deregulation and Asian engagement. Furthermore, APEC was a framework that could promote closer relations between two of Australia's most important partners, the United States and Japan. The former was its most important ally and second largest trade partner, and the latter its largest trade partner. At the same time, APEC brought for Australia, through its annual Leaders Meetings, regular access to a meeting of the leaders of some of the world's most important countries. In other words, compared with other members, APEC was a significantly 'deep' issue for Australia. In the 1990s, the Australian government felt the need to maintain and promote APEC's momentum somehow, and, considering the intentions of the United States, it perceived that APEC needed concrete results especially in the area of regional trade liberalization. Thus, for Australia, a successful conclusion of the EVSL consultations implied not only gaining direct economic benefits from liberalization but also activating APEC itself. However, Australian industries were demanding the vigorous utilization of the ITA model for EVSL. In particular, expectations from the domestic agricultural and food industries were very high. Moreover, the electoral support base of the National Party, which formed the Coalition government with the Liberal Party, were basically 'regional' (or country) areas where primary industry, including agriculture, predominated, and the general election was expected to be held by the end of 1998 (the election was held in October in fact, just before the APEC Ministerial and Leaders Meetings were held in Kuala

Lumpur). This election factor was also behind the government's campaign to try to give significant publicity to EVSL and, as a result, boost domestic industries' expectations. Meanwhile, the ALP, the opposition party, had a strong sense that it was the founder and main promoter of APEC. Hence, the ALP criticized the government's EVSL policy, arguing that it was not making enough efforts to ensure its success. In sum, Australia's domestic preferences for EVSL became homogeneous throughout the government, the Parliament and industries, so that the size of its win-set shrank like that of the United States.

The EVSL policy making process and the structure of the win-set in Japan were almost exactly the same as in the past. Domestic policy coordination was conducted by a limited number of ministries, mainly MITI and MAFF. The policy making tradition (or 'institution') that each ministry had the veto power on policies which would influence industries of its jurisdiction was alive and well, and MAFF vetoed liberalization in four EVSL sectors, namely fish and fish products, forest products, food and oilseeds and oilseed products, under its fundamental principle of 'not to commit liberalization that goes beyond the Uruguay Round agreement' (Chapter 4). The argument over EVSL packaging, which surfaced at SOM and Trade Ministers Meeting in the first half of 1998, had the effect of politicizing the issue in Japan. The opposition against liberalizing the above four sectors, fish and forest products in particular because they were included in the Front Nine sectors, from the *norin-zoku* parliamentarians and the agricultural, fishery and forestry interest groups, was activated and strongly backed the MAFF position. Under these circumstances, the size of Japan's win-set depended on the nature of choices at Level I. If the Level I agreement was presented as a binary choice (the EVSL package or no-agreement), Japan could do nothing but to choose no-agreement (the status-quo). However, if the Level I choices were continuous according to the voluntarism principle of APEC, the areas that Japan could accept (number of columns in Figure 2.2) must have been relatively large. The preferences of the government (ministries) and industries for EVSL were not necessarily homogeneous, but the veto exercised by MAFF and the movement for the EVSL package at Level I correlatively had the effect of making its win-set homogeneous in a negative sense. For the Japanese government, this development must have been unexpected at the start of the EVSL consultations.

The distinctive feature that the case study on Korea raised in terms of the EVSL policy making process was that the Korean government decided its policies not so much by considering whether the liberalization itself would generate economic benefits for domestic industries. Rather, the case study resolved, decisions were made through 'rational' judgments on which EVSL policy direction would promote the maximum domestic political support for the government. In Korea, pluralism in policy making was underdeveloped (described as 'undeveloped sub-government' in Chapter 7), and the connections between domestic industries and the National Assembly and/or the government were limited. Thus, on the one hand, it was relatively easy for the government (President) to control bureaucratic institutions. In fact, President Kim Dae-Jung could carry out administrative reform soon after he came to office in early 1998. On the foreign economic policy making front, he successfully concentrated domestic coordination and international negotiation functions in one ministry, the MOFAT. On the other hand, however, whether the general public supported the policies had to be gauged by the stances of the mass media and the approval ratings of the government through opinion polls. Thus, the government's policies could not avoid showing 'populist' tendencies. EVSL policy was not an exception and it was decided from the standpoint of maximizing political support. At that time, the most important factor was the currency (economic) crisis which broke in Korea in November 1997. The Korean government was originally reluctant to commit to liberalization beyond the Uruguay Round agreement, which meant that the size of its initial win-set was small. However, the currency crisis forced the government to make every effort to restore the credibility of the Korean economy urgently. Then what the Korean government faced was the trade off between the domestic support which could be gained by restoring international credibility through liberalization commitments under EVSL and the loss of support from domestic industries that were targeted by EVSL. For about a year after the end of 1997, the tone of mass media reports, which were critical of the government, placed priority on the restoration of international credibility and, thus, became pro-liberalization. At the SOM held in April 1998, the government announced the change in its EVSL policy and opted for positive liberalization, aiming to maximize domestic political support. Consequently, the size of its win-set continued to expand during 1998. However, after the failure at the Kuala Lumpur Ministerial Meeting in December to reach an agreement on the liberalization element, EVSL was no longer useful to the Korean government as a tool to draw political support. Coincidentally, the mass media began to emphasize the protection of the economically weak, and the government did not hesitate to redirect its foreign economic policy, including EVSL, toward a much more passive stance. During 1999, the Korean win-set for EVSL shrank rapidly to its original size.

The EVSL policy making processes in Thailand and Indonesia were similar, in the sense that their bureaucratic institutions played the major roles, and the coordination between the government and domestic industries did not go well. Also, they were similar in expressing their support for EVSL but not responding favorably to the demand of the pro-liberalization group in the actual consultations at Level I.

In the Thai case, the Ministries of Commerce and Finance played the major part in domestic coordination and international consultations, but the ministries in charge of domestic industries, such as the Ministries of Industry and Agriculture, were not actively involved in the process. Policy coordination between the two major ministries, Commerce and Finance, seemed to have gone well. The Ministry of Commerce invited representatives from the appropriate ministries and industrial groups for consultations during the periods of making Thai nominations for EVSL sectors, during the process of EVSL sector selection at the SOM level, and after fifteen sectors were selected for EVSL. In such domestic consultations, however, domestic industries' feedback was not active. Prior to sector selection, they were confused by the ambiguous nature of what they could achieve through EVSL, as well as when and how it would occur. After sector selection, they had trouble with the definition of energy, environmental and other products. The high standard of technology used in the civil aircraft sector did not help Thai industries understand what EVSL was about. Meanwhile, the government tried to settle its EVSL policy quickly in order to keep pace with the Level I consultation schedule. As a result, policy coordination among the Ministries of Commerce and Finance, domestic industries and the industrial ministries was insufficient. Subsequently, as the policy making process proceeded, concerns were raised from the latter two on liberalization even in the sectors that their own government had proposed or supported. Though the Thai government announced that it would participate in EVSL in all Front Nine sectors, its win-set could only have limited size in reality. This was because, for the Thai government, APEC liberalization had a lower policy priority than AFTA. Thailand was a strong advocate of AFTA, taking the initiative in deepening and expanding it. Thus, Thailand could not participate in EVSL if it contained measures which might diminish the meaning of AFTA. In the EVSL consultations, the Thai government insisted on such options as to start reducing tariffs in or after 2003 and to set target end-rates to be higher than 5 per cent for some products and in some sectors. The government even expected that tariff reductions for certain products would end in 2020 (if this became the case, EVSL would no longer be 'early' liberalization). The reason why the government asserted these options was because it wanted to secure the benefits from AFTA before EVSL. The Thai win-set did not allow EVSL to go beyond the AFTA commitments both in tariff rates and the implementation schedule (see Chapter 2 and Appendix 4). Domestic preferences for EVSL in Thailand could be judged as basically heterogeneous since there were concerns raised in certain sectors. But at the same time, on the point that 'commitments beyond AFTA were unacceptable,' policy preferences could be seen as homogeneous.

In Indonesia, the central role in domestic policy coordination was played by DIT. The fact that consultations between the government and domestic industries were held on EVSL can be seen as a significant development (Chapter 9), considering that decision making during the Soeharto period (until May 1998) was conducted in a top-down manner and opinions of domestic industries were rarely taken into account (or maybe only the opinions of the Soeharto family enterprises were heard?). Indeed, it seemed that the government and industries reached agreements on liberalization in sectors such as fish and fish products, forest products and medical equipment. However, there were too many restrictions to carry out sufficient domestic coordination. First, the Indonesian government lacked the resources to perform efficient domestic coordination. It lacked the ability to conduct research to analyze how EVSL would affect respective sectors of the domestic economy, and it seemed that DIT could not coordinate the consultations between other ministries and industry groups of each EVSL sector well. The inefficient coordination might be seen as having been inevitable, as the government (DIT) could not have been well accustomed to such activities. Second, the currency crisis that occurred in July 1997 was an additional and decisive blow. The crisis brought chaos not only to Indonesia's economy but also to its political and social systems, and government and industries were preoccupied with handling the situation. It is not hard to imagine that, for the Indonesian government, policy priority for EVSL dropped dramatically. In the end, EVLS policy making seems to have been left almost entirely to DIT, and coordination with domestic industries became insufficient and unbalanced. As in Korea, restoration of the international credibility of its economy was urgently required in Indonesia during the currency crisis, so that it was difficult for the government to stop or drastically weaken its commitments to APEC liberalization, including EVSL. Moreover, because the Bogor target was set by the strong initiative of the then President Soeharto, the government felt obliged to continue participating in the APEC liberalization process (Chapter 9). Thus, the Indonesian government declared that it would participate in all sectors of EVSL. The actual stance of Indonesia presented at Level I, nevertheless, did not conform to the proposals by SOM (see Chapter 2 and Appendix 4). Indonesia showed relatively positive attitudes on liberalization in the sectors that it nominated or supported, but its stances on other sectors were very much passive. These facts indicated that Indonesia's win-set for EVSL was small in size, and that domestic (in Indonesia's case, almost the same as 'the government's') preferences were heterogeneous.

The examination of the sizes and structures of members' win-sets for EVSL so far can be summarized as follows. The United States and Australia had highly homogeneous domestic preferences. As their homogeneities were created through active government involvement, the expectations from domestic industries rose and the size of win-sets shrank. The responses of the members directly hit by the currency crisis showed sharp contrast. The Korean government, backed by dominant public opinion to prioritize restoration of the international credibility of the domestic economy, continued enlarging its win-set during 1998, while Thailand and Indonesia presented their passive liberalization plans on the whole according to their heterogeneous domestic preferences, contrary to the announcement of their intentions to participate positively in every EVSL sector. The sizes of their win-sets were basically small. Japan and Thailand had their fundamental principles of 'not to make commitments beyond the Uruguay Round agreement' and 'not to make commitments beyond AFTA' respectively, so that the sizes of their win-sets were limited from the very start of the Level I consultations.

As summarized, the sizes of win-sets of most EVSL participating members were small and their structure, as a whole, was diversified and heterogeneous. Therefore, an overlapping area of all members' win-sets was hard to find from the beginning and reaching an agreement at Level I was difficult. The actual Level I consultations could not close the gap and consolidate each member's stance as explained in Chapter 2 (see also Appendix 4). However, the two-level game model suggests that, if negotiators had heterogeneous domestic preferences on the negotiated issue, striking an agreement was possible through creating an overlapping area of win-sets by enlarging mutual win-sets via domestic/international side-payments (or concessions) and/or issue linkages. Why were such attempts not made in the EVSL consultations? The following sections will try to answer this question.

The EVSL sector selection process and the level of members' expectations

The fact that each member nominated its desirable sectors for EVSL in mid-1997 after domestic coordination clearly illustrated that there already were 'continuous' choices at Level II before the start of the sector selection process at Level I. The EVSL consultations saw frequent interactions between Level I and II. Those interactions cannot be perceived through the original two-level game model that assumed a simple directionality between Level I and II: a provisional (and binary) agreement at Level I to be ratified or rejected at Level II. Here, it will be shown that vast gaps emerged among the levels of members' expectations for EVSL through the interactive sector selection process.

The United States nominated nine sectors for EVSL, the most of any member, and all of them were selected. The final fifteen EVSL sectors covered most US interests and did not include sectors unfavorable to its domestic industries. When nominating sectors, the United States took other members' circumstances and nominations into account. It did not nominate agriculture-related sectors because it expected strong opposition from Japan, Korea, Taiwan and others. Domestic industries did not criticize the administration for that. The US decision not to nominate agriculture can be understood as an attempt to enlarge the win-sets of Japan, Korea, Taiwan and others. It can also be understood in the same context that the United States once tried to persuade Australia not to nominate the food sector.

As unilateral and conscious efforts were made to exclude 'sensitive' sectors for other members from EVSL, it seems that both the US administration and domestic industries understood that they had actually enlarged the win-sets of others. This understanding had the effect of raising their expectations for EVSL. The US acceptance (or concession) of including trade facilitation and Ecotech elements in EVSL to accommodate the participation of developing economies further encouraged a tendency towards raised expectations. Even before the start of concrete consultations on the Front Nine sectors, the US administration and industries seemed to have become increasingly 'hawkish' based on the misconception that their own win-set, as well as other members', was fairly large in size. In reality however, because of the homogeneity of the domestic constituencies' preferences and their hawkish expectations, the win-set of the United States was very small. Domestic constituencies demanded a complete victory from their negotiators at Level I, which restricted their capacity to compromise. The US win-set for EVSL shrank substantially as early as the conclusion of the sector selection process, contrary to the high expectations prevailing for EVSL.

Australia was in a similar position to that of the United States in respect of EVSL sector selection. From the five nominations that Australia made, three sectors were selected for EVSL. One of its nominations not selected was 'nuisance tariffs,' a proposal to remove already low tariff rates of 2 per cent or less. The nomination of nuisance tariffs did not target any specific industrial sectors and it could be categorized as a trade facilitation measure. Though the automobile sector was included in EVSL, tariff reduction was not set as a goal. Other sensitive sectors for Australia, such as TCF, were not included in EVSL. On the other hand, what Australia most wanted to be included in EVSL were the agriculture-related sectors. This was understandable considering the trade structure of the Australian economy and the political support base of the National Party explained earlier. Australia nominated the food sector for EVSL and it was selected in due course, but domestic coordination for its nomination was not necessarily without obstacles. In Australia, there were some domestic industry groups that worried about the inclusion of the agriculture-related sectors in EVSL. Their concern was that, if agriculture-related sectors were included in EVSL, the whole initiative might end in rupture, since agriculture had always been problematic in any trade negotiations. It was symbolic that the agricultural and food industries in Australia acknowledged 'the toughest negotiation was at home' (Chapter 6). Domestic coordination for the nominations saw the development of a compromise that Australia would not nominate unprocessed agricultural products, instead nominating food as a processed product. Non-agriculture-related industries accepted the government's and food industry's assertion that the problem could be avoided by excluding sensitive products for other members from coverage in the food sector, through extensive product-by-product examinations. After this domestic coordination process, the gains that the Australian agricultural and food industries could expect from EVSL became significantly smaller compared with those anticipated originally (Chapter 6). From all this domestic process, the Australian government and the agricultural and food industries understood (in fact, misunderstood) that their efforts to make concessions unilaterally to other members, such as Japan, Korea and Taiwan, had the effect of expanding those members' win-sets. This misunderstanding had the effect of fuelling the expectations of the government and domestic industries for EVSL to even higher levels.

In contrast to the US and Australian cases, Korea's nominations were only three (government procurement, steel and steel products and petrochemicals) and none of them were selected for EVSL. The sectors for which Korea expressed its support were government procurement (nominated also by Mexico), automobiles, telecommunication and information MRA, competition policy, intellectual property rights and investment (see Appendix 2). All these sectors did not aim for trade liberalization (tariff reduction). The Korean attitude on sector nomination and support implied that Korea was not sure whether its economy could achieve very much from EVSL. The exclusion of its nominations from EVSL, steel and petrochemicals in particular, must have further lowered Korea's expectations for the initiative. In 1997, President Kim Young-Sam, who was in his last days in office, made clear that Korea would not liberalize its market beyond the Uruguay Round commitments. The Korean government had the impression that the proliberalization members had expanded EVSL suddenly (Chapter 7). The Korean government made a dramatic policy change toward supporting liberalization in early 1998, but it was for the purpose of maximizing political support, not because the government re-evaluated the potential economic gains that EVSL could bring and expanded its expectations.

Indonesia nominated three sectors, and two of them (fish and fish products and forest products) were selected. It supported three sectors (oilseeds and oilseed products, natural and synthetic rubber and toys) and all of them were included in EVSL. Since five of its six nominated or supported sectors were selected, the 'success rate' of Indonesian nominations/support was not bad at all. Under such circumstances, relatively homogeneous domestic preferences could be expected, but this was not necessarily the case for Indonesia. In addition to the simple fact that there existed ten other sectors that it did not nominate or support, the main focus of EVSL for Indonesia was on fish and fish products and forest products, which were expected to become major non-oil/natural gas export products. Other sectors had only marginal significance for Indonesia. Appendix 4 confirms that Indonesia's interests in EVSL concentrated on the two sectors and lots of reservations were made in other sectors on the SOM proposals.

Thailand won five sectors from its seven nominations. Two nominations not selected were canned/processed vegetables and fruit and rice/rice products, both of which were sensitive for members such as Japan, Korea and Taiwan. All of the five sectors it supported were included in EVSL. The success rate of ten out of eleven was relatively high, thus it could be assumed so were Thai expectations for EVSL. However, as explained earlier, those expectations were under the condition that EVSL did not exceed its AFTA commitments. Since the pro-liberalization members urged 'beyond-AFTA commitments' as the consultations proceeded, Thai expectations for EVSL must have diminished rapidly.

In terms of having limited expectations for EVSL, Japan was similar to Indonesia and Thailand. Japan nominated eight sectors for EVSL and three of them (environmental goods and services, fertilizers and natural and synthetic rubber) were adopted. The number of sectors that Japan supported reached sixteen, but only seven of them were selected. Japan nominated or supported ten of the fifteen EVSL sectors after all, but its success rate was relatively low (see Appendix 2). The characteristics of Japan's nominations/support were that many of them were not major export products (such as fertilizers, beer and barley malt, brown distilled spirits or bicycles) and some had no relation to tariff reduction (such as competition policy, government procurement or intellectual property rights). These tendencies were in sharp contrast to those of the United States or Australia, and it seemed to imply that, from the start, Japan did not expect much benefit from EVSL for its economy, which had been in recession since the early 1990s. A crucial question remained: why did the Japanese government accept the selection of fishery and forestry for the final fifteen EVSL sectors, which subsequently became the focus of (and the obstacles for) consultations in 1998? Surprisingly, according to Appendix 2, Japan even supported the selection of forest products. With hindsight, it seems that it can only be explained by the Japanese government's 'naive' belief that the APEC principle of 'voluntary action' would be applied to EVSL without doubt, but this point will be touched upon later.

To summarize, gaps existed among the levels of members' expectations for EVSL even before the sector selection process at Level I, and the process could not fill these gaps. In other words, the sector selection process and selected sectors could not expand members' win-sets and their overlaps. Furthermore, the United States and Australia misunderstood that the unilateral concessions they were making at this point enlarged other members' win-sets and, as a result, fueled domestic expectations for EVSL. Backed by those 'excessive' expectations, the pro-liberalization coalition pushed ahead with the EVSL packaging at Level I, while members with low or limited expectations were swept along in the strong initiative.

The nature of choices at Level I: coalition, packaging and critical mass

During 1997, the sector nominations were carried out as continuous choices first at Level II. Subsequently, the sector selections conducted at Level I were also continuous choices. The central questions now are: in 1998, why could a 'consensus' on whether the agreement should be made as binary choices (the package) or as continuous choices (voluntary actions) *not* be gained; and why did the Level I consultations proceed until the Kuala Lumpur Ministerial Meeting in November without resolving this issue?

The United States played a major role in promoting the EVSL package by forming a pro-liberalization coalition with Australia, Canada and New Zealand by mid-1997. As pointed out in Chapter 5, US liberalization policy under the APEC framework had become very active since 1993. Though other members, especially those from Asia, expressed concerns about this US attitude, the US administration did not see inconsistencies between its policy and the APEC principles (Chapter 5). This US policy tendency was brought to EVSL, recognizing that the strong support from the APEC forum was crucial for the success of the ITA initiative at the WTO in 1996. Domestically, no opposition was raised to the original stance of the administration either from officials or industries throughout the EVSL process, as the homogeneous policy preferences of and agreement between the administration and industries remained intact. In other words, the United States tied its own hands through the hawkishness of its domestic expectations. For the United States, Japan's attitude of rejecting liberalization in certain sectors was nothing but 'protectionism.' Moreover, as Japan's objections to the EVSL package were based on its commitment to the APEC principle of voluntarism, the United States became worried that it could stimulate the opposition of other members, which were potentially negative to EVSL, and have damaging effects on its attempt to create a 'critical mass' at Level I. Hence, US policy toward Japan aimed to soften it up, mainly by 'external pressure,' as well as to isolate it from other members.

From Japan's point of view, the government must have agreed to the inclusion of fish and fish products and forest products in EVSL because it believed any APEC activities would be operated in 'cafeteria style' under the voluntarism principle. For this reason, Japan stood firm in opposing any move to force members to act under the APEC framework. In other words, the Japanese government tenaciously opposed the EVSL packaging because the initiative went totally against what it believed to be at the core of the APEC principles. As explained earlier, unless the Level I agreement allowed continuous choices, the size of Japan's win-set was zero.

It seems, however, that it was only Japan that raised strong opposition to the packaging of EVSL from the start, and continued to oppose it. Even before the EVSL sectors were selected, the Thai government stated that APEC members should not be forced to act against their will, and after sector selection, it understood that early agreements should be made where possible, but that it would not be a problem to leave some areas, on which agreements could not be achieved quickly, for a while (Chapter 8). Indonesia's attitude was similar to that of Thailand. In short, these members' basic notions on how EVSL should be operated were the same as that of Japan. However, Thailand and Indonesia (and other members that were opposed to the EVSL package) did not argue their cases directly at the Level I consultations like Japan did. Instead, these members expressed full participation in EVSL on the one hand, and made a lot of reservations to the SOM proposals for concrete action on the other. Most of their reservations must have been unacceptable for the promoters of the EVSL package, but under these circumstances, there was a strong possibility of inducing 'voluntary defection' by the potential anti-packaging members if agreements similar to the SOM proposals were pushed ahead at Level I. In reality, the binary choice agreement (the EVSL package) that the pro-liberalization members pursued was turning more and more into continuous choices as the consultations proceeded. Thailand and Indonesia maintained their stance of following the majority by distancing themselves from the argument over whether EVSL should be operated as a package or by voluntary action, and they closely monitored the possibility of critical mass formation. As a result, these members were able to secure a position where there would be no need to change their policy preferences for liberalization drastically, whether critical mass for the EVSL package was successfully formed or not.

As these members maintained the 'wait-and-see' position, Japan's efforts to form an anti-packaging coalition, which were activated from mid-1998, were slow to come to fruition. While the overall tone of the Kuching Trade Ministers Meeting in June 1998 supported the packaging, it did not define what 'voluntarism' meant for EVSL, and for APEC in general. In September, the Japanese government sent its trade, agriculture, fishery and forestry related ministers to Northeast and Southeast Asian members to persuade them to openly back its position against the packaging, but the attempts were not visibly effective (Chapter 4). There were essentially two reasons why the EVSL package, an issue that clearly did not have overall support from members, had to be brought into the Ministerial Meeting: the domestic conditions of the pro-liberalization coalition members were generally hawkish; and a potential anti-packaging coalition had not firmed.

Nevertheless, just before the opening of the Kuala Lumpur Ministerial Meeting (14–15 November 1998), Thailand and Indonesia, along with China, Malaysia and the Philippines, took a step toward Japan's position and explicitly opposed the EVSL package. Their actions can be understood according to the explanation developed in Chapter 3, where the necessity of expanding the original two-level game model was pointed out: participants with inferior negotiation/response/adjustment abilities at Level I and II would choose the status quo in the very last stage of multilateral Level I negotiations. In the context of EVSL, the interpretation can be made that, when it became certain that the Ministerial Meeting would be held without a prior compromise between the pro-liberalization members and Japan, other members that had not been able to cope with the pace of EVSL consultations and, thus, strategically maintained 'wait-and-see' stance, openly expressed their doubt about (or opposition to) the packaging. In addition, it was very possible that the Japanese government's announcement, made just four days prior to the Ministerial Meeting, that 'it would spend about 2.7 billion yen to assist fishery and forestry industries in Asian countries for the next five years' worked as a 'side-payment' in a negative sense to get some members to oppose (or not to subscribe to) the EVSL package. For instance, the Indonesian government felt that it should not be making any arguments which would ignore Japan's opinions during the economic crisis, since Japan was already one of the major donor countries of official development assistance for Indonesia (Chapter 9). Putnam's original two-level game model assumed that side-payments could only enlarge the win-set of a negotiation partner. The above case shows the possibility of side-payments being used for the purpose of preventing certain agreements by reducing the win-sets of counterparts in a multilateral Level I negotiation.

Though Korea's economic size was not small, its policy change toward supporting liberalization in 1998 was not an important factor in creating critical mass for the liberalization element of EVSL. Given this fact, it can be seen that critical mass formation had become very difficult as early as at the stage when Japan directed its determined opposition to the packaging. In any case, the failure of the attempt at critical mass formation for the EVSL package was settled when members other than Japan raised direct opposition (or explicit discontent) at Level I.

Liberalization strategies, costs of no-agreement and issue depths

Though the EVSL consultations attracted the media's attention, partly due to the sharp confrontation between Japan and the United States, participants' perceptions of 'costs of no-agreement' in general were surprisingly low. This can be seen as the other factor contributing to the EVSL packaging proceeded at Level I despite explicit and implicit opposition. The perceptions of the costs of no-agreement depended on how each member was designing its liberalization strategy, hence how it conceived the relations between the WTO and APEC liberalization frameworks, at the time when it was widely expected that the launch of a new round of WTO trade negotiations was imminent.

The US Clinton administration, which was expecting to reproduce the ITA model, recognized that EVSL was the place to examine what should and could be brought to the WTO negotiations (Chapter 5). The absence of 'fast-track' trade negotiating authority during the whole period of EVSL consultations did not cause a problem in terms of domestic procedures, because it was still not too late to obtain it from Congress at the start of the WTO new round. After the Kuala Lumpur Ministerial Meeting, the USTR explained that the results of the EVSL consultations were not a failure for the United States (Chapter 5). On the one hand, it must have been hard for the administration to admit to failure over EVSL, as it had played a major role in inducing homogeneous domestic preferences and raised expectations. On the other hand, the results were not really a failure for the United States because the 'agreement' to negotiate the liberalization element of Front Nine sectors at the WTO was consistent with its original EVSL strategy, at least as a procedure. In other words, the no-agreement on the EVSL package at APEC was surely a blow for the United States, but it was not so great as to cause the need to change its WTO policy. Moreover, for the United States, the EVSL consultations were also useful as an 'experiment' to draw out other members' policies for the WTO new round. In particular, the US administration understood that it had been able to get Japan to commit to trade negotiations on agriculture, and fishery and forestry products in the new round. Both politically and economically, APEC was just another 'means' for the United States, while its issue depth was notably limited.

For Japan to commit to liberalization talks in the agriculture, fishery and forestry sectors outside the WTO framework just before the launch of the new round was totally irrational. It was even more so to do it at APEC, where voluntarism was a core principle. The fact that domestic side-payments, such as the one provided when the government accepted the partial opening of the domestic rice market at the Uruguay Round, were not even talked about for EVSL illustrated the determination of the government. The MAFF announcement just after the Kuala Lumpur Ministerial Meeting that the results were a sweeping victory for Japan (Chapter 4) symbolically demonstrated that the cost of no-agreement for the EVSL package was negative (i.e. the benefit of no-agreement was positive) for Japan. Generally, the APEC issues for Japan have been perceived to have considerable depth, as Japan played a central role in its establishment along with Australia, and as it was the only forum that had the participation of members from East and Southeast Asia, North America and Oceania, all important partners for Japan's diplomacy. However, Japan carried out its original opposition to the EVSL package to the end, despite its initial isolation. A possible interpretation of Japan's attitude was that APEC activities were important politically and economically so long as they did not interfere with its overall liberalization strategy. To prevent the APEC liberalization initiative from conflicting with its general trade strategy, Japan needed APEC to operate according to the principle of voluntarism. Since the serious confrontation between Japan and the United States could weaken the US commitments to APEC, which would result in the weakening of APEC itself as an international forum, it could be seen that, for Japan, APEC was not a value to be protected at all costs.

The Korean stance prior to 1998 indicated that APEC had a lower priority than the WTO in its trade policy and liberalization strategy. Also, as explained earlier, the change in its trade policy in early 1998 to actively involve itself in APEC liberalization including EVSL was made because the government expected the change to maximize its domestic political support, no matter what results would eventually develop from the EVSL initiative. If the EVSL package was agreed, the Korean government could accept it without much domestic opposition, and if it was not agreed, the government could still achieve the best possible result (the maximization of domestic political support). In other words, the outcome of the EVSL consultations was not of primary importance for the Korean government, and the cost of no-agreement was negative from the beginning. Korea's liberalization policy, including EVSL, became very passive again when the tone of the domestic mass media turned from restoration of economic credibility to the protection of the economically weak after the Kuala Lumpur Ministerial Meeting. It clearly showed that the Korean liberalization strategy had returned to its original position, pre-1998.

APEC policies in Thailand had been decided by a few of the policy making elite according to their perceptions of national interest. Their perception of Thailand's national interests in international trade were based on AFTA; APEC was not a significant aspect for their liberalization strategy. For Thailand, APEC was not the only liberalization framework (Chapter 8) and it was certainly not the most important. This situation did not change during the EVSL process. The Thai policy of following the majority at the Level I consultations was an attempt to monitor the climate for the emergence of a critical mass, and to ride the winning horse if possible. This could be understood as a typical strategy by negotiation participants unable to have a direct influence on the development of a critical mass. This strategy itself implied that the cost of no-agreement for the EVSL package was low for Thailand. In addition, due to a lack of human and other resources, concluding the consultations on fifteen EVSL sectors and implementing concrete measures within the period of several years was difficult for Thailand (Chapter 8). For a country prioritizing trade liberalization through AFTA, to concentrate resources on EVSL would not have been a wise option.

Indonesia's EVSL policy, after the economic crisis in particular, became negative in reality, though the government maintained its ostensible commitment. This passive attitude toward EVSL was in sharp contrast to the agreement reached among the ASEAN countries to accelerate AFTA liberalization around the same time. For Indonesia's liberalization strategy, as for Thailand's, APEC was not the only liberalization framework to rely on and not the most important, either. However, according to Chapter 9, APEC was recognized as a deep issue for Indonesia. Besides the perception that APEC trade and investment liberalization and facilitation and Ecotech would increase potential export opportunities for Indonesia (and all other members), APEC was an important forum in which Indonesia participated on an equal basis with powers such as the United States, Japan and China. Nonetheless, Chapter 9 pointed out that APEC had significant issue depth for Indonesia so long as it remained a 'consultation' forum, not a 'negotiation' institution. Indonesia recognized that the possibility of maintaining equal status with the region's powers would decrease if agreements with binding force were negotiated at APEC. Since EVSL, as its process proceeded, was perceived to be departing from 'consultations' (voluntary actions) to 'negotiations' (the package), the cost of no-agreement for Indonesia, for which liberalization under the APEC framework was not a priority, must also have been lowered.

Australia might be the member that saw no-agreement on EVSL as having the highest cost. The reasons behind Australia's promotion of the EVSL package along with the United States included: the government's belief in the need to maintain APEC's momentum by achieving concrete results in liberalization to maintain the US commitment to APEC; the government's major role in inducing homogeneous domestic policy prefer-ences for EVSL; declining domestic confidence in the effects of the decades-long program of structural adjustment and liberalization/deregula-tion, which had increased pressure on the government to deliver economic results; the government's need to shore up rural electoral support; and the government's belief that EVSL was a good opportunity to make up for its recent failures in Asia-Pacific diplomacy. Under these circumstances, the government lost sight of the balance among several policy objectives embodied in APEC. As explained in Chapter 6, APEC was always an issue with significant depth for Australia. What was lost by the failure to achieve agreement on the liberalization element of EVSL was not only economic benefit. After the Kuala Lumpur Ministerial Meeting, however, the govern-ment became seriously concerned about the possibility of doing further damage to APEC if the consultations on the liberalization of the Back Six sectors continued in 1999. For Australia, APEC as an institution, and the cooperation capital that APEC had accumulated, were far more important than the almost wrecked EVSL. For the purpose of saving APEC, the Australian government even played a role in persuading the United States to accept the proposal to refer the liberalization element of the Back Six sectors to the WTO, without detailed consultations on the contents. In other words, the policy change was made because the Australian government once more realized the depth of the APEC issue for the country.

As examined so far, the costs of no-agreement on EVSL were generally low (thus, the status quo did not entail a great loss) and the depth of the APEC issue was limited for most members. This conjuncture provided an incentive for the pro-liberalization coalition to push the EVSL package aggressively even though there was strong opposition, and for members that considered the principle of voluntarism as one of the most important to stubbornly reject the initiative. Australia, for which the APEC issue had considerable depth, was an exception, but a number of factors made it belong to the pro-liberalization coalition and prevented it from seriously seeking a compromise to bridge the gap until the Kuala Lumpur Ministerial Meeting.

The influence of the Asian economic crisis

The ways in which the Asian economic (currency) crisis influenced the EVSL policies of each member varied, and it is not possible to understand how this influence was reflected in the Level I consultations from a single aspect.

The crisis did not necessarily affect each member's liberalization policy in a negative way, making agreement at Level I more difficult. Some members that were not affected directly by the crisis, such as the United States, argued that the crisis made structural adjustment through liberalization even more important and necessary; while those directly hit by the crisis felt it was hard to raise strong opposition to EVSL because they desperately needed monetary assistance from the IMF, the institution where the will and policy of the United States had the strongest influence. In addition, the crisis did not affect domestic preferences for liberalization policies in most members examined in the case studies, and there were few cases in which the new negotiators at Level I, due to the changes in the governments, had different policy preferences and basic policy directions from their predecessors. The only exception was Korea. Its drastic EVSL policy changes, twice during the process between 1998 and 1999, were for the purpose of maintaining the legitimacy of the government under the specific conditions of the crisis. However, since the first policy change in the first half of 1998 was a significant expansion of its win-set for the Front Nine sectors, it could not have a negative influence on the formation of the critical mass for the Level I agreement.

Rather, the main impact of the economic crisis on EVSL was that it severely lowered the policy priority of EVSL in the foreign economic policies of crisis-affected members, and reduced the resources available for the domestic and international consultations and coordination. In general, it seems reasonable to assume that the quality and quantity of resources that developing countries can mobilize for a study on how liberalization in specific sectors would affect the domestic economy and regional trade flows cannot match those of developed countries even at normal times. The EVSL process was an exception. The Thai and Indonesian governments lacked the ability to mobilize resources to conduct comprehensive econometric analyses as DFAT and the Productivity Commission of Australia were able to at several times in a short period of time. These members had no choice but to allocate their scarce resources toward responding to the economic crisis. In Indonesia, the political, economic and social conditions were totally different from the time when President Soeharto played a central role in shaping the Bogor Declaration in 1994, and the Thai government insisted that the problem was not in liberalization itself but in the lack of preparation for it (Chapter 8). The Thai and Indonesian cases clearly showed that they considerably lost their abilities to negotiate at Level I and to coordinate at Level II because of the crisis.

Consensus that was not shared

So far, the factors that contributed to the failure of EVSL consultations to reach an agreement on the liberalization element have been examined from various aspects: each member's policy making process, the sizes and structures of their win-sets, the level of expectations for EVSL, the perception of the cost of no-agreement and issue depth, and the impact of the Asian economic crisis. All these have been demonstrated as important factors. However, what lies behind all of them, and the most important factor in explaining the failure, was the lack of common and clear understandings on the modality and objectives of APEC liberalization. In reality, the 'consensus' incorporated in past Joint Statements of the Ministerial Meetings and Declarations of the Leaders Meetings were not shared by all members.

All APEC activities are supposed to be carried out under the 'voluntarism' principle. Furthermore, all APEC liberalization measures, including EVSL, are supposed to be conducted under the general principles for liberalization/facilitation set by the OAA. The point is that the United States, Australia and the others that pushed the EVSL package, and Japan which rejected the initiative, did not believe their respective behaviors were contrary to APEC principles. For instance, the United States had a view that 'voluntarism doesn't mean countries can do whatever they want' (Chapter 5), so that it saw Japan's rejection of liberalization in the fishery and forestry sectors as protectionism. On the other hand, Japan understood that to choose not to participate in certain measures in certain sectors in EVSL was a legitimate right based on the voluntarism principle. Both Japan and the United States must have realized their differences in interpreting the APEC principles during the process of EVSL consultations, if not before. However, to modify their beliefs in order to seek compromise was almost impossible: their domestic accords were too solid; their costs of no-agreement were too low; and the EVSL issue did not have sufficient depth.

What the APEC principles of 'voluntarism,' 'flexibility,' 'comprehensiveness' and others meant and what they did not mean were ambiguous, therefore each member interpreted them in a way favorable to itself. In the Statements of the Chair of the Trade Ministers Meetings and the Joint Statements of the Ministerial Meeting during the period of EVSL consultations, the following words and phrases repeatedly appeared: 'early voluntary liberalization ... pursuing comprehensive liberalization ...' (the Montreal Trade Ministers Meeting, May 1997); '[EVSL] is conducted on the basis of the APEC principle of voluntarism ...' (the Vancouver Ministerial Meeting, November 1997); 'flexibility would be required ... [in order to] consider the final agreements/arrangements of each sector in its entirety ...' (the Kuching Trade Ministers Meeting, June 1998), 'The EVSL initiative, undertaken through ... voluntarism, is an integrated approach to liberalization ...' (the Kuala Lumpur Ministerial Meeting, November 1998). These words and phrases could not lead the Level I consultations toward an agreement. Furthermore, 'the significance of the commitment taken by the highest levels (of member governments)' that the United State and others used to insist that agreement had to be reached could not be of any assistance in bringing about the converging of the Level I consultations in one direction, since there were differences in understandings on what the Leader of each member had committed to (i.e. the EVSL package or EVSL through voluntary action). In APEC, in the first place, what was meant by 'free and open trade and investment' has never been clearly stated, nor has it ever been resolved whether 'free and open trade and investment,' if and when established, would be applied to outsiders without any conditions according to 'open regionalism' in its purest form.

These ambiguous APEC principles were necessary and effective in bringing agreement among as many members as possible, including developing ones, to the newly formed regional economic cooperation forum, and in formulating long-term and general objectives among diversified members. However, ironically, these principles became obstacles for forming a critical mass to decide and implement concrete liberalization measures under the EVSL initiative.

Implications for APEC activities

The EVSL consultations virtually failed at the Ministerial Meeting in November 1998 and the attempts to control damage during the following year were unsatisfactory. How, then, would the results of EVSL affect APEC and its activities in the years to come? In concluding, this topic will be briefly touched upon.

The fact that members did not share a consensus on how and what should be achieved in APEC liberalization needs to be addressed as the first issue raised by the EVSL episode. On the other hand, through the process, it was reconfirmed that binding cooperation measures could not be agreed on and implemented under the APEC framework. The EVSL package, an attempt to attach binding force to a part of APEC liberalization activities, was ultimately rejected. In other words, it was endorsed that the 'voluntarism' principle meant that APEC members could decide freely in which cooperation schemes, or in which part of cooperation schemes, they should participate, though pressure from peers existed. What is interesting and worth noting in relation to this was that the review of the OAA guidelines was agreed at the Ministerial and Leaders Meetings in Brunei in November 2000 (APEC Ministerial Meeting 2000: paragraph 9; APEC Leaders Meeting 2000: attachment 1). It may not be wrong to assume that the failure of EVSL was at least one of the reasons for the OAA guideline review. As a result, the IAP Peer Review process has been introduced since 2002 to improve members' IAPs and monitor their implementation. However, regarding 'how' to achieve those objectives, to make agreed cooperation measures more binding than the level confirmed through the EVSL process (thus, making liberalization measures more credible) would be difficult.

Second, some points regarding the formation of critical mass were raised by the EVSL episode. As explained at the beginning of this chapter, APEC liberalization has an aspect which seeks to create critical mass, since active but unorganized liberalization attempts would raise the serious risk of free riding. There seem to be two basic implications that can be drawn from the failure of EVSL to create critical mass. First, to generate critical mass through APEC liberalization, it appears that at a minimum the participation of the two regional economic powers, Japan and the United States, is needed. In the EVSL case, the United States, Canada, Australia, New Zealand and some others formed a coalition to push the packaging initiative, but this group was not sufficient to form critical mass. The consultations were carried on without clear prospect of success or failure in critical mass formation, because of Japan's opposition. Hence, second, in APEC activities, especially in liberalization, formation of critical mass appears possible only on subjects and substances on which Japan and the United States can agree. The ITA succeeded in gaining critical mass within APEC, because there existed a basic agreement between Japan and the United States (and Canada and the EU) at the Quadrilateral Trade Ministers Meeting prior to the APEC Ministerial and Leaders Meetings in 1996.

Third, the EVSL process revisited the problem of what role APEC could play among many other liberalization frameworks, given its distinctive characteristics. It should be remembered that it was during an 'inter-round' period after the successful conclusion of the Uruguay Round that APEC began to take seriously the goal of regional liberalization. However, APEC liberalization conducted under the voluntarism principle cannot have the binding power of a WTO round. It is, rather, natural for APEC liberalization (voluntary and non-discriminative regional tariff and NTB reduction) to stagnate when a WTO round is underway, or just prior to the launch of a round. During the period between the launch of the round and the conclusion of negotiations, APEC, as a whole, can show its support for the round just like it did for the Uruguay Round. However, it will become increasingly difficult to carry out its own liberalization initiatives independent of the WTO. It is symbolic that the focus of the APEC agenda has shifted from liberalization to Ecotech measures, such as capacity building for the implementation of WTO commitments and action plans to respond to the 'new economy,' since 2000.

Fourth, it should be pointed out that, after the EVSL failure, movement to establish free trade agreements (FTAs) in the Asia-Pacific region has been increasing in recent years. In addition to the United States, Canada, Chile and Mexico, which have had the FTA formation in their minds for some time as a part of their liberalization strategies, Japan, Korea, Singapore, Australia, New Zealand and others have changed their traditional trade policies from concentrating on multilateralism. Though the discriminatory nature of FTAs and the 'open regionalism' concept of APEC are potentially contradictory, responses from the APEC forum so far have been to state that those FTAs should be consistent with the WTO rules and APEC principles and goals. They have also stated that FTAs could promote regional and multilateral liberalization, but failed to specify 'how' (APEC Leaders Meeting 2000: paragraph 28; APEC Trade Ministers Meeting 2001: paragraph 22,

2003; APEC Ministerial Meeting 2002). APEC is yet to demonstrate clearly what role it can play to bridge the (WTO) multilateral liberalization process and FTAs to make sure that the latter does not hinder the former.

Lastly, the progress of APEC liberalization depends heavily on the contemporary international and regional economic environment, even more so than other liberalization frameworks. The ASEAN members' decisions to join APEC as its original members in 1989 were drastic changes of their foreign policies, considering their traditional attitudes towards the establishment of an international institution in the Asia-Pacific region. It was also somewhat surprising that Indonesia, as a host economy, played a central role in shaping the Bogor Declaration in 1994, considering the level of protection of its market at the time and its traditional trade policies. Moreover, the fact that all Asian members, except for Malaysia, accepted Indonesia's initiative without clear reservations was epoch-making. What lay in the background of all these phenomena was high rates of economic growth of developing economies in East and Southeast Asia from the mid-1980s to the mid-1990s, using the foreign direct investment inflows and export expansion as leverage. Currently, all these members are still suffering from the legacy of the economic crisis which has lowered the policy priority of APEC liberalization. However, when economic recoveries get on track and the new WTO round is concluded, there may be a possibility that they would reactivate their interests in and commitments to APEC liberalization. After all, liberalization under the APEC cooperation framework is not completely calculable but, at the same time, cannot be totally ignored.

Appendix 1

The APEC EVSL process: a consolidated chronology

19 November 1995	APEC Leaders endorse the Osaka Action Agenda. The OAA states 'APEC economies will identify industries in which the progressive reduction of tariffs (and non-tariff measures) may have positive impact on trade and economic growth in the Asia-Pacific region or for which there is regional industry support for early liberalisation' (Part One, Section C).
26–28 September 1996	The Quadrilateral Ministers Meeting held in Seattle. Canada, Japan, the United States and the EU agree to promote the ITA at the WTO Ministerial Conference in Singapore in December.
25 November 1996	APEC leaders, issuing their Declaration following their meeting in Subic, The Philippines, instruct their Ministers to 'identify sectors where early voluntary liberalisation would have a positive impact on trade, investment, and economic growth in the individual APEC economies as well as in the region, and submit to us their recommendations on how this can be achieved' (paragraph 8).
9–13 December 1996	ITA is finalized and signed by twenty-nine members at the WTO Ministerial Conference in Singapore.
8–10 May 1997	APEC Trade Ministers meet in Montreal. They instruct officials to undertake studies and report back to them by August on possible sectors for early liberalization, based on tariff and non-tariff dimensions, facilitation and Ecotech, and fullest possible private sector input, with a view to creating critical mass for stimulating broader sectoral action through the WTO.

15 July 1997	On the deadline set by the SOM, thirteen APEC members nominate sixty-two sectors covering over thirty sectors for early liberalization. The CTI and SOM held in St John's in August provide officials with the opportunity collectively to review and assess the nominations; trade officials begin to consolidate overlapping nominations, refining elements contained in various proposals, and clarifying indications of support.
27–28 September 1997	ABAC finalizes a report to Leaders at the meeting in Santiago. In the report, ABAC selects eight sectors (industries and sub-components) to recommend to the official sector selection process.
27–28 October 1997	An informal SOM is held in Singapore further to advance work on reviewing and assessing nominations, consolidating overlapping nominations, refining elements contained in various proposals and clarifying indications of support. The list of sectors is consolidated to forty-one following this meeting.
21–22 November 1997	The EVSL Annex of the Joint Statement of the APEC Ministerial Meeting in Vancouver takes note of the forty-one sectors proposed for review and consideration by officials, taking it as an indication of the 'high level of support in the region for further trade liberalisation.' They select fifteen sectors based on their consideration of 'the levels of support for, the economic significance of, and the internal balance that has been developed within, specific proposals.' They also emphasize the APEC principle of voluntarism 'whereby each economy remains free to determine the sectoral initiatives in which it will participate.' Further, they 'recommend that Leaders endorse members beginning immediately to complete work on these proposals through finalising the scope of coverage, flexible phasing, measures covered and implementation schedule, including choice of measures and instruments for implementation based on the existing proposals, for each of these sectors.' They suggest such work should be done in the first half of 1998 for implementation beginning in 1999.
25 November 1997	The Vancouver APEC Leaders' Declaration states 'we welcome the action taken to accelerate by two years the timetable for the identification of sectors

for early voluntary liberalization, a decision that underlines our determination to advance the pace of liberalization in the region and globally. We endorse the agreement of our Ministers that action should be taken with respect to early voluntary liberalization in 15 sectors, with nine to be advanced throughout 1998 with a view to implementation beginning in 1999. We find this package to be mutually beneficial and to represent a balance of interests. We instruct Ministers responsible for trade to finalize detailed targets and timelines by their next meeting in June 1998. To sustain this momentum, we further instruct that the this year to be brought forward for consideration of additional action next year.'

December 1997	The CTI starts to work on defining programs for the Front Nine sectors, forms 'Specialist Groups' for each sector.
16–17 February 1998	The first status reports for the Front Nine sectors are submitted by the CTI to the SOM held in Penang. The SOM instructs CTI to progress proposals.
27 Feb–3 March 1998	ABAC Meeting in Mexico City. ABAC sets up the EVSL Task Force.
20–24 April 1998	Special CTI on EVSL is held in Kuala Lumpur. CTI asks each member to provide comments on proposals.
1–3 May 1998	At a meeting in Sydney, ABAC endorses the EVSL initiative and urges all APEC members to partici pate in comprehensive and credible sectoral packages.
18–20 June 1998	Revised status reports gathered by CTI are submitted to the SOM held in Kuching. These reports provide information on product coverage, measures of actions and implementation schedule in each sector. The SOM proposes that the final agreements on EVSL should be endorsed in their 'entirety.'
22–23 June 1998	APEC Trade Ministers Meeting held in Kuching. The Statement of the Chair indicates that specific concerns have been raised by individual economies in each sector (paragraph 3), while it acknowledges that there is emerging consensus on product coverage, target end rates and target end dates (paragraph 4). The Statement also says that participation in the nine sectors and all three measures

(liberalization, facilitation and Ecotech) in each sector will be essential (paragraph 5), indicating the intention of 'packaging.' Flexibility will be in the form of longer implementation periods and developing economies should be allowed such flexibility in principle (paragraph 6). In reality, the Meeting meets deadlock over Japan's refusal to accept the liberalization elements of some EVSL proposals.

Chile and Mexico withdraw from the EVSL process, arguing that APEC's trade liberalization agenda should be carried out on a comprehensive basis.

4–6 September 1998   ABAC finalizes the annual report to Leaders at the Taipei Meeting. A Japanese representative in charge of EVSL strongly argues that Japan will not participate in the tariff reduction in the forestry, fishery and oilseeds sectors, but concedes to sign on the final report to avoid the collapse of the whole ABAC process. The report backs the position of the Statement of the Chair of the June Trade Ministers Meeting and urges that the EVSL process should be inclusive, comprehensive and credible.

13–15 September 1998   The SOM in Kuantan again fails to resolve the EVSL issue as some countries try to ensure maximum flexibility to minimize the impact on their economies. While Japan has shown more flexibility, China has become less flexible, arguing the plan must be 'realistic.'

15 October 1998   Media reports that the US, Canada, Hong Kong, Singapore and Australia are intensifying diplomatic efforts to persuade Japan to back EVSL in order to avoid sending further signals of APEC's weakness during the Asian financial crisis.

9 November 1998   Japan offers to accelerate its tariff cuts in other areas to compensate for its refusal to do so on forestry and fisheries products.

10 November 1998   Japan makes final decision to reject liberalization in the fisheries and forestry sectors. Also, Japan decides to make an offer of a 27 billion yen package to Asian APEC members to assist their fisheries and forestry sectors.

14–15 November 1998   APEC Ministerial Meeting in Kuala Lumpur. Ministers decide to refer the tariff element of the Front Nine sectors to the WTO for further negotiations. The Joint Statement declares that Ministers reached consensus in implementing the facilitation and Ecotech measures for the nine sectors.

18 November 1998   APEC Leaders Meeting in Kuala Lumpur. The Declaration blandly welcomes 'the progress achieved on the EVSL package of nine sectors. We instruct Ministers of participating economies to implement the agreement reached on these sectors and further advance work on the remaining six sectors, demonstrating our commitment to the liberalisation process amidst the financial crisis in the region' (paragraph 19).

26 January 1999   New Zealand, the host member of APEC in 1999, submits liberalization proposals for the Front Nine sectors to the WTO. The initiative is now called the 'Accelerated Tariff Liberalization' and communication with WTO officials starts in Geneva.

8–9 February 1999   The SOM in Wellington recognizes the importance of developing number of 'deliverables' in NTMs, facilitation and Ecotech elements for EVSL sectors to restore APEC's credibility.

6–7 May 1999   The SOM, held in Christchurch, agrees to propose that the tariff element of the Back Six sectors also be referred to the WTO.

29–30 June 1999   APEC Trade Ministers Meeting in Auckland agrees that the atmosphere within the WTO is now positive for the negotiation of the tariff elements of the remaining six EVSL sectors; Ministers resolve that the tariff elements of the remaining six EVSL sectors should be negotiated in the WTO. The Ministers develop a table of NTMs, facilitation and Ecotech measures for the fifteen EVSL sectors and compile a list of eight 'deliverables.'

12–13 August 1999   The SOM in Rotorua receives lists of more 'deliverables' on sector-to-sector basis from CTI.

9–10 September 1999   APEC Ministerial Meeting in Auckland is uncontroversial on EVSL as the tariff element has gone out of scope. Ministers add four more measures to the list of deliverables for NTMs, facilitation and Ecotech. Discussion centers on how APEC should deal with the WTO Ministerial Conference in November. In general, Ministers agree that APEC should contribute to the launch of the new WTO round which should be broad-based including industrial tariffs; the new round is to be ratified as a single package within three years; and that economies may liberalize early but are required to remain in negotiations until the entire package is ready.

13 September 1999   APEC Leaders' Declaration following the Auckland meeting does not mention sectoral liberalization. Its compromise on the common APEC position in the WTO is to call for 'a balanced and sufficiently broad-based agenda to be concluded within three years as a single package which does not preclude the possibility of early results on a provisional basis.'

Appendix 2

APEC Early Voluntary Sectoral Liberalization SOM Chair Indicative Worksheet (as of 21 November 1997)

Proposals	Sponsors	Support, Unqualified	Others
Food sector Measures: APEC facilitation work (especially standards) intensified. APEC Ecotech activities intensified. Food sub-sectors (tariffs, NTMs) studied. Tariffs eliminated, reduced or harmonized	Australia	Hong Kong, New Zealand	Brunei, Canada, Papua New Guinea, Singapore, Thailand, United States
Fish sector Measures: Tariffs eliminated. NTMs removed. Subsidies removed. SPS measures inconsistent with international agreements removed. Ecotech program to facilitate liberalization	Brunei, Canada, Indonesia[1], New Zealand, Thailand	Hong Kong	Australia, Malaysia, Papua New Guinea, Singapore, United States
Rice and rice products. Measures: Tariffs reduced. NTMs including GP subsidies, import restrictions relaxed /abolished	Thailand		Australia, New Zealand, Papua New Guinea, United States
Beer and barley malt. Measures: Tariffs eliminated for beer. Tariffs, NTMs and export subsidies eliminated for barley malt	Canada		Australia, Japan, New Zealand, Papua New Guinea, United States
Oilseeds and oilseed products. Measures: Tariffs eliminated. NTMs, export subsides and other trade distorting measures eliminated. APEC Ecotech work intensified	Canada, Malaysia, United States		Australia, Brunei, Indonesia, New Zealand, Papua New Guinea, Singapore, Chinese Taipei

Canned /processed vegetables and fruit Measures: Tariffs reduced. NTMs abolished. Strict inspection requirements replaced by specific standards. MRA established.	Thailand		Australia, Brunei, New Zealand , Papua New Guinea, Singapore
Fresh /unprocessed vegetables and fruit Measures: Tariffs and NTMs removed. Subsidies frozen (domestic support) or eliminated (export subsidies). SPS measures aligned with international standards. Ecotech to support liberalization	New Zealand		Australia, Brunei, Singapore, Thailand United States
Brown distilled spirits Measures: Tariffs phased out and bound.	Canada		Japan, New Zealand, Papua New Guinea, United States
Energy secto, Measures: Tariffs removal accelerated, NTMs identified and addressed, Barriers and impediments to services identified and removed, Transparent government procurement policies adopted, APEC facilitation work intensified, Standard coordinated in APEC	Australia, Thailand,[2] United States	Singapore	Hong Kong, Japan, New Zealand, Papua New Guinea, Chinese Taipei
Chemicals (comprehensive, Measures: Tariffs reduced and eliminated, NTMs made more transparent and reduced, Customs and regulatory procedures facilitated and reduced, Standards harmonization, Investment liberalization	United States, Singapore, Australia, Hong Kong	Canada	Japan, Malaysia, New Zealand, Papua New Guinea, Thailand
Petrochemicals Measures: Tariffs harmonized and eliminated	Korea	Singapore	New Zealand, United States
Fertilizers, Measures: Tariffs eliminated, NTMs aligned with international standards, Ecotech	Canada	Singapore, Thailand	Japan, New Zealand, Papua New Guinea, Chinese Taipei, United States

Fertilizers, Measures: Tariffs removed	Japan	Singapore, Thailand	New Zealand, Papua New Guinea, Chinese Taipei
Films, Measures: Tariffs removed	Japan	Singapore	New Zealand, Papua New Guinea, United States
Forest Products Measures: Tariffs removed, NTMs studied, Codes aligned with international standards, SPS measures aligned with international standards, Ecotech	Canada, Indonesia[3], New Zealand, United States[4]	Hong Kong, Singapore	Australia, Japan, Chinese Taipei, Thailand
Gems and jewelry, pearls, precious metals and articles thereof, Measures: Tariffs reduced /eliminated, NTMs reduced /eliminated	Thailand, Chinese, Taipei[5]		Australia, Canada, Hong Kong, Malaysia, New Zealand, Papua New Guinea, Singapore, United States
Steel and steel products, Measures: Tariffs reduced /eliminated, Ecotech to promote sustainable development	Korea		Canada, Japan, New Zealand, Papua New Guinea, Singapore, United States
Non-ferrous metals, Measures: Tariffs harmonized /phased out, NTMs identified and eliminated, Export restrictions eliminated	Australia		Canada, New Zealand, Papua New Guinea, Singapore, United States
Environmental goods and services, Measures: Tariffs eliminated, Services trade liberalized, NTMs identified and addressed, APEC Ecotech and project work intensified	Canada, Japan, Chinese, Taipei, United States	Hong Kong, Singapore	Australia, Malaysia, New Zealand, Papua New Guinea
Transport equipment, Measures: Tariffs removed	Japan	Singapore	New Zealand, Papua New Guinea
Automotive sector, Measures: Standards /regulations harmonized, TILF measures identified, Ecotech work intensified	United States	Singapore	Australia, Canada, Japan, Korea, New Zealand, Papua New Guinea
Bicycles, Measures: Tariffs and NTMs removed	China		Japan, New Zealand, Papua New Guinea, Singapore

Civil Aircraft Measures: Customs duties and charges eliminated	Canada	Japan, Singapore, Chinese Taipei, United States	Australia, New Zealand, Papua New Guinea
Medical equipment, associated services and instruments Measures: Tariffs eliminated, NTMs identified and addressed, Services liberalized, Technical assistance in consultation with the private sector	United States, Singapore	Hong Kong	Australia, Japan, New Zealand, Papua New Guinea, Thailand
Medical instruments and apparatus Measures: Tariffs and NTMs reduced /eliminated, Technical cooperation in R &D promoted	Thailand	Singapore	Australia, Canada, Japan, New Zealand, Papua New Guinea, United States
Scientific equipment, Measures: Tariffs removed	Japan	Singapore	Australia, New Zealand, Papua New Guinea
Natural and synthetic rubber Measures: Tariffs and NTMs reduced /eliminated Ecotech	Thailand Japan		Australia, Canada, Indonesia, New Zealand, Papua New Guinea, Singapore, Chinese Taipei
Toys Measures: Tariffs progressively reduced to zero NTMs identified, consulted on and eliminated progressively	China, Hong Kong, Singapore, United States	Australia, Canada, New Zealand	Brunei, Indonesia, Malaysia, Papua New Guinea, Chinese Taipei, Thailand
Footwear Measures: Tariffs reduced, NTMs addressed and eliminated, Ecotech to promote technical assistance, technology transfer and investment promotion	Indonesia	Chinese Taipei	New Zealand, Papua New Guinea, Singapore, Thailand
Precision engineering /machinery Measures: Tariffs eliminated	Singapore		Hong Kong, Japan, New Zealand, Papua New Guinea
Consumer electronics, Measures: Tariffs removed	Singapore		Hong Kong, Japan, New Zealand, Papua New Guinea

Telecommunications and information equipment Measures: MRA for test results and certification implemented	United States	Canada, Japan, Singapore	Australia, Hong Kong, Korea, New Zealand, Papua New Guinea, Chinese Taipei
Musical instruments Measures: Tariffs removed	Japan		New Zealand, Papua New Guinea, Singapore
Accounting services Measures: Transparency of market access enhanced. Market access restrictions reduced	China		Australia, New Zealand, Papua New Guinea
Competition policy Measures: Technical assistance to develop competition policy /legislation	Mexico	Chinese Taipei	Japan, Korea, New Zealand, Papua New Guinea, United States
Government procurement Measures: Non-binding principles developed, Adherence to WTO /GPA	Korea		Japan, New Zealand, Papua New Guinea, Chinese Taipei
Government procurement Measures: Databases established	Mexico	Korea, Chinese Taipei	Japan, New Zealand, Papua New Guinea
Intellectual property rights Measures: Measures related to well-known marks identified /harmonized, IPR protection for geographical indications implemented, Marks /patents registration procedures identified /harmonized, Procedures for enforcing copyrights /neighboring rights identified	Mexico		Japan, Korea, New Zealand, Papua New Guinea, Chinese Taipei, United States
Investment Measures: Elements of a liberalised investment environment and policy options for voluntary inclusion in IAPs identified, Transparency exchanges	Japan		Canada, Korea, New Zealand, Papua New Guinea, Chinese Taipei

Nuisance tariffs Measures: Tariffs with an applied MFN rate of less than 2 % removed, possible exclusion of products imported in bulk consignments or of high unit value	Hong Kong, Australia, Chile, New Zealand	Brunei, Canada, Singapore	Malaysia
Applied tariff reduction across all sectors Measures: Applied tariffs reduced by 25 % on a weighted average basis (15 % minimum cut)	Chile, Hong Kong		Singapore

Source: APEC Ministerial Meeting (1997a).

Notes:

[1] Indonesia is in the process of confirming the full scope of product sub-categories that it is able to endorse within the nominated HS product codes

[2] Thailand reserves its position with respect to the services component of the proposal

[3] Indonesia's support relates to certain HS Chapters only

[4] The United States has yet to determine whether its support includes Ch. 46

[5] Excluding NTMs

Appendix 3

Sectors for Early Voluntary Sectoral Liberalization – summary of scope of coverages (as of December 1998)

Sectors	Scope of coverage	Target end rates	Target end dates
Forest Products	HS ex 3804, ex 3806, 44, ex 46, 47, 48, 49, ex 9401, ex 9403, ex 9406	Elimination	ex HS 38, HS 44, ex HS 46, ex HS 94, 1 January 2002 (Developed Economies), 1 January 2004 (Developing Economies), HS 47, 48, 49: 1 January 2000 (Developed Economies), 1 January 2002 (Developing Economies)
Fish and fish products	HS 0301–0307, ex 0511, ex 1504, ex 1603, 1604, 1605, ex 2301, ex 2309	Elimination	By 31 December 2005
Toys	HS 9501: Wheeled toys designed to be ridden by children, HS 9502: Dolls representing only human beings, HS 9503: Other toys; reduced-size (scale) models; puzzles of all kinds, HS 9504: Articles for funfair, table or parlor games, HS 9505: Festive, carnival or other entertainment articles	Elimination	By 2000–2005
Gems and jewelry	HS 71	Elimination / reduction to 0–5 %	By 2005
Chemicals	HS 28–39 inclusive, except: 2905.43, 2905.44, 3301, 3501 – 3505, 3809.10, 3824.60	Chemical Tariff Harmonization Agreement rates, (0, 5.5, 6.5 %)	By 2001 (current tariff rates $\leqq$ 10 %). By 2004 (current tariff rates > 10 %)
Medical equipment and instruments	HS 2844.40, 3822, 8419.20, 8713, 8714.20, 9018, 9019, 9021, 9022, 9023, 9024, 9025, 9026, 9027, 9028, 9030, 9031, 9032, ex 8149.90, 9402.10, 9402.90	Elimination	By 1 January 2001
Environmental goods and services	Goods: 109 items[1]. Services[2]	Elimination	By 200X (four years from agreement)
Energy	Coal, electricity and gas items: twelve six-digit tariff lines from HS Chapter 27[3]. Energy-related products and equipments: 137 six-digit tariff lines from HS Chapters 73, 82, 84, 85, 87[3]. Services[4]	Elimination	By 1 July 2004

Source: WTO (1999a, 1999b).

Notes: [1] See WTO (1999b: Annex III.2)

[2] Consolidated list of services being developed as outlined in CTI Status Report on the Environment Sector, 27 May 1998. Further work required

[3] Scope of product coverage being developed based on Attachment A to the CTI Status Report on the Energy Sector, 27 May 1998

[4] Scope of services is as per Attachment B to the CTI Status Report on the Energy Sector, 27 May 1998

Appendix 4

Appendix 4. Summary of reservations to the Kuching product coverage, target end rates and target end dates (as of 23 December 1998)

Sector Target end rate Target end date	Extended phasing				End rate proposal		Exclusions
	Target end date + up to 2 yrs	Target end date + 3–5 yrs	Target end date + 6–10 yrs Inclusive	Target end date +11 yrs. and above	Target end rate + up to and including 5%	Target end rate + more than 5%	
Gems and jewelry 0–5% 2005		10[5] CHIN 13[3] MAL			48[3] IND 1[3] JPN		25[3] CHIN 5[4] PHIL
Toys 0% 2000–2005		22[1.3] CHIN 4[3] KOR 27[3] MAL 67[3] THAI 30[1] BRU			15[1] BRU 17[1.3] CHIN 10[4(b)] JPN 35[3] MAL 86[4(b)] PHIL 67[3] THAI	15[1] BRU 9[1.3] CHIN	5[4(a)], 18[1]IND 14[1] PHIL ex 5[4(c)]) PHIL 25[1] THAI
Chemicals CTHA rates 2001/2004	3.1[3] MAL 3.0 THAI	0.1[3] AUS 0.8[3] CHIN 19.5 PHIL 7.3[3)] CT 6.3 THAI	1.1[3] BRU 31[3] CHIN 1.5[3] MAL 57 THAI	22[3] MAL 32.4 THAI	28.2[3] IND 0.2[3] MAL 5.4 PHIL	3.3[3] IND	0.1[4(b)] BRU 63[3] CHIN 0.6[3] IND 0.9 THAI
Medical equipment and instruments 0% 2001	33[3]KOR 1[2.3] MAL 31[3] CT	32[3] CHIN 0.4[3] KOR 3[3] PNG 100[4(b)] PHIL 10[3] CT 93[2] THAI	50[4] BRU 3[3] CHIN 6[3] MAL 5[2] THAI		50[4] BRU 36[3] CHIN 80[3,4] IND 30[3] MAL 100[4(b)] PHIL 79[2] THAI	2[3] IND 3[3] PNG	64[2,3] CHIN 8[2,3] CT 2[2] THAI
Fish and fish products 0% 2003/2005	1[3] AUS 72[4(b)] PHIL 4[2]THAI	87[3] CHIN 2[3] MAL 3[3] US 13[3] KOR	3[3] MAL		87[3] CHIN 16[3] MAL 100[4(b)] PHIL 23[2] THAI	96[3] PNG	100 JPN 15[3] KOR 100 CT 3[1] THAI 1[2] CHIN 2[3] KOR
Forest products** 0% 2000–2004	3 AUS 29 IND 11 KOR 2 MAL 51 CT 27 THAI	2 AUS 85 CHIN 16 KOR 1 MAL 86 PNG 5 THAI	21BRU 4 CHIN 19 KOR 8 MAL 11 THAI	1 MAL 2 THAI	25 BRU 8 CHIN 28 IND 12 MAL 97 PHIL 1 CT 27 THAI	40 CHIN 1 IND 53 PNG	3 CHIN 31 JPN 12 KOR 1 MAL 9 CT 50 THAI
Energy** 0% 1 July 2004	9 AUS 3 CHIN 71 IND **** CT 26 THAI	54 AUS **** CT2 2*** US 9 KOR	34 MAL 15 THAI	13 MAL 21 THAI	23 IND 3 JPN 48 MAL 99 PHIL 62 THAI	48 IND	44 CHI 1 PHIL **** CT 36 THAI
Environmental goods and services** 0% 2003	5 AUS 94 PHIL 1 CT 5, ex 1 THAI 1 US	7 CT	27 BRU 17* KOR 5 MAL	17 MAL 5 THAI	27 BRU 59 MAL 94 PHIL 10 ex 1 THAI	1 MAL	35 BRU 84 CHIN 11 JPN 7 KOR 7 MAL 6 PHIL 2, ex 13 CT 95 THAI

Notes:

1   Moral/religious grounds
2   Technical definitional grounds
3   Domestic sensitivity grounds
4   Others: (a) children educational grounds; (b) traditional crafts/cultural grounds;
      (c) public safety reasons; (d) national tariff policy; and (e) national security

* No end date specified but is assumed not to go beyond 2010

** Information provided was at HS 6/8-digit level

*** No end date specified but is assumed not to go beyond 2010; specific flexibility required
      will take into account end date ultimately agreed and any other forms of flexibility
      endorsed

**** Revised reservation list to be provided

N.B. The above summary does not yet fully reflect the reservations of the following
      economies for which further information would need to be provided:
      - Forest products: Japan;
      - Energy: Papua New Guinea, China and Chinese Taipei

Source: WTO (1999a).

Bibliography

In English

ABAC (1997) *Report to the Economic Leaders – APEC Means Business: ABAC's Call to Action*, November.
—— (1998) *Report to the APEC Economic Leaders – APEC Means Business: Restoring Confidence, Regenerating Growth*, November.
Adlan, D. N. (1998) *Speech to the Third APEC Ministers Conference on Regional Science and Technical Cooperation*, 21 October.
AF&PA (1998) *Annual Report*, Washington D.C.: AF&PA.
—— (1999) *Press Release*, 13 December.
Aggarwal, Vinod K. and Charles E. Morrison (1999) 'APEC as an International Institution,' paper presented to the 25th Pacific Trade and Development (PAFTAD) Conference on 'APEC: The Challenges and Tasks in the 21st Century,' 16–18 June.
Anek, Laothamatas (1992) *Business Association and the New Political Economy of Thailand*, Boulder: Westview Press.
APEC CTI (1998) *Chair's Summary Record of Discussion*, the third CTI meeting of 1998, September, Kuantan.
—— (1999) *Summary of Work Plans/Progress on NTMs, Facilitation and Ecotech in EVSL Sectors*, August, Rotorua.
APEC Leaders Meeting (1994) *APEC Economic Leaders' Declaration of Common Resolve*, 15 November, Bogor, (http://www.apecsec.org.sg/virtualib/econlead/bogor.html).
—— (1995a) *APEC Economic Leaders' Declaration for Action*, 19 November, Osaka, (http://www.apecsec.org.sg/virtualib/econlead/osaka.html).
—— (1995b) *The Osaka Action Agenda: Implementation of the Bogor Declaration*, 19 November, Osaka, (http://www.apecsec.org.sg/virtualib/history/osaka/osakaact.html).
—— (1996) *APEC Economic Leaders' Declaration: From Vision to Action*, 25 November, Subic, (http://www.apecsec.org.sg/virtualib/econlead/subic.html).
—— (1997) *APEC Economic Leaders' Declaration: Connecting the APEC Community*, 25 November, Vancouver, (http://www.apecsec.org.sg/virtualib/econlead/vancouver.html).
—— (1998) *APEC Economic Leaders' Declaration: Strengthening the Foundation for Growth*, 18 November, Kuala Lumpur, (http://www.apecsec.org.sg/virtualib/econlead/malaysia.html).
—— (1999) *APEC Economic Leaders' Declaration: The Auckland Challenge*, 13 September, Auckland, (http://www.apecsec.org.sg/virtualib/econlead/nz.html).
—— (2000) *APEC Economic Leaders' Declaration: Delivering to the Community*, 16 November, Bandar Seri Begawan, (http://www.apecsec.org.sg/virtualib/econlead/brunei.html).

APEC Ministerial Meeting (1989a) *Joint Statement*, November, Canberra, (http://www.apecsec. org .sg/virtualib/minismtg/mtgmin89.html).

—— (1989b) *Chairman's Summary Statement*, November, Canberra, (http://www.apecsec.org. sg/virtualib/minismtg/mtgmin89.html).

—— (1990) *Joint Statement*, July, Singapore, (http://www.apecsec.org.sg/virtualib/minismtg /mtgmin90.html).

—— (1991) *Joint Statement*, November, Seoul, (http://www.apecsec.org.sg/virtualib/mini smtg/ mtgmin91.html).

—— (1993) *Joint Statement*, November, Seattle, (http://www.apecsec.org.sg/virtualib/mini smtg/mtgmin93.html).

—— (1995) *Joint Statement*, November, Osaka, (http://www.apecsec.org.sg/virtualib/mini smtg/mtgmin95.html).

—— (1996) *Joint Statement*, November, Manila, (http://www.apecsec.org.sg/virtualib/mini smtg/mtgmin96.html).

—— (1997a) *SOM Chair's Report to Ministers on EVSL*, 21 November, Vancouver.

—— (1997b) *Joint Statement*, November, Vancouver, (http://www.apecsec.org.sg/virtualib /mini smtg/mtgmim97.html).

—— (1998) *Joint Statement*, November, Kuala Lumpur, (http://www.apecsec.org.sg/virtu-alib/minismtg/mtgmim98.html).

—— (1999) *Joint Statement*, September, Auckland, (http://www.apecsec.org.sg/virtualib/ minismtg/mtgmim99.html).

—— (2000) *Joint Statement*, November, Bandar Seri Begawan, (http://www.apecsec.org.sg/ virtualib/ minismtg/mtgmin2000.html).

—— (2002) *Joint Statement*, October, Los Cabos, (http://www.apecsec.org.sg/virtualib/ minismtg/mtgmin2002.html).

APEC SOM (1998a) *Chair's Summary Conclusion of the Second Senior Officials Meeting for the Tenth APEC Ministerial Meeting*, June, Kuching.

—— (1998b) *Chair's Summary Conclusion of the Third Senior Officials Meeting for the Tenth APEC Ministerial Meeting*, September, Kuantan.

—— (1999a) *Summary Conclusions of the First APEC Senior Officials Meeting for the Eleventh Ministerial Meeting*, February, Wellington.

—— (1999b) *Summary Conclusions of the Second APEC Senior Officials Meeting of the Eleventh Ministerial Meeting*, May, Christchurch.

APEC Trade Ministers' Meeting (APEC Meeting of Ministers Responsible for Trade) (1996) *Statement of the Chair*, July, Christchurch, (http://www.apecsec.org.sg/virtualib/mini smtg/mtgtrd96.html).

—— (1997) *Statement of the Chair*, May, Montreal, (http://www.apecsec.org.sg/virtualib/ minismtg/mtgtrd97.html).

—— (1998) *Statement of the Chair*, June, Kuching, (http://www.apecsec.org.sg/virtualib/ minismtg/mtgtrd98.html).

—— (1999) *Statement of the Chair*, June, Auckland, (http://www.apecsec.org.sg/virtualib/ minismtg/mtgtrd99.html).

—— (2001) *Chair's Statement*, June, Shanghai, (http://www.apecsec.org.sg/virtualib/ minismtg/mtgtrd2001.html).

—— (2003) *Statement of the Chair*, June, Khon Kaen, (http://www.apecsec.org.sg/virtualib/ minismtg/mtgmrt2003.html).

Australia–US Ministerial Consultations (1998) *Joint Communiqué*, July, Sydney.

Barnett, Michael (1990) 'High Politics Is Low Politics: The Domestic and Systemic Sources of Israeli Security Policy, 1967–1977,' *World Politics*, vol. 42, no. 4, July, pp. 529–62.

Beazley, Kim (1999) 'Winning in the Global Economy: Trade Policy for the New Millennium,' Monash APEC Lecture, 18 June, Melbourne.

Beeson, Mark (1996) 'APEC: Nice Theory, Shame about the Practice,' *Australian Quarterly*, vol. 68, no. 2, pp. 35–50.

Bergsten, C. Fred (1996) 'An Asian Push for World-Wide Free Trade,' *The Economist*, 6 January, pp. 76–7.

—— (1999) 'A New Trade Liberalization Strategy for APEC,' mimeo.

Chia, Siow Yue (ed.) (1994) *APEC: Challenges and Opportunities*, Singapore: Institute of Southeast Asian Studies.

Cook, P. (1998a) *Speech to the Australian Institute of Export (NSW) Ltd Royal Automobile Club*, 29 May, Sydney.

—— (1998b) 'The Asian Crisis and Australia's Agricultural and Resources Sectors,' speech to the Australian Agricultural and Resources Economists Society, 20 November, Sydney.

—— (1999) 'APEC: Meeting the Challenge of the New Millennium,' *ALP Policy Discussion Paper*, June, Canberra.

Cotton, James and John Ravenhill (eds) (2001) *The National Interest in a Global Era: Australia in World Affairs 1996–2000*, Melbourne: Oxford University Press.

Davidson, Paul J. (1997) *The Legal Framework for International Economic Relations*, Singapore: Institute of Southeast Asian Studies.

Dee, P., A. Hardin and M. Schuele (1998) *APEC Early Voluntary Sectoral Liberalisation*, Productivity Commission Staff Research Paper, Canberra: AusInfo.

Destler, I. M. (1995) *American Trade Politics*, 3rd edition, Washington D.C.: Institute for International Economics/Twentieth Century Fund.

—— (1996) *The National Economic Council: A Work in Progress*, Washington D.C.: Institute for International Economics.

——(1998) 'Foreign Economic Policy under Bill Clinton,' in Scott (ed.) (1998), pp. 89 - 107.

Destler, I. M. and Peter J. Balint (1999) *The New Politics of American Trade: Trade, Labor and the Environment*, Washington D.C.: Institute for International Economics.

Deyo, Frederic C. (ed.) (1987) *The Political Economy of the New East Asian Industrialism*, Ithaca: Cornell University Press.

DFAT (1997a) *In the National Interest: Australia's Foreign and Trade Policy White Paper*, Canberra: National Capital Printing.

—— (1997b) *Sectoral Trade Liberalisation in APEC: Some Preliminary Statistics, Industry Consultations*, March/April, Canberra: DFAT.

Diebold, William Jr (1996) 'From the ITO to GATT – and Back?' in Kirshner (ed.) (1996), pp. 152–73.

Dieter, Herbert (1997) 'APEC and the WTO: Collision or Co-operation?' *The Pacific Review*, vol. 10, no. 1, pp. 19–38.

Downer, Alexander and Tim Fischer (1998) *Joint Statement*, 12 May, Kuala Lumpur.

Downs, George W. and David M. Rocke (1995) *Optimal Imperfection?: Domestic Uncertainty and Institutions in International Relations*, Princeton: Princeton University Press.

Doyle, Michael W. (1986) 'Liberalism and World Politics,' *American Political Science Review*, vol. 80, no. 4, December, pp. 1151–69.

—— (1997) *Ways of War and Peace: Realism, Liberalism, and Socialism*, New York: W. W. Norton.

Drysdale, Peter (1997) 'APEC and WTO: Complementary or Competing?' paper prepared for the ISEAS APEC Roundtable 1997 on 'APEC – Sustaining the Momentum,' 6 August, Singapore.

Drysdale, Peter and W. Lu (1996) 'Australia's Export Performance in East Asia,' *Pacific Economic Paper*, no. 259, September.

Elek, Andrew (1995) 'APEC Beyond Bogor: An Open Economic Association in the Asia-Pacific Region,' *Asian Pacific Economic Literature*, vol. 9, no. 1, May.

Evans, Peter B. (1993) 'Building an Integrative Approach to International and Domestic Politics: Reflections and Projections,' in Evans, Jacobson and Putnam (eds) (1993), pp. 397–430.

Evans, Peter B., Harold K. Jacobson and Robert D. Putnam (eds) (1993) *Double-Edged Diplomacy: International Bargaining and Domestic Politics*, Berkeley: University of California Press.

Fayle, P. (1998) 'Department of Foreign Affairs and Trade, Testimony to the Joint Standing Committee on Foreign Affairs, Defence and Trade,' 30 March.

Finger, J. Michel (1991) 'The GATT as an International Discipline over Trade Restrictions: A Public Choice Approach,' in Vaubel and Willett (eds) (1991).

Fischer, Tim (1998a) *Speech to the Silver Perch Industry Forum*, 14 March, Port Macquarie.

—— (1998b) 'Firing on All Cylinders: The Dynamic LNG Industry,' speech to the 12th Liquid Natural Gas Industry International Conference, 14 May, Perth.

—— (1998c) *Media Statement following the APEC Ministerial Meeting*, 15 November, Kuala Lumpur.

Fukushima, Glenn S. (1994) 'The Role of Government in High Tech Trade,' in Waldenberger (ed.) (1994).

Funabashi, Yoichi (1995a) *Asia Pacific Fusion: Japan's Role in APEC*, Washington D.C.: Institute for International Economics.

Garnaut, Ross (1994) 'Open Regionalism: Its Analytic Basis and Relevance to the International System,' *Journal of Asia Economics*, vol. 5, no. 2, pp. 273–90.

—— (1999) 'APEC Ideas and Reality: History and Prospects,' paper presented to the 25th Pacific Trade and Development (PAFTAD) Conference, 16–18 July, Osaka.

Garrett, Geoffrey and Peter Lange (1995) 'Internationalization, Institutions and Political Change,' *International Organization*, vol. 49, no. 4, Autumn, pp. 627–55.

Garten, Jeffrey E. (1997) 'Business and Foreign Policy,' *Foreign Affairs*, vol. 76, no. 3, pp. 67–79.

Gibbons, P. (1997) 'The Impact of the WTO ITA Agreement,' paper presented at 'CITER 2: The Second Annual Conference on International Trade Education and Research: Free Trade in Information Technology and Telecommunications,' 4–5 December, University of Melbourne.

Gourevitch, Peter (1978) 'The Second Image Reversed: The International Sources of Domestic Politics,' *International Organization*, vol. 32, no. 4, pp. 881–911.

—— (1996) 'Squaring the Circle: The Domestic Sources of International Cooperation,' *International Organization*, vol. 50, no. 2, Spring, pp. 349–73.

Hannah, T. (1999) 'APEC and the WTO: Two Tracks to Trade Liberalisation,' speech, 23 April.

Hewitt, Joanna (1999) 'Australian Ambassador to APEC, Department of Foreign Affairs and Trade, Testimony to the Foreign Affairs, Defence and Trade References Committee,' 18 February.

Higgott, Richard (1993) 'Competing Theoretical Approaches to International Cooperation: Implications for the Asia-Pacific,' in Higgott, Leaver and Ravenhill (eds) (1993), pp. 290–311.

Higgott, Richard and Andrew F. Cooper (1990) 'Middle Power Leadership and Coalition Building: Australia, the Cairns Group and the Uruguay Round of Trade Negotiations,' *International Organization*, vol. 44, no. 4, Autumn, pp. 589–632.

Higgott, Richard, R. Leaver and J. Ravenhill (eds) (1993) *Pacific Economic Relations in the 1990s: Cooperation or Conflict?* Boulder: Lynne Rienner Publishers.

Hooke, M. (1998) 'Executive Director, Australian Food and Grocery Council, Testimony to the Foreign Affairs, Defence and Trade References Committee', 6 March.

Howard, John (1998) *Speech to the National Farmers' Federation 46th Council Meeting*, 24 November, Canberra.

Iida, Keisuke (1993) 'When and How Do Domestic Constraints Matter?' *Journal of Conflict Resolution*, vol. 37, pp. 403–26.

Ikenberry, G. John (1986) 'The State and Strategies of International Adjustment,' *World Politics*, vol. 39, no. 1, pp. 53–77.

—— (1988) 'Market Solutions for State Problems: The International and Domestic Politics of American Oil Decontrol,' in Ikenberry, Lake and Mastanduno (eds) (1988), pp. 151–77.

Ikenberry, G. John, David A. Lake and Michael Mastanduno (eds) (1988) *The State and American Foreign Policy*, Ithaca: Cornell University Press.

Industry Commission (1997) *Automotive Industry Report Volume I*, Report no. 58, 26 May, Canberra.

Jackson, John (1989) *The World Trading System: Law and Policy of International Economic Relations*, Cambridge, Massachusetts: MIT Press.

—— (1998) *The World Trade Organization: Constitution and Jurisprudence*, Chatham House Papers, London: Pinter.

Johnson, Chalmers (1987) 'Political Institution and Economic Performance: The Government–Business Relationship in Japan, South Korea and Taiwan,' in Deyo (ed.) (1987).

Jung, Yong-duck and Keunsei Kim (1997) 'The State Institutions and Policy Capabilities: A Comparative Analysis of the Administrative Reforms in Japan and Korea,' paper presented at the 17th World Congress of the International Political Science Association, August 17–21, Seoul.

Kahler, Miles (1992) 'Multilateralism with Small and Large Numbers,' *International Organization*, vol. 46, no. 2, Summer, pp. 681–708.

—— (1995) *International Institutions and the Political Economy of Integration*, Washington D.C.: The Brookings Institution.

Katzenstein, Peter J. (ed.) (1978) *Between Power and Plenty: Foreign Economic Policies of Advanced Industrial States*, Madison: University of Wisconsin Press.

—— (1985) *Small States in World Markets: Industrial Policy in Europe*, Ithaca: Cornell University Press.

Keating, Paul (1998) 'Implications for the Strategic Architecture of the Asian Hemisphere: APEC's Sixth Leaders Summit Meeting,' 22 September, Shanghai.

Kelly, Paul (1992) *The End of Certainty*, Sydney: Allen and Unwin.

Keohane, Robert O. (1986) 'Reciprocity in International Relations,' *International Organization*, vol. 40, no. 1, Winter.

Keohane, Robert O. and Helen V. Milner (eds) (1996) *Internationalization and Domestic Politics*, Cambridge: Cambridge University Press.

Keohane, Robert O. and Joseph S. Nye (1977) *Power and Interdependence: World Politics in Transition*, Boston: Little, Brown.

Kirshner, Orin (ed.) (1996) *The Bretton Woods–GATT System: Retrospect and Prospect after Fifty Years*, Armonk: M. E. Sharpe.

Kissinger, Henry A. (1966) 'Domestic Structure and Foreign Policy,' *Daedelus*, no. 95, Spring, pp. 503–29.

Krasner, Stephen D. (1978a) *Defending the National Interest: Raw Materials Investments and U.S. Foreign Policy*, Princeton: Princeton University Press.

—— (1978b) 'United States Commercial and Monetary Policy: Unravelling the Paradox of External Strength and Internal Weakness,' in Katzenstein (ed.) (1978).

—— (1987) *Asymmetries in Japanese–American Trade*, Berkeley: The University of California Press.

—— (1991) 'Global Communications and National Power: Life on the Pareto Frontier,' *World Politics*, vol. 43, no. 3, April, pp. 336–66.

Krauss, Ellis S. (1993) 'U.S.–Japan Negotiation on Construction and Semiconductors, 1985–1988,' in Evans, Jacobson and Putnam (eds) (1993).

Lawrence, Robert Z. (1996) *Regionalism, Multilateralism and Deeper Integration*, Washington D.C.: The Bookings Institution.

Lincoln, Edward J. (1999) *Troubled Times: US–Japan Trade Relations in the 1990s*, Washington D.C.: Brookings Institution Press.

Lopez, Carolina Albero and Jacint Soler Matutes (1998) 'Open Regionalism versus Discriminatory Trading Agreements,' *ASEAN Economic Bulletin*, vol. 14, no. 3, pp. 253–72.

Lowi, Theodore J. (1979) *The End of Liberalism: The Second Republic of the United States*, 2nd edition, New York: W. W. Norton & Company.

Mansfield, Edward D. and Helen V. Milner (1999) 'The New Wave of Regionalism,' *International Organization*, vol. 53, no. 3, Summer.

Martin, Pierre (1994) 'The Politics of International Structural Change: Aggressive Unilateralism in American Trade Policy', in Stubbs and Underhill (eds) (1994).

Mastanduno, Michael, David A. Lake and G. John Ikenberry (1989) 'Toward a Realist Theory of State Action,' *International Studies Quarterly*, no. 33, pp. 457–74.

Mayer, Frederick W. (1992) 'Managing Domestic Differences in International Negotiations: The Strategic Use of Internal Side-Payments,' *International Organization*, vol. 46, no. 4, pp. 798–818.

Milner, Helen V. (1988) 'Trading Places: Industries for Free Trade,' *World Politics*, vol. 40, no. 3, April, pp. 350–76.

—— (1997) *Interests, Institutions and Information: Domestic Politics and International Relations*, Princeton: Princeton University Press.

Moravcsik, Andrew (1993) 'Introduction: Integrating International and Domestic Theories of International Bargaining,' in Evans, Jacobson and Putnam (eds) (1993), pp. 1–42.

—— (1997) 'Taking Preferences Seriously: A Liberal Theory of International Politics,' *International Organization*, vol. 51, no. 4, Autumn, pp. 513–53.

Morgenthau, Hans J. (1949) *Politics Among Nations: The Struggle for Power and Peace*, New York: Knopf.

Nesadurai, Helen E. S. (1996) 'APEC: A Tool for US Regional Domination?' *The Pacific Review*, vol. 19, no. 1, May.

Ogita, Tatsushi (2001) 'On Principles of APEC,' *IDE APEC Study Center Working Paper Series*, 00/01, no. 4, Chiba: Institute of Developing Economies.

Ogita, Tatsushi and Daisuke Takoh (1997) 'The Making of Osaka Action Agenda and Japan's Individual Action Plan: The APEC Policy Making Process in Japan Revisited,' *IDE APEC Study Center Working Paper Series*, 96/97, no. 7, Tokyo: Institute of Developing Economies.

O'Halloran, Sharyn (1994) *Politics, Process and American Trade Policy*, Ann Arbor: University of Michigan Press.

Okamoto, Jiro (1995) 'ASEAN's New Role in the Asia Pacific Region: Can It Be a Driving Force of Wider Regional Cooperation?' *Pacific Economic Papers*, no. 245, July.

Pastor, Robert A. (1981) *Congress and the US Foreign Economic Policy, 1926–1976*, Berkeley: University of California Press.

Petri, Peter A. (1999) 'APEC and the Millennium Round,' paper for discussion at the 25th PAFTD Conference on 'APEC: Its Challenges and Tasks in the 21st Century', 16–18 June, Osaka.

Putnam, Robert D. (1988) 'Diplomacy and Domestic Politics: the Logic of Two-level Games,' *International Organization*, vol. 42, no. 3, pp. 427–60.

Quad Meeting (Quadrilateral Trade Ministers Meeting) (1996a) *Chairman's Statement*, April.

—— (1996b) *Chairperson's Summary*, September.

Reisman, Simon (1996) 'The Birth of a World Trading System: ITO and GATT' in Kirshner (ed.) (1996), pp. 82–6.

Risse-Kappen, Thomas (1991) 'Public Opinion, Domestic Structure and Foreign Policy in Liberal Democracies,' *World Politics*, vol. 43, no. 1, July, pp. 479–512.

—— (1994) 'Ideas Do Not Float Freely: Transnational Coalitions, Domestic Structures and the End of the Cold War,' *International Organization*, vol. 48, no. 2, Spring, pp. 185–214.

Rogowski, Ronald (1989) *Commerce and Coalition: How Trade Affects Domestic Political Alignments*, Princeton: Princeton University Press.

Ruggie, John G. (1982) 'International Regimes, Transactions and Change: Embedded Liberalism in the Postwar Economic Order,' *International Organization*, vol. 36, no. 2, Spring, pp. 379–415.

Saxonhouse, Gary R. (1996) 'Comments' on Dr. Yamazawa's paper presented to 'The Emerging WTO System and Perspectives from East Asia' Symposium at the University of Michigan, 28–30 August, *Joint US–Korea Academic Studies*, vol. 7.

Schelling, Thomas. C. (1978) *Micro Motives and Macro Behavior*, New York: W. W. Norton.

Schoppa, Leonard J. (1997) *Bargaining with Japan: What American Pressure Can and Cannot Do*, New York: Columbia University Press.

Schweller, R. L. (1992) 'Domestic Structure and Preventive War,' *World Politics*, vol. 38, no. 1, October, pp. 25–57.

Scott, James M. (ed.) (1998) *After the End: Making US Foreign Policy in the Post-Cold War World*, Durham, NC: Duke University Press.

Snape Richard H., Lisa Gropp and Tas Luttrell (1998) *Australian Trade Policy 1965–1997. A Documentary History*, St Leonards: Allen & Unwin.

Soesastro, Hadi (1994) 'The Institutional Framework for APEC: An ASEAN Perspective' in Chia (ed.) (1994), pp. 36–53.

Stubbs, Richard and Geoffrey R. D. Underhill (eds) (1994) *Political Economy and the Changing Global Order*, London: Macmillan.

Suthiphand Chirathivat (1997) 'APEC Policy Making Process of Thailand,' paper presented to the International Workshop on 'Economic Policy in APEC and Impediments to Trade in APEC,' organized by the Institute of Developing Economics (IDE), 12–13 February 1997.

Tjokroamidjojo, Bintoro and Djadmiko (1999) *Economic Reform and Structural Adjustment to Respond to the Financial Crisis*, unpublished paper.

TPCC (1995) *The National Export Strategy: Third Report to the United States Congress*, Washington D.C.: US Government Printing Office.

US Council of Economic Advisers (1994) *Economic Report of the President, Transmitted the Congress, February 1994*, together with the Annual Report of the Council of Economic Advisers, Washington D.C.: US Government Printing Office.

—— (1995) *Economic Report of the President, Transmitted the Congress, February 1995*, together with the Annual Report of the Council of Economic Advisers, Washington D.C.: US Government Printing Office.

US Department of Commerce (1998) *Remarks of US Under-Secretary for International Trade David L. Aaron at the American Chamber of Commerce*, 9 September, Kuala Lumpur.

US Department of Commerce, International Trade Administration (1995) *The Big Emerging Markets: 1996 Outlook and Sourcebook*, Lanham: Bernan Press.

US Department of Commerce, Trade Compliance Center, Market Access and Compliance, International Trade Administration (1999) *An Analysis of the Importance of the Accelerated Tariff Liberalization (ATL) Initiative to US Exports and Jobs*, September.

US Department of State (1997) *Asia-Pacific Economic Cooperation (APEC)*, Fact Sheet released by the Bureau of East Asia and Pacific Affairs, 6 November.

—— (1998) *Why APEC Matters to Americans*, fact sheet released by the Bureau of East Asian and Pacific Affairs, 26 October.

US House of Representatives (1998) *Hearing before the Subcommittee on Asia and the Pacific of the Committee on International Relations*, One Hundred Fifth Congress, First Session, 6 November, Washington D.C.: US Government Printing Office.

US President (1994a) 'Remarks and a Question-and-Answer Session at Waseda University in Tokyo, July 7, 1993,' *Public Papers of the Presidents of the United States, William J. Clinton 1993*, Book I, Washington D.C.: US Government Printing Office.

—— (1994b) 'Remarks to the Seattle APEC Host Committee, November 19, 1993,' *Public Papers of the Presidents of the United States, William J. Clinton 1993*, Book II, Washington D.C.: US Government Printing Office.

US Senate (1999) *Senate Concurrent Resolution 48 Acknowledges APEC's Key Role in Region*, 28 July.

USTR (1994) *1994 Trade Policy Agenda and 1993 Annual Report of the President of the United States of the Trade Agreements Program*, Washington D.C.: US Government Printing Office.

—— (1995) *1995 Trade Policy Agenda and 1994 Annual Report of the President of the United States of the Trade Agreements Program*, Washington D.C.: US Government Printing Office.

—— (1998a) *U.S. Trade Representative Hails APEC Progress on Trade*, for immediate release, 23 June.

—— (1998b) *Bershefsky Welcomes APEC Sectoral Agreement Plans to Move Initiative to WTO*, news release, 15 November.

—— (1999) *1999 Trade Policy Agenda and 1998 Annual Report of the President of the United States Agreements Program*, Washington D.C.: US Government Printing Office.

USTR and White House Council on Environmental Quality (1999) *Accelerated Tariff Liberalization in the Forest Products Sector: A Study of the Economic and Environment Effects*, November.

US White House (1997) *Press Briefing by Assistant to the President for International Economic Policy Dan Tarullo, and Deputy National Security Advisor Jim Steinberg on Upcoming APEC Summit*, 20 November.

Van Hoof, G. J. H.(1983) *Rethinking the Sources of International Law*, Deventer: Kluwer.

Vaubel, Roland and Thomas D. Willett (eds) (1991) *The Political Economy of International Organizations*, Boulder: Westview Press.

Verdier, Daniel (1994) *Democracy and International Trade: Britain, France and the United States, 1860–1990*, Princeton: Princeton University Press.

—— (1998) 'Domestic Responses to Capital Market Internationalization under the Gold Standard, 1870–1914,' *International Organization*, vol. 52, no. 1, Winter, pp. 1–34.

Vogel, David (1987) 'Government–Industry Relations in the United States: An Overview,' in Wilks and Wright (eds) (1987), pp. 92–116.

Waldenberger, Franz (ed.) (1994) *The Political Economy of Trade Conflicts*, New York: Springer-Verlag.

Waltz, Kenneth N. (1959) *Man, the State and War: A Theoretical Analysis*, New York: Columbia University Press.

—— (1979) *Theory of International Politics*, Reading: Addison-Wesley.

Wendt, Alexander E. (1987) 'The Agent-Structure Problem in International Relations Theory,' *International Organization*, vol. 41, no. 3, Summer, pp. 335–70.

Wesley, Michael (1997) 'The Politics of Exclusion: Australia, Turkey and Definitions of Regionalism,' *The Pacific Review*, vol. 10, no. 4, pp. 523–55.

—— (2001) 'Australia and the Asian Crisis,' in Cotton and Ravenhill (eds) (2001), pp. 301–24.

Wilks, Stephen and Maurice Wright (eds) (1987) *Comparative Government–Industry Relations: Western Europe, the United States and Japan*, Oxford: Clarendon Press.

Winham, Gilbert R. (1992) *The Evolution of International Trade Agreements*, Toronto: University of Toronto Press.

Wright, J. (1997) 'Department of Industry, Science and Technology, Testimony to the Foreign Affairs, Defence and Trade Resources Committee,' 24 November.

WTO (1996) *Ministerial Declaration on Trade in Information Technology Products*, December, (http://www.wto.org/wto/goods/inftech.htm).

—— (1999a) *APEC's 'Accelerated Tariff Liberalisation' (ATL) Initiative, Communication from New Zealand*, WT/GC/W/138, 26 January.

—— (1999b) *APEC's Accelerated Tariff Liberalisation (ATL) Initiative, Communication from New Zealand, Addendum*, WT/GC/W/138/Add.1, 22 April.

——(2001) *Trading into the Future*, March, (http://www.wto.org/english/res_e/ doload_e/tif.pdf).

Zakaria, F. (1992) 'Realism and Domestic Politics,' *International Security*, vol. 17, no. 1, Summer, pp. 462–83.

In Indonesian

Syahperi, Johan S. (1999) *APEC: Dari Kuala Lumpur ke Auckland* [APEC: From Kuala Lumpur to Auckland], paper presented at the Centre for Strategic and International Studies, 5 August.

In Japanese

Funabashi, Yoichi (1995b) *Ajia Taiheiyo Fyujyon* [Asia Pacific Fusion], Tokyo: Chuo Koron Sha.

Hosokawa, Hisashi (1999) *Daikyosojidai no Tsusho Senryaku* [Trade Strategy in the Mega Competition Era], Tokyo: Nihon Hoso Shuppan Kyokai.

Hosoya, Chihiro and Tomohito Shinoda (eds) (1998) *Shinjidai no Nichibei Kankei* [Japan–US Relations in the New Era], Tokyo: Yuhikaku.

Inoguchi, Takashi and Tomoaki Iwai (1987) *'Zokugiin' no Kenkyu: Jiminto Seiken wo Gyujiru Syuyakutachi* [A Study on *Zoku Giin*], Tokyo: Nihon Keizai Shimbun Sha.

Itoga, Shigeru (1994) 'Kunibetsu Bunseki – Tai' [Country Analysis – Thailand], in Itoga (ed.) (1994), pp. 246–62.

—— (ed.) (1994) *Ugokidasu ASEAN Keizaiken: 2008 nen eno Tembo* [ASEAN Economic Sphere in Motion: Prospect for the Year 2008], Tokyo: Institute of Developing Economies.

JIPRS (Japan Industrial Policy Research Institute) (ed.) (1999) *Kankoku no Keizaitaisei Kaikaku ni Kansuru Chosa Kenkyu* [A Study on Economic Regime Reform in Korea], Tokyo: JIPRI.

Kawanaka, Takeshi (1995) 'Tonan Ajia Shokoku to APEC' [Southeast Asian Countries and APEC], in Miyachi and Onishi (eds) (1995), pp. 92–110.

Kikuchi, Tsutomu (1995) *APEC: Ajia Taiheiyo Shinchitsujo no Mosaku* [APEC: Searching for a New Order in the Asia-Pacific], Tokyo: The Japan Institute of International Affairs.

—— (1998) *AjiaTaiheiyo no Chiikishugi to Nichibei Kankei* [Regionalism in the Asia Pacific and Japan–US Relations], in Hosoya and Shinoda (eds) (1998), pp. 180–225.

Kimiya, Tadashi (1999) 'Kankoku ni okeru Keizaikiki to Roshikankei Rejimu no Tenkai: Ro-Shi-Sei Iinkai no Katsudo wo Chushin ni [The Development of the Labor-Management Relation Regime in Korea under the Economic Crisis] in JIPRS (ed.) (1999).

Kokusaiho Gakkai (ed.) (1975) *Kokusaiho Jiten* [The Dictionary of International Law], Tokyo: Kajima Shuppankai.

Kusano, Atsushi (1991) *Amerika Gikai to Nichibei Kankei* [The US Congress and Japan–US Relations], Tokyo: Chuo Koron Sha.

—— (1997) *Seisaku Katei Bunseki Nyumon* [An Introduction to Policy Process Analysis], Tokyo: University of Tokyo Press.

Kuwahara, Teruji (1975) 'Sogoshugi' [Reciprocity], in Kokusaiho Gakkai (ed.) (1975), pp. 416–18.

Medhi Krongkaew (1999) 'APEC no Yukue: Aratana 10 Nen ni Muketa Tembo' [The Future of APEC: Prospects for the New Decade], *Jetoro Sensa* [JETRO Sensor], December, pp. 98–9.

Miyachi, Soshichi and Takeo Onishi (eds) (1995) *APEC: Nihon no Senryaku* [Japan's Strategy Towards APEC], Tokyo: Waseda University Press.

Miyazato, Seigen and Hisakazu Usui (eds) (1992) *Shin Kokusai Seijikeizai Chitsujo to Nichibei Kankei* [New International Political Economic Order and Japan–US Relations], Tokyo: Dobunkan.

Nagao, Satoru (1994) *'Uruguai Raundo Nogyo Kosho to EC: 2 Leberu Gemu Apurochi ni yoru Bunseki'* [Uruguay Round Agricultural Negotiations and the European Community: A Study Through Putnam's Two-Level Games Approach], *Kokusai Seiji*, no. 106, pp. 105–21.

Nakano, Minoru and Jae-Ho Yeom (1998) 'Seisaiku Kettei Kozo no Nikkan Hikaku: Bunseki Wakugumi to Jirei Bunseki' [A Comparative Analysis of Policy Making Structure in Japan and South Korea: A Conceptual Framework and Case Study], *Revaiasan* [Leviathan], no. 23, pp. 78–109.

Ohashi, Hideo (1998) *Beichu Keizai Masatsu: Chugokukeizai no Kokusaitenkai* [US–China Economic Friction], Tokyo: Keiso Shobo.

Onishi, Yutaka and Masahiko Tatebayashi (1998) 'Shocho Saihen no Nikkan Hikaku Kenkyu' [A Comparative Study on Ministerial Reform in Japan and South Korea], *Revaiasan* [Leviathan], no. 23, pp. 126–50.

Oyane, Satoshi (1992) ' *"MFA Regimu" Teppai no Seisaku Katei'* [Political Process in the Abolition of the MFA Regime], in Miyazato and Usui (eds) (1992).

Suehiro, Akira (2000) 'Zaisei Kinyu Seisaku: Chuo Ginko no Dokuritsusei to Soshiki no Noryoku' [Fiscal and Monetary Policy: The Autonomy of the Central Bank and Organizational Capability], in Suehiro and Higashi (eds) (2000), pp. 59–114.

Suehiro, Akira and Shigeki Higashi (eds) (2000) *Tai no Keizai Seisaku: Seido, Soshiki, Akuta* [Economic Policy in Thailand: The Role of Institutions and Actors], Chiba: Institute of Developing Economies.

Takano, Yuichi (ed.) (1988) *Kokusaikankeiho no Kadai* [Issues in the Law of International Relations], Tokyo: Yuhikaku.

Takase, Tamotsu (ed.) (1993) *Zoho Gatto to Uruguai Raundo* [The GATT and the Uruguay Round], Tokyo: Toyo Keizai Shimpo Sha.

Takase, Tamotsu and Kiyotaka Akasaka (1993) 'Gatto no Gensoku' [The Principles of the GATT], in Takase (ed.) (1993), pp. 37–56.

Tsujinaka, Yutaka, Chung-Hee Lee and Jae-Ho Yeom (1998) 'Nikkan Riekidantai no Hikaku Bunseki: 1987 Nen Minshuka Igo no Kankoku Dantai Jyokyo to Seiji Taisei' [A Comparative Analysis of South Korean and Japanese Interest Associations: Korean Civil Society and its Political Regime Since 1987], *Revaiasan* [Leviathan], no. 23, pp. 18–49.

Yamamoto, Soji (1988) 'Kokusai Keizaiho ni Okeru Sogoshugi no Kino Henka' [Functional Change of Reciprocity in International Economic Law] in Takano (ed.) (1988).

Yoon, Chang-Jung (1995) *Kimu Yon Samu Daitoryo to Seigadai no Hitobito: Kankoku Seiji no Kozo* [President Kim Young-Sam and the People of the Blue House], Tokyo: Chuo Koron Sha.

Zengyoren (ed.) (1999) *Heisei 10 Nendo Zengyoren Gyosei Taisaku Houkokusho* [1998 Zengyoren Fisheries Policy Action Report], Tokyo: Zengyoren.

In Korean

Bark, Taeho, Woo-Sik Moon and Jin-Hyun Paik (1998) *APEC JuYoHabEuiEui HoeWonGugByeol IHaengE GwanHan YeonGu* [Strengthening Compliance with APEC Agreement: A Study on Member States' Compliance with APEC Agreement], Seoul: KIEP.

Cho, Yong-Gyun (1996) *APEC MuYeog/TuJa JaYuHwaE DaeHan HanGugEui GiPonIhJang* [Position on the Liberalization of Trade and Investment in APEC], Seoul: The Institute of Foreign Affairs and National Security.

International Economic Bureau, MOFAT (1999) *ChoeGun APEC DongHyang* [The Current Trend of APEC], Winter.

Jin, Chang Soo (1998) 'HanIlEoEobHyeobJeongE GwanHan IlBonEui JeongChaegGwa DaeEungBangHyang' [The Japanese Policy for Korea–Japan Fishing Negotiation and the Korean Approach to it], paper reported to the government.

KIEP (1998) 'HyangHu 2NyeonEui DaeOeGyeongJeJeongChaeg YeoKeon Gwa GwaJe' [The Conditions and Problems of our Foreign Economic Policy for the Next Two Years], mimeo.

Kim, Chang-Seon (1998) 'BunYaByeol JaBalJeog JoGiJaYuHwa: ChuJin HyoenHwang Gwa DaeChaeg' [Early Voluntary Sectoral Liberalization: Its Promoting Situation and Countermeasure], paper presented at the Seminar on 'APEC SinOeGyoJeonRyag Eui MoChaeg: GwaJeWa DaeEungBangHyang' [In Search of the New Foreign Strategy of APEC: Problems and Approaches], KIEP.

Kim, Ho-sup (1997) 'Ssal SiJang GaeBangJoengChaegEui HanIl BiGyo' [Comparative Analysis of the Policy of Rice Market Release in Korea and Japan], paper presented at the Workshop on the Study of the Political Economy of Japan and Korea, the Center of Asian Studies, Korea University, Seoul.

Kim, Tae-hyeon, Seok-Chin Ryu and Jin-yeong Jeong (eds) (1995) *OeGyo Wa JoengChi: SeGyeHwa SiDaeEui GugJeHyoebSangNonRiWa JeonRyag* [Diplomacy and Domestic Politics: The Logic and Strategy of International Negotiations of the Global Era], Orum.

Kwon, Yeong-Joo and Yutaka Onishi (1999) 'Han-Il HaengJeongGaeHyeogEui BiGyo' [A Comparative Study of Administrative Reform in Korea and Japan], paper presented at the Seminar of Korean Association of Modern Japanology, Pusan.

MITI (1997) *TongSangSanEobBaegSeo* [White Paper of International Trade and Industry].

MOCIE (1998) *SanEobJaWonBaegSeo* [White Paper of Commerce, Industry and Energy].

Nam, Sang-Jeong (1998) 'APEC Eui HyeonAnGwa GagGugEui JeonRyag' [The Problems of APEC and the Strategies of Nations], paper presented at the Seminar on 'APEC SinOeGyo-JeonRyag Eui MoChaeg: GwaJaWa DaeEungBangHyang' [In Search of New Foreign Strategy of APEC: Problems and Approaches], KIEP.

Regional Cooperation Division, MOFAT (1998) *ChoeGun APEC DongHyang* [The Current Trend of APEC], Autumn.

—— (1999) *99 APEC Je2Cha GoWiGwanRiHoeEui* [The Report on the Result of APEC/SOM2].

Ro, Jae Bong (1997) 'APEC HyeonHwangGwa HyangHuGwaJe' [The Situation of APEC and Problems for the Future], *DaeOeGyeongJeJeongChegYeonGu* [KIEP Global Economic Review], vol. 1, no. 1, pp. 125–59.

Shin, Yeong-tae, Myeong-saeng Jeong, Lim-yeong Ma and Jae-hyeong Ahn (1998) *APEC SuSan-BunYa JoGiJaYuHwaEui YeongHyangGwa DaeChaeg* [The Influence and Countermeasure of Early Liberalization of Marine Products at APEC], Seoul: Korea Maritime Institute.

Son, Jungshik and Hongyul Han (1998) *APEC BiGwanSe JangBaegEui HyeonHwang* [Non-Tariff Barriers in APEC Economies], Seoul: KIEP.

Song, Yoocheul (1998a) 'APEC BunYaByeol JaYuHwaEui JinRoWa JeongCheg GwaJe' [The Promoting Situation and the Korean Problems of APEC/EVSL], paper presented at the Policy Seminar on 'APEC MuYeogJaYuHwaEui ChuJinGwa HanGugEui JeonRyag: 98APEC MuYeogJangGwanHoeEuiEui JuYoGwaJeWa JeonRyag KIEP JeongCheg' [Promotion of Trade Liberalization in APEC and the Strategy of Korea: The Main Theme and our Strategy of APEC Trade Ministers' Meeting in 1998], KIEP, pp. 15–24.

—— (1998b) 'APEC JaBalJeog BunYaByeol JoGiJaYuHwaEui NonEui HyeonHwangGwa DaeEung BangAn' [The Discussing Situation of APEC/EVSL], *KIEP SeGyeGyeongJe* [KIEP Global Economic Review], vol. 1, no. 2.

WTO Division, MOFAT (1999) *Je2Cha DaeOeGyeongJeJoJeongWiWonHoe GaeChoe* [Summary of the Second Foreign Economy Adjustment Committee].

Yang, Su-Gil (1997) 'BaenKuBeo APEC JeongSangHoeEuiEui EuiEuiWa URiEui DaeEung' [The Significance of the APEC Leaders' Meeting in Vancouver and our Response], paper presented at the Symposium on 'ATaeGyeongJeEui GyaJeWa BaenKuBeo APEC JeongSangHoeEui' [The Problems of the Asia-Pacific Economy and the APEC Leaders' Meeting in Vancouver], KIEP.

In Thai

University Affairs Agency (1998) *Aepekh Naa Ruu* [An Introduction to APEC], Bangkok.

Index

For Product Safety Concerns and Information please contact our EU
representative GPSR@taylorandfrancis.com
Taylor & Francis Verlag GmbH, Kaufingerstraße 24, 80331 München, Germany

www.ingramcontent.com/pod-product-compliance
Lightning Source LLC
Chambersburg PA
CBHW061141220326
41599CB00025B/4312

* 9 7 8 0 4 1 5 6 5 2 8 8 9 *